THE POEMS AND PROSE OF Mary, Lady Chudleigh

$18.95

THE POEMS AND PROSE OF Mary, Lady Chudleigh

EDITED BY
Margaret J. M. Ezell

New York Oxford
OXFORD UNIVERSITY PRESS
1993

Oxford University Press

Oxford New York Toronto
Delhi Bombay Calcutta Madras Karachi
Kuala Lumpur Singapore Hong Kong Tokyo
Nairobi Dar es Salaam Cape Town
Melbourne Auckland Madrid
and associated companies in
Berlin Ibadan

Published by Oxford University Press, Inc.,
200 Madison Avenue, New York, New York 10016

Library of Congress Cataloging-in-Publication Data

Chudleigh, Mary, Lady. 1656–1710.
The Poems and Prose of Mary, Lady Chudleigh:
edited by Margaret J. M. Ezell
p. cm. -- (Women writers in English 1350–1850)
1. Women—England—Literary collections. 2. Women and literature—England—History—17th century.
I. Ezell, Margaret J. M. II. Title. III. Series.
PR3346.C6A6 1993 828'.409--dc20 92-16922
ISBN 0-19-507874-8 (cloth)
ISBN 0-19-508360-1 (paper)

This volume was supported in part by the National Endowment for the Humanities, an independent federal agency.

Printing (last digit):
9 8 7 6 5 4 3 2 1

Printed in the United States of America
on acid-free paper

This volume is dedicated to
Elsie Duncan-Jones, a never-failing source
of inspiration and encouragement

CONTENTS

The Ladies Defence: Or, The Bride-Woman's Counsellor Answer'd

Poems on Several Occasions

The Song of the Three Children Paraphras'd

Essays upon Several Subjects in Prose and Verse

FOREWORD

Women Writers in English 1350–1850 presents texts of cultural and literary interest in the English-speaking tradition, often for the first time since their original publication. Most of the writers represented in the series were well known and highly regarded until the professionalization of English studies in the later nineteenth century coincided with their excision from canonical status and from the majority of literary histories.

The purpose of this series is to make available a wide range of unfamiliar texts by women, thus challenging the common assumption that women wrote little of real value before the Victorian period. While no one can doubt the relative difficulty women experienced in writing for an audience before that time, or indeed have encountered since, this series shows that women nonetheless had been writing from early on and in a variety of genres, that they maintained a clear eye to readers, and that they experimented with an interesting array of literary strategies for claiming their authorial voices. Despite the tendency to treat the powerful fictions of Virginia Woolf's *A Room of One's Own* (1928) as if they were fact, we now know, against her suggestion to the contrary, that there were many "Judith Shakespeares," and that not all of them died lamentable deaths before fulfilling their literary ambitions.

This series is unique in at least two ways. It offers, for the first time, concrete evidence of a rich and lively heritage of women writing in English before the mid-nineteenth century, and it is based on one of the most sophisticated and forward-looking electronic resources in the world: the Brown University Women Writers Project textbase (full text database) of works by early women writers. The Brown University Women Writers Project (WWP) was established in 1988 with a grant from the National Endowment for the Humanities, which continues to assist in its development.

Women Writers in English 1350–1850 is a print publication project derived from the WWP. It offers lightly-annotated versions based on single good copies or, in some cases, collated versions of texts with more complex editorial histories, normally in their original spelling. The editions are aimed at a wide audience, from the informed undergraduate through professional students of literature, and they attempt to include the general reader who is interested in exploring a fuller tradition of early texts in English than has been available through the almost exclusively male canonical tradition.

SUSANNE WOODS
General Editor

ACKNOWLEDGMENTS

Producing a book is always a cooperative project; producing a series of books such as Women Writers in English becomes more of a cooperative crusade. What began as a small specialized research project has developed into an adventure in literature, computing, and publishing far beyond our initial abstract conception.

At Brown University, many administrators have given the Women Writers Project invaluable support, including President Vartan Gregorian, Provost Frank Rothman, Dean of the Faculty Bryan Shepp, and Vice President Brian Hawkins. Vital assistance has come from the English Department, including chairs Walter Davis, Stephen M. Foley, and Elizabeth D. Kirk, and from staff members at Computing and Information Services, particularly Don Wolfe, Allen Renear, and Geoffrey Bilder. Maria Fish has staffed the Women Writers Project office through crises large and small.

At Oxford University Press, Elizabeth Maguire and Claude Conyers have been both patient and visionary.

Ashley Cross, Julia Deisler, and Lisa Gim shared with me their excitement about teaching early women writers, as have many other faculty members and graduate students at Brown and elsewhere. My friends and colleagues locally in Brown's Computing in the Humanities Users Group and internationally in the Text Encoding Initiative, especially Michael Sperberg-McQueen, have stimulated my thinking about texts and the electronic uses and encoding of texts. Syd Bauman and Grant Hogarth have sustained me in the computer and publishing aspects of the project.

Students are the life's blood of the Women Writers Project, and all of the students who have passed through our offices are part of this volume. Most particularly, among those who worked on *The Poems and Prose of Mary, Lady Chudleigh* were Stephanie Bell, Lisa Billowitz, Amanda Deaver, Nina Greenberg, Thomas R. Harshman, B. Jessie Hill, Deborah Hirsch, Daniel J. Horn, Katie Lott, Leslie Stern, Michele Tepper, and Amanda Zabriskie.

Other students have contributed mightily to the spirit and vitality of the WWP: Carolyn Cannuscio, Lisa Chick, John Fitzgerald, Mithra

Irani, Anthony Lioi, Jason R. Loewith, Carole E. Mah, Elizabeth Soucar, Susan B. Taylor, and Elizabeth Weinstock.

My personal thanks go especially to Sarah Finch Brown and Julia Flanders for their extraordinary dedication to the project, their meticulous scholarship, and their support through the final production details.

ELAINE BRENNAN
Managing Editor

ACKNOWLEDGMENTS

I gratefully acknowledge the assistance of several libraries and my colleagues and friends in the preparation of this edition. Librarians at the Folger Shakespeare Library, the British Library, the Bodleian Library, the Wellcome Institute for the History of Medicine, the West Country Studies Library in Exeter, University of Michigan Library, and the Humanities Research Center at the University of Texas made my task easier with their help. In particular, I am grateful to Jennie Rathbun at the Houghton Library, Mrs. M. Rowe at the Devon Record Office, and Mary L. Robertson at the Huntington Library. The Texas A&M University Honors Program and the Interdisciplinary Group for Historical Literary Studies at Texas A&M University helped to support the time spent in preparing the groundwork for this edition.

In the preparation of this text, I am indebted first and foremost to the skills of Elizabeth Hageman and Elaine Brennan. Sharon Valiant, Moira Ferguson, Ruth Perry, Peter Beal, and Peter Blayney all generously shared information with me. I am also grateful for the advice and assistance of Lena Cowen Orlin, David R. Anderson, Grace Buonocore, Jeffrey N. Cox, Donald R. Dickson, John S. Ezell, Wendy Motooka, James Fitzmaurice, and the members of my Folger Institute seminar, who generously bore with me during the editing process.

MARGARET J. M. EZELL

INTRODUCTION

"You were no sooner gone," wrote John Dryden to his publisher Jacob Tonson in 1697, "but I felt in my pocket, & found my Lady Chudleighs verses; which this Afternoon I gave Mr. [William] Walsh to read in the Coffee house. His opinion is the same with mine, that they are better than any which are printed before the Book [the commendatory verses in Dryden's translation of Virgil]: so thinks also Mr. Wycherley."[1] By the time the former Poet Laureate and his aging libertine literary friends made their endorsement of Chudleigh to one of the period's most important publishers, Mary, Lady Chudleigh had been practicing the art of poetry for over twenty years. Her writings appeared in print only during the last ten years of her life, but her development as a poet and essayist neatly spanned the second half of the seventeenth century. In her printed volumes—*The Ladies Defense* (1701), *Poems* (1703), and *Essays upon Several Subjects* (1710)—we can observe her responses to the changing literary scene and social concerns which faced writers during this time.

In particular, Lady Chudleigh's verse and essays spoke to the concerns of her contemporary women readers. "The following Poems were written at several Times, and on several Subjects," she opens her volume of verse; "If the Ladies, for whom they are chiefly design'd, and to whose Service they are intirely devoted, happen to meet with any thing in them that is entertaining, I have all I am at." Her first published work was the long dialogue poem *The Ladies Defence* (1701), written to refute stifling notions of wifely subservience expressed in *The Bride-Woman's Counsellor* (1699), a marriage sermon by John Sprint. The most frequently anthologized poem by her, "To the Ladies," with its striking opening line ("Wife and Servant are the same"), appeared in her first published collection of verse in 1703. This poem seems to have appealed strongly to her eighteenth-century female readers: contemporary copies of it, for example, can be found transcribed on the flyleaf of

1. *The Letters of John Dryden*, ed. Charles E. Ward (Durham, N.C.: Duke Univ. Press, 1942), 98–100.

the Shakespeare First Folio owned by Elizabeth Brockett and also in Elizabeth Dottin's manuscript volume of Bishop Henry King's poems.[2] "'Twas thine O Chudleigh (name for ever dear / Whilst wit and virtue claim the lay sincere!)," wrote Mary Scott over sixty years after Chudleigh's death, "Boldly t'assert great Nature's equal laws, / And plead thy helpless injur'd sex's cause."[3] For the twentieth-century reader, Chudleigh's life and writings still raise issues of central importance in our understanding of the role of women as authors and readers in the seventeenth and early eighteenth centuries, including her education as a writer, her audience, and her subsequent reception in literary histories.

Mary Lee, the future Lady Chudleigh, was baptized in the parish of Clyst St. George, Devon, on 19 August 1656.[4] Her birth occurred less than a year after her parents, Richard Lee and Mary Sydenham, were married by a Justice in London on 28 August 1655, an event later recorded in her mother's parish, Wynford Eagle, Dorset, on 31 August. Mary was the oldest child in the family, and she also survived the longest: the parish register of Clyst St. George reveals that two of her siblings died in childhood (her brother William [1662–67] and sister Martha [1672–72]) and that her other brother, Richard (1676–1701), died before her, leaving his wife Agnes to raise their two young children, Richard and Mary, all still residing in the parish of Clyst St. George.

Mary Lee's mother, Mary Sydenham (1632–1701), immortalized as "Philinda" by her daughter, came from the illustrious Sydenham family of Wynfold Eagle, Dorset. Mary Lee's uncles included Colonel William Sydenham, who fought on Parliament's side during the Civil War and served as a member of Richard Cromwell's council, and Dr. Thomas Sydenham, who was famous in the history of medicine for his studies of epidemic diseases. Dr. Sydenham was also a friend of the scientist

2. Folger Library STC 22273 No. 23, fourth flyleaf ^{v}; Bodleian Library (hereafter BOD) MS Malone 22, f. 2^{v}.

3. Mary Scott, *The Female Advocate* (London, 1774).

4. *The Registers of Clyst St. George, County Devon 1565–1812*, transcribed by John Lomax Gibbs (London, 1899), 41.

Richard Boyle and the philosopher John Locke; Sydenham was the physician to Anne Finch, Viscountess Conway, the Neoplatonist writer. Thus, through her mother's side of the family, Mary Lee had a network of intellectually inclined relatives living in Dorset and in the Chelsea area of London, relatives who appear to have shared the engagement with issues of natural history and metaphysics which Chudleigh displays so confidently in her own writings.

On her father's side, the Lees of Winslade appear in the parish registers from the 1620s onward. Little is known about the family, except that Richard Lee, like his father William before him, was a substantial man of property, who used "esq" after his name on leasing documents; one source lists him as "Richard Lee of Westminister," implying that in addition to his land in Devon, the family had London connections as well.[5] The Lee family owned a house called Winslade, which was demolished by the middle of the eighteenth century, sometime after it was sold to the Spicer family. Winslade appears on eighteenth-century maps as lying 3–4 miles southeast of Exeter and some twelve miles, as the crow flies, from Mary Chudleigh's future home in Ashton at Place Barton.

Mary Lee married into an equally well-established family. The Chudleighs of Ashton had been lords of the manor since 1320, and branches of the family were scattered throughout Devon and London. The line into which she married was, like her mother's family, distinguished for its activities on the Parliamentary side during the Civil War. Sir George Chudleigh, the first baronet, worked actively against the king at the beginning of the conflict, as did his son James, a major-general who died from his wounds in 1643. After his son's death, the first baronet ceased his opposition, and by the time of the Restoration, the Chudleigh family was again firmly in the Royalist camp.[6] The second baronet, Mary Chudleigh's father-in-law, married Elizabeth Fortesque from nearby Fillegh, and they had at least five children. Mary Chudleigh's brother-in-law Hugh established a branch of the family in

5. Devon Record Office, MS 53/6/Box 35 and MS 49/1/75/2; *Report and Transactions of the Devonshire Association* 19 (1887): 340.

6. Maxwell Adams, "A Brief Account of Ashton Church and of Some of the Chudleighs of Ashton, in Devon," *Transactions of the Devonshire Association for the Advancement of Science, Literature and Art* 31 (1899): 185–98.

Westminister with his wife Susanna and their children; the Ashton parish register reveals that her sisters-in-law married locally, Elizabeth in 1675 to John Hunt of Chudleigh, Devon, and Grace in 1678 to Thomas Gibbon of Exeter.[7] In the 1670s, her father, husband, and brother-in-law Thomas Gibbon pursued business interests together, which suggests that the families worked together profitably.[8]

Mary Lee and George Chudleigh were married in Clyst St. George, 25 March 1674, and their first child, Mary, was baptized and buried there (20 September 1676–9 January 1677). Mary Chudleigh then disappears from the registers anywhere in England and Scotland for seven years;[9] she reappears in the parish of Clyst St. George with the baptism of George (the eventual fourth baronet) on 21 August 1683. Between August 1683 and September 1693, Mary Chudleigh gave birth on the average of every two years. Clearly, she was able to bear children after the death of her first child, so the seven year gap in the baptism records is a mystery: it may imply a separation, or travel abroad, or, on the other hand, simply a series of miscarriages which were not recorded.

Two more of her children were baptized in her family's parish church—Richard, 4 November 1685 and Thomas, 11 August 1687—before the family moved to Ashton. She buried her son Richard in Ashton in 1688. Her father-in-law, Sir George Chudleigh, died in 1691, at which time her husband inherited the title. No record has been found of the death of her mother-in-law, Elizabeth Fortesque. Her death, however, might explain Mary Chudleigh's move from the Lee family parish in Winslade to the Chudleigh's family seat, Place Barton, sometime in 1688.

Of her children born between 1683 and 1693, only George and

7. Devon Record Office, MS Ashton Parish Register.

8. Devon Record Office, MS 49/1/76/1 and 57/3/10/4.

9. There is an inaccurate reference to a poem addressed to Lady Chudleigh appearing in 1684 in Hilda Smith and Susan Cardinale's *Women and Literature of the Seventeenth Century: An Annotated Bibliography Based on Wing's Short-Title Catalogue* (Greenwood, N.J.: Garland Press, 1990), 26. The description of item 128B, "W.C.," *Poems on Several Occasions* (1684), suggests that Chudleigh was one of several women to whom verses were addressed, but the content of this volume does not match the account given of it and no poem to Chudleigh or any other women appears there.

Thomas survived to become adults with families of their own.[10] One hardly need search much further for explanations of the persistent note of melancholy and stoicism one finds in Chudleigh's verse and essays which can be dated from the 1690s than the deaths of four of her six children, including both of her daughters, at very young ages. The years immediately preceding the publication of her poems were particularly bleak. The death of her youngest child, Eliza Maria (1693–1701/2), followed closely those of her mother and brother Richard. Considered against this background, her decision to open her volume of verse with an ode on the death of the young Duke of Gloucester, the only child of Queen Anne to survive infancy but who died from smallpox in 1700 when he was eleven, takes on added poignancy.

Also, during those years in which she prepared her work for publication, Chudleigh herself was severely ill with a form of crippling rheumatism which eventually took her life. In a letter to her friend and fellow poet Elizabeth Thomas dating from 1701/2, Chudleigh invited her to visit Ashton, but warned, "Ashton is healthly enough in the Summer, but I cannot be here in the Winter without hazarding my Life."[11] In 1703 she wrote Thomas from Exeter where she had moved for her health that "my Body sinks under the Pressure, and will not keep Pace with my Mind."[12] In spite of deteriorating health during this period, however, she was completing her final book, the volume of prose and verse meditations *Essays upon Several Subjects.*

---

10. George became the fourth baronet; he married Frances Davies and had four daughters. It was this branch of the family to whom George Ballard applied for information about Mary Chudleigh; Ballard's correspondent in Exeter, Dr. Lyttelton, had dinner with Lady Chudleigh's granddaughters and got their subscriptions for Ballard's *Memoirs;* they also supplied him with the original documents Ballard used. See BOD MS Ballard 42, ff. 136, 141, 149. Her other son, Thomas, married a distant cousin, Henrietta Chudleigh, and became the governor of the Chelsea Hospital; his daughter, Elizabeth Chudleigh, achieved notoriety for appearing either topless or in transparent muslin at the king's masquerade in 1749, the year before her grandmother's poems celebrating retirement from the vanity of society were reprinted. She became the Duchess of Kingston and attained a permanent place in history as the only woman to be tried by the House of Lords for bigamy. See Beatrice Curtis Brown, *Elizabeth Chudleigh, Duchess of Kingston* (London: Gerald Howe, 1927).

11. *Pylades and Corinna: Or, Memoirs of the Lives, Amours, and Writings of Richard Gwinnett . . . and Mrs. Elizabeth Thomas,* 2 vols. (London: 1731), 2:267.

12. *The Poetical Works of Philip Late Duke of Wharton,* 2 vols. (London, 1731), 2:114.

Chudleigh's last known letter, written from Exeter and dated 8 October 1710, was a reply to Sophia, Electress of Hanover, to whom she had dedicated the just recently published *Essays upon Several Subjects* and who had responded with a letter complimenting her on the volume. Chudleigh excuses the delay in responding to this flattering acknowledgment, but states that "I was so very ill, as to be in danger of Death: I continued in that deplorable state for several days; and extremely weak, for several weeks."[13] Her son Thomas wrote to Sophia in January 1711 that his mother had received great joy from the Princess's letter and had temporarily regained "that strength and ease which she had not known during the continuance of a long sickness; she with great earnestness and pleasure imployed that last remaines of Life in dictating the acknowledgements of Her thanks and gratitude; which in obedience to Her dying commands I presume to send."[14] She died 15 December 1710, having been confined to her room for a long period before her death.[15]

It has been the practice for commentators to supplement the bare facts of Chudleigh's life by reading the content of her poems as though they were strictly autobiographical, confessional accounts of her personal situation. Until now, the lack of information about Chudleigh from any source other than George Ballard's printed life of her in *Memoirs of Several Ladies of Great Britain* (1752) has led to critics inferring the events of her life from the topics treated in her poems; certainly, the poems on the death of her mother and her daughter encourage such a biographical reading of her texts. New biographical evidence, however, suggests how such inferential readings have been misleading.

In particular, Chudleigh's attacks on her generation's notions of a wife's duties and a husband's powers should be viewed in the context of Chudleigh's overall career as a writer whose work shows both her control of contemporary genres and her experiments with them. In these volumes, we see a movement from a Restoration lyricist and satirist, pri-

13. British Library MS Stowe 223, f. 398.

14. British Library MS Stowe 224, f. 1.

15. George Ballard, *Memoirs of Several Ladies of Great Britain,* 1752, ed. Ruth Perry (Detroit: Wayne State Univ. Press, 1985), 356.

marily writing pastorals and lyrics, to a philosophic essayist and religious devotionalist, using a mixture of prose meditation and celebratory verse which marks the last stage of her literary efforts. In the preface to *Essays upon Several Subjects*, she herself places her early satire, *The Ladies Defence*, in this framework; "the whole was designed as a Satyr on Vice," she explains in the preface to Essays, "and, not, as some have maliciously reported, for an Invective on Marriage."

Her works read as a whole—a long dialogue poem and two collections of poetry and prose—constitute less a coherent autobiographical chronicle of the events of her life than a continuous philosophical exploration of human passions and the ways to live a truly harmonious life, at peace with one's passions. To explore these intense emotions, we find Chudleigh using a range of genres most popular among Restoration writers, including the lyric and the ode. Chudleigh states in the preface to her first volume that in her poetry her readers will "find a Picture of my Mind, my Sentiments all laid open to their View":

> They'll sometimes see me cheerful, pleas'd, sedate and quiet; at other times griev'd, complaining, struggling with my Passions, blaming myself, endeavouring to pay a Homage to my Reason, and resolving for the future, to support all the Troubles, all the uneasinesses of Life, and then by unexpected Emergencies, unforeseen Disappointments, sudden and surprizing Turns of Fortune, discompos'd, and shock'd till I have rallied my scatter'd Forces, got new Strength, and by making an unweary'd Resistance, gain'd the better of my Afflictions, and restor'd my Mind to its former Tranquility.

Although she dedicated her works to queens and princesses, Chudleigh's poetry and prose speak universally in their exploration of what it means to live a good life. In writing poetry and meditations, Lady Chudleigh seemed to find that harmony which she believed was lacking in her society.

One of the most frequent explanations by her later biographers of Mary Chudleigh's references to her "solitary life" and melancholy found in the prefaces to the volumes and her letters to Elizabeth Thomas is that Mary Chudleigh's marriage was not a happy one, and that she fretted away in enforced rural domesticity. The *Dictionary of National Biography* asserts that "the marriage was far from happy, and Lady

Chudleigh found little pleasure, except in retirement and reading." *The Macmillan Dictionary of Women's Biography* summarizes her life even more bluntly, stating simply that she was "born in Devon, unhappily married to a local landowner."[16] A biographer of her granddaughter, Elizabeth Chudleigh, carries this pattern of autobiographical reading of "Wife and Servant" to such an extent that Mary Chudleigh is presented to us as a crabby figure in a sour domestic tragedy, a "disappointed and passionate woman [who] tolled out her life. She died unmourned and unregretted in 1710 and at her own request was buried without a memorial."[17]

Since Mary Chudleigh herself wrote little about her own marriage and nothing specifically about her husband, this domestic discord is largely inferred from the subject matter of her two satires and from remarks made in letters written toward the end of her life. She warned Londoner Elizabeth Thomas, for example, that should she visit Devon, "you will find very little agreeable Company here, most of the Persons you will converse with, will speak a Language you will hardly understand; you will find us as rough and unpolished as our Country."[18] "Ashton does boast an excellent library," however, and "what you want in Conversation, you shall make up in Books." In another letter to Thomas written several years later, Chudleigh states that if she had not made "my Books and my Thoughts to be the most agreeable Companions, and had I not betime accustomed my selfe to their Conversation, perhaps I should have been as unhappy as any of my Sex."[19] As we have seen, however, Chudleigh's later years were filled with more trials than simply a lack of compatibility with her spouse; she continues this letter, "now, I thank God, I cannot only patiently, but chearfully, bear a great many Things which others would call Afflictions, Life and Death are Things very indifferent to me."

If, on the other hand, Sir George was indeed the boorish country

---

16. *The Macmillan Dictionary of Women's Biography*, ed. Jennifer S. Uglow, 2nd ed. (New York: Macmillan, 1989), 110.

17. Elizabeth Mavor, *The Virgin Mistress: The Life of the Duchess of Kingston* (London: Chatto Windus, 1964), 23–24.

18. *Pylades and Corinna*, 2:267. 19. *Wharton*, 2:112–13.

squire such as Chudleigh caricatures in the person of Sir John Brute in *The Ladies Defence* and as subsequent generations of biographers have made him out to be, it seems odd that he would have permitted his wife to publish pieces satirizing him or to have sanctioned the subsequent editions of them after her death. What Lady Chudleigh does say about him specifically occurs in a letter written toward the end of her life to Elizabeth Thomas. In 1703 Chudleigh told Thomas that she had been busy writing the pieces which would be published as the *Essays upon Several Subjects in Prose and Verse* (1710) and that "you shall see them if I come to London this Winter, but that I believe I shall not, because I find Sir *George* will not leave the Country, and 'twill be Melancholly for me to be alone in Lodging, it tired me the last Winter."[20] While certainly wistful, this does not read like the letter of a person either constrained from travelling or anxious to flee an unhappy relationship.

If one wishes to infer biographical circumstance from the content of Chudleigh's verses, indeed one could counter the negative view of matrimony found in "To the Ladies" with Chudleigh's ideal lover described in "The Wish." "Would but indulgent Fortune send / To me a kind, and faithful Friend," begins the female speaker,

> One Pious, Lib'ral, Just and Brave,
> And to his Passions not a Slave:
> In whom I safely may confide,
> And with him all my Cares divide,
> . . . .
> Who charm'd with Wit, and inward Graces,
> Despises Fools with tempting Faces;
> And still a beauteous Mind does prize
> Above the most enchanting Eyes.

We have no certain means, at this point, of knowing whether Sir George most closely resembled the husband in Chudleigh's poems who finds his greatest pleasure conversing with his livestock and treating his wife like a "Turkish Slave" or the lover who has the sense to prize wit in a woman and "a beauteous Mind."

We can also enlarge our understanding of Chudleigh's participation

---

20. *Wharton*, 2:113.

in Restoration literary life beyond that offered in Ballard's printed text by examining the patterns of authorship she followed and the reception history of her publications. While we do not know the dates of composition for many of the works in her first volume of poetry, we do know that Chudleigh's circumstances from childhood through married maturity gave her the opportunity to cultivate literary acquaintances, pursue her studies of the classics, and, in the final stages, to establish a public reputation as an author. In the patterns of authorship she followed, she shows the typical pattern of writing first for a select coterie audience and later for a commercial public, a pattern which can be seen in the careers of many of her contemporaries, both male and female.

The extensive connections of her family on both sides were important for the young poet. The memoir of Mary Chudleigh written by a family member for her eighteenth-century biographer George Ballard makes it clear that she was educated by her father and encouraged in her literary and antiquarian pursuits by both her mother's and father's families. Chudleigh appears to have begun her career as a poet at an early age. "She was ever from her infancy addicted to reading and [had] naturally a genius for poetry," her relative informed Ballard.[21] The very first reference we have to Mary Chudleigh comes from a Sydenham cousin writing to his uncle Thomas Sydenham, the physician, about her intellectual pursuits. William Sydenham wrote from Wynfold Eagle in November 1675 that "my uncle Lees and coson Chidleighs reterne for Devon again"; "whilst my coson Chidleighs were here, shee being a great lover of Antiquities, desired me and as I formerly promised her, to have one of the Roman Barrowes to bee digged up[;] as you know on the Downes are plenty in this County especially."[22] The family memoir of her notes that poetry and "History were her beloved studies," and her fascination with classical literature and ancient history marks every aspect of her writing.[23]

In particular, we find a fascination with "rational theology," the

21. BOD MS Ballard 74, f. 301^{r}.

22. Kenneth Dewhurst, *Dr. Thomas Sydenham (1624–1689): His Life and Original Writings* (London: The Wellcome Historical Medical Library, 1966), 166.

23. BOD MS Ballard 74, f. 301^{r}.

philosophical attempt to harmonize science and theology, in Chudleigh's long poems such as "The Resolution" and "The Song of the Three Children" as well as in her prose meditations. In her verse, she cites writers such as the naturalist John Ray and the cosmographer Thomas Burnet, whose works on the history of the planet and of the universe seek to create a moralized history of natural phenomenon. Throughout her texts, Chudleigh returns repeatedly to the image of the "dancing atoms," a reference to the classical theory set forth by Epicurus and Lucretius in which the movement of infinite atoms in infinite space, not the whims of the gods, are responsible for actions in nature. In her treatment of it, Chudleigh converts the classical model into a Christian one, having all creation from lightning bolts to sea serpents, from individual "atoms" to all of humanity, joining together to praise their heavenly maker. In her longest poem, "The Song of the Three Children," based on an apocryphal addition to the Book of Daniel in which the three young men cast into the fiery furnace of Nebuchadnezzar sing the Lord's praises, Chudleigh essentially redescribes key moments in the earth's history from the Bible—the Creation, the Flood, and the Apocalypse—using the song of science.

Chudleigh's poetry and prose display an impressive knowledge of classical philosophy, science, and history. As the family memoir also notes, "not understanding any Languages besides her own she was forc'd to content herself with reading the best translations." Commenting on this problem in seventeenth-century female education, Judith Drake, in *An Essay in Defence of the Female Sex* (1696), noted, however, that "'tis possible for an ingenious Person to make a considerable progress in most parts of Learning, by the help of English only," since through "the obliging Humour" of translators, "scarce any thing either Ancient or Modern that might be of general use either for Pleasure, or Instruction is left untouch'd."[24] Lady Chudleigh lived during a great period of English verse translation of the classics, and her writings clearly reflect her study of them. The list of authors she recommends for her female readers in the preface to *The Ladies Defence* and the poem "The Resolution" include Seneca, Plutarch, Epictetus, Horace, Ovid, Virgil, Lucre-

24. Judith Drake, *An Essay in Defence of the Female Sex* (London, 1696), 41–42.

tius, Theocritus, Juvenal, and Persius. In particular, the allusions in her poetry and prose highlight the central importance of John Dryden's translations of the complete works of Virgil (1696) and Plutarch's *Lives* (1683–86) in the literary landscape of the latter part of the Restoration.

Through her marriage, Lady Chudleigh moved from being a simple reader and admirer of Dryden's works into being a part of Dryden's wide-reaching literary circle. One of the most important literary connections she made was with her husband's distant cousins, the Clifford family at Ugbrook Park, located some four miles from the Chudleigh seat at Ashton. The first Lord Clifford of Charles II's "Cabal" was Dryden's patron, and Dryden is believed to have translated several sections of Virgil while staying at Ugbrook. He was such a frequent and respected visitor that a particular scenic viewpoint was called "Dryden's Seat," and he, in turn, dedicated his translation of Virgil's *Pastorals* to Hugh, the second Lord Clifford.[25] It is clear from Dryden's letter to Tonson that it was at Ugbrook Park that he became aware of Mary Chudleigh's poetry: Dryden wished to have her verses on his translation of Virgil printed in the second edition of it, but he warned Tonson to wait until he had heard from "Lord Clifford whether My Lady will put her name to them or not."

In addition to professional men of letters such as Dryden, Chudleigh also numbered among her acquaintances several well-known devotional writers and essayists, including Mary Astell and John Norris of Bemerton, poets such as Elizabeth Thomas, and a circle of admiring amateurs. In addition to her sisters-in-law residing in Exeter and nearby, the Clifford family also may have formed part of this literary group. Apart from Lord Clifford himself, known for his patronage of the arts, the Clifford household also included several women who may have shared Chudleigh's literary tastes and formed part of her literary circle, including Clifford's wife Anne Preston, a contemporary of Mary Chudleigh, and at times three of his unmarried sisters.

Members of Chudleigh's literary group appear to have exchanged verses and to have used pastoral pen names. Chudleigh herself used the

25. Cyril Hughes Hartmann, *Clifford of the Cabal* (London: Heinemann, Ltd., 1937), 291; James Anderson Winn, *John Dryden and His World* (New Haven: Yale Univ. Press, 1987), 477.

name "Marissa" in her correspondence with Elizabeth Thomas ("Corinna"). In addition to poems commenting on the verses by her women friends, such as "To Eugenia, on her Pastoral," several of her poems use the device of "Marissa" in dialogue with other women. It is used most strikingly as a method of examining and controlling her intense grief over the deaths of her mother and daughter. Chudleigh also used imaginary dialogues much more lightheartedly, as in "The Inquiry: A Dialogue between Cleanthe and Marissa," in which the two women attempt to decide whether a miser, a pedant, or an awkward "whining lover" is the biggest fool.

Apart from Elizabeth Thomas and Mary Astell ("Almystrea"), the identities of these women—"Cleanthe," "Clorissa," "Lucinda," and "Eugenia"—remain a mystery at this point. It was to entertain such a group, Chudleigh explains in her preface to *Essays upon Several Subjects*, that she wrote *The Ladies Defence*, "who, when they read it, were pleas'd to tell me they lik'd it, and desir'd me to Print it." It is not known, for example, whether the Eugenia of Chudleigh's poem is the same who wrote the first response in 1699 to Sprint's sermon, *The Female Preacher* (published by H. Hill, the same printer who produced Sprint's sermon); this was reissued as *The Female Advocate* in 1700, and is frequently misattributed to Chudleigh in bibliographies.

"Eugenia," too, signs herself as a "Lady of Quality," but her sharp-edged prose reproof to Sprint is very different in tone and tactics from Chudleigh's verse dialogue. "Ladies," Eugenia begins, "If you inquire who I am, I shall only tell you in general, that I am one that never yet came within the Clutches of a Husband; and therefore what I write may be the more favourably interpreted as not coming from a Party concern'd."[26] Eugenia claims a small acquaintance with Greek and Latin and to "having adventur'd a little abroad into the World, and endeavour'd to understand Men and Manners"; not even in Italy and Spain, she declares, do men demand from their wives "a Slavery so abject as this [Sprint] would fain persuade us to" (vi). While Chudleigh informs her readers in the "Preface" to *The Ladies Defence* that Sprint himself sent her a copy of the sermon ("of whom, notwithstanding he has been pleas'd to

26. Eugenia, *The Female Advocate* (London, 1700), v.

treat us with the utmost Severity and Neglect, I think my self oblig'd in Justice to say, that he is a Person of Learning"), Eugenia declares that she had it from "a Gentleman who I am sure was very far in it from the design of the Author," and she characterizes the sermon as "Rude and Scandalous" and Sprint himself as a "Levite" deserving to be rebuked.

Eugenia and Chudleigh share an admiration for the writings of Mary Astell, whom they cite in their refutations of Sprint. As Astell's biographer Ruth Perry has recently noted, Chudleigh depicts the author of *A Serious Proposal to the Ladies* (1694), *Letters Concerning the Love of God* (1695) with John Norris, and *Some Reflection Upon Marriage* (1700) as her inspiration, both as a writer "Attracted by the Glory of your Name, / To follow you in all the lofty Roads of Fame" and as one who lives a life of Platonic bliss, "a nobler Path to tread, / And from Tyrannick Custom free."[27] The intense strain of neoplatonism found in Chudleigh's writings, in poems such as "The Observation," "Solitude," and "The Choice" and in essays such as "Of Death" and "Of Friendship," suggests how much in sympathy Chudleigh was with the writings of Astell and Norris.

It appears from Elizabeth Thomas's correspondence that Chudleigh and Astell knew one another personally. A friendship seems plausible, given the location of Chudleigh's Sydenham relatives in Chelsea where Astell lived. Elizabeth Thomas, who herself wrote a poem lauding Almystrea, was, on the other hand, apparently snubbed by Astell. Even though the contact between Thomas and Astell was made through a mutual friend, John Norris of Bemerton, Astell's behavior led Thomas to write to Chudleigh for an explanation of Astell's attitude towards her.[28] On this occasion, Chudleigh was able to assure Thomas that Norris, at least, was "very much your Friend." She follows this reassurance with a detailed physical description of Norris, suggesting that she, unlike Thomas, knew the Platonist poet and essayist in person rather than just through correspondence.[29] Thomas, on her side, forwarded Chudleigh's letters to the London physician-poet-translator Dr. Samuel

27. Ruth Perry, *The Celebrated Mary Astell: An Early English Feminist* (Chicago: Univ. of Chicago Press, 1986), 107–8.

28. *Ibid.*, 266. 29. *Wharton*, 2:110–11.

Garth. Garth was a friend of Dryden and early encourager of Pope, a translator of Ovid, and a member of the Kit-Cat Club; unfortunately, no record of the substance of Chudleigh's correspondence remains to reveal whether it was of a medical or literary nature.[30]

Through Mary Chudleigh's letters and her poems addressed to other poets we gain some sense of her involvement in the literary life of her day. She was, however, never a charismatic social figure at the center of a group of literati in the way that Katherine Philips perhaps was and Lady Mary Wortley Montagu would become. Lady Chudleigh was able nevertheless (for all her protestations of how dull the Devon natives were and how lonely London lodgings could be) to participate directly in London literary life. Her first printer, John Deeve (or Deere), was a minor bookseller, who dealt mostly in law books and is referred to by his contemporaries only as being "unfortunate"; her next printer, however, was Bernard Lintott, a prominent and influential figure, who published Pope, Gay, Steele, and Nicholas Rowe.[31]

Although her writings did not appear in print until 1701, less than a decade before her death, her poems enjoyed four editions, and individual poems have appeared in anthologies throughout the eighteenth and nineteenth centuries and up to the present day. As we have seen, her first readers were family and friends. With her introduction to the literary world represented by Dryden at Ugbrook Park and the publication of *The Ladies Defence*, she moved into a new mode of authorship. She became a public figure, a poet whom strangers read; they sought her friendship and they sent their own verses to her for comment. Chudleigh, too, had her female followers who after her death celebrated the life and works of "Marissa."

Elizabeth Thomas began their friendship by writing to Chudleigh and sending some of her own work. "Your acceptance of that worthless Present [Thomas's poems] was not only infinitely beyond its Deserts, but even the Vanity of my most presumptuous Wishes," Thomas begins

30. *Wharton*, 2:115.

31. Henry R. Plomer, ed., *A Dictionary of the Printers and Booksellers who were at Work in England, Scotland, and Ireland from 1668–1725* (Oxford: Oxford Bibliographical Society, 1922), 103.

her second letter, "at the same time when I rejoice at my good Fortune, I cannot but blush at the exchange you will make by entering into a Correspondence with one who has neither Genius enough to answer your inimitable Letters, nor Merit sufficient to preserve those kind Thoughts you have entertained of her."[32] Chudleigh sounds rather surprised at the attention, protesting, "The weak Defence I have made for my Sex, is ... far from deserving the Thanks you are pleased to give me both in your obliging Letter, and your admirable Verses."[33]

The titles of the three poems Thomas wrote praising Chudleigh mark the milestones in Chudleigh's progress through the world of public authorship: "To the Lady Chudleigh, the Anonymous Author of the *Lady's Defence*," "To the Lady Chudleigh, on Printing her Excellent Poems," and, finally, "On the Death of the Lady Chudleigh, An Ode."[34] In these verses, Thomas continually praises Chudleigh for her ability to combine "wit" with "learning"; she holds up for admiration Chudleigh's "solid Judgment" which "sparkles in each Line." Thomas declares that she wishes to be able to "... praise the Beauties of each sparkling Line: / Show, with what solid Pleasures they delight, / How Wit, and Learning, in your Works unite."[35]

Terms of praise such as these are continued in Chudleigh's biographical entries in eighteenth- and nineteenth-century sources. Over forty years after her death, George Ballard, having collected information about her for several years, published her life in *Memoirs of Several Ladies of Great Britain* (1752), the text which would act as the principal source of information about her for subsequent literary biographers. In the eighteenth century, these included Theophilus Cibber's entry on her in *The Lives of the Poets* (1753), the anonymous *Biographium Fæmineum* (1766) which is directly based on Ballard, and in the nineteenth century, Mary Hays's *Female Biography* (1803), Jane Williams's *The Literary Women of England* (1861) and, eventually, her entry in *The Dictionary of National Biography.*

32. *Pylades and Corinna,* 2:264.

33. *Wharton,* 2:107.

34. Elizabeth Thomas, *Miscellany Poems* (London, 1722).

35. Thomas, "To the Lady Chudleigh, on Printing her Excellent Poems," *Poems,* 150.

No hesitation or qualifications disturb the praise of Chudleigh's life and writings by those scholars and friends George Ballard consulted in compiling the first critical assessment of her in the mid-eighteenth century. It appears to have been Ballard's practice to send out copies of the works of the women he was studying to receive comments on it from academic friends at Oxford and his various antiquarian contacts. One contact who provided much useful information to Ballard, Thomas Rawlins, recommended Chudleigh in 1743 as a likely candidate for Ballard's volume, describing her as "ye Author of severall Admirable Poems & other useful Discourses & for rare Wit & Learning & Eloquence as well as Piety and Virtue was justly esteemed ye Honr & Glory of her Sex."[36]

Ballard's friend William Parry, a clergyman at Shipton, wrote enthusiastically to Ballard in 1747 that "I own my obligations to you for favouring me with the sight of Lady Chudleigh's ingenious Essays; they discover a very great and uncommon Degree of Piety and Learning, and a noble Contempt of those Vanities which the Generality of Ladies of her Rank too eagerly pursue."[37] Parry was so taken with Chudleigh's prose meditations that "I have writ to a Friend in London to purchase it for me."

Individual poems by Chudleigh remained alive for readers in the numerous biographical accounts based on Ballard and in anthologies of women's verses compiled during the eighteenth and nineteenth centuries. Cibber printed "On the Death of my dear Daughter Eliza Maria Chudleigh" in his life of her in 1753. Colman and Thornton in their 1755 edition of *Poems by Eminent Ladies* included "To the Ladies," "To Eugenia, on her Pastoral," "The Resolve," "The Inquiry," "A Dialogue of Lucian Paraphrased," and all of *The Ladies Defence;* this generous selection was reduced by the 1780 edition to "To the Ladies," "The Resolve," and "The Inquiry." Alexander Dyce's *Specimens of British Poetesses* (1827) offered "To the Ladies" and "The Resolve," a selection replicated by Frederic Rowton in *The Female Poets of Great Britain* (1853), who lauded her for her "clever championship of her sex at a time when the female mind was far too little esteemed," although he

36. BOD MS Ballard 41, f. 250^{r}. 37. BOD MS Ballard 40, ff. 82^{v}–83^{r}.

cautioned his female readers that the advice given to women to remain single in "To the Ladies" was less worthy than her defense of them.

Although a scattered few of her verses remain immortal in anthologies, as Ballard notes, Chudleigh herself was buried without a monument or inscription at Ashton. However, the description of her provided by George Russell, who also translated the Latin texts included in the volume for Ballard, serves admirably to place her life and writings in the context of her times. Ballard found it so apt that he included Russell's assessment word for word in the *Memoirs.* Russell, summarizing Chudleigh's merits for his time and later generations, declares that her works stand revealed as

> the delib'rate results of a long exercise in the world improv'd with Reading, Regulated by Judgment, soften'd by good breeding, and heighten'd with sprightly thoughts and elevated Piety. Her stile often runs of itself into a kind of Poetical measure, I dare say the authoress never observ'd it—Her soul was harmonious, no wonder her Expressions are the same.[38]

Selected Bibliography

Ballard, George. *Memoirs of Several Ladies of Great Britain who have been Celebrated for their Writings or Skill in the Learned Languages, Arts and Sciences* (1752). Edited by Ruth Perry. Detroit: Wayne State Univ. Press, 1985.

Coleman, Antony. "The Provok'd Wife and The Ladies Defense." *Notes and Queries,* n.s. 17 (March 1970): 88–91.

Perry, Ruth. "Chudleigh, Mary." In *A Dictionary of British and American Women Writers, 1660–1800.* Edited by Janet Todd. London: Methuen, 1987.

Smith, Hilda. *Reason's Disciples: Seventeenth-Century English Feminists.* Urbana: Univ. of Illinois Press, 1982.

Williamson, Marilyn. *Raising Their Voices: British Women Writers, 1650–1750.* Detroit: Wayne State Univ. Press, 1990.

38. BOD MS Ballard 37, ff. 133^{r-v}.

Note on the Text and Sources

After her death, Chudleigh's poems were reprinted several times by Lintott. The second edition, published the year before her death, contained *The Ladies Defence*, which she states in the Preface to *Essays upon Several Subjects* was added by Lintott to the original edition without her permission; this version was reprinted in 1713, with slight modifications in pagination. The third edition appeared in 1722 with the label "corrected," but the only difference from the 1709 edition is found in the title page, ornaments, and pagination. The final edition in 1750 is unchanged in content from the previous ones.

Several of Chudleigh's letters to Elizabeth Thomas are held at the Bodleian Library, contained in the volume of letters (including those of Pope) which Thomas sold to the bookseller Edmund Curll. These appear printed in *Pylades and Corinna* (1731) and *The Poetical Works of Philip Late Duke of Wharton* (1731). Chudleigh's last letter to Princess Sophia is at the British Library.

Ballard copied directly from the family memoir that Chudleigh left in manuscript "two tragedies, two operas, a masque, some of Lucian's dialogues done into verse, 'Satyrical Reflections on Saqualio,' in imitation of one of Lucian's dialogues, with several small poems on various occasions" (355).[39] Although some recent sources refer to manuscripts of Chudleigh's being held by the Huntington and Houghton Libraries, such citations appear to be mistaken. None of Chudleigh's literary manuscripts seem to have survived; there are, however, contemporary transcriptions of some of her works, such as are cited in the text above. A report of the Devonshire Association in 1887 records that no trace of the Chudleigh MSS had turned up in response to two separate queries, and recent searches have proved equally unsuccessful.

The texts for this edition were taken from the 1701 edition of *The Ladies Defence*, Folger Shakespeare Library (shelf number PR 3346 C7 L3 Cage); the 1703 edition of *Poems on Several Occasions*, incorporating the errata, Huntington Library (shelf mark 58020), and the 1710

39. *Report and Transactions of the Devonshire Association for the Advancement of Science, Literature and Art* 19 (1887): 340–41 (341).

edition of *Essays upon Several Subjects*, Folger Shakespeare Library (shelf number 166-748q).

Obvious printers' errors have been silently emended, but eighteenth-century variants in punctuation and orthography have been retained. In dialogue poems, abbreviated speaker names have been spelled out for consistency, and those verse paragraphs have not been indented. Some portions of various texts were originally printed in an italic font; they have been printed here in a roman font for readability; in the same way, multiple layers of emphasis, particularly in poem or essay titles, have been reduced.

The Ladies Defence

OR,

THE BRIDE-WOMAN'S COUNSELLOR ANSWER'D:

A Poem in a Dialogue Between

Sir John Brute, Sir William Loveall,

Melissa, and a Parson

{ 1701 }

TO ALL INGENIOUS LADIES

Ladies,

The Love of Truth, the tender Regard I have for your Honour, joyn'd with a just Indignation to see you so unworthily us'd, makes me assume the Confidence of imploying my Pen in your Service. The Knowledge I had of my Inability for so great a Task, made me for a while stifle my Resentments, as thinking it much better privately to lament the Injuries that were done you, than expose you by a weak Defence to the fresh Insults of a Person, who has not yet learnt to distinguish between Railing and Instruction, and who is so vain as to fancy, that the Dignity of his Function will render every thing he thinks fit to say becoming: But when I found that some Men were so far from finding fault with his Sermon, that they rather defended it, and express'd an ill-natur'd sort of Joy to see you ridicul'd, and that those few among 'em who were Pretenders to more Generosity and good Humour, were yet too proud, too much devoted to their Interest, and too indulgent to their Pleasures, to give themselves the Trouble of saying any thing in your Vindication, I had not the Patience to be Silent any longer. Besides it vex'd me to think he should have the Satisfaction of believing, that what by the Malice of some, the Neutrality of others, and the Sacredness of his Character, he was secur'd from all Opposition, and might triumph over you at his Pleasure: it also troubl'd me to find that but one of our own Sex had the Courage to enter the Lists with him: I know there are several other Ladies, who, if they wou'd be so kind to themselves, and you, as to undertake the Quarrel, wou'd manage it with more Learning, Eloquence and Address, than I dare pretend to, as being infinitely my Superiours in all the Indowments of the Mind; but since they think fit to decline it, I hope they will permit me to enter the Field, and try my Fortune with our mighty Antagonist. I assure 'em I do not do it out of an ambitious desire of being talk'd of, or with hopes of having it said, I can Write well; no, if I know my own Heart, I am far from any such Vanity, as being too well

Line 8. **Person:** John Sprint, author of *The Bride-Woman's Counsellor* (1699).

Line 21. **one … Sex:** Eugenia, author of *The Female Preacher* (1699), reprinted as *The Female Advocate* (1700).

acquainted with my own Insufficiency, to entertain any such unbecoming Thoughts of my mean Performance. The following Poem is intirely the Result of that great Concern and Zeal I have for your Reputation; and if it happens to do you any Service, I have all that I aim at; and the only Favour I have to beg of you is, that you will be so generous as to receive it into your Protection, and so obliging as to let the Affection with which 'twas written, compensate for its Faults. I am sorry *Mr. Sprint* should have any occasion given him for so severe an Invective, and I heartily wish my Sex wou'd keep a stricter Guard over their Passions, and amidst all the various Occurrences of Life, consult neither their Ease, the Gratification of their Humour, nor the Satisfaction of others, when 'tis in Opposition to their Reason; but having rightly inform'd themselves what ought to be done on each Emergency, go steadily on, without being disturb'd either at Unkindnesses, Reproaches, Affronts or Disappointments; that all who see 'em may have just cause to conclude, from the Regularity of their Actions, the Calmness of their Tempers, and the Serenity of their Looks, that there are no Uneasinesses within, and that they are infinitely better pleas'd with the secret Plaudits of their own Consciences, than they would be with the flattering Acclamations of a deceitful inconstant World; but such an Evenness, such a Tranquility of Mind, is not attainable without much Study, and the closest Application of Thought; it must be the work of Time, and the Effect of a daily Practice. But perhaps, while I am indeavouring to make you happy, and shewing you the way to transmit your Names with Honour to succeeding Ages, my kindness may be misconstru'd, and I thought guilty of unpardonable Arrogancy, for presuming to prescribe Rules to Persons, who already know much more than I can teach 'em. To free my self from this Imputation, I solemnly declare, That what I write is wholly intended for such as are on the same Level with my self, and have not been blest with a learned and ingenious Education, and cannot boast of such a strength of Resolution, such a constancy of Mind, such a depth of Reason and solidity of Judgment, as is requisite, in order to the obtaining that desirable Firmness, and, (if I may be allow'd to call it so) Inflexibility of Soul, which I have been recommending; and not for those who, by the greatness of their Virtue, and the Sublimity of their Wit, are rais'd to a

Line 48. **Plaudits:** praise.

Height above me; on such I content my self to gaze at an awful distance, and am pleas'd to see, notwithstanding what has been said to the contrary by some envious Detractors, still among us Women that are shining Examples of Piety, Prudence, Moderation, Patience, and all other valuable Qualities; by such as these I should take it as a Favour to be instructed; and would they by a generous Condescension give themselves the Trouble of directing us in the management of our Lives, we should be for ever bound to pay 'em the highest Retributions. 'Tis only to such as are in the lowest Form, to the meanest Proficients in the School of Virtue, that I take the Liberty of giving Advice. So well, so intirely well I love my Sex, that if 'twere in my Power they shou'd be all wholly faultless, and as much admir'd for the Comprehensiveness of their Knowledge, as they are now despis'd for their Ignorance, and have Souls as beauteous as their Faces, Thoughts as bright and sparkling as their Eyes: And in what Station so ever Providence thinks fit to place 'em, I would earnestly desire 'em, as a thing exceedingly for their Honour, to be careful to observe a just Decorum, and neither suffer themselves to be transported with Joy when they are Happy, or dispirited when they are Miserable; but to be humble, kind, sincere, and easie of Access, when Great, Liberal when Rich, Sedate, Chearful and Contented when Poor, free from Revenge, and ready to forgive when injur'd, the same when reproach'd or applauded, when caress'd, or neglected: And if it is their hard Fortune to be marry'd to Men of brutish unsociable Tempers, to Monsters in Humane Shape, to Persons who are at open defiance with their Reason, and fond of nothing but their Folly, and under no other Government but that of their irregular Passions, I would perswade them to struggle with their Afflictions, and never leave contending, 'till they have gain'd an absolute Victory over every repining Thought, every uneasie Reflection: And tho' 'tis extreamly difficult, yet I wou'd advise 'em to pay 'em as much Respect, and to obey their Commands with as much readiness, as if they were the best and most indearing Husbands in the World; this, will not only put a stop to the invidious Censures of their spightful Enemies, but give 'em the possession of that inward Joy, that unspeakable Satisfaction, which naturally arises from the apprehension of having done good and audable Actions: In order to the

Line 97. **invidious**: liable to cause resentment.

gaining such a happy disposition of Mind, I would desire 'em seriously to consider what those things are which they can properly call their own, and of which Fortune cannot deprive 'em, and on these alone they ought to terminate their Desires, and not vainly extend 'em to those things which are not within their Power, as Honours, Riches, Reputation, Health, and Beauty; for they being Goods which they cannot bestow on themselves, and of which they may have but a very transient possession, they ought to enjoy 'em with indifferency, and look on 'em only as Gifts, which the Almighty Donor freely and liberally gives, and which he may, when he thinks fit, resume without the least injustice: This, if often and heedfully reflected on, will make 'em moderate their Desires, and teach 'em never with Earnestness to wish for any thing that has no dependance on 'em, nor to entertain an Aversion for things that 'tis not in their Power to avoid. I would have them also to consider that those things which are generally accounted Evils, as Poverty, Disgraces, the loss of Children and Friends, with all other Calamities incident to the Humane Nature, are not really so; for if they were, they would be so to all, which 'tis evident they are not. Poverty, which is so much dreaded by some, and too often shunn'd at the expence both of their Conscience and Honour, has been courted by others; and there have been Persons who have look'd on their Wealth as a Burden, and thrown it off as an unnecessary Load, esteeming themselves rich enough when they have had wherewithall to satisfie their Hungar and their Thirst, and to defend themselves from the Injuries of the Weather. 'Tis but little that Nature desires, and we may be as happy in Cottages as in Pallaces. Disgrace, if they are satisfi'd of their own Innocency, ought to give 'em no disturbance. 'Tis but a Phantom, and subsists only in the Imagination. Reproachful injurious Language can do them no hurt, unless they themselves contribute to it. The having it said they are Proud, Passionate, Censorious, Extravagant or whatsoever else Malicious People are pleas'd to accuse them of, does not make them so, neither will they be the less regarded by those who are throughly acquainted with their innate Worth and Value. 'Tis to the few Wise and Virtuous they ought to indeavour to approve themselves; as for the unthinking many, the Giddy Multitude, who are ready to Deifie this Day, those whom they will despise, vilifie, and affront tomorrow, 'tis below 'em to court their Favour, or desire their Approbation; their Applauses being as little to be valu'd as their Censures. As for their

Children and Friends, they, like the former, are of the number of those Goods to which they have no right, and are to be parted with not repiningly, but thankfully; their injoying them so long being a favour, for which they ought to make a grateful Acknowledgment, and not to gratifie a selfish, disingenuous Humour, by murmuring at the All-wise Disposer of Events, who knows much better than they what is good and convenient for them; and as long as their Virtue, their Prudence, their Patience, their Integrity are left, they may retire into themselves, and there be happy without any other Company; neither are Sickness and Death altogether so formidable as they are generally represented; the First may be overcome by a Mind resolv'd and constant; and amidst the greatest Pains 'tis some Consolation to think 'twill be Glorious and Honourable to indure them with Courage. As for the Last, which is look'd on as the most terrible and shocking of all those things which are commonly call'd Evils, as being the Privation of Life, and a thing abhorrent to Nature, 'tis no more than drawing the Curtain, and inlarging the Prospect: 'Twill give them a Writ of Ease, a kind Discharge from all the Numerous Miseries of Life, and place them at once beyond the reach of Envy, and the Power of Fortune. That such great and momentous Truths as these may become familiar to their Minds, I would perswade 'em, instead of spending so much of their Time in reading Plays and Romances, to bestow a part of it in studying Moral Philosophy, which they will find to be of very great use toward the bettering and informing of their Understandings, the improving their Judgments, and the regulating their Wills and Affections: From what I have said, I would not have it thought I dislike Plays and Romances; I assure you I think 'em very innocent, and very agreeable Diversions, especially the First. Tragedies fill the Mind with noble Ideas, and inspire us with great and generous Sentiments; and Comedies show us our Faults in the clearest Light; in them we see our Weaknesses expos'd, and all our darling Follies ridicul'd; and 'tis our selves alone we ought to blame, if we receive no Advantage from them, for they instruct at the same time they entertain. But the Books I would chiefly recommend, next to the Sacred Scripture, and Devotional Discourses, are, *Seneca's Morals,* together with those of

Line 171. **Seneca:** Stoic philosopher (d. A.D. 65) who educated Nero and wrote numerous compositions on moral subjects.

Plutarch; and the Philosophy of *Epictetus;* that excellent Man, who in the worst of Times, and the most vicious Court in the World, kept his Integrity inviolable, and was still true to his Principles, and constant to himself amidst all the Inconveniencies, Discouragement and Disgraces that attended him: Neither the Indisposition of his Body, nor the Barbarity of a Savage Master, nor that Poverty in which he spent his Life, cou'd make him do or say any thing unworthy of himself, or unbecoming a Philosopher. I would likewise recommend to them *Gassendi's Morals,* I mean, theThree Discourses of Happiness, Virtue and Liberty, collected from his Works by the learned Monsieur *Bernier.* To these I desire 'em to add both Ancient and Modern Histories; in the reading of which they will see the Rise and Fall of mighty Monarchies, great Kingdoms springing from their Ruines, and little States supporting themselves for several Ages amidst numerous and powerful Enemies, by the force of good Laws, and the advantages of just and prudent Institutions, together with the Mischiefs that Luxury, Pride, Ambition, Avarice, and the desire of absolute Dominion have often involv'd 'em in. They will there also see Men rais'd from the Dust, from low and obscure Beginnings, and exalted to the greatest Height of Power, the utmost extent of Humane Glory; and then all on a sudden, by an unexpected reverse of Fate, a strange and surprizing turn of Fortune, depriv'd of all their Grandeur, and reduc'd to their Original meanness. Princes sometimes on Thrones, and sometimes in Prison. Good Men induring the Punishments due to Vice, and vicious Men receiving the Rewards belonging to Vertue. There they will find a *Socrates* dying by Poyson, a *Regulus* expiring in Torments, an *Aristides,*

Line 172. **Plutarch**: celebrated Roman historian (A.D. 46–120) and author of *Moralia* and *De cohibenda ira;* Dryden compiled a translation of his *Lives of the Noble Grecians and Romans* in 1683–86. **Epictetus**: Stoic philosopher (c. A.D. 60–140), born a slave and freed by Nero, whose thoughts on austerity, humility, patience, and contempt of riches were collected by a student under the title *Enchiridion.*

Line 179. **Gassendi**: Pierre Gassendi (1592–1655), a friend of Galileo and Pascal, whose work attempted to unite Christianity and natural science; his works were translated by François Bernier (1620–88).

Line 196. **Socrates**: Stoic philosopher (469–399 B.C.), whose life was a search for truth and the exposure of fraud and vanity; he was sentenced to death by drinking hemlock. **Regulus**: Roman consul in 267 and 256 B.C.; the emblem of heroic constancy, he was captured by the Carthaginians and sent as a hostage to urge peace terms with the Roman senate, but instead he convinced the Romans to reject them, whereupon he was severely tortured by his captors. **Aristides**: celebrated Athenian soldier and judge (fl. 484 B.C.), called "Aristides the Just," who died in poverty.

Camillus and *Rutilius* banish'd by their ungrateful Country-Men, a *Pompey* treacherously slain, a *Cæsar* murder'd by his Friends, a *Belisarius* begging his Bread, and a *Mauritius* with his whole Family falling by the Hands of a rebellious Subject. Sure such Objects as those will keep them from wondering at little Accidents, or grieving at trifling Disappointments, from sinking under every small Affliction, and make them entertain a very low Opinion of Humane Greatness; such Vicissitudes as these will let 'em see there's no dependance on any thing here; neither Virtue, Knowledge, Prudence, Quality, nor Power; neither the greatest Obligations, the closest Ties of Conscience and Honour, nor yet a Spotless Innocency of Life, and irreprovable Integrity of Manners, are able to defend their Possessors from the Outrages of Fortune, or from the invenom'd Tongues, and bloody Designs of cruel and ambitious Men. If they should find themselves tyr'd, and their Minds too much sadden'd by these melancholy Reflections, I would advise 'em to read the Poets, and acquaint themselves with all the Finenesses of those great Masters of Wit and Language, *Homer, Anacreon, Theocritus, Lucretius, Manilius, Virgil, Horace, Ovid, Juvenal,* and *Persius,* are now naturaliz'd, and wear an

---

Line 197. **Camillus**: Camillus L. Furius (d. 365 B.C.), a famed Roman general who was banished for distributing the spoils of war but who came back to rescue Rome when it was besieged by the Gauls. **Rutilius**: P. Rutilius Rufus, Roman consul during reign of Sylla (ca. 70 B.C.), banished for his virtues and opposition to vice.

Line 198. **Pompey**: a famous Roman general (B.C. 106–48) who formed the first triumvirate with Julius Caesar and Crassus in B.C. 60; he was stabbed in the back by Septimus, formerly one of his trusted soldiers. **Belisarius**: a great general during the reign of Justinian (527–65 A.D.), who after defeating the Vandals and the Goths was accused of conspiracy; his eyes were put out, and he ended life as a wandering beggar.

Line 213. **Anacreon**: Greek lyric poet (ca. 570?–488? B.C.) who wrote mainly about love and wine. **Theocritus**: Greek poet of Sicily (3rd century B.C.) who is said to have created the genre of pastoral poetry. **Lucretius**: Roman poet (ca. 99–55 B.C.), whose main work was a six-book philosophical poem, *De Rerum Natura*, using Epicurus's "atomic" theory of the universe to oppose a view that events in this world can only be understood as the actions of the gods; he proposed instead that virtue is the true source of all peace and tranquility; it was translated by Dryden, appearing in *Sylvae* (1685). **Manilius**: Marcus Manilius, author of works on astronomy written during the reign of Augustus and Tiberius (ca. A.D. 10–30), translated by Edward Sherburne in 1675. **Virgil**: Publius Virgilius Maro (70–19 B.C.), author of the *Aeneid.*

Line 214. **Horace***:* Quintus Horatius Glaccus (65–8 B.C.), Roman lyric poet who celebrated the good life in retirement and offered moderation as the key to happiness. **Ovid:** Ovidius Naso (43 B.C.–A.D. 17), Roman poet, author of *Metamorphoses*, translated by Dryden and Garth. **Juvenal**: Roman satirist (A.D. 60–ca. 130) who wrote sixteen satires on the depravity of contemporary society, translated by Dryden. **Persius:** Roman satirist (A.D. 34–62) whose six satires were influenced by Stoic philosophy; also translated by Dryden.

English Dress; and we have the happiness to have Poets of our own, who for their good Sense, flight of Fancy, Purity of Stile, and Elevation of Thought, deserve the highest admiration. And that the Men may have no just Cause to upbraid them with their being ignorant of any thing that is worthy of their Knowledge, I would also perswade 'em to read such Books as treat of the several Parts of the Earth, and which give *Geographical* Descriptions of Places; they will find the Travels of ingenious, inquisitive Men infinitely delightful, and they will every where in their Relations meet with things very entertaining, and diverting, as well as useful, it being extreamly pleasant to observe the different Opinions, Manners, Customs, Interests, and Habits of the several Inhabitants of the World, and to know what is remarkable in each Country, and peculiar to it. Such Studies as these, together with those which I have mention'd before, will so wholly imploy their Thoughts, and so intirely fill up those Intervals of Time which they can spare from their Domestick Affairs, and the necessary Concerns of Life, that they will have no leisure to inquire into the Transactions of their Neighbourhood, or to make uncharitable Reflections on their Conduct; nor will there be any Room left for the ordinary Impertinences of Conversation: They will know how to entertain themselves, and others, both advantagiously and agreeably, and will be always easie and pleas'd, whether alone, or in Company; neither the Badness of their Husbands, the Unkindnesses of their Friends, the Censoriousness of an envious malicious World, nor the most unwelcome Turns of Fortune will give them any Trouble, or disturb their Repose. I beg your pardon for the length of this Address, and for the liberty I have taken to speak my Thoughts so freely, which I do not doubt but you will readily grant to one, who has no other Design but that of doing you Justice, nor no higher Ambition, than that of letting the World see with how much Sincerity, Respect and Ardour, she is,

Ladies, Your most Humble and Devoted Servant.

M—y C——

THE PREFACE TO THE READER

The Book, which has been the occasion of the insuing Poem, was presented to me by its Author, of whom, notwithstanding he has been pleas'd to treat us with the utmost Severity and Neglect, I think my self oblig'd in Justice to say, that he is a Person of Learning. What his Reasons were for using us so roughly, I know not; perhaps he did it to let us see his Wit, who has had the ill Fortune to converse with Women of ungovernable Tempers, whose Passions have got the Ascendant of their Reason; such I think cannot be too harshly treated, and the greatest kindness that can be done 'em, is to bring 'em (if 'tis possible) to the Knowledge of themselves, and their Duty, and by shewing them their Faults, indeavour to depress those towring Imaginations. But 'tis hard that all should suffer for the Failures and Indiscretions of some; that those who are willing to give up themselves intirely to the Conduct of Reason, who make it their Study to live according to the strictest Rules of Vertue, and are so far from indulging themselves in their Follies, that they esteem Reproofs as the greatest Favours that can be shown 'em, and are contented that all Mankind should be Judges of their Actions; whom Passions cannot byass, nor Interest tempt, nor Ill Usage provoke to do or say any thing unworthy of themselves, should be rank'd with Criminals, and have no Deference pay'd 'em: 'Tis for their Sakes alone I have made the following Remarks. I have done it by way of Dialogue, and those Expressions which I thought would be indecent in the Mouth of a Reverend Divine, are spoken by Sir *John Brute*, who has all the extraordinary Qualifications of an accomplish'd Husband; and to render his Character compleat, I have given him the Religion of a Wit, and the good Humour of a Critick. I am afraid the Clergy will accuse me of Atheism for making *Sir John* speak so irreverently of them; but before they condemn me, I beg 'em to be so just as to consider, that I do not speak my own Thoughts, but what one might rationally suppose a Man of his Character will say on such Occasions: And to prevent their hav-

---

Line 2. **its Author**: John Sprint, who resided in Sherbourn, Dorset, author of *The Bride-Woman's Counsellor* (1699).

ing any misapprehensions of me, I do assure 'em, that for all such of their Order as are pious and ingenuous Men, whose Conversations are instructive, and whose Lives are conformable to those holy Truths they teach, none can have a higher Veneration than I: And if such as these find any thing in my Poem that they dislike, they will oblige me in letting me know it, and I promise 'em I will retract it. Had he treated us with a little more Respect, and instead of the surly Sourness of a Cynick, express'd himself with the good Humour of an English Man, and the soft and indearing Mildness of a Christian, I should have thought my self oblig'd to have return'd him Thanks for his Instructions. That we are generally less Knowing, and less Rational than the Men, I cannot but acknowledge; but I think 'tis oftener owing to the illness of our Education, than the weakness of our Capacities. The learned *F. Malebranch* says, *'Tis in a certain Temperature of the Largeness and Agitation of the Animal Spirits, and conformity with the Fibres of the Brain, that the Strength of Parts consists;* and he tells us, That Women are sometimes blest with that just Temperature, and are Learned, Couragious, and capable of every thing; and instead of that nauseous Jargon, and those impertinent Stories with which our Maids usually entertain us in our younger Years, taught the Languages of the Schools, and accustom'd to the reading of Histories, and Books of Morality; and did our Husbands treat us with that Kindness, that Sincerity, I will not say with that Respect, for fear that should be thought too much for a Wife, but only with that common Civility which is due to Strangers, they would meet with a grateful return, and have much less reason to complain. Would the Men do me the honour to take my Advice, I am confident they would for the future have less occasion to complain. First; I would have them be more judicious in their Choice, and prefer Virtue and good Sense, before either Riches, Beauty or Quality; these, joyn'd with an agreeable Humour, will make them happier than the greatest Affluence of Wealth, or than all the Charms of a lovely Face; and if 'tis their good Fortune to meet with such, I would in the second Place perswade 'em to treat them with all that Affection and Tenderness which they deserve, and leave intirely to their management the Affairs of the Kitchen, and those other little Concerns of the Family which seem to be below their inspection. And Lastly, I would have them look upon them as Friends, as Persons fit to be confided in, and trusted with their Designs, as such whose Interest is inseparably united with theirs: by such Methods as these, they would not only win their Love, but preserve it, and engage 'em to a reciprocal Esteem; and when once they have secur'd their Affection, they need not doubt of their Obedience; the desire to please will render the most difficult Commands easie. Should I give a particular Answer to each Paragraph, I should not only tire the Readers Patience, but my own, for which Reason I intend only to take notice of some very remarkable things, such as his saying, We make it our business before we are married to lay Snares for Hearts, and imprint, Come love me, in the pleasantness of our Looks, in the neatness of our Dress, in the Discretion of our Words, and in the Obligingness of our Deportment. Now what can be vainer than to think, that while the Men are Admirers of themselves, and aim at nothing but their own Satisfaction, the Women should be wholly destitute of Self-love, and do nothing to please themselves; or that Pleasantness, Vivacity and Chearfulness, which are the Effects of an internal Joy and Tranquility of Mind, should continue when the Cause ceases? Perhaps before they were marry'd, they had nothing to discompose them, no Cares to disturb their Thoughts, no Unkindnesses to resent, nothing to pall their Delights; but now the case may be alter'd; they may meet with a thousand Discouragements, with Troubles capable of altering the gayest Temper; and what influences the Mind, is ordinarily apparent in the Countenance, and discovers it self by a melancholy dejected Air, and too often occasions an Incoherency in the Discourse, a Neglect in the Dress, and an indecent Carelessness and Moroseness in the Carriage; so that all those things with which he upbraids us, ought to be rather look'd on as our Misfortune, than our Fault; and if he would have us to be such as we formerly were, he must perswade the Men to be the same they were when they made their first Addresses; and not, when marryed, think of making Innovations, or of introducing *Persian* Customs; neither give the Ribbon Weavers the Trouble of making Motto's on our Ribbons, or us the fatigue of imbroidering *Love*, *Honour* and *Obey*, on our Head Dresses, for fear, after all our labour, such Ornaments shou'd appear as ridiculous

---

Line 97. **Persian Customs:** In Sprint's sermon, he makes a reference to Persian women who wear the emblem of a foot on their headdresses to show their submission to their husbands.

and antiquated as *Passive Obedience* wou'd, if 'twere to be worn by him and the rest of his Brethren. But yet permit me to say, 'twould be very difficult for a rational ingenious Woman, were she Mistress of never so much Vertue, and blest with the greatest Strength of Resolution, if 'twere her ill Fortune to be married to a foolish, passionate, stingy, sottish Husband, to have as high an Esteem for him, as if he had all those good Qualities which she sees, and cannot but like in others: and I think she may be allow'd secretly to wish, that he were as wise, as generous, as temperate, as such a Man, as much a Master of his Passions, as obliging, and sincere as another. There is one thing which I think does more contribute to the Unhappiness of the married State, than any of those which he has mention'd, and that is, Parents forcing their Children to Marry contrary to their Inclinations; Men believe they have a right to dispose of their Children as they please; and they think it below them to consult their Satisfaction: 'Tis no matter what their Thoughts are, if the Fathers like, 'tis enough: And is it rational to suppose, that such Matches can ever be fortunate? If the Men are prudent, they will carry it civilly to their Wives; and the Women if they are discreet, will be obsequious and respectful to their Husbands, but there cannot be that Friendship, that Tenderness, that Unity of Affection which ought to be in that sacred State. I could say much more on so copious a Subject, but I fear I have already weary'd my Reader, to whose Trouble I will not add, by making trifling Apologies for what I have written: The liberty I take, I am willing to give, and the ingenious Author may, if he pleases, Animadvert as freely on my Book, as I have done on his; if he finds any thing in it that can justly give him any Offence, I beg his Pardon for it; and I do assure him, that what I have writ is wholly the Result of that great Concern and Kindness I have for my Sex, and is so far from proceeding from the least Disrespect to him, that I am ready to own to the whole World, that I think for his Piety he deserves an universal Esteem.

Line 101. **Passive Obedience**: unthinking or unquestioning acceptance of authority.

The Ladies DEFENCE:

Or, a Dialogue Between

Sir *John Brute,* Sir *William Loveall, Melissa,* and a *Parson*

Sir John. Welcome, thou brave Defender of our Right;
'Till now, I thought you knew not how to Write:
Dull heavy Morals did your Pens imploy;
And all your business was to pall our Joy:
With frightful Tales our Ears you still did grate,
And we with awful Reverence heard you prate;
Heard you declaim on Vice, and blame the Times,
Because we impudently shar'd your Crimes;
Those darling Sins you wholly wou'd ingross:
And when disturb'd, and fretting at your loss,
With whining Tones, and a pretended Zeal,
Saw you the Rancour of your Minds Reveal:
Till now, none of your Tribe were ever kind,
Good Humour is alone to you confin'd;
You, who against those Terrours of our Lives,
Those worst of Plagues, those Furies call'd our Wives,
Have shew'd your Anger in a Strain Divine,
Resentment sparkles in each poignant Line.
Sure you've the Fate of wretched Husbands met,
And 'tis your own Misfortune you regret;
You cou'd not else with such a feeling Sense
Expatiate on each Fault, and Blazon each Offence.
How happy, O Sir *William,* is your Life!
You have not known the Trouble of a Wife:
Your Rural Cares you undisturb'd can mind,
And 'midst your Brutal Subjects Pleasure find:

Title. **Sir John Brute**: brutal husband in Sir John Vanbrugh's *The Provoked Wife* (1697).
Line 26. **Brutal Subjects**: livestock.

Your Snowy Flocks you with delight can view,
They are both innocent, and pretty too:
And when from Business you your Thoughts unbend,
You can with Joy the Noble Chase attend,
Or when you please Drink freely with a Friend.
No frowning Female stands observing by,
No Children fright you with their hideous Cry;
None dare contend; none your Commands dispute;
You like the Great *Mogul*, are Absolute:
Supream in all things; from our Slavery free,
And tast the Sweets of envy'd Liberty.

Sir William. The beauteous Sex I ever did revere,
And can't with patience these Reflections hear:
To them I've long a constant Homage pay'd,
And with Delight each Charming Face survey'd.
I've had of Mistresses a numerous Store,
The Fam'd *Anacrean* could not boast of more;
Yet each was Good, each with Perfections blest,
And each by turns has triumph'd in my Breast.
That I'm unmarry'd, is my Fate, not Choice:
I in a happy Bondage should rejoyce;
And thank my Stars, if they wou'd yet incline
Some lovly She to be for ever mine:
Then wonder not to hear me take their Part,
And plead for the dear Idols of my Heart.
Spightful Invectives shou'd no Patrons find,
They are the Shame, and Venom of the Mind.

Parson. Not led by Passion, but by Zeal inspir'd,
I've told the Women what's of them requir'd:
Shew'd them their Duty in the clearest Light,
Adorn'd with all the Charms that cou'd invite:

Line 35. **Great Mogul**: ruler of the Mohammedan-Tartar empire in India.

Line 43. **Anacrean**: Anacreon; Greek lyric poet (570?–488? B.C.) who wrote mainly about love and wine.

Taught them their Husband to Obey and Please,
And to their Humours sacrifice their Ease:
Give up their Reason, and their Wills resign,
And every Look, and every Thought confine.
Sure, this, Detraction you can't justly call?
'Tis kindly meant, and 'tis address'd to All.

Melissa. Must Men command, and we alone obey,
As if design'd for Arbitrary Sway:
Born petty Monarchs, and, like *Homer's* Gods,
See all subjected to their haughty Nods?
Narcissius-like, you your own Graces view,
Think none deserve to be admir'd but you:
Your own Perfections always you adore,
And think all others despicably poor:
We have our Faults, but you are all Divine,
Wisdom does in your meanest Actions shine:
Just, Pious, Chast, from every Passion free,
By Learning rais'd above Humanity.
For every Failure you a Covering find;
Rage is a Noble Bravery of Mind:
Revenge, a Tribute due to injur'd Fame;
And Pride, but what transcendant Worth does claim:
Cowards are Wary, and the Dull are Grave,
Fops are Genteel, and Hectoring Bullies Brave:
Such as live High, regardless of Expence,
Are Generous Men, and ever bless'd with Sense:
Base Avarice Frugality you call,
And he's a prudent Man who grasps at all:
Who to be Rich, does Labour, Cheat, and Lie;
Does to himself the Sweets of Life deny,
And wretched lives, that he may wealthy dye.
Thus to each Vice you give some specious Name,
And with bright Colours varnish o're your Shame.

Line 68. **Narcissius-like**: in Greek myth, Aphrodite made Narcissus fall in love with his own reflection in a pool of water because he spurned the love of one of her nymphs, Echo.

But unto us is there no Deference due?
Must we pay all, and look for none from you?
Why are not Husbands taught as well as we;
Must they from all Restraints, all Laws be free?
Passive Obedience you've to us transferr'd,
And we must drudge in Paths where you have err'd:
That antiquated Doctrine you disown;
'Tis now your Scorn, and fit for us alone.

Parson. Love and Respect, are, I must own, your due,
But not till there's Obedience paid by you:
Submission, and a studious Care to please,
May give a Right to Favors great as these:
But if Subjection is by you deny'd,
You'll fall the unpitty'd Victims of your Pride:
We then all Husband justly may appear,
And Talk, and Frown, 'till we have taught you Fear.

Sir John. Yes, as we please, we may our Wives chastise,
'Tis the Prerogative of being Wise:
They are but Fools, and must as such be us'd.
Heaven! how I blush to see our Pow'r abus'd:
To see Men doat upon a Female Face,
And all the Manly Roughness of their Sex disgrace!

Melissa. Not thus you talk'd when you *Lenera* lov'd,
By softer Passion, sure, your Soul was mov'd,
Then at her Feet, false Man, you flattering lay,
And pray'd, and vow'd, and sigh'd your Hours away;
Admir'd her Face, her Shape, her Mein, her Air,
And swore that none was so divinely fair;
None had such Charms, none else the wondrous Art
To gain th' intire possession of your Heart.
Having expended your whole Stock of Sense,
And quite exhausted all your Eloquence,

Line 117. **Mein:** mien; air, manner.

When not one Phrase was left of all your Store,
Asham'd to have it known you were so poor,
You made your Silence want of words supply,
And look'd, as if your Love wou'd make you die:
Shew'd all your Art, your Native Guile display'd,
And gaz'd till you had won the thoughtless Maid.

Sir John. I lov'd her, 'till to her I was confin'd:
But who can long to what's his own be kind?
Plagues seize the Wretch who ty'd the cursed Knot,
Let him be damn'd: Eternally forgot.

Melissa. There spoke the Husband; all the fiend reveal'd:
Your Passion utters what's by most conceal'd.
O that my Sex safe Infidels would live,
And no more Credit to your Flatteries give.
Mistrust your Vows, despise your little Arts,
And keep a constant Guard upon their Hearts.
Unhappy they, who by their Duty led,
Are made the Partners of a hated Bed;
And by their Fathers Avarice or Pride,
To Empty Fops, or Nauseous Clowns are ty'd;
Or else constrain'd to give up all their Charms
Into an old ill-humour'd Husbands Arms,
Who hugs his Bags, and never was inclin'd
To be to ought besides his Money kind,
On that he dotes, and to increase his Wealth,
Wou'd Sacrifice his Conscience, Ease and Health,
Give up his Children, and devote his Wife,
And live a Stranger to the Joys of Life.
Who's always positive in what is Ill,
And still a Slave to his imperious Will:
Averse to any thing he thinks will please,
Still Sick, and still in love with his Disease:
With Fears, with Discontent, with Envy curst,

Line 142. **Clowns**: peasants.

To all uneasie, and himself the worst.
A spightful Censor of the present Age,
Or dully jesting, or deform'd with Rage.
These call for Pity, since it is their Fate;
Their Friends, not they, their Miseries create:
They are like Victims to the Alter led,
Born for Destruction, and for Ruine bred:
Forc'd to sigh out each long revolving Year,
And see their Lives all spent in Toil and Care.
But such as may be from this Bondage free,
Who've no Abridgers of their Liberty;
No cruel Parents, no imposing Friends,
To make 'em wretched for their private Ends,
From me shall no Commiseration have,
If they themselves to barbarous Men inslave.
They'd better Wed among the Savage kind,
And be to generous Lyons still confin'd;
Or match'd to Tygers, who would gentler prove
Than you, who talk of Piety and Love,
Words, whose Sense, you never understood,
And for that Reason, are nor kind, nor good.

Parson. Why all this Rage? we merit not your hate;
'Tis you alone disturb the Marriage State:
If to your Lords you strict Allegiance pay'd,
And their Commands submissively obey'd:
If like wise Eastern Slaves with trembling Awe
You watch'd their Looks, and made their Will your Law,
You wou'd both Kindness and Protection gain,
And find your duteous Care was not in vain.
This, I advis'd, this, I your Sex have taught;
And ought Instruction to be call'd a Fault?
Your Duty was I knew the harder part;
Obedience being a harsh, uneasie Art:
The Skill to Govern, Men with ease can learn;
We're soon instructed in our own Concern.
But you need all the Aid that I can give,

To make you unrepining Vassals live.
Heav'n, you must own, to you has been less kind,
You cannot boast our Steadiness of Mind,
Nor is your Knowledge half so unconfin'd;
We can beyond the Bounds of Nature see,
And dare to Fathom vast Infinity.
Then soar aloft, and view the Worlds on high,
And all the inmost Mansions of the Sky:
Gaze on the Wonders, on the Beauties there,
And talk with the bright Phantoms of the Air:
Observe their Customs, Policy and State,
And pry into the dark Intrigues of Fate:
Nay more than this, we Atoms can divide,
And all the Questions of the Schools decide:
Turn Falsehood into Truth, and Impudence to Shame,
Change Malice into Zeal, and Infamy to Fame,
Makes Vices Virtues, Honour but a Name.
Nothing's too hard for our Almighty Sense,
But you, not blest with *Phœbus* influence,
Wither in Shades; with nauseous Dulness curst,
Born Fools, and by resembling Idiots Nurst.
Then taught to Work, to Dance, to Sing and Play,
And vainly trifle all your Hours away,
Proud that you've learn't the little Arts to please,
As being incapable of more than these:
Your shallow Minds can nothing else contain,
You were not made for Labours of the Brain;
Those are the Manly Toils which we sustain.
We, like the Ancient Giants, stand on high,
And seem to bid Defiance to the Sky,
While you poor worthless Insects crawl below,
And less than Mites t'our exhalted Reason show.
Yet by Compassion for your Frailties mov'd,
I've strove to make you fit to be belov'd.

Line 210. **Phœbus**: Apollo, Greek god of the sun and of poetry.

Sir John. That is a Task exceeds your utmost Skill,
Spite of your Rules, they will be Women still:
Wives are the common Nusance of the State;
They all our Troubles, all our Cares create,
And more than Taxes, ruin an Estate.
Wou'd they, like *Lucifer*, were doom'd to Hell,
That we might here without disturbance dwell,
Then we should uncontroul'd our Wealth imploy,
Drink high, and take a full Repast of Joy:
Damn Care, and bravely roar away our Time,
And still be busied in some noble Crime.
Like to the happier Brutes, live unconfin'd,
And freely chuse among the Female kind.
So liv'd the mighty Thunderer of old,
Lov'd as he pleas'd, and scorn'd to be controul'd:
No Kindred Names his Passion cou'd restrain:
Like him I'll think all Nice Distinctions vain;
And tir'd with one, to a new Mistress fly,
Blest with the Sweets of dear Variety.

Melissa. To live at large a Punishment wou'd prove
To one acquainted with the Joys of Love.
Sincere Affection centers but in one,
And cannot be to various Objects shown.
Wou'd Men prove kind, respectful, just and true,
And unto us their former Vows renew,
They wou'd have then no Reason to complain,
But 'till that time Reproofs will be in vain.
Some few perhaps, whom Virtue has refin'd;
Who in themselves no vicious Habits find,
Who sway'd by Reason, and by Honour led,
May in the thorny Paths of Duty tread;
And still unweary'd with your utmost Spight,
In the blest Euges of their Minds delight:

Line 239. **Thunderer**: Jove or Zeus. Line 258. **Euges**: exclamations of praise.

But still the most will their Resentment show,
And by deplor'd effects let you their Anger know.

Sir William. She's in the right. They still wou'd virtuous prove,
Were they but treated with Respect and Love,
Your barbarous Usage does Revenge produce,
It makes 'em bad, and is their just Excuse.
You've set 'em Copies, and dare you repine,
If they transcribe each black, detested Line?

Parson. I dare affirm those Husbands that are ill,
Were they unmarried, wou'd be faultless still.
If we are cruel, they have made us so;
What e'er they suffer, to themselves they owe:
Our Love on their Obedience does depend,
We will be kind, when they no more offend.

Melissa. Of our Offences who shall Judges be?

Parson. For that great Work Heav'n has commission'd me.
I'm made one of his Substitutes below,
And from my Mouth unerring Precepts flow;
I'll prove your Duty from the Law Divine,
Celestial Truth in my Discourse shall shine.
Truth drest in all the Gaieties of Art,
In all that Wit can give, or Eloquence impart.
Attend, attend, the August Message hear,
Let it imprint a reverential Fear.
'Twill on your Mind a vital Influence have,
If while I speak, you're Silent as the Grave.
The sacred Oracles for deference call,
When from my Oily Tongue they smoothly fall.
First, I'll by Reason prove you should obey,
Next, point you out the most compendious way,
And then th' important Doctrine I'll improve,

Line 288. **compendious**: summarizing large amounts concisely.

These are the Steps by which I mean to move.
And first, because you were by Heav'n design'd
To be the Comforts of our Nobler Kind:
For us alone with tempting Graces blest,
And for our Sakes by bounteous Nature drest.
With all the choicest Beauties of her Store,
And made so fine, that she cou'd add no more.
And dare you now, as if it were in Spight,
Become our Plagues, when form'd for our Delight?
Consider next, we are for you accurst,
We sinn'd, but you, alas! were guilty first.
Unhappy *Eve* unto her Ruin led,
Tempted by Pride, on the bright Poyson fed;
Then to her thoughtless Husband gave a Part,
He eat, seduc'd by her bewitching Art.
And 'twas but just that for so great a Fault
She shou'd be to a strict Subjection brought;
So strict, her Thoughts should be no more her own,
But all subservient made to him alone.
Had she not err'd, her Task had easie been,
He ow'd his change of Humour to her Sin.
From that unhappy Hour he Peevish grew;
And she no more of solid Pleasure knew.
His Looks a sullen Haughtiness did wear,
And all his Words were Scornful, or Severe;
His Mind so rough, Love could not harbour there.
The gentle God in hast forsook his Seat,
And frighted fled to some more soft Retreat:
His Place was by a thousand Ills possest,
The crouding Dæmons throng'd into his Breast,
And left no Room for tender Passions there:
His Sons with him in the sad Change did share.
His Sourness soon Hereditary grew;
And its Effects are still perceiv'd by you.
With all your Patience, all your Toil and Art,
You scarce can keep the surly Husband's Heart.
Your Kindness hardly can Esteem create;

Yet do not blame him, since it is his Fate:
But on your Mother *Eve* alone reflect;
Thank her for his Moroseness and Neglect:
Who with a fond indulgent Spouse being blest,
And like a Mistress Courted, and Carest,
Was not contented with her present State,
But must her own Unhappiness create;
And by ill Practices his Temper spoil,
And make what once was easie, prove a Toil.
If you wou'd live as it becomes a Wife,
And raise the Honour of a marry'd Life,
You must the useful Art of wheedling try,
And with his various Humours still comply:
Admire his Wit, praise all that he does do,
And when he's vex'd, do you be pettish too:
When he is sad, a cloudy Aspect wear,
And talk to him with a dejected Air:
When Rage transports him, be as mad as he,
And when he's pleas'd, be easie, gay and free.
You'll find this Method will effectual prove,
Inhance your Merit, and secure his Love.

Sir John. It wou'd: But Women will be Cross and Proud;
When we are merry, Passionate and Loud:
When we are angry, then they frolick grow,
And Laugh, and Sing, and no Compliance show.
In Contradictions they alone delight,
Are still a Curse, and never in the Right.
By Heav'n I'd rather be an Ape, or Bear,
Or live with Beggers in the open Air,
Expos'd to Thunder, Lightning, Want and Cold,
Than be a Prince, and haunted with a Scold.
Those noisie Monsters much more dreadful are,
Than threatning Comets, Plagues, or bloody War.
Grant Providence (if such a Thing there be)
They never may from Hoarsenesses be free.
May on their Tongues as many Blisters grow

As they have Teeth; and to increase their Woe,
Let their Desires by Signs be still convey'd,
And talking be for ever Penal made.

Parson. Hold, hold: I can't these Interruptions bear;
If you don't me, these sacred Truths revere.
Now, Madam, I'll instruct you to obey,
And as I promis'd, point you out the way.
First, to your Husband you your Heart must give,
He must, alone in your Affection live.
What e'er he is, you still must think him blest,
And boast to all that you are truely blest;
If Fools should laugh, and cry 'tis but a Jest,
Yet still look Grave, and vow you are Sincere,
And undisturb'd their ill-bred Censures bear.
Do what you can his Kindness to ingage,
Wink at his Vices, and indulge his Rage.
How vain are Women in their youthful Days,
How fond of Courtship, and how proud of Praise,
What Arts they use, what Methods they devise,
To be thought Fair, Obliging, Neat and Wise.
But when they're marry'd, they soon careless grow,
Neglect their Dress, and no more Neatness show:
Their Charms are lost, their Kindness laid aside,
Smiles turn'd to Frowns, their Wisdom into Pride,
And they or Sullen are, or always Chide.
Are these the ways a Husband's Love to gain?
Or won't they rather heighten his Disdain?
Make him turn Sot, be troublesome and sad,
Or if he's fiery, Cholerick and Mad.
Thus they their Peace industriously destroy,
And rob themselves of all their promis'd Joy.

Line 391. **Cholerick:** angry.

Next, unto him you must due Honour pay,
And at his Feet your Top-knot Glories lay;
The *Persian* Ladies Chalk you out the way:
They humbly on their Heads a Foot do wear,
As I have Read, but yet the Lord knows where:
That Badge of Homage graceful does appear,
Wou'd the good Custom were in fashion here.
Also to him you inward Reverence owe;
If he's a Fool, you must not think him so;
Nor yet indulge one mean contemptuous Thought,
Or fancy he can e're commit a Fault.
Nor must your Deference be alone confin'd
Unto the hid Recesses of your Mind,
But must in all your Actions be display'd,
And visible to each Spectator made.
With him, well pleas'd, and always chearful live,
And to him still respectful Titles give.
Call him your Lord, and your good Breeding show,
And do not rudely too familiar grow:
Nor like some Country Matrons call him Names,
As *John,* or *Geffrey, William, George* or *James;*
Or what's much worse, and ne're to be forgot,
Those courser Terms of Sloven, Clown, or Sot;
For tho' perhaps they may be justly due,
Yet must not, Madam, once be spoke by you:
Soft winning Language will become you best;
Ladies ought not to Rail, tho' but in Jest.
Lastly, to him you Fealty must pay,
And his Commands without dispute obey.
A blind Obedience you from Guilt secures,
And if you err, the Fault is his, not yours.
What I have taught you, will not tiresom prove,
If as you ought, you can but truely love:

Line 395. **Top-knot Glories**: reference to Sprint's approval of Persian women who wear an emblem of a foot on their headdresses to signal their submission.

Line 421. **Fealty**: loyalty.

Honour and Homage then no Task will be;
And we shall, sure, as few ill Husbands see,
As now good Wives: They'l Prodigies appear,
Like Whales and Comets, shew some Danger near.
Now to Improvement I with hast will run,
Be short in that, and then my Work is done.
To you, Sir, First, I will my self apply,
To you, who are more fortunate than I,
And yet are free from the dire Gordian Tye.
You that Religion ought to love, and praise,
Which does you thus above the Females raise;
Next me admire, who can such Comments make,
And kindly wrest the Scripture for your Sake:
And now if you dare try a marry'd State,
You'l have no Reason to accuse your Fate,
Since I have told 'em, if they'll be good Wives,
Thy must Submit, and flatter all their Lives.
You, who already drag the Nuptial Chain,
Will now have no occasion to complain,
Since they beyond their Sphere no more will towr,
But for the future own your Sovereign Pow'r:
And being indue'd by this Advice of mine,
To you their Sense and Liberty resign:
Turn Fools and Slaves, that they the more may please.
Now it is fit for Gifts so vast as these,
We should some little Gratitude express,
And be more Complaisant in our Address:
Bear with their Faults, their weaknesses of Mind,
When they are Penitent, we shou'd be kind.
And that their Faith we may the more secure,
For them some Inconveniencies indure:
When they're in Danger, their Defenders prove;
'Twill shew at once, our Valour, and our Love.
But let it be our more immediate Care

Line 435. **Gordian Tye**: complex situation, seemingly unbreakable union; here a reference to marriage.

To make 'em these unerring Rules revere.
Bid 'em attentively each Precept read;
And tell 'em, they're as holy as their Creed:
Besure each Morning 'ere they Eat or Pray,
That they with Care the sacred Lesson say:
This, will our Quiet, and their Souls secure,
And both our Happiness, and theirs ensure.
I on their Duty cou'd with ease inlarge,
But I would not too much their Memories charge;
They're weak, and shou'd they over-loaden be,
They'll soon forget what has been said by me;
Which Heav'n avert! since it much Thought has cost,
And who wou'd have such wond'rous Rhetorick lost?

Melissa. A Mouse the labouring Mountain does disclose,
What rais'd my Wonder, my Derision grows.
With mighty Pomp you your Harangue begun,
And with big Words my fixt Attention won.
Each studied Period was with Labour wrought,
But destitute of Reason and of Thought.
What you meant Praise upon your selves reflects,
Each Sentence is a Satyr on your Sex.
If we on you such Obloquies had thrown,
We had not, sure, one peaceful Minute known:
But you are Wise, and still know what is best,
And with your selves may be allow'd to Jest.

Parson. How dare you treat me with so much neglect?
My sacred Function calls for more Respect.

Melissa. I've still rever'd your Order as Divine;
And when I see unblemish'd Vertue Shine,
When solid Learning, and substantial Sense,
Are joyn'd with unaffected Eloquence;
When Lives and Doctrines of a Piece are made,

Line 476. **Harangue**: tirade. Line 482. **Obloquies**: verbal abuse.

And holy Truths with humble Zeal convey'd;
When free from Passion, Bigottry and Pride,
Not sway'd by Interest, nor to Parties ty'd,
Contemning Riches, and abhorring Strife,
And shunning all the noisie Pomps of Life,
You live the aweful Wonders of your Time,
Without the least suspicion of a Crime:
I shall with Joy the highest Deference pay,
And heedfully attend to all you say.
From such, Reproofs shall always welcome prove,
As being th' Effects of Piety and Love.
But those from me can challenge no Respect,
Who on us all without just Cause reflect:
Who without Mercy all the Sex decry,
And into open Defamations fly:
Who think us Creatures for Derision made,
And the Creator with his Work upbraid:
What he call'd Good, they proudly think not so,
And with their Malice, their Prophaneness show.
'Tis hard we should be by the Men despis'd,
Yet kept from knowing what wou'd make us priz'd:
Debarr'd from Knowledge, banish'd from the Schools,
And with the utmost Industry bred Fools.
Laugh'd out of Reason, jested out of Sense,
And nothing left but Native Innocence:
Then told we are incapable of Wit,
And only for the meanest Drudgeries fit:
Made Slaves to serve their Luxury and Pride,
And with innumerable Hardships try'd,
Till Pitying Heav'n release us from our Pain,
Kind Heav'n to whom alone we dare complain.
Th' ill-natur'd World will no Compassion show;
Such as are wretched, it wou'd still have so:
It gratifies its Envy and its Spight;
The most in others Miseries take Delight.
While we are present they some Pity spare,

And Feast us on a thin Repast of Air:
Look Grave and Sigh, when we our Wrongs relate,
And in a Complement accuse our Fate:
Blame those to whom we our Misfortunes owe,
And all the Signs of real Friendship show.
But when we're absent, we their Sport are made,
They fan the flame, and our Oppressors aid;
Joyn with the Stronger, the victorious Side,
And all our Suff'rings, all our Griefs deride.
Those generous Few, whom kinder Thoughts inspire,
And who the Happiness of all desire;
Who wish we were from barbarous Usage free,
Exempt from Toils, and shameful Slavery,
Yet let us unreprov'd, mispend our Hours,
And to mean Purposes imploy our nobler Pow'rs.
They think if we our Thoughts can but express,
And know but how to Work, to Dance and Dress,
It is enough, as much as we should mind,
As if we were for nothing else design'd,
But made, like Puppets, to divert Mankind.
O that my Sex would all such Toys despise;
And only Study to be Good, and Wise:
Inspect themselves, and every Blemish find,
Search all the close Recesses of the Mind,
And leave no Vice, no Ruling Passion there,
Nothing to raise a Blush, or cause a Fear:
Their Memories with solid Notions fill,
And let their Reason dictate to their Will.
Instead of Novels, Histories peruse,
And for their Guides the wiser Ancients chuse,
Thro' all the Labyrinths of Learning go,
And grow more humble, as they more do know.
By doing this, they will Respect procure,
Silence the Men, and lasting Fame secure;
And to themselves the best Companions prove,
And neither fear their Malice, nor desire their Love.

Sir William. Had you the Learning you so much desire,
You, sure, wou'd nothing, but your selves admire:
All our Addresses wou'd be then in vain,
And we no longer in your Hearts shou'd Reign:
Sighs wou'd be lost, and Ogles cast away,
You'd laugh at all we do, and all we say.
No Courtship then durst by the Beaux be made
To any thing above a Chamber Maid.
Gay Cloaths, and Periwigs wou'd useless prove;
None but the Men of Sense wou'd dare to love:
With such, Heav'n knows, this Isle does not abound,
For one wise Man, Ten thousand Fools are found;
Who all must at an awful distance wait,
And vainly curse the rigour of their Fate.
Then blame us not if we our Interest Mind,
And would have Knowledge to our selves confin'd,
Since that alone Pre-eminence does give,
And rob'd of it we should unvalu'd live.
While You are ignorant, We are secure,
A little Pain will your Esteem procure.
Nonsense well cloath'd will pass for solid Sense,
And well pronounc'd, for matchless Eloquence:
Boldness for Learning, and a foreign Air
For nicest Breeding with th' admiring Fair.

Sir John. By Heav'n I wish 'twere by the Laws decreed
They never more should be allow'd to Read.
Books are the Bane of States, the Plagues of Life,
But both conjoyn'd, when studied by a Wife:
They nourish Factions, and increase Debate,
Teach needless things, and causeless Fears create.
From Plays and Novels they learn how to Plot,
And from your Sermons all their Cant is got:
From those they learn the damn'd intrieguing way
How to attract, and how their Snares to lay:

Line 569. **Ogles**: leers. Line 571. **Beaux**: dandies, men overly concerned with fashion.

How to delude the Jealous Husband's Care,
Silence his Doubts, and lull asleep his Fear:
And when discover'd, by the Last they're taught
With Shews of Zeal to palliate their Fault;
To look Demure, and talk in such a Strain,
You'd swear they never would be ill again.

Parson. You're in the Right: Good things they misapply;
Yet not in Books, but them, the Fault does lie:
Plays are of use to cultivate our Parts,
They teach us how to win our Hearers Hearts:
Soft moving Language for the Pulpit's fit,
'Tis there we consecrate the Poet's Wit:
But Women were not for this Province made,
And shou'd not our Prerogative invade;
What e'er they know shou'd be from us convey'd:
We their Preceptors and their Guides shou'd prove,
And teach them what to hate, and what to Love.
But from our Sermons they no ill can learn,
They're there instructed in their true Concern;
Told what they must, and what they must not be;
And shew'd the utmost Bounds of Liberty.

Sir William. Madam, since we none of your Beauty share,
You shou'd content your selves with being Fair:
That is a Blessing, much more Great, than all
That we can Wisdom, or can Science call:
Such beauteous Faces, such bewitching Eyes,
Who wou'd not more than musty Authors prize?
Such wondrous Charms will much more Glory yield
Than all the Honours of the dusty field:
Or all those Ivy Wreaths that Wit can give,
And make you more admir'd, more reverenc'd live.
To you, the knowing World their Vows do pay,
And at your Feet their learned Trophies lay;
And your Commands with eager hast obey.

By all my Hopes, by all that's Good I swear,
I'd rather be some celebrated Fair,
Than wise as *Solon*, or than *Crœsus* Heir.
Or have my Memory well stuff'd with all
Those Whimseys, which they high-rais'd notions call.

Melissa. Beauty's a Trifle merits not my Care.
I'd rather *Æsop's* ugly Visage wear,
Joyn'd with his Mind, than be a Fool, and Fair.
Brightness of Thought, and an extensive View
Of all the Wonders Nature has to shew;
So clear, so strong, and so inlarg'd a Sight
As can pierce thro' the gloomy Shades of Night,
Trace the first Heroes to their dark Abodes,
And find the Origine of Men and Gods:
See Empires rise, and Monarchies decay,
And all the Changes of the World survey:
The ancient and the modern Fate of Kings,
From whence their Glory, or Misfortune springs;
Wou'd please me more, than if in one combind,
I'd all the Graces of the Female Kind.
But do not think 'tis an ambitious Heat,
To you I'll leave the being Rich and Great:
Your's be the Fame, the Profit, and the Praise;
We'll neither Rob you of your Vines, nor Bays:
Nor will we to Dominion once aspire;
You shall be Chief, and still your selves admire.
The Tyrant Man may still possess the Throne;
'Tis in our Minds that we wou'd Rule alone:
Those unseen Empires give us leave to sway,
And to our Reason private Homage pay:

Line 635. **Solon**: Athenian lawgiver and statesman (638–ca. 558 B.C.). **Crœsus**: the last king of Lydia, known for his enormous wealth (reigned 560–546 B.C.).

Line 639. **Æsop's ... Visage**: the author of the *Fables*, believed to have been a deformed slave.

Line 656. **Vines, nor Bays**: allusion to the Roman custom of crowning successful poets and generals with garlands; signs of achievement and victory.

Our struggling Passions within Bounds confine,
And to our Thoughts their proper Tasks assign.
This, is the Use we wou'd of Knowledge make,
You quickly wou'd the good Effects partake.
Our Conversations it wou'd soon refine,
And in our Words, and in our Actions shine:
And by a pow'rful Influence on our Lives,
Make us good Friends, good Neighbours, and good Wives.
Of this, some great Examples have been shown,
Women remarkable for Virtue known:
Jealous of Honour, and upright of Life,
Serene in Dangers, and averse to Strife:
Patient when wrong'd, from Pride and Envy free,
Strangers to Falsehood and Calumny:
Of every noble Quality possest:
Well skill'd in Science, and with Wisdom blest.
In Ancient *Greece,* where Merit still was crown'd,
Some such as these in her Records were found.
Rome her *Lucretia,* and her *Porcia* show,
And we to her the fam'd *Cornelia* owe:
A Place with them does Great *Zenobia* claim;
With these I cou'd some modern Ladies Name,
Who help to fill the bulky Lists of Fame:
Women renown'd for Knowledge, and for Sense,
For sparkling Wit, and charming Eloquence.
But they're enough: at least to make you own,
If we less Wise and Rational are grown,
'Tis owning to your Management alone.
If like th' Ancients you wou'd generous prove,
And in our Education shew your Love;

Line 681. **Lucretia**: Lucretia, wife of Tarquinius, who was raped by Sextus, son of Tarquin, the king of Rome; she killed herself after urging her husband to avenge her. **Porcia**: Portia, the wife of Brutus, who committed suicide after his death.

Line 682. **Cornelia**: mother of Tiberius and Gaius Gracchus; she refused to wed a king in favor of marrying a Roman citizen.

Line 683. **Zenobia**: queen of Palmyra who fought against the Romans and invaded Asia Minor and Egypt.

Into our Souls wou'd noble Thoughts instill,
Our Infant-Minds with bright Ideas fill:
Teach us our Time in Learning to imploy,
And place in solid Knowledge all our Joy:
Perswade us trifling Authors to refuse,
And when we think, the useful'st Subjects chuse:
Inform us how a prosperous State to bear,
And how to Act when Fortune is severe:
We shou'd be Wiser, and more blameless live,
And less occasion for your Censures give:
At least in us less Failings you wou'd see,
And our Discourses wou'd less tiresom be:
Tho' Wit like yours we never hope to gain,
Yet from Impertinence we should refrain,
And learn to be less Talkative and Vain.
Unto the strictest Rules we should submit,
And what we ought to do, think always fit.
Never dispute, when Duty leads the way,
But its Commands without a Sigh Obey.
To Reason, not to Humour, give the Reins,
And be the same in Palaces and Chains.
But you our humble Suit will still decline;
To have us wise was never your Design:
You'll keep us Fools, that we may be your Jest;
They who know least, are ever treated best.
If we do well, with Care it is conceal'd;
But every Errour, every Fault's reveal'd:
While to each other you still partial prove,
Can see no Failures, and even Vices love.
The bloody Masters of the martial Trade,
Are prais'd for Mischiefs, and for Murders pay'd.
The noisy Lawyers, if they can but bawl,
Soon grace the Wool-sacks, and adorn the Hall.
The envy'd Great, those darling Sons of Fame,

Line 725. **Wool-sacks**: the name of the seat of the Lord Chancellor in the House of Lords in Parliament.

Who carry a Majestic Terrour in their Name;
Who like the Demy Gods are plac'd on High,
And seem th' exalted Natives of the Sky:
Who sway'd by Pride, and by Self-love betray'd,
Are Slaves to their imperious Passions made,
Are with a Servile Awe by you rever'd;
Prais'd for their Follies, for their Vices fear'd.
The Courtier, who with every Wind can veer,
And midst the Mounting Waves can safely steer;
Who all can flatter; and with wond'rous grace,
Low cringing Bows, and a designing Face,
A smiling Look, and a dissembl'd Hate,
Can hug a Friend, and hasten on his Fate,
Has your Applause; his Policy you praise;
And to the Skies his prudent Conduct raise.
The Scholar, if he can a Verb decline,
And has the Skill to reckon Nine times Nine,
Or but the Nature of a Fly define;
Can Mouth some Greek, and knows where *Athens* stood,
Tho' he perhaps is neither Wise, nor Good,
Is fit for *Oxford;* where when he has been,
Each Colledge view'd, and each grave Doctor seen,
He mounts a Pulpit, and th' exalted Height
Makes Vapours dance before his troubl'd Sight,
And he no more can see, nor think aright.
Yet such as these your Consciences do Guide,
And or'e your Actions and your Words preside.
Blame you for Faults which they themselves commit,
Arraign your Judgment, and condemn your Wit:
Instil their Notions with the greatest Ease,
And Hood-wink'd lead you where so e'er they please.
The formal Justice, and the jolly Knight,
Who in their Money place their chief delight;
Who watch the Kitchin, and survey the field,
To see what each will to their Luxury yield:
Who Eat and Run, then Quarrel, Rail and Drink,
But never are at leisure once to Think:

Who weary of Domestick Cares being grown,
And yet, like Children, frighted when alone,
(Detesting Books) still Hunt, or Hawk, or Play,
And in laborious Trifles wast the Day,
Are lik'd by you, their Actions still approv'd,
And if they're Rich, are sure to be belov'd.
These are the Props, the Glory of the State,
And on their Nod depends the Nation's Fate:
These weave the Nets, where little Flies betray'd,
Are Victims to relentless Justice made,
While they themselves contemn the Snares that they
    have laid;
As Bonds too weak such mighty Men to hold
As scorn to be by any Laws controul'd.
Physicians with hard Words and haughty Looks,
And promis'd Health, bait their close-cover'd Hooks:
Like Birds of Prey, while they your Gold can scent,
You are their Care, their utmost help is lent;
But when your Guineas cease, you to the *Spaw* are sent,
Yet still you Court 'em, think you cannot die
If you've a Son of *Æsculapius* by.
The Tradesmen you Caress, altho' you know
They wealthy by their Cheats and Flatteries grow;
You seem to credit every Word they say,
And as they sell, with the same Conscience pay:
Nay to the Mob, those Dregs of Humane kind,
Those Animals you slight, you're wond'rous kind;
To them you Cring, and tho' they are your Sport,
Yet still you fawn, and still their Favour Court.
Thus on each other daily you impose,
And all for Wit, and dextrous Cunning goes.
'Tis we alone hard Measure still must find;
But spite of you, we'll to our selves be kind:

Line 781. **Guineas**: gold coins of considerable value. **Spaw**: spa or health resort.

Line 783. **Æsculapius**: in Greek and Roman myth, the god of healing and medicine.

Line 790. **Cring**: cringe, grovel servilely.

Your Censures slight, your little Tricks despise,
And make it our whole Business to be wise.
The mean low trivial Cares of Life disdain,
And Read and Think, and Think and Read again,
And on our Minds bestow the utmost Pain.
Our Souls with strictest Morals we'll adorn,
And all your little Arts of wheedling Scorn;
Be humble, mild, forgiving, just and true,
Sincere to all, respectful unto you,
While as becomes you, sacred Truths you teach,
And live those Sermons you to others Preach.
With want of Duty none shall us upbraid,
Where-e'er 'tis due, it shall be nicely pay'd.
Honour and Love we'll to our Husbands give,
And ever Constant and Obedient live:
If they are Ill, we'll try by gentle ways
To lay those Tempests which their Passions raise;
But if our soft Submissions are in vain,
We'll bear our Fate, and never once complain:
Unto our Friends the tenderest kindness show,
Be wholly theirs, no separate Interest know:
With them their Dangers and their Suff'rings share,
And make their Persons, and their Fame our Care.
The Poor we'll feed, to the Distress'd be kind,
And strive to Comfort each afflicted Mind.
Visit the Sick, and try their Pains to ease;
Not without Grief the meanest Wretch displease:
And by a Goodness as diffus'd as Light,
To the pursuit of Vertue all invite.
Thus will we live, regardless of your hate,
Till re-admitted to our former State;
Where, free from the Confinement of our Clay
In glorious Bodies we shall bask in Day,
And with inlightened Minds new Scenes survey.
Scenes, much more bright than any here below,
And we shall then the whole of Nature know;
See all her Springs, her secret Turnings view,

And be as knowing, and as wise as you.
With generous Spirits of a Make Divine,
In whose blest Minds Celestial Virtues shine,
Whose Reason, like their Station, is sublime,
And who see clearly thro' the Mists of Time,
Those puzling Glooms where busy Mortals stray,
And still grope on, but never find their way.
We shall, well-pleas'd, eternally converse,
And all the Sweets of Sacred Love possess:
Love, freed from all the gross Allays of Sense,
So pure, so strong, so constant, so intense,
That it shall all our Faculties imploy,
And leave no Room for any thing but Joy.

Line 842. **Allays:** alloys; mixtures of precious and base metals.

Poems on Several Occasions

{ 1703 }

TO THE QUEEN'S MOST EXCELLENT MAJESTY

MADAM,

'Tis not without awful Thoughts and a trembling Hand that these Poems are laid at your Royal Feet. The Address has too much Confidence; the Ambition is too aspiring; But to whom should a Woman unknown to the World, and who has not Merit enough to defend her from the Censure of Criticks, fly for Protection, but to Your *Majesty?* The Greatest, the Best, and the most Illustrious Person of Your Sex and Age.

That wonderful Condescension, that surprizing Humility, and admirable Sweetness of Temper, which induc'd Your *Majesty* to accept a Congratulatory Ode on Your happy Accession to the Crown, give Ground to hope that from a Goodness and Generosity boundless as Yours, I may promise my self both Pardon and Protection, who am, with the profoundest Veneration,

MADAM, Your Majesty's most Loyal, most Humble, and most Obedient Servant,

MARY CHUDLEIGH.

Title. Queen Anne (1665–1714), who ascended the throne in 1702.

PREFACE

The following Poems were written at several Times, and on several Subjects: If the Ladies, for whom they are chiefly design'd, and to whose Service they are intirely devoted, happen to meet with any thing in them that is entertaining, I have all I am at. They were the Employment of my leisure Hours, the innocent Amusement of a solitary Life: In them they'll find a Picture of my Mind, my Sentiments all laid open to their View; they'll sometimes see me cheerful, pleas'd, sedate and quiet; at other times griev'd, complaining, struggling with my Passions, blaming my self, endeavouring to pay a Homage to my Reason, and resolving for the future, with a decent Calmness, and unshaken Constancy, and a resigning Temper, to support all the Troubles, all the uneasinesses of Life, and then by unexpected Emergencies, unforeseen Disappointments, sudden and surprizing Turns of Fortune, discompos'd, and shock'd, till I have rallied my scatter'd Forces, got new Strength, and by making an unweary'd Resistance, gain'd the better of my Afflictions, and restor'd my Mind to its former Tranquillity.

'Tis impossible to be happy without making Reason the Standard of all our Thoughts, Words and Actions, and firmly resolving to yield a constant, ready, and cheerful Obedience to its Dictates. Those who are govern'd by Opinion, inslav'd to Custom, and Vassals to their Humors, are Objects of Pity, if such as are wretched by their own Choice, can be properly said to deserve Commiseration. They act by no steady Principles, are always restless, disturb'd, and uneasie; sometimes agitated by one Passion, and sometimes by another, fretting about Trifles, and lamenting the Loss of such Things, as others would think it a part of their Felicity to be without.

What we generally call Misfortunes, what we fancy to be Miseries, are not really so; they exist only in the Imagination, are Creatures of the Brain, Troubles of our own forming, and like Phantoms vanish as soon as Reason shines clear.

Would we contract our Desires, and learn to think that only necessary, which Nature has made so, we should be no longer fond of Riches, Honours, Applauses, and several other Things which are the unhappy

Occasions of much Mischief to the World, which unavoidably involve Mankind in great Misery, and draw after them a long Train of Vice; and doubtless were we so happy as to have a true Notion of the Dignity of our Nature, of those great Things for which we are design'd, and of the Duration and Felicity of that State to which we are hastning, we should scorn to stoop to mean Actions, blush at the very Thoughts of doing any thing below our Character, and look on the little worthless Concerns of Life, *viz.* on the amassing Treasures, the gaining Titles, the making a pompous Appearance, and the gratifying our Appetites, as Trifles below our Care, and unworthy of our Thoughts, Things too mean to be the Business, much less the Delight of rational Beings, of such as were created for nobler, and much more sublime Employments: We should then without Regret, or at least with Patience and a becoming Submission to the Divine Pleasure, see our selves depriv'd of those Things which we now falsly fancy to be constituent Parts of our Happiness; we should then, if Death wounds us in the tenderest part of our Souls, robs us of what 'tis most allowable for us to prize, snatches from us our dearest Relations, our best, our darling Friends, look on them as Persons not lost, but only remov'd to better, more blissful Habitations, and where we may reasonably flatter our selves with the hope, that they may have the same Kindness for us, the same Friendship, the same Inclinations, the same Readiness to do us obliging Offices, and where we shall very shortly meet again, and renew our Endearments, and where our Love shall be as lasting as our Souls, as great as our Happiness.

The way to be truly easie, to be always serene, to have our Passions under a due Government, to be wholly our own, and not to have it in the Power of Accidents, of things foreign to us to ruffle and disturb our Thoughts, is to retire into our selves, to live upon our own Stock, to accustom our selves to our own Conversation, to be pleas'd with nothing but what strictly and properly speaking, we may justly pretend a Right to; of which kind, such things can never be said to be, of which 'tis in the Power of Fortune to deprive us.

No Joy but what results from virtuous Actions, no Pleasure but what arises from a Sense of having done what we ought, no Acquisition but that of Wisdom, no Applause but that of Conscience, is truly desirable; such Delights as these, such valuable Treasures, are the Things I would recommend to my Sex: I would have them no longer solicitous about

Impertinences, anxious about Trifles, Slaves to their own Humors, and a Prey to every mean designing Flatterer; I would not have them employ more Time in beautifying their Faces, in rendring themselves agreeable, than in adorning their Minds, and enriching their Understandings: There is a noble Disdain, a becoming and allowable Pride; 'tis commendable to scorn to be below others in Things that are essentially Praise-worthy, and they may be permitted to put a true Value on themselves, when instead of exciting them to Vanity, giving them wrong Notions of Perfection, false Ideas of their own Merits, it tends only to the raising them above those mean despicable Things, those contemptible Accomplishments of which the most are proud: I beg their Pardon for presuming so freely to advise them, and I own it to be a Fault which nothing but the Zeal I have for them can excuse.

These Poems begin with a very long one on the Death of the Duke of *Glocester:* Tho' I never had the Honour to view the fair Original, so that I pretend not to draw from the Life, yet having had from Persons on whom I can well depend, a just and full Character of him, as of a Prince of wonderful Hopes, and who at his first Appearance, in his Dawn of Life, the Morning of his Age, discover'd a shining Merit, a more than ordinary Propensity to Knowledge, a winning Sweetness of Temper, join'd with a Generosity becoming his Birth: In a word, all those great and distinguishing Qualities which raise his Royal Parents as much above those of their own Rank, as their sublime Dignity has elevated them above the meanest of the People, I thought so great a Loss would sufficiently justifie all I cou'd say on that Subject, and render the Length of it excusable.

On the Death of his Highness the Duke of *Glocester*

1.

I'le take my Leave of Business, Noise and Care,
And trust this stormy Sea no more:
Condemn'd to Toil, and fed with Air,
I've often sighing look'd towards the Shore:
And when the boistrous Winds did cease,
And all was still, and all was Peace,
Afraid of Calms, and flatt'ring Skies,
On the deceitful Waves I fixt my Eyes,
And on a sudden saw the threatning Billows rise:
Then trembling beg'd the Pow'rs Divine,
Some little safe Retreat might be for ever mine:
O give, I cry'd, where e'er you please,
Those Gifts which Mortals prize,
Grown fond of Privacy and Ease,
I now the gaudy Pomps of Life despise.
Still let the Greedy strive with Pain,
T'augment their shining Heaps of Clay;
And punish'd with the Thirst of Gain,
Their Honour lose, their Conscience stain:
Let th'ambitious Thrones desire
And still with guilty hast aspire;
Thro' Blood and Dangers force their Way,
And o'er the World extend their Sway,
While I my time to nobler Uses give,
And to my Books, and Thoughts entirely live;
Those dear Delights, in which I still shall find
Ten thousand Joys to feast my Mind,
Joys, great as Sense can bear, from all its Dross refin'd.

Title. **Duke of Glocester:** Queen Anne's only child to survive infancy, the Duke of Glocester, died in 1700 at age 11 from smallpox.

2.

The Muse well pleas'd, my choice approv'd,
And led me to the Shades she lov'd:
To Shades, like those first fam'd Abodes
Of happy Men, and rural Gods;
Where, in the World's blest Infant State,
When all in Friendship were combin'd
And all were just, and all were kind;
E're glitt'ring Show'rs, dispers'd by *Jove*,
And Gold were made the Price of Love,
The Nymphs and Swains did bless their Fate,
And all their mutual Joys relate,
Danc'd and sung, and void of Strife.
Enjoy'd all Harmless Sweets of Life;
While on their tuneful Reeds their Poets play'd,
And their chast Loves to future Times convey'd.

3.

Cool was the place, and quiet as my Mind,
The Sun cou'd there no Entrance find:
No ruffling Winds the Boughs did move:
The Waters gently crept along,
As with their flowry Banks in Love:
The Birds with soft harmonious Strains,
Did entertain my Ear;
Sad *Philomela* sung her Pains,
Express'd her Wrongs, and her Despair;
I listen'd to her mournful Song,
The charming Warbler pleas'd,
And I, me thought, with new Delight was seiz'd:
Her Voice with tender'st Passions fill'd my Breast,
And I felt Raptures not to be express'd;
Raptures, till that soft Hour unknown,
My Soul seem'd from my Body flown:

Line 51. **Philomela**: in Greek myth, Philomela was raped by Tereus, king of Thrace, who then cut out her tongue to silence her; she was changed into a nightingale by the gods.

Vain World, said I, take, take my last adieu,
I'le to my self, and to my Muse be true,
And never more phantastick Forms pursue:
Such glorious Nothings let the Great adore,
Let them their airy *Juno's* court,
I'le be deceiv'd no more,
Nor to the Marts of Fame resort:
From this dear Solitude no more remove,
But here confine my Joy, my Hope, my Love.

4.

Thus were my Hours in Extasies employ'd,
And I the secret Sweets of Life enjoy'd:
Serene, and calm, from every Pressure free,
Inslav'd alone by flatt'ring Poesie:
But Oh! how pleasing did her Fetters prove!
How much did I, th'endearing Charmer Love!
No former Cares durst once my Soul molest,
No past Unkindness discompos'd my Breast;
All was forgot, as if in *Lethe's* Stream
I'd quench'd my Thirst, the past was all a Dream:
But as I pleas'd my self with this unenvy'd state,
Behold! a wondrous Turn of Fate!
A hollow Melancholy Sound
Dispers'd an awful Horror round,
And hideous Groans thro' all the Grove resound
Nature the dismal Noise did hear,
Nature her self did seem to fear:
The bleating Flocks lay trembling on the Plains;
The Brooks ran murmuring by,
And Echo to their Murmurs made reply:
The lofty Trees their verdant Honours shake;
The frighted Birds with hast their Boughs forsake,
And for securer Seats to distant Groves repair.

Line 64. **Juno**: in Roman myth, the wife of Jupiter and queen of heaven.

Line 77. **Lethe's Stream**: in Greek myth, the river in Hades whose waters cause forgetfulness.

The much wrong'd *Philomel* durst now no more
Her former Injuries deplore;
Forgot were all her moving Strains
Forgot each sweet melodious Air;
The weaker Passion, Grief, surrendred to her Fear.

5.

A sudden Gloom its dusky Empire spread,
And I was seiz'd with an unusual dread:
Where e'er I look'd, each Object brought affright:
And I cou'd only mournful Accents hear,
Which from th'adjacent Hills did wound my Ear;
Th'adjacent Hills the gen'ral Horror share:
Amaz'd I sat, depriv'd of all Delight,
The Muse was fled, fled ev'ry pleasing Thought,
And in their Room were black Ideas brought,
By busie Fear, and active Fancy wrought.
At length the doleful Sound drew near,
And lo, the British Genius did appear!
Solemn his Pace,
Dejected were his Eyes,
And from his Breast thick thronging Sighs arise:
The Tears ran down his venerable Face,
And he with Lamentations loud fill'd all the sacred Place.

6.

He's Dead he cry'd! the young, the much belov'd!
From us too soon, Ah! much too soon remov'd!
Snatch'd hence in his first Dawn, his Infant Bloom!
So fell *Marcellus* by a rigorous Doom.
The Good, the Great, the Joy, the Pride of *Rome!*

Line 92. **Philomel**: Philomela. Line 108. **British Genius**: Dryden.

Line 117. **Marcellus**: the descendant and namesake of the great Roman general who defeated Hannibal; celebrated in the *Aeneid* as a youth of great promise who died young.

But Oh! he wants like him a *Maro* to rehearse
His early worth in never dying Verse:
To sing those rising Wonders which in him were seen;
That Morning light which did it self display,
Presaging earnest of a glorious Day;
His Face was Charming, and his Make Divine,
As if in him assembl'd did combine
The num'rous Graces of his Royal Line:
Such was *Ascanius*, when from flaming *Troy*
Pious *Æneas* led the lovely Boy,
And such the God when to the *Tyrian* Queen
A welcom Guest he came;
And in his Shape caress'd th' illustrious Dame
And kindled in her Breast the inauspicious Flame.

7.

But this, alas! was but th' exterior part;
For the chief Beauties were within:
There Nature shew'd her greatest Art,
And did a Master-piece begin:
But ah! the Strokes were much too fine,
Too delicate to last:
Sweet was his Temper, generous his Mind,
And much beyond his Years, to Martial Arts inclin'd:
Averse to Softness, and for one so young,
His Sense was manly, and his Reason strong:
What e'er was taught him he would learn so fast
As if 'twas his design
When he to full Maturity was grown,
Th'applauding World amaz'd should find
What e'er was worthy to be known,
He with the noblest Toil had early made his own.

Line 119. **Maro**: the poet Virgil, Publius Virgilius Maro (70–19 B.C.), author of the *Aeneid*, whose works were translated by Dryden in 1697.

Line 127. **Ascanius**: son of Aeneas. Line 129. **Tyrian Queen**: Dido.

8.

Such, such was he, whose Loss I now lament;
O Heav'n! why was this matchless Blessing sent!
Why but just shewn, and then, our Grief to raise,
Cut off in the beginning of his Days!
Had you beheld th'afflicted Royal Pair
Stand by that Bed, where the dear Suff'rer lay
    To his Disease a helpless Prey,
And seen them gaze on the sad doubtful Strife,
Between contending Death, and strugling Life,
Observ'd those Passions which their Souls did move,
    Those kind Effects of tender'st Love;
    Seen how their Joys a while did strive
    To keep their fainty Hopes alive,
    But soon alas! were forc'd to yield
        To Grief and dire Despair,
        The short contested Field:
    And them in that curst Moment view'd,
    When by prevailing Death subdu'd,
Breathless and pale, the beauteous Victim lay,
When his unwilling Soul was forc'd away
    From that lov'd Body which it lately blest,
That Mansion worthy so divine a Guest,
You must have own'd, no Age could ever show
A sadder Sight, a Scene of vaster Woe.

9.

Sorrow like theirs, what Language can express!
Their All was lost, their only Happiness!
The good *Ægeus* could not more be griev'd
    When he the Sable Flag perceiv'd,
Than was the Prince; but we this difference find,

Line 161. **fainty**: faint, sickly, languid; inclined to swoon.

Line 175. **Ægeus**: in Greek myth, the king of Athens and the father of Theseus, who, when he saw his son's ships returning with black sails, wrongly believed Theseus had been killed by the Minotaur and killed himself in despair.

The last was calmer, more resign'd,
And had the stronger, more Majestick Mind:
He knew Complaints could give him no Relief,
And therefore cast a Veil upon his sullen Grief;
Th'afflicted Princess could not thus controul
The tender Motions of her troubled Soul:
Unable to resist, she gave her Sorrows way,
And did the Dictates of her Grief obey:
Maternal Kindness still does preference claim,
And always burns with a more ardent Flame:
But sure no Heart was ever thus opprest,
The Load is much too great to bear;
In sad Complaints are all her Minutes spent,
And she lives only to lament:
All soft Delights are Strangers to her Breast:
His unexpected Fate does all her Thoughts ingross,
And she speaks nothing but her mighty Loss.
So mourn'd *Andromache* when she beheld
Astyanax expos'd to lawless Pow'r,
Precipitated from a lofty Tow'r:
Depriv'd of Life the Royal Youth remain'd
And with the richest *Trojan* Blood the Pavement stain'd:
Speechless she gaz'd, and by her Grief impell'd,
Fearless amidst the *Græcian* Troops she run,
And to her panting Bosom clasp'd her mangl'd Son.

10.

As thus he spoke *Britannia* did appear,
Attended by a Sylvan Throng,
And with her brought the River Nymphs along:
He's dead! he's dead! the Genius loudly cry'd,

Line 195. **Andromache**: in Greek myth, the wife of the Trojan warrior Hector, who saved her son Astyanax from the flames when Troy was burnt, only to see him thrown from the city walls by Ulysses.

Line 203. **Britannia**: poetic name of the personification of Britain.

Line 204. **Sylvan Throng**: a group of woodland spirits.

On whose dear Life you did so much depend,
He's dead, He's dead, she mournfully reply'd:
Heav'n would not long the mighty Blessing lend:
Some envious Pow'r, who does my Greatness fear,
Foreseeing if he shou'd to Manhood live,
He'd glorious Proofs of wondrous Valor give:
To distant Lands extend his Sway,
And teach remotest Nations to obey:
Resolv'd no pow'rful Art his Life should save,
Nor I should longer my lov'd *Gloucester* have.
No more they said, but to their Sighs gave way,
The Nymphs and Swains all griev'd no less than they.
He's dead! he's dead! they weeping said;
In his cold Tomb the lovely Youth is laid,
And has too soon, alas! too soon the Laws of Fate obey'd.
No more, no more shall he these Groves adorn,
No more by him shall flow'ry Wreaths be worn:
No more, no more we now on him shall gaze,
No more divert him with our rural Lays,
Nor see him with a godlike Smile receive our humble Praise.
Their loud Laments the Nereids hear,
And full of Grief, and full of Fear,
Their watry Beds in haste forsake;
And from their Locks the pearly Moisture shake:
All with one Voice the much lov'd Youth lament,
And in pathetic Strains their boundless Sorrow vent.

11.

Upon the Ground I pensive lay;
Complain'd and wept as much as they:
My Country's Loss became my own,
And I was void of Comfort grown.
He's dead! he's dead! with them I cry'd,
And to each Sigh, each Groan reply'd.

Line 227. **Nereids**: river nymphs.

The *Thracian* Bard was not more mov'd,
When he had lost the Fair he lov'd;
When looking back to please his Sight
With all that could his Soul delight,
He saw her sink int' everlasting Night.
The Sorrows of the Princess pierc'd my Heart,
And I, me thought, felt all her Smart:
I wish'd I cou'd allay her Pain,
Or part of her Affliction share;
But Oh! such Wishes are in vain,
She must alone the pond'rous Burthen bear.
O Fate unjust! I then did cry,
Why must the young, the virtuous die!
Why in their Prime be snatch'd away,
Like beauteous Flow'rs which soon decay,
While Weeds enjoy the Warmth of each succeeding Day?

12.

While thus I mourn'd, a sudden Light the Place o'er spread
Back to their genuine Night the frighted Shadows fled:
Dilating Skies disclos'd a brighter Day,
And for a glorious Form made way;
For the fam'd Guardian of our Isle:
The wondrous Vision did with Pomp descend,
With awful State his kind Approaches made,
And thus with an obliging Smile
To the much griev'd *Britannia* said,
No more, my much lov'd Charge, no more
Your time in useless Sorrows spend;
He's blest whose Loss you thus deplore:
Above he lives a Life Divine,
And does with dazling Splendor shine:

Line 239. **Thracian Bard**: Orpheus, who, in the Greek myth, lost his chance to bring his wife Eurydice back from the dead when he turned and looked at her before they left Hades.

Line 259. **Guardian ... Isle:** St. George.

I met him on th' Æthereal Shore,
With Joy I did th' illustrious Youth embrace,
And led him to his God-like Race,
Who sit inthron'd in wondrous State,
Above the Reach of Death or fate:
The *Caledonian* Chiefs were there,
Who thro' the World have spread their Fame,
And justly might immortal Trophies claim:
A long Descent of glorious Kings,
Who did, and suffer'd mighty things:
With them the *Danish* Heroes were,
Who long had ancient Kingdoms sway'd,
And been by Warlike States obey'd:
With them they did their Honours share,
With them refulgent Crowns did wear,
From all their Toils at length they cease,
Blest with the Sweets of everlasting Peace.

13.

Among the rest, that beauteous suff'ring Queen
Who'd all the turns of adverse Fortune seen;
Robb'd of a Crown, and forc'd to mourn in Chains,
And on a Scaffold end her num'rous Pains
Receiv'd him with a cheerful Look,
And to her Arms her dearest Off-spring took:
Next came the martyr'd Prince, who liv'd to know
The last Extremities of woe:
Expos'd unjustly to his People's hate,
He felt the Rigor of remorseless Fate.
Virtue and spotless Innocence,
Alas! are no Defence:

Line 269. **Æthereal Shore**: heaven's gate.

Line 274. **Caledonian Chiefs**: ancient Scottish rulers, a reference to the Stuarts.

Line 286. **beauteous ... Queen**: Mary Stuart, Queen of Scots (1542–87), executed by Queen Elizabeth I.

Line 292. **martyr'd Prince**: Charles I, king of England (1625–49), executed by Parliament.

They rather to the Rage expose
Of bloody and relentless Foes:
Too fierce they shine, too glaring bright,
The Vicious cannot bear their Light.
Next came his Son, who long your Sceptre sway'd,
And whom his Subjects joyfully obey'd;
Then last of all the fair *Maria* came,
Who lately grac'd the *British* Throne;
And there with a reviving Splendor shone,
But made a short, a transient Stay,
By Death from all her Glories snatch'd away:
How vain is Beauty, Wealth, or Fame,
How few the Trophies of a boasted Name!
Death can't be brib'd, be won by none:
To Slaves and Kings a Fate a like, a like Regard is shown.

14.

All these the lovely Youth carest,
And welcom'd him to their eternal Rest:
Welcome, they said, to this our blissful Shore,
To never ending Joys, and Seats Divine,
To Realms where clear unclouded Glories shine,
Here you may safely stand and hear the Billows roar,
But shall be toss'd on that tempestuous Sea no more:
No more shall grieve, no more complain,
But free from Care, and free from Pain,
With us for ever shall remain.
While thus they spoke, celestial Musick play'd,
And welcom! welcom! every Angel said:
With eager hast their Royal Guest they crown'd,
While welcom! welcom! echo'd all around,
And fill'd th' Æthereal Court with the loud cheerful Sound.

Line 302. **his Son**: Charles II, king of England (1660–85).

Line 304. **Maria:** Queen Mary II, eldest child of James II; queen of England (1689–94).

15.

He said; and to superior Joys return'd;
Britannia now no longer mourn'd:
No more the Nymphs, no more the Swains,
With Lamentations fill'd the Plains:
The Muse came back, and with her brought
Each sprightly, each delightful Thought:
Kindly she rais'd me from the Ground,
And smiling wip'd my Tears away:
While Joy, she said, is spread around,
And do's thro' all the Groves resound,
Will you to Grief a Tribute pay,
And mourn for one who's far more blest,
Than those that are of Crowns possest?
No more, no more you must complain,
But with *Britannia* now rejoice:
Britannia to the Choir above
Will add her charming Voice:
Not one of all her beauteous Train
But will obsequious prove;
And each will try who best can sing,
Who can the highest Praises bring;
Who best describe his happy State,
And best his present Joys relate.
Hark! Hark! the Birds are come again,
And each renews his sweet melodious Strain.
Clear is the Skie, and bright the Day,
Among the Boughs sweet Zephyrs play,
And all are pleas'd, and all are gay.
And dare you still your Grief express,
As if you wish'd his Honours less,
And with an envious Eye beheld his Happiness?

Line 354. **Zephyrs**: breezes.

16.

Ah! cruel Muse, with Sighs I said,
Why do you thus your Slave upbraid?
I neither at his Bliss repine;
Nor is't my choice to disobey:
Your Will, you know, has still been mine;
And I would now my ready def'rence pay:
But Oh! in vain I strive, in vain I try,
While my lov'd Princess grieves, I can't comply:
Her Tears forbid me to rejoice,
And when my Soul is on the Wing,
And I would with *Britannia* sing,
Her Sighs arrest my Voice.
But if once more you'd have me cheerful prove,
And with your Shades again in Love,
Strive by your Charms to calm her troubled Mind;
Let her the Force of pow'rful Numbers find:
And by the Magick of your Verse restore
Her former Peace, then add Delights unknown before
Let her be blest, my Joys will soon return,
But while she grieves, I ne'er can cease to mourn.

On the Vanities of this Life: A Pindarick Ode

1.

What makes fond Man the trifle Life desire,
And with such Ardor court his Pain?
'Tis Madness, worse than Madness, to admire
What brings Ten thousand Miseries in its Train:
To each soft moment, Hours of Care succeed,
And for the Pleasures of a Day,
With Years of Grief we pay;
So much our lasting Sorrows, our fleeting Joys exceed.

In vain, in vain, we Happiness pursue,
        That mighty Blessing is not here;
        That, like the false misguiding Fire,
Is farthest off, when we believe it near:
        Yet still we follow till we tire,
        And in the fatal Chase Expire:
        Each gaudy nothing which we view,
        We fancy is the wish'd for Prize,
Its painted Glories captivate our Eyes;
Blinded by Pride, we hug our own Mistake,
And foolishly adore that Idol which we make.

2.

Some hope to find it on the Coasts of Fame,
And hazard all to gain a glorious Name;
    Proud of Deformity and Scars,
They seek for Honour in the bloodiest Wars;
        On Dangers, unconcern'd, they run,
        And Death it self disdain to shun:
    This, the Rich with Wonder see,
        And fancy they are happier far
        Than those deluded Heroes are:
    But this, alas! is their Mistake;
        They only dream that they are blest,
For when they from their pleasing Slumbers wake,
They'll find their Minds with Swarms of Cares opprest,
        So crouded, that no part is free
            To entertain Felicity:
        The Pain to get, and Fear to lose,
        Like Harpies, all their Joys devour:
        Who such a wretched Life wou'd chuse?
Or think those happy who must Fortune trust?
That fickle Goddess is but seldom just.
Exterior things can ne'er be truly good,

Line 36. **Harpies**: in the *Aeneid*, foul, winged monsters who snatched away food from the starving Trojans.

Because within her Pow'r;
This the wise Ancients understood,
And only wish'd for what wou'd Life sustain;
Esteeming all beyond superfluous and vain.

3.

Some think the Great are only blest,
Those God-like Men who shine above the rest:
In whom united Glories meet,
And all the lower World pay Homage at their Feet:
On their exalted Heights they sit in State,
And their Commands bind like the Laws of Fate:
Their Regal Scepters, and their glitt'ring Crowns,
Imprint an awful Fear in ev'ry Breast:
Death shoots his killing Arrows thro' their Frowns;
Their Smiles are welcom, as the Beams of Light
Were to the infant World, when first it rose from Night.
Thus, in the Firmament of Pow'r above,
Each in his radiant Sphere does move,
Remote from common View;
Th'admiring Croud with Wonder gaze,
The distant Glories their weak Eyes amaze:
But cou'd they search into the Truth of Things,
Cou'd they but look into the Thoughts of Kings;
If all their hidden Cares they knew,
Their Jealousies, their Fears, their Pain,
And all the Troubles of their Reign,
They then wou'd pity those they now admire;
And with their humble State content, wou'd nothing more desire.

4.

If any thing like Happiness is here,
If any thing deserves our Care,
'Tis only by the Good possest;
By those who Virtue's Laws obey,
And cheerfully proceed in her unerring Way;

Whose Souls are cleans'd from all the Dregs of Sin,
From all the base Alloys of their inferior Part,
And fit to harbour that Celestial Guest,
Who ne'r will be confin'd
But to a holy Breast.
The pure and spotless Mind,
Has all within
That the most boundless Wish can crave;
The most aspiring Temper hope to have:
Nor needs the Helps of Art,
Nor vain Supplies of Sense,
Assur'd of all in only Innocence.

5.

Malice and Envy, Discontent, and Pride,
Those fatal Inmates of the Vicious Mind,
Which into dang'rous Paths th' unthinking Guide,
Ne'er to the pious Breast admittance find.
As th' upper Region is Serene and clear,
No Winds, no Clouds are there,
So with perpetual Calms the virtuous Soul is blest,
Those Antepasts of everlasting Rest:
Like some firm Rock amidst the raging Waves
She stands, and their united force outbraves;
Contends, till from her Earthly Shackles free,
She takes her flight
Into immense Eternity,
And in those Realms of unexhausted Light,
Forgets the Pressures of her former State.
O'er-joy'd to find her self beyond the reach of Fate.

6.

O happy Place! where ev'ry thing will please,
Where neither Sickness, Fear, nor Strife,
Nor any of the painful Cares of Life,

Line 92. **Antepasts**: foretastes.

Will interrupt her Ease:
Where ev'ry Object charms the Sight,
And yields fresh Wonder and Delight,
Where nothing's heard but Songs of Joy,
Full of Extasie Divine,
Seraphick Hymns! which Love inspire,
And fill the Breast with sacred Fire:
Love refin'd from drossy Heat,
Rais'd to a flame sublime and great,
In ev'ry Heav'nly Face do's shine,
And each Celestial Tongue employ:
What e'er we can of Friendship know,
What e'er we Passion call below,
Does but a weak Resemblance bear,
To that blest Union which is ever there,
Where Love, like Life, do's animate the whole,
As if it were but one blest individual Soul.

7.

Such as a lasting Happiness would have,
Must seek it in the peaceful Grave,
Where free from Wrongs the Dead remain.
Life is a long continu'd Pain,
A lingring slow Disease.
Which Remedies a while may ease,
But cannot work a perfect Cure:
Musick with its inchanting Lays,
May for a while our Spirits raise,
Honour and Wealth may charm the Sense,
And by their pow'rful Influence
May gently lull our Cares asleep;
But when we think our selves secure,
And fondly hope we shall no future Ills endure,
Our Griefs awake again,
And with redoubl'd Rage augment our Pain:
In vain we stand on our Defence,
In vain a constant Watch we keep,

In vain each Path we guard;
Unseen into our Souls they creep,
And when they once are there, 'tis very hard
With all our Strength to force them thence;
Like bold Intruders on the whole they seize,
A Part will not th' insatiate Victors please.

8.

In vain, alas! in vain,
We Reason's Aid implore,
That will but add a quicker Sense of Pain,
But not our former Joys restore:
Those few who by strict Rules their Lives have led,
Who Reason's Laws attentively have read;
Who to its Dictates glad Submission pay,
And by their Passions never led astray,
Go resolutely on in its severest Way,
Could never solid Satisfaction find:
The most that Reason can, is to persuade the Mind,
Its Troubles decently to bear,
And not permit a Murmur, or a Tear,
To tell th' inquiring World that any such are there:
But while we strive our Suff'rings to disown,
And blush to have our Frailties known;
While from the publick View our Griefs we hide,
And keep them Pris'ners in our Breast,
We seem to be, but are not truly blest;
What like Contentment looks, is but th' Effect of Pride:
From it we no advantage win,
But are the same we were before,
The smarting Pains corrode us still within;
Confinement do's but make them rage the more:
Upon the vital Stock they prey,
And by insensible degrees they wast our Life away.

9.

In vain from Books we hope to gain Relief,
Knowledge does but increase our Grief:
The more we read, the more we find
Of th' unexhausted Store still left behind:
To dig the wealthy Mine we try,
No Pain, no Labour spare;
But the lov'd Treasure too profound does lie,
And mocks our utmost Industry:
Like some inchanted Isle it does appear;
The pleas'd Spectator thinks it near;
But when with wide spread Sails he makes to shore,
His Hopes are lost, the Phantom's seen no more:
Asham'd, and tir'd, we of Success despair,
Our fruitless Studies we repent,
And blush to see, that after all our Care,
After whole Years on tedious Volumes spent,
We only darkly understand
That which we thought we fully knew;
Thro' Labyrinths we go without a Clue,
Till in the dang'rous Maze our selves we lose,
And neither know which Path t'avoid, or which to chuse.
From Thought to Thought, our restless Minds are tost,
Like Ship-wreck'd Mariners we seek the Land,
And in a Sea of Doubts are almost lost.
The *Phœnix* Truth wrapt up in Mists does lie,
Not to be clearly seen before we die;
Not till our Souls free from confining Clay,
Open their Eyes in everlasting Day.

Line 195. **Phœnix**: the legendary phoenix is reborn from its own ashes.

To *Almystrea*

1.

Permit *Marissa* in an artless Lay
To speak her Wonder, and her Thanks repay:
Her creeping Muse can ne'er like yours ascend;
She has not Strength for such a towring Flight.
Your Wit, her humble Fancy do's transcend;
She can but gaze at your exalted Height:
Yet she believ'd it better to expose
Her Failures, than ungrateful prove;
And rather chose
To shew a want of Sense, than want of Love:
But taught by you, she may at length improve,
And imitate those Virtues she admires.
Your bright Example leaves a Tract Divine,
She sees a beamy Brightness in each Line,
And with ambitious Warmth aspires,
Attracted by the Glory of your Name,
To follow you in all the lofty Roads of Fame.

2.

Merit like yours, can no Resistance find,
But like a Deluge overwhelms the Mind;
Gives full Possession of each Part,
Subdues the Soul, and captivates the Heart.
Let those whom Wealth, or Interest unite,
Whom Avarice, or Kindred sway
Who in the Dregs of Life delight;
And ev'ry Dictate of their Sense obey,
Learn here to love at a sublimer Rate,
To wish for nothing but exchange of Thoughts,
For intellectual Joys,

Title. **Almystrea**: anagram of Mary Astell, author of *A Serious Proposal to the Ladies* (1694) and *Some Reflections Upon Marriage* (1700).

Line 1. **Marissa**: Chudleigh's *nom de plume*.

And Pleasures more refin'd
Than Earth can give, or Fancy can create.
Let our vain Sex be fond of glitt'ring Toys,
Of pompous Titles, and affected Noise,
Let envious Men by barb'rous Custom led
Descant on Faults,
And in Detraction find
Delights unknown to a brave gen'rous Mind,
While we resolve a nobler Path to tread,
And from Tyrannick Custom free,
View the dark Mansions of the mighty Dead,
And all their close Recesses see;
Then from those awful Shades retire,
And take a Tour above,
And there, the shining Scenes admire,
Th' Opera of eternal Love;
View the Machines, on the bright Actors gaze,
Then in a holy Transport, blest Amaze,
To the great Author our Devotion raise,
And let our Wonder terminate in Praise.

To *Clorissa*

1.

To your lov'd Bosom pleas'd *Marissa* flies;
That place where sacred Friendship gives a Right,
And where ten thousand Charms invite.
Let others Pow'r and awful Greatness prize;
Let them exchange their Innocence and Fame
For the dear Purchase of a mighty Name:
Let greedy Wretches hug their darling Store,
The tempting Product of their Toils adore,
And still with anxious Souls, desire and grasp at more:
While I disdain to have my Bliss confin'd
To things which Fortune can bestow, or take,

To things so foreign to the Mind,
And which no part of solid Pleasure make:
Those Joys of which I am possest
Are safely lodg'd within my Breast,
Where like deep Waters, undisturb'd they flow,
And as they pass, a glassy smoothness show:
Unmov'd by Storms, or by th' Attacks of Fate,
I envy none, nor wish a happier State.

2.

When all alone in some belov'd Retreat,
Remote from Noise, from Bus'ness, and from Strife,
Those constant curst Attendants of the Great;
I freely can with my own Thoughts converse,
And cloath them in ignoble Verse,
'Tis then I tast the most delicious Feast of Life:
There, uncontroul'd I can my self survey,
And from Observers free,
My intellectual Pow'rs display,
And all th' opening Scenes of beauteous Nature see:
Form bright Ideas, and enrich my Mind,
Enlarge my Knowledge, and each Error find;
Inspect each Action, ev'ry Word dissect,
And on the Failures of my Life reflect:
Then from my self, to Books, I turn my Sight,
And there, with silent Wonder and Delight,
Gaze on th' instructive venerable Dead,
Those that in Virtue's School were early bred,
And since by Rules of Honour always led;
Who its strict Laws with nicest Care obey'd,
And were by calm unbyass'd Reason sway'd:
Their great Examples elevate my Mind,
And I the force of all their Precepts find;
By them inspir'd, above dull Earth I soar,
And scorn those Trifles which I priz'd before.

3.

Next these Delights Love claims the chiefest Part,
That gentle Passion governs in my Heart:
Its sacred Flames dilate themselves around,
And like pure Æther no confinement know:
  Where ever true Desert is found,
  I pay my Love and Wonder too:
  Wit, when alone, has Pow'r to please,
  And Virtue's Charms resistless prove;
    But when they both combine,
    When both together shine,
Who coldly can behold a Glory so Divine?
  Since you, *Clorissa*, have a Right to these,
    And since you both possess,
You've, sure, a double title to my Love,
    And I my fate shall bless,
For giving me a Friend, in whom I find
United, all the Graces of the Female kind.

4.

Accept that Heart your Merit makes your own,
And let the Kindness for the Gift attone:
Love, Constancy, and spotless Truth I bring,
These give a Value to the meanest Thing.
O! let our Thoughts, our Interests be but one,
Our Griefs and Joys, be to each other known:
In all Concerns we'll have an equal Share,
Enlarge each Pleasure, lessen ev'ry Care:
  Thus, of a thousand Sweets possest,
  We'll live in one another's Breast:
When present, talk the flying Hours away,
When absent, thus, our tender Thoughts convey;
  And, when by the Decrees of Fate
  We're summon'd to a higher State,
We'll meet again in the blest Realms of Light,
And in each other there eternally delight.

To Mr. *Dryden*, on his excellent Translation of *Virgil*

1.

Thou matchless Poet, whose capacious Mind
Contains the whole that Knowledge can impart,
Where we each charming Science find,
And ev'ry pleasing Art:
Permit my Muse in plain unpolish'd Verse,
In humble Strains her Wonder to rehearse:
From her low Shade she lifts her dazl'd Sight,
And views the Splendor and amazing Height:
See's boundless Wit, in artful Numbers play,
And like the glorious Source of Day,
To distant Worlds both Light and Heat convey.

2.

Before the happy Birth of Light,
E'er Nature did her forming Pow'r display,
While blended in their native Night,
The Principles of all things lay;
Triumphant Darkness did her self dilate,
And thro' the Chaos with resistless Sway
Her dusky Horrors spread;
Such in this Isle was once our wretched State:
Dark melancholy Night her sable Wings display'd,
And all around her baleful Influence shed;
From Gloom, to Gloom, with weary'd Steps we stray'd,
Till *Chaucer* came with his delusive Light,
And gave some transient Glimm'rings to the Night:
Next kinder *Spencer* with his Lunar Beams
Inrich'd our Skies, and wak'd us from our Dreams:
Then pleasing Visions did our Minds delight,

Title. Dryden translated the complete works of Virgil into English verse beginning in1680; he published *The Works of Virgil* in 1697.

And airy Spectres danc'd before our Sight:
Amidst our Shades in antick Rounds we mov'd,
And the bright entertaining Phantoms lov'd.

3.

With *Waller* our first Dawn of Light arose,
He did the Beauties of the Morn disclose:
Then *Milton* came, and *Cowley* blest our Eyes;
With Joy we saw the distant Glory rise:
But there remain'd some Footsteps of the Night,
Dark Shadows still were intermix'd with Light:
Those Shades the mighty *Dryden* chas'd away,
And shew'd the Triumphs of refulgent Day:
  Now all is clear, and all is bright,
  Our Sun from his Meridian height
   Darts kindly down reviving Rays
And one continu'd Splendor crowns our Days.

4.

This Work, great Poet, was reserv'd for thee,
None else cou'd us from our Confinement free:
By thee led on, we climb the sacred Hill,
And our pleas'd Eyes with distant Prospects fill:
View all th' Acquests thy conqu'ring Pen has made,
  Th' immortal Trophies of thy Fame:
And see, as if we stood on Magick Ground,
Majestick Ghosts with verdant Laurels crown'd:
Illustrious Heroes, ev'ry glorious Name,
That can a Place in ancient Records claim:
Among the rest, thy *Virgil's* awful Shade,
Whom thou hast rais'd to bless our happy Land,
Does circl'd round with radiant Honours stand:
He's now the welcom Native of our Isle,

Line 40. **Meridian:** midday. Line 47. **Acquests:** acquisitions.

And crowns our Hopes with an auspicious Smile;
With him we wander thro' the Depths below,
And into Nature's Close Recesses go;
View all the Secrets of th'infernal State,
And search into the dark Intriegues of Fate:
Survey the Pleasures of th'*Elysian* Fields,
And see what Joys the highest Region yields.

5.

What Thanks, thou gen'rous Man, can we repay,
What equal Retributions make,
For all thy Pains, and all thy Care,
And all those Toils, whose kind Effects we share?
Our Language like th'*Augean* Stable lay,
Rude and uncleans'd, till thou by Glory mov'd,
Th' *Herculean* Task didst undertake,
And hast with Floods of Wit th'offensive Heaps remov'd:
That ancient Rubbish of the *Gothick* Times,
When manly Sense was lost in trifling Rhimes:
Now th'unform'd Mass is to Perfection wrought;
Thou hast inlarg'd our Knowledge, and refin'd our Thought.
Long mayst thou shine within our *British* Sphere,
And may not Age, nor Care,
The sprightly Vigor of thy Mind impair:
Let Envy cease, and all thy Merits own,
And let our due Regards in Praise be ever shown:
And when from hence thou shalt remove
To bless th'harmonious World above,
May thy strong Genius on our Isle descend,
And what it has inspir'd, eternally defend.

Line 68. **Augean Stable**: in Greek myth, the huge stable housing the oxen herd of Augeas, king of Greece, which was never cleaned until Hercules was assigned to do it as one of his twelve labors.

Line 72. **Gothick Times**: medieval period; here, crude, barbaric times.

Song

1.

Why *Damon*, why, why, why so pressing?
The Heart you beg's not worth possessing:
Each Look, each Word, each Smile's affected,
And inward Charms are quite neglected:
  Then scorn her, scorn her, foolish Swain,
  And sigh no more, no more in vain.

2.

Beauty's worthless, fading, flying;
Who would for Trifles think of dying?
Who for a Face, a Shape, wou'd languish,
And tell the Brooks, and Groves his Anguish,
  Till she, till she thinks fit to prize him,
  And all, and all beside despise him?

3.

Fix, fix you Thoughts on what's inviting,
On what will never bear the slighting:
Wit and Virtue claim your Duty,
They're much more worth than Gold and Beauty:
  To them, to them, your Heart resign,
  And you'll no more, no more repine.

To *Eugenia*

Methinks I see the Golden Age agen,
Drawn to the Life by your ingenious Pen:
Then Kings were Shepherds, and with equal Care
'Twixt Men and Sheep, did their Concernments share:
There was no need of Rods and Axes then,
Crooks rul'd the Sheep, and Virtue rul'd the Men:
Then Laws were useless, for they knew no Sin,
From Guilt secur'd by Innocence within:
No Passion but the noblest, fill'd each Breast,
They were too good to entertain the rest:
Love, which is now become an Art, a Trade,
It self to them with all its Sweets convey'd;
Indulgent Nature their kind Tutress prov'd,
And as she taught, without Deceit, they lov'd:
Thus did they live; thus they employ'd their Hours;
Beneath cool Shades, on Banks of fragrant Flow'rs,
They sat and listen'd, while their Poets sung
The Praises of the Brave, the Wise, the Young;
What e'er was Good, or Great, their Theme they made,
To Virtue still a Veneration paid;
But Love did in each Song Precedence claim,
And in soft Numbers they made known their Flame:
Poets by Nature are to Love inclin'd;
To them, the Lover's God was ever kind:
They still observ'd his Laws, and all their Care
Was to win Fame, and to oblige the Fair:
But ah! dear Friend, those happy Days are past;
Hard Fate! that only what is ill should last!
Unhappy we! born in the Dregs of Time,
Can ne'er to their vast height of Virtue climb;

Title. **Eugenia:** possibly the same "Eugenia" who wrote *The Female Preacher* (1699), also called *The Female Advocate* (1700), a prose rebuttal to Sprint's sermon *The Bride-Woman's Counsellor,* which inspired Chudleigh's *The Ladies Defence*.

Line 1. **Golden Age:** a period of time long past when life was idyllic; in Ovid, the first period of man, a pastoral idyll.

But lie immers'd in Vice, forsaken quite
Of those pure Joys which did their Souls delight:
We live disguis'd, nor can each other trust,
But only seem obliging, kind and just,
To serve our low Designs; by Int'rest sway'd,
That pow'rful God by all Mankind obey'd!
Nor are those Vices in the Town alone,
The Country too does with the Pressure groan:
For Innocence (once our peculiar boast)
Is now with all her Train of Virtues lost;
From hence to the divine Abodes retir'd
Here undeserv'd, as well as undesir'd:
Yet some imperfect Footsteps still are seen,
That future Times may know they once have been:
But oh! how few will tread that sacred way;
By Vice, or Humor, most are led astray:
Those few who dare be good, must live alone
To all Mankind, except themselves, unknown:
From a mad World, to some obscure Recess,
They must retire, to purchase Happiness:
Yet of this wretched Place so well you've writ,
That I admire your Goodness and your Wit,
And must confess your excellent Design
To make it with its native lustre shine:
To hide its Faults, and to expose to view
Nought but its Beauties, is becoming you.

Song: To *Lerinda*

Cease, Dear *Lerinda*, cease admiring
  Why Crouds and Noise I disapprove;
What e'er I see abroad is tiring;
  O let us to some Cell remove;
Where all alone our selves enjoying,
  Enrich'd with Innocence and Peace,
On noblest Themes our Thoughts employing,
  Let us our inward Joys increase:
And still the happy Taste pursuing,
  Raise our Love and Friendship higher,
And thus the sacred Flames renewing,
  In Extasies of Bliss expire.

Song

1.

When Daphne first her Shepherd saw,
  A sudden Trembling seiz'd her;
Honour her wandring Looks did awe,
  She durst not view what pleas'd her.

2.

When at her Feet he sighing lay,
  She found her Heart complying;
Yet wou'd not to her Love give way,
  To save her Swain from dying.

3.

The little God stood laughing by
  To see her dextrous feigning;
He bid the blushing Fair comply,
  The Shepherd leave complaining.

The Wish

Would but indulgent Fortune send
To me a kind, and faithful Friend,
One who to Virtue's Laws is true,
And does her nicest Rules pursue;
One Pious, Lib'ral, Just and Brave,
And to his Passions not a Slave;
Who full of Honour, void of Pride,
Will freely praise, and freely chide;
But not indulge the smallest Fault,
Nor entertain one slighting Thought:
Who still the same will ever prove,
Will still instruct, and still will love:
In whom I safely may confide,
And with him all my Cares divide:
Who has a large capacious Mind,
Join'd with a Knowledge unconfin'd;
A Reason bright, a Judgment true,
A Wit both quick, and solid too:
Who can of all things talk with Ease,
And whose Converse will ever please:
Who charm'd with Wit, and inward Graces,
Despises Fools with tempting Faces;
And still a beauteous Mind does prize
Above the most enchanting Eyes:
I would not envy Queens their State,
Nor once desire a happier Fate.

The Elevation

1.

O how ambitious is my Soul,
How high she now aspires!
There's nothing can on Earth controul,
Or limit her Desires.

2.

Upon the Wings of Thought she flies
Above the reach of Sight,
And finds a way thro' pathless Skies
To everlasting Light:

3.

From whence with blameless Scorn she views
The Follies of Mankind;
And smiles to see how each pursues
Joys fleeting as the Wind.

4.

Yonder's the little Ball of Earth,
It lessens as I rise;
That Stage of transitory Mirth,
Of lasting Miseries:

5.

My Scorn does into Pity turn,
And I lament the Fate
Of Souls, that still in Bodies mourn,
For Faults which they create:

6.

Souls without Spot, till Flesh they wear,
Which their pure Substance stains:
While thy th'uneasie Burthen bear,
They're never free from Pains.

Friendship

Friendship is a Bliss Divine,
And does with radiant Lustre shine:
But where can that blest Pair be found
That are with equal Fetters bound?
Whose Hearts are one, whose Souls combine,
And neither know or Mine, or Thine;
Who've but one Joy, one Grief, one Love,
And by the self same Dictates move;
Who've not a Frailty unreveal'd,
Nor yet a Thought that is conceal'd;
Who freely one another blame,
And strive to raise each other's Fame;
Who're always just, sincere, and kind,
By Virtue, not by Wealth, combin'd;
Whose Friendship nothing can abate,
Nor Poverty, nor adverse Fate,
Nor Death it self: for when above,
They'll never, never, cease to love,
But with a Passion more refin'd,
Become one pure celestial Mind.

The Happy Man

He is the happy Man whose constant Mind
Is to th' Enjoyment of himself confin'd:
Who has within laid up a plenteous Store,
And is so rich that he desires no more:
Whose Soul is always easie, firm, and brave,
And much too great to be Ambition's Slave:
Who Fortune's Frowns without Concern can bear,
And thinks it less to suffer, than to fear:
Who, still the same, keeps up his native State,

Unmov'd at all the Menaces of Fate:
Who all his Passions absolutely sways,
And to his Reason cheerful Homage pays,
Who's with a *Halcyon* Calmness ever blest,
With inward Joy, untroubl'd Peace, and Rest:
Who while the Most with Toil, with Guilt, and Heat,
Lose their dear Quiet to be Rich and Great,
Both Business, and disturbing Crouds does shun,
Pleas'd that his Work is with less Trouble done:
To whom a Grove, a Garden, or a Field,
Much greater, much sublimer Pleasures yield,
Than they can find in all the Charms of Pow'r,
Those splendid Ills which so much Time devour:
Who more than Life, his Friends and Books can prize,
And for those Joys the noisie world despise:
Who when Death calls, no Weakness does betray,
Nor to an unbecoming Fear give way;
But to himself, and to his Maxims true,
Lies smiling down, and bids Mankind adieu.

A Dialogue between *Alexis* and *Astrea*

Alexis. Come, fair *Astrea*, let us for a while
Beneath this pleasant Shade our Cares beguile:
In kind Discourses let us pass away
The tiresom Heat, and Troubles of the Day:
The Gods no greater Blessing can bestow
Than mutual Love, 'tis all our Bliss below.

Astrea. But Men, false Men, take Pleasure to deceive,
And laugh, when we their Perjuries believe;

Line 13. **Halcyon Calmness**: a perfectly still and motionless state; dead still water, named for the myth of Alcyone and Ceyx.

Their Languishments, and all their other Arts,
Their Sighs, and Vows, are only Snares for Hearts.

Alexis. Think not, unjust *Astrea*, all are so,
Alexis will a deathless Passion show.
May the severest of all Plagues, your Hate,
And all the Rigors of an angry Fate,
With all those Curses that to Guilt are due,
Fall on my Head, when I am false to you.
A Love like mine, can no decrease admit;
A Love, inspir'd by Virtue, and by Wit,
Like its immortal Cause, will ever last,
And be the same, when Youth, and Beauty's past:
Nor need *Astrea* blush to own my Flame,
Or think 'twill prove a Blemish to her Fame,
Since 'tis as pure, as Spotless as her Mind,
Bright as her Eyes, from all its Dross refin'd.

Astrea. When Humors are alike, and Souls agree,
How sweet! how pleasant must that Union be!
But oh! that Bliss is but by few possest,
But few are with the Joys of Friendship blest.
Marriage is but a fatal Lott'ry made,
Where some are Gainers, but the most betray'd:
The mild and froward, cruel and the kind,
Are in unequal Chains by Fate confin'd:
Most are a Sacrifice to Interest made,
Interest, and Gold, now more than Love persuade:
To conqu'ring Gold, the most themselves submit,
That has more Charms, than Beauty, Youth, or Wit:
Unhappy they! whom Riches thus unite,
Whom Wealth does to the sacred Band invite:
The languid Passion quickly will expire,
Wealth can ne'er keep alive the dying Fire:
Virtue the *Hymenæan* Torch shou'd light,

Line 41. **Hymenæan Torch**: marriage torch.

'Tis that alone preserves its Lustre bright:
The Rich and Great let the vain World admire,
Neither their Gold, nor Grandeur, I desire;
Virtue, and Love, to me's a great Estate,
I wish no more, but leave the rest to Fate.

Alexis. Let Kings for Empire, and for Crowns contend,
Let them their Arms to distant Realms extend:
I envy none, no not the Pow'rs above,
I've all I covet in *Astrea's* Love.

Astrea. How blest are we! nothing our Hearts can sever,
Not Death it self, we'll love, we'll love for ever.

Alexis. But we must part; hard Fate will have it so,
Alexis must from his *Astrea* go.
Yes, we must part; O th'afflicting Sound!
It shakes my Breast, my very Soul does wound.
Is there no way, this Misery to shun,
Ye cruel Gods! what has *Alexis* done
To merit this severe, this rig'rous Fate?
Had you no way, but this, to shew your Hate?

Astrea. Cease these Complaints; while you possess my Heart,
While there you live, can we be said to part?
Our Thoughts shall meet, they ne'er can be confin'd,
We'll still be present to each other's Mind:
I'll view you with my intellectual Sight,
And in th'indearing Object take Delight:
My faithful Mem'ry shall your Vows retain,
And in my Breast you shall unrival'd reign.

Alexis. And your dear Image shall my Solace prove,
On that I'll gaze, to that I'll sigh my Love:
To that a thousand tender things I'll say,
And fancy that does ev'ry Sigh repay:

Each word approves by an obliging Smile,
As if it kindly wou'd my Griefs beguile:
Thus, will I languish out the tedious Day,
Thus, will I pass my saddest Hours away.

Astrea. What tho' by Fate our Bodies are confin'd,
Nought can obstrust the Journies of the Mind:
A virtuous Passion will at distance live,
Absence to that will a new Vigor give,
Which still increases, and grows more intense,
The farther 'tis remov'd from the mean Joys of Sense.

To the Ladies

Wife and Servant are the same,
But only differ in the Name:
For when that fatal Knot is ty'd,
Which nothing, nothing can divide:
When she the word *obey* has said,
And Man by Law supreme has made,
Then all that's kind is laid aside,
And nothing left but State and Pride:
Fierce as an Eastern Prince he grows,
And all his innate Rigor shows:
Then but to look, to laugh, or speak,
Will the Nuptial Contract break.
Like Mutes she Signs alone must make,
And never any Freedom take:
But still be govern'd by a Nod,
And fear her Husband as her God:
Him still must serve, him still obey,
And nothing act, and nothing say,
But what her haughty Lord thinks fit,

Who with the Pow'r, has all the Wit.
Then shun, oh! shun that wretched State,
And all the fawning Flatt'rers hate:
Value your selves, and Men despise,
You must be proud, if you'll be wise.

To the *Queen's* most Excellent *Majesty*

1.

MADAM,
Permit me at Your Royal Feet to lay
This humble Off'ring of a trembling Muse;
        Permit me there to pay
This Tribute to transcendent Merit due;
To that transcendent Merit which conspicuous is in You.
Bold is th'Address, and the Presumption high!
But she all meaner Objects does refuse,
    To this vast height will fly,
And hopes Your Goodness will th'ambitious Flight excuse.
I strove a while her Ardor to conceal,
    Unseen it burnt within my Breast;
But now impetuous grows, and will it self reveal;
    'Tis much too strong to be supprest.
What was at first but Warmth, now to a Flame do's rise,
    On you she gazes with admiring Eyes,
    And ev'ry lower Object does despise:
Pardon her Transports, since from Zeal they spring,
    And give her Leave of You to sing;
Of You, the noblest Theme that she can chuse,
Of You, who're with Ten thousand Graces fraught,
Of You, who far exceed the widest Bounds of Thought:
In whom as to their Centre Lines are drawn,
All those bright Qualities in one combine,
Which did till now with scatter'd Glory shine;
    Appear'd till now but in their Dawn:

You're the Meridian Splendor of Your Line;
And on Your Sex entail a lasting Fame:
We shall be ever proud of Your illustrious Name.

2.

Long may You reign, long fill the *British* Throne,
And make the haughty *Gallick* Foe our *English* Valor own:
Assert the Rights of Your Imperial Crown;
And vie with ancient Heroes for Renown:
Tread in his Steps whom Fate has snatch'd away,
Like him the Terror of Your Arms display;
But longer, longer much Your happy Subjects sway,
His mighty Acts cou'd not the Victor save,
        Those Conquests he had gain'd
        Cou'd not preserve his Life:
Death to his vast Designs a Period gave,
Sent him amidst his Triumphs to the Grave:
For You he fought, for You he Wreaths obtain'd,
    For You he strove to humble *France:*
For You has been the Toil, for You the Strife,
    For You the Battels he has won,
    The wondrous things which he has done:
    To him there nothing now remains,
But empty Fame, that mean Reward for all his Pains.
Heav'n brought him here Your Grandeur to advance,
    That was the kind Design of Fate,
And took him hence when he had aggrandiz'd Your State.
    To You he all his Trophies yields,
To You the dusty Honours of the bloody Fields:
He at Your Feet lays all his Lawrels down.
And adds his great Atchievements to the Glories of
        Your Crown.

Line 28. **entail**: bequeath, leave as a legacy. Line 31. **Gallick Foe**: French.

Line 34. **Tread . . . Steps**: William III, who died in 1702.

3.

If Poets may to Prophesie pretend,
If they're allow'd to pry,
Into the hidden Secrets of Futurity,
They dare presage, You will Your Pow'r extend,
And spite of *Salic* Laws, the *Gallick* throne ascend:
For You that noble Task's assign'd,
'Tis You are born Mankind to free,
From arbitrary Sway, and hateful Tyranny:
You, none but You, are for that Work design'd;
We no where cou'd a fitter Champion find:
Go on great Heroin, and exalt Your Name,
Go fearless on in the bright Tracks of Fame:
When Beauty leads, and Virtue shows the Way,
The Men will soon with joyful hast obey,
None then will shew a greater Zeal than they:
They for Your Service with a noble Pride
Will all Your Enemies defie,
Will all their Vain Efforts deride,
And strive who first for You shall die;
Who first th' ambition'd Honour have,
Who first lie down in the contested Grave.

4.

Where You reside, may Pleasures still abound,
May blooming Joys disperse themselves around,
And may there nothing there but soft Delights be found:
Still may Your Subjects make Your Bliss their Care,
Contending Parties in Your Cause unite:
No more within our *British* Sphere
May threatning Clouds appear,
Or deafning Storms affright,
But all be calm, and all be bright;

Line 59. **presage**: foretell.

Line 60. **Salic Laws**: the founding law of France, which prohibits women from succeeding to the throne.

Bright as those virtues which adorn Your Mind,
Those Virtues, which we no where else can in Perfection find.
May Heav'n indulgent to Your Wishes prove,
And make You still chief Object of its Love:
Bless You with all the Favours it can give,
And let You in a num'rous Off-spring live;
An Off-spring worthy of Your Princely Line,
Great as Your Merit, like Your self Divine.

5.

My pious Pray'rs have quick Acceptance found,
Propitious Omens Heaven is pleas'd to send,
Pleas'd Nature does this glorious Change approve;
On You she seems t'attend
Commission'd from Above:
Each Hour of Your auspicious Reign,
Has been with wondrous Blessings crown'd;
The Sun restores his Heat again,
Again restores reviving Rays,
Again we're blest with radiant Days:
No noxious Vapors now dare rise,
No Streams of Earth pollute the Skies,
Back to their gloomy Source each darkning Atom flies:
A balmy Sweetness fills the Air,
Health and Pleasure revel there;
The Flow'rs rise beauteous from the Ground,
And spread their fragrant Odors round;
The Trees prepare
Their verdant Crowns to wear;
Amidst their Boughs soft Zephyrs play:
And in low whisp'ring Murmurs their glad Homage pay:
The warbling Birds resound Your Praise,
And welcom You with cheerful Lays:
Joy does in every Face appear,
In ev'ry Face is seen to smile;
A Joy till now to us unknown,
A Joy which You cou'd give alone;

You to Your Subjects are more dear,
To us the happy Natives of this Isle,
Than Life, and all the Pleasures we possess below,
All, all the gay Delights Your *Albion* can bestow,
Which rich in You, and Your immortal Fame,
The Title now of Fortunate may claim,
And justly be allow'd to glory in so great a Name.

The Resolution

Yes, dear *Philistris*, in my lov'd Retreat
I will the Malice of my Stars defeat:
I've not deserv'd my Fate, and therefore dare
To brave my Fortune when 'tis most severe:
While Innocence and Honour guard my Breast,
I shall in spite of my worst Foes be blest:
In spite of all the Rage the Furies can inspire,
When into mortal Breasts they breath infernal Fire,
With Eyes that dart malignant Horrors round,
And Voices which affright with their tremendous Sound,
They fiercely may the cruel Fight begin,
And hope by Violence the Day to win;
But all in vain; I'll smiling ward each Blow,
And where my Duty calls undaunted go:
Secure within, their Shock I dare sustain,
My Souls impassive, and can feel no Pain:
I've secret Joys, Delights to them unknown,
In Solitude I never am alone:
Books are the best Companions I can find,
At once they please, at once instruct the Mind.

Line 124. **Albion:** England.

Fam'd *Rochester,* who *Athens's* Plague has writ
With all the Charms of Poetry and Wit,
Does Honour on his sacred See bestow;
At once its Glory, and its Blessing too:
Him I with Pleasure read, each well weigh'd Line,
Delights my Soul, his Thoughts are all Divine.

With awful Fear on *Stillingfleet* I gaze,
His wondrous Knowledge and deep Sense my ravish'd
Soul amaze:

Smooth *Tillotson* affords no less Delight,
None ever did with more Exactness write,
Or with more Clearness each dark Text unfold,
He sacred Truths intelligibly told:
Strong are his Reasons, and his Language fine,
And like his Subjects, ev'ry where Divine;

Much the learn'd *Sarum's* pompous Stile do's please,
His Thoughts, tho' lofty, are express'd with Ease:
What e'er he writes so captivates the Mind,
We there the Strength of pow'rful Reason find:
See human Nature to its Zenith rais'd,
And Virtue with a winning Sweetness prais'd;
So charming made, and so majestick too,
We're forc'd to Love, what awfully we view:

Line 21. **Rochester**: Francis Atterbury (1662–1732), bishop of Rochester, noted as a preacher and a writer. He was involved in the controversy over the authentication of *The Epistles of Phalaris* (1695), which were supposedly written by the tyrannical ruler in 600 B.C.

Line 23. **See**: the jurisdiction of a bishop.

Line 27. **Stillingfleet**: Edward Stillingfleet (1635–99), bishop of Worcester, whose text *The Irenicum* urged compromises with the Presbyterians.

Line 29. **Tillotson**: John Tillotson (1630–94), archbishop of Canterbury, a latitudinarian whose sermons were much admired by Dryden.

Line 35. **Sarum**: Gilbert Burnet (1643–94), bishop of Salisbury and author of *The History of the Reformation* (1724–34). **pompous**: grand.

Thou wondrous Man! who can enough admire
The amazing Force of that celestial Fire,
Which thro' each Line do's sacred Warmth inspire?
To darkest Minds clear dazling Light convey,
Refulgent Beams of intellectual Day!

Th'ingenious *Norris* in a flowing Strain,
With various Scenes of Wit do's entertain;
Sometimes in Prose he sweetly do's invite,
And then in Verse takes an unbounded Flight:
Plato reviv'd, we in his Writings find,
His Sentiments are there, but more refin'd.
'Twould be too tedious if I all should name,
Who have a just, unquestion'd Right to Fame.

O happy *Albion!* in thy Clergy blest,
In Sons that are of ev'ry Grace possest!
May they increase, and like ascending Light
Chase hence those Spectres that are pleas'd with Night,
Nor can endure a Glory so divinely bright:
Those restless Troublers of the Churches Peace;
May their Attacks, and their Reproaches cease;
While she supported by Almighty Love,
Securely on the wat'ry Deep do's move;
In sacred Pomp on swelling Surges rise,
And all the Monsters of the Main despise.

Philosophers next these, are my Delight;
O let me learn from them to think aright:
Contending Passions timely to restrain,
And o'er my self a happy Conquest gain:

Line 47. **Refulgent**: shining brightly, glittering.

Line 48. **Norris**: John Norris (1657–1715), rector of Bemerton, Christian Platonist, and author of *An Essay Towards the Theory of an Ideal and Intelligible World* (1701–4), a study of Melbrance's spiritual Cartesianism; his correspondence with Mary Astell was published under the title *Letters Concerning the Love of God* (1695).

Line 52. **Plato reviv'd**: Neoplatonism. Line 66. **Monsters of the Main**: sea creatures.

To stand unalter'd at the Turns of Fate,
And undejected in the worst Estate.

With Secret Pleasure I the Lives survey
Of those great Men who Virtue did obey,
And went unweary'd on in her steep painful Way;
Their bright Examples fortifie my Mind,
And I within both Strength and Calmness find:

When I am wrong'd, or treated with Neglect,
I on the patient *Socrates* reflect;
That virtuous Man, who was severely try'd,
Who injur'd liv'd, and much more injur'd dy'd:
Methinks I see him laugh'd at on the Stage,
And made a Victim to the Poets Rage;
Expos'd, and ridicul'd, while he sits by,
And calmly bears their spiteful Calumny:
In him none coul'd the least Emotion find,
He bore Reproaches with a constant Mind,
And bravely met that Fate, which Fate for him design'd;
That Fate, which he persuaded was to shun;
But he resolv'd to keep the Glory he had won:
His Fame, to him than Life, was much more dear,
And Death was what he ne'er had learnt to fear:
Brave to the last, and to his Virtue true,
Without Concern he bid his Friends adieu,
And with a free, untroubl'd, cheerful Air,
Did for another, better State prepare,
And smiling drank the welcome Cure of all his Care:
That happy Draught, that Balm for all his Grief,
His best, his last, his only sure Relief.

O who wou'd live, that with such ease could go
From this vile World, this dismal Scene of Woe,
Where most are false, and no Compassion show,
Where our Misfortunes but a Jest are made,
Where by pretended Friends we're most betray'd:

Where Men are to their Int'rest wholly ty'd,
Slaves to their glitt'ring Gold, and to their Pride,
And where Ambition, and Self-love as sovereign
Lords preside:
Where Kindness only do's to Words extend,
And few are truly that which they pretend,
And where the greatest Prodigy's a Friend.

Thrice happy Times when Riches were despis'd,
And Men for innate Worth were only priz'd:
When none to Titles their respect did pay,
Nor were to Bribes a mercenary Prey:
When all to rural Cares their Thoughts did bend,
And on their harmless Flocks with Peace attend;
When underneath some cool delightful Shade,
They to their Nymphs their artless Courtship made,
And were with kindest Vows, and unfeign'd Truth repaid:
When Constancy their highest Boast became,
And Friend was held the most endearing Name;
When nothing ill was harbour'd in the Mind,
But all were pious, gen'rous, just and kind.
But that blest Age, alas! was quickly past,
What's eminently good can never last:
Short was the peaceful *Saturn's* Golden Reign:
But oh! this Iron Age do's still remain.

Betimes the Vicious their Insults began,
And fatal was Integrity to Man:
The virtuous still to Hardships were inur'd,
And still the Drudgeries of Fate indur'd:
Saw Fools admir'd, and wealthy Fops carest,

Line 126. **Saturn's Golden Reign**: in the first book of Ovid's *Metamorphoses*, translated by Dryden and published in the miscellany *Examen Poeticum* (1693), the first of the four ages of time was the reign of Saturn, father of Jupiter, which was typified as a time of idyllic, pastoral happiness, "When man yet new / No rule but uncorrupted reason knew"; the current age, the Iron Age, is the time when evil rules and "Truth, modesty, and shame, the world forsook."

And Rebels with Imperial Purple drest:
Knaves made the Props of an unthinking State,
When Truth and Justice shou'd support the Weight:
Ill Men ador'd, and prais'd above the Skies,
While at their Feet neglected Merit lies,
And *Regulus* amidst his Tortures dies:

An *Aristides* from his *Athens* sent,
From his ungrateful Town to Banishment:

A *Cato* bleeding in the noblest Cause,
A Victim to his Honour, and the Laws:
He reads with Pleasure of th'immortal State,
And then with hast anticipates his Fate;
With the same Courage he for *Rome* had fought,
He for his Soul a welcom Passage sought.

A *Petus* strugling with a Tyrant's Rage,
A suff'ring *Arria*, Wonder of her Age!
The best of Wives, the kindest, truest Friend;
Her Spouse in all his Troubles did attend:
His Grief was hers, and so was all his Care;
Well pleas'd she was with him the worst of Ills to share.
When he was doom'd by his own Hand to die,
She beg'd him with the Sentence to comply;
Told him a wretched Life deserv'd no Care,

Line 138. **Regulus**: Marcus Atilius Regulus, Roman consul in 267 and 256 B.C.; captured by the Carthaginians, he was sent as a hostage to urge peace terms with the Roman senate, but instead he convinced the Romans to reject them, whereupon he was severely tortured by his captors.

Line 139. **Aristides**: celebrated Athenian solder and judge (fl. 484 B.C.), called "Aristides the Just," who died in poverty.

Line 141. **Cato**: a Stoic known for his simple life, straightforward speech, and self-denying service, who opposed Julius Caesar, warning the senate to beware Caesar's ambition; after being defeated by Caesar's troops, Cato fatally stabbed himself in 46 B.C.

Lines 147–48. **Petus ... Arria**: Arria was the wife of a Roman senator, Pætus Cecinna, who was accused of being in a conspiracy against Claudius and ordered sent to Rome by sea. Arria accompanied him and once at sea, she stabbed herself and presented the sword to her husband, who, inspired by her example, also killed himself (A.D. 42).

And that a *Roman* never ought to fear:
Bid him remember with what noble Pride
The valiant *Curtius*, and the *Decii* dy'd;
And how th'immortal *Brutus* Death's griesly Form defy'd:
But when she saw her Reasons could not move,
She gave a vast, a wondrous Proof of Love:
With hast she snatch'd his Poniard from his Side,
And with her dearest Blood the fatal Weapon dy'd;
Then drawing it undaunted from her Breast,
And with a Look that no Concern exprest,
She smiling gave it to his trembling Hand,
And said, O *Petus*, thus, thy Fate command:
Thus, *Cæsar's* Malice, and thy Stars defie;
Believe me, 'tis not difficult to die.
She said no more; he sighing clos'd her Eyes,
And taught by her, with conscious Blushes dies;
Asham'd to think for such a noble Deed
He shou'd th' Example of a Woman need.

An *Epictetus* in a *Nero's* Court,
The best of Men, a Slave, and Fortune's Sport.

A *Belisarius*, blind, despis'd, and poor,
Seeking precarious Alms from Door, to Door;
And meanly striving to prolong his Breath,
To save a Life more to be fear'd, than Death:

Line 158. **Curtius ... Decii**: according to Roman myth, Lacus Curtius sacrificed his life to close a chasm that appeared in the Roman forum and that soothsayers declared could only be filled if Rome's greatest treasures were thrown into it; Curtius declared that valor and bravery were Rome's greatest treasures and, fully armed, rode his horse into the chasm. The Decii were members of the family of Decius, who sacrificed themselves in battle to serve Rome.

Line 159. **griesly**: grisly, causing fear or disgust.

Line 174. **Epictetus**: a Stoic philosopher (ca. A.D. 60–140), born a slave and freed by Nero, whose thoughts on austerity, humility, patience, and contempt of riches were collected by a student under the title *Enchiridion*. **Nero**: Roman emperor (A.D. 36–68), noted for barbaric cruelty; he ordered the executions of his mother, Seneca, Lucan, and Petronius.

Line 176. **Belisarius**: a great general during the reign of Justinian (A.D. 527–63), who after defeating the Vandals and the Goths was accused of conspiracy; his eyes were put out, and he ended life as a wandering beggar.

While Earth-born Monsters, a degen'rous Race,
Rise from their Slime, and fill the heav'nly Space;
Where, for a while, like Meteors they amaze,
And fright the World with their portentous Blaze;
Till having wasted all their Stock of Light,
They fall unpity'd from their tow'ring Hight,
And lie despis'd in the dark Shades of Night.

Thus Hist'ry Shews the World in its rude Infant State,
And does the Progress of Mankind relate;
By what slow Steps they first to Greatness rose;
Does all their Arts, their Policies disclose:

There, I behold th' *Assyrian* Empire rise,
And *Babel's* lofty Tow'rs insult the Skies:
See mighty *Cyrus* all their Hopes defeat,
And place himself in the Imperial seat:
From whence I see the great *Darius* fall,
And the *Pellean* Youth possest of all:
Him, full of Glory, full of God-like Fire
I see amidst adoring Crouds expire:
Young *Ammon* all his boasted Conquests quit,
And early to the Laws of Fate submit:
He, whose Ambition towr'd above the Skies,
Now with a Spot of Earth scarce cover'd lies;
And in a dark, a narrow, silent Grave,
Sleeps undistinguish'd from his meanest Slave.

I next observe the Western Empire rise,
The *Roman* Eagles wanton in the Skies:
Those Birds of *Jove* clap their extended Wings,

Line 193. **Cyrus**: King of Persia (reigned 559–529 B.C.) who invaded Assyria and took the city of Babylon.

Line 196. **Pellean Youth**: Alexander the Great (356–323 B.C.).

Line 199. **Ammon**: Alexander the Great was declared a god, "the son of Jupiter Ammon," at Ammon's temple.

While with the clattering Sound the wide *Expansum* rings:
See Royal Shepherds an Usurper chase,
And on his Throne their injur'd Grandsire place;
With happy Omens the Foundations lay
Of that great City which the World must sway:
See *Rome's* rash Builder, the Derider kill,
And a dear Brother's Blood relentless spill.

O what is Man, if by his Passion led!
Lions and Tigers with less cause we dread:
They much the gentler, much the kinder prove,
Whom nothing can against their Species move:
But Men each other's Ruin still design,
They break thro' all the Ties, the Laws Divine:
Nor Blood, nor Friendship, can their Rage restrain,
Intreaties all are lost, and Tears are shed in vain:
Slaves to their Will, they ev'ry Vice obey,
And on their Actions no Restriction lay.

This fatal Truth the sad *Lucretia* found;
Methinks in Tears I see her almost drown'd;
Confus'd she sits among her grieving Friends,
While each to her distressful Tale attends:
Trembling and Pale, with Sighs, and downcast Eyes,
The moving Rhetorick of her Sorrow tries:
And then by her own Hand with wondrous Courage dies.

Line 208. **Expansum**: open spaces.

Line 209. **Royal Shepherds**: in Roman myth, twin brothers Romulus and Remus deposed Amulius and restored their grandfather Numitor as the king of Alba Longa, the city that was the precursor of Rome; Remus was then killed by Romulus when they argued about founding the city of Rome.

Line 225. **Lucretia**: Lucretia, wife of Tarquinius, who was raped by Sextus, son of Tarquin, the king of Rome; she killed herself after urging her husband to avenge her.

Pride of thy Sex! thy Glory still shall live,
To thee we will our loudest Plaudits give:
My Muse with Joy shall celebrate thy Fame,
And make the Groves resound with thy immortal Name.
Th' amaz'd Beholders view the breathless Fair,
And for a just, a quick Revenge prepare:
The proud *Tarquinius* with his guilty Race
They from his undeserv'd Dominions chase:
Govern'd by Consuls then, with Freedom blest,
And of the noblest Parts of Earth possest,
Rome long enjoy'd the Glories she had won;
But was inthrall'd at length by her victorious Son,
To his superior Fortune she gave way,
But did not long his Tyranny obey:
The *Roman* Soul exerts it self once more,
T'assert lost Rights, and Liberty restore;
The mighty *Cæsar* to their Rage did yield,
Nor could the Goddess her lov'd Off-spring shield.
See, full of Wounds, the Hero gasping lies,
And fiercely rolling his Majestick Eyes,
Seems to call Vengeance from his Kindred Skies.

How vain is Greatness, and how frail is Pow'r!
Those who above their Fellow Mortals tow'r,
Who with a Word can save, or with a Word destroy,
Can't to themselves insure one Moment's Joy:
But soon may tumble from their slippery State,
And feel the Pressures of an adverse Fate.

Sure for our selves if we our Terms could make,
We should not Life on such Conditions take;
Life, which subjects us to Ten thousand Ills,
And ev'ry Minute with new Trouble fills:
By which to Fortune we're still Captives made,
And to the worst of Tyrannies betray'd;
Captives to her, who makes Mankind her Sport,
Who slights the best, and does the basest court;

Who low with Earth the mighty *Pompeys* lays,
And from the Dust does *Aniello's* raise.

When such Reflections, such sad Thoughts as these
On my dejected Soul begin to seize,
To pleasant Studies I my self apply,
And feast upon the Sweets of Poetry;
Those luscious Banquets which the Mind invite,
Where all is to be found that can delight.

Sometimes in *Homer* I the *Grecians* view,
See, what the King, and injur'd Husband do;
See, tow'ring *Ilium* compass'd round with Foes,
And for her sake her Sons their Lives expose;
Her valiant Sons, who prodigal of Blood,
Long in Defence of their lov'd Country stood:
See, from their Seats superior Pow'rs descend,
And on the *Phrygians* and the *Greeks* attend,
And with indecent warmth among themselves contend.
View fierce *Achilles* full of Grief and Rage,
Victorious *Hector* with redoubl'd Strength engage:
Revenge to ev'ry Blow new Force does give;
The Hopes of *Ilium* must no longer live:
Fate signs his Doom; the Godlike Hero falls,
And thrice his Body's drag'd around the *Trojan* Walls:
The *Cyprian* Goddess mourns her Favourite slain,
And loud Laments fill all the *Idalian* Plain.

Line 267. **Pompey**: Roman general (106–48 B.C.) who formed the first triumvirate with Julius Caesar and Crassus in 60 B.C.; he was stabbed in the back by Septimus, formerly one of his trusted soldiers.

Line 268. **Aniello**: Tomaso Aniello, also called Masaniello (1620–47), the son of a fisherman who led a popular revolt in Naples against the ruling Spanish nobility, urging the people to kill all aristocrats.

Line 277. **Ilium**: In Virgil's *Aeneid*, Troy. Line 282. **Phrygians**: Trojans.

Line 290. **Cyprian Goddess**: Aphrodite.

Line 291. **Idalian Plain**: on the island of Cyprus, Idalia was sacred to Aphrodite.

The wise *Ulysses* does my Wonder raise,
Who can enough his prudent Conduct praise?
With his ill Fortune he did long contest,
And was not with the sight of his lov'd Princess blest:
The Royal Mourner for his Absence wept,
And from her Heart intruding Princes kept;
In vain they sigh'd, in vain Addresses made,
They cou'd not by their utmost Arts persuade:
To her first Vows she still did constant prove,
Doubly secur'd by Honour, and by Love.

The Prince of *Lyricks,* full of heav'nly Fire,
Well pleas'd I read, and as I read, admire;
Of Gods and Heroes, and of God-like Kings,
He with unequal'd Strength, and Sweetness sings:
Sometimes his Muse flies near, and keeps in Sight,
Then on a sudden takes a towring Flight,
And soars as high as the bright Realms of Light.
The help of mean and servile Art disdains,
While in each charming Line luxuriant Nature reigns:
His pregnant Fancy from its Boundless Store,
Selects the richest, and the noblest Oar,
Which his unerring Judgment so refines,
That thro' the whole a pleasing Lustre shines;
Virtue's the darling Subject of his Lays,
In ev'ry Ode he Piety displays,
And to the Gods due Veneration pays.
Great was the Pow'r of his immortal Song,
That could his Fame in ancient *Greece* prolong:
Twice save his House, when *Thebes* was made a Prey
Untouch'd that stood, while *Thebes* in Ashes lay.

Line 302. **Prince of Lyricks**: Pindar (ca. 522–443 B.C.), lyric poet.

Line 320. **Twice ... House**: When Alexander the Great destroyed Thebes in 335 B.C. he ordered that Pindar's house be spared.

The Force of Numbers warlike *Sparta* knew,
For her what Wonders did *Tyrtæus* do!
He sung the Glories which on Fame attend;
And Honour gain'd by those who shall the State defend:
Who full of Courage, full of Heat Divine,
No Hazards for their Gods, and Laws, decline;
Who fear not Death, when the Reward is Praise,
That blest Exchange for all their coming Days:
The listning Soldiers with fresh Ardor fir'd;
As if they were by *Mars* himself inspir'd,
With furious Transports to the Field repair'd,
And met those Dangers, which before they fear'd:
Nothing *Messene* from their Rage could shield,
She to her former Lords was forc'd to yield:
She who to Martial Pow'r would not submit,
Was made a Prey to all-commanding Wit.

Theocritus in soft harmonious Strains,
Describes the Joys of the *Sicilian* Swains,
When with their Flocks they grace the flow'ry Plains,
And on their Pipes to listning Beauties play,
Who with their kind Regards the lov'd Musicians pay:
He, Nature in her native Plainness drew,
He, who the Springs of tender'st Passions knew,
Did Love in all its Infant Graces shew;
Love, unacquainted with deceitful Arts,
And only aiming at Exchange of Hearts.

Line 323. **Tyrtæus**: Greek elegiac poet (fl. 684 B.C.) who inspired the Spartans to victory with his war songs.

Line 331. **Mars**: Roman god of battle. Line 334. **Messene**: city conquered by the Spartans.

Line 338. **Theocritus**: Greek poet of Sicily (3rd century B.C.) who is said to have created the genre of pastoral poetry.

Lucretius with his Philosophick Strains,
My Mind at once delights, and entertains:
Thro' Paths untrod, I see him fearless go;
His Steps I tread, with eager hast to know:
With him explore the boundless Realms of Chance,
And see the little busie Atoms dance:
See, how without Direction they combine,
And form a Universe without Design,
While careless Deities supremely blest,
Enjoy the Pleasures of eternal Rest,
Resolv'd that nothing here their Quiet shall molest.
Strange that a Man of such a Strength of Thought,
Could think a World was to Perfection brought
Without Assistance from the Pow'rs above,
From the blest Source of Wisdom, and of Love!
All frightful Thoughts he from my Soul does chase,
And in their room glad, bright Ideas place:
Tells me that Happiness in Virtue lies,
And bids me Death, that dreaded Ill, despise:
That Phantom, which if we but judg'd aright,
Would never once disturb, nor once affright;
The shocking Prospect of a future State,
Does in our Souls an anxious Fear create;
That unknown Somewhere which we must explore,
That strange, that distant, undiscover'd Shore,
Where we must land, makes us the Passage dread:
But were we by inlightned Reason led,
Were false Opinions banish'd from the Mind,
And we to the strict Search of Truth inclin'd,
We sure shou'd meet it with as much Delight
As the cool Pleasures of a silent Night,

Line 348. **Lucretius**: Roman poet (ca. 99–55 B.C.), whose main work was a six-book philosophical poem, *De Rerum Natura*, using Epicurus's "atomic" theory of the universe to oppose a view that events in this world can only be understood as the actions of the gods; he proposes instead that virtue is the true source of all peace and tranquility; it was translated by Dryden, appearing in *Sylvae* (1685).

And to our Graves with Cheerfulness should run,
Pleas'd that our tedious Task of Life were done.

Virgil with sacred Raptures fills my Mind,
In him I unexhausted Treasures find:
While he my ravish'd Soul does entertain,
Malice and Rage employ their Shafts in vain:
Easie and pleas'd, by him I'm led along,
And hear the wise *Silenus's* charming Song:
Among his Nymphs and Swains with Pleasure live,
And to their Musick glad Attention give:
Then hear his Shepherds for some Prize contend,
And see his Husbandmen their much lov'd Toil attend:
Next with him to the burning *Ilium* go,
Where he displays Ten thousand Scenes of Woe:
Amidst the Flames the pious Prince I View,
Fearless, unmov'd, his great Designs pursue:
Like great *Alcides* he with Toil and Pain,
To th'utmost Height of Glory did attain,
And unrelenting *Juno's* Hate sustain;
A due Reward at length his Virtue found,
And he with Glory and with Love was crown'd.

Horace is full of Wit, and full of Art,
My Mind he pleases, and inflames my Heart,
And fills my Breast with his Poetick Fire:
O that he cou'd his wondrous Heat inspire:
But mine's a pale, a languid, feeble Flame,
Wholly unworthy such a Poet's Name:

Line 381. **Virgil**: Dryden translated Virgil's *Pastorals*, the sixth of which is Silenus's song, which describes the formation of the universe.

Line 391. **Ilium**: in Virgil's *Aeneid*, Troy.

Line 395. **Alcides**: in classical mythology, Hercules, son of Zeus and Alcmena; Juno or Hera, Zeus's wife, persecuted him.

Line 400. **Horace**: Quintus Horatius Glaccus (65–8 B.C.), Roman lyric poet who celebrated the good life in retirement and offered moderation as the key to happiness.

My humble Muse her Eyes can only raise,
Pleas'd that she has the Liberty to her Gaze,
And Leave to offer up the Tribute of her Praise.

When by soft moving *Ovid* I am told,
Of those strange Changes which were wrought of old,
When Gods in Brutal Shapes did Mortals court,
And unbecoming Actions made their Sport,
When helpless Wretches fled from impious Pow'rs,
And hid themselves in Birds, Beasts, Trees, and Flow'rs:
When none from Outrage cou'd securely dwell,
But felt the Rage of Heav'n, of Earth, and Hell:
Methinks, I see those Passions well exprest,
Which play the Tyrant in the Mortal Breast:
They to Ten thousand Miseries expose,
And are our only, and our deadly Foes:
They like the Vultur on our Entrails prey,
And in our Path the Golden Apple lay,
But from us snatch our dear *Euridices* away.
Up the steep Hill the pond'rous Torment roll,
And cheat with empty Shews the famish'd Soul:
Those who are still submitted to their Sway,
Must in the gloomy Realms of *Pluto* stay,
And never more re-visit cheerful Day:
But those who're from their earthly Dross calcin'd,
Who tast the Pleasures of a virtuous Mind,

Line 409. **Ovid**: Ovidius Naso (43 B.C.–A.D. 17), Roman poet, author of *Metamorphoses*.

Line 422. **Golden Apple**: in Greek myth, Atalanta lost a race when she picked up three golden apples her suitor Hippomenes had dropped in her path.

Line 423. **Euridice**: in Greek myth, the wife of Orpheus. She was snatched back into Hades when he could not resist looking back at her before they were completely away from it.

Line 424. **Up ... roll**: in Greek myth, Sisyphus was condemned to roll a large rock eternally up a steep hill.

Line 427. **Pluto**: in Roman myth, god of the underworld.

Line 429. **Dross**: base materials. **calcin'd**: reduced to ashes by flames.

Who'd rather chuse to die, than once their Conscience stain,
Who midst Temptations Innocence retain,
And o'er themselves an undisputed Empire gain:
In th'*Elysian* Fields shall be for ever blest,
And with the Happy, there enjoy the Sweets of Rest.

How well does he express unhappy Love!
Each Page does melt, and ev'ry Line does move.
The fair *Oenone* does so well complain,
That I can't chuse but blame her faithless Swain:
Good *Hypermnestra* much laments her Fate,
Forsaken *Phyllis* her deplor'd Estate;
Her absent Lord sad *Laodamia* mourns,
And *Sappho* for her perjur'd *Phaon* burns:
O wondrous Woman! Prodigy of Wit!
Why didst thou Man to thy fond Heart admit?
Man, treacherous Man, who still a Riddle proves,
And by the Dictates of his Fancy moves,
Whose Looks are Snares, and ev'ry Word a Bait,
And who's compos'd of nothing but Deceit?
What Pity 'twas thou shouldst to Love give way,
To Love, to vicious Love, become a Prey,
And by a guilty, inauspicious Flame,
Eclipse the Splendor of so bright a Name.

Line 434. **Elysian Fields**: in Greek myth, paradise, the home of the blessed after death.

Line 438. **Oenone**: in Greek myth, a nymph of Mt. Ida, who was loved and betrayed by Paris; after she was abandoned by him for Helen of Troy, she committed suicide.

Line 440. **Hypermnestra**: in Greek myth, one of the daughters of Danaus; she refused her father's order to kill her husband.

Line 441. **Phyllis**: in Ovid's *Heroides*, translated by Dryden, Phyllis was deserted by her lover Demophoön.

Line 442. **Laodamia**: in Greek myth, the wife of Protesilaus, the first warrior to be killed in the Trojan war; she committed suicide after his death.

Line 443. **Sappho**: the Greek poet who supposedly killed herself when rejected by Phaon.

On *Juvenal* I look with great Delight,
Both he and *Persius* with much Keeness write,
They gravely teach, as well as sharply bite.

Think not to th'ancient Bards I am alone confin'd,
They please, but never shall ingross my Mind;
In modern Writers I can Beauties find.
Phœbus has been propitious to this Isle,
And on our Poets still is pleas'd to Smile.

Milton was warm'd by his enliv'ning Fire,
Who *Denham*, *Waller*, *Cowley* did inspire,
Roscommon too, whom the learn'd World admire:

The tuneful *Dryden* felt his hottest Rays,
And long with Honour wore his freshest Bays:
The Arts, the Muses, and the Graces try
To raise his Name, and lift him to the Skie,
And bless him with a Fame that ne'er shall die:
But he is gone! extinguish'd is that Light,
Which with its Lustre so long charm'd our Sight:
Yet at his Loss we dare not once repine,
While we see *Dorset* with such Glory shine,

Line 455. **he and Persius**: two Roman satirists, whose satires were translated by Dryden in one volume, *The Satires of Juvenal and Persius* (1692).

Line 460. **Phœbus**: in classical myth, Apollo, god of the sun and of poetry.

Line 463. **Denham**: Sir John Denham (1615–69), poet and translator best known for his long topographical poem *Cooper's Hill* (1642), and his paraphrase of part of the *Aeneid*. **Waller**: Edmund Waller (1606–87), lyric poet, best known for his polished verses celebrating Lady Dorothy Sidney, "Sacharissa." **Cowley**: Abraham Cowley (1618–67), lyric and elegiac poet, who introduced the form of the rhetorical ode imitated by Dryden.

Line 464. **Roscommon**: Wentworth Dillon, 4th earl of Roscommon (1633–85), author of a translation of Horace's *Ars Poetica* (1680) and *Essay on Translated Verse* (1684).

Line 470. **he is gone**: Dryden died in 1700.

Line 473. **Dorset**: Charles Sackville, 6th earl of Dorset (1638–1706), friend and patron of Dryden and Prior, who also wrote lyrics and satires.

While we see *Normanby* adorn the Skies,
And *Halifax* with dazling Brightness rise
That fam'd Triumvirate of Wit and Sense,
Who Laws to the whole Under-world dispence;
Whose Praise for me t'attempt, would be a Fau't,
So much are they beyond the highest flight of Thought.

Granville the Charms of Virtue does rehearse,
Bright it appears in his majestick Verse:
Forsaken Honesty's his chief Delight,
To That, and Honour, he does all invite:
Commends that Peace, that Quiet of the Mind,
Which those enjoy, who to themselves confin'd
Forsake the noisie World, and leave its Cares behind,
Who live in Shades, where true Contentment's found,
And fly from Courts, as from unhallow'd Ground.
How wondrous good has he *Chryseis* made!
How full of Charms is that fair Captive Maid!
What noble Proofs of Kindness does she give!
For her *Atrides* she can wretched live!
Whom she so much above her self does prize,
That when his Safety in the Balance lies,
From his lov'd Sight, and all her Bliss she flies;
And rather than his Happiness destroy,
Will take an everlasting leave of Joy.
Such an Affection, such a gen'rous Flame,
Sure, the severest Censor cannot blame.
As firm, as lasting, would our Friendships prove,

Line 474. **Normanby**: John Sheffield, 3rd earl of Mulgrave, later 1st Duke of Buckingham and Normanby (1648–1721), was Dryden's patron; he also wrote *An Essay on Satire* (1680) and *An Essay upon Poetry* (1682).

Line 475. **Halifax**: Charles Montagu, earl of Halifax (1661–1715), author of *An Epistle to Charles Earl of Dorset* (1690), which celebrates the victory of William III in Ireland.

Line 480. **Granville**: George Granville, baron Lansdowne (1667–1735), author of *Heroick Love: A Tragedy* (1698), based on Homeric legends of tragic love.

Line 489. **Chryseis**: in the *Iliad,* the daughter of Chryses, a priest of Apollo, who was given to Agamemnon as his concubine.

Line 492. **Atrides**: Agamemnon.

If, as we ought, we knew but how to love:
Did Honour chuse, and Truth unite our Hearts,
If we were free from sordid wheedling Arts,
From Av'rice, Pride, and Narrowness of Mind,
We shou'd to others, as our selves be kind,
And all the Pleasures of a virtuous Union find.
The lov'd Commerce would more and more endear,
We with our Friends in all Concerns should share,
With them rejoice, and grieve, and hope, and fear;
And by Degrees to such an Ardor rise,
That we for them should Life it self despise,
And much above our own, their Satisfaction prize.

Than *Dennis* none with greater Judgment writes,
Fancy with Vigor in his Stile unites.

A Place with these, *Vanbrook* may justly claim,
His Thoughts are full of Wit, and full of Flame:
Instructing Sharpness runs thro' ev'ry Page;
His *Æsop's* the *Thersites* of our Age.

Than *Garth* none can with greater Smoothness write,
Just is his Stile, his Satyr is Polite:
Not rude like those which in the Woods are bred,
Each piercing Truth's with courtly Softness said:
But when he glorious Actions does rehearse,
And makes the Great the Subject of his Verse,
He soars aloft above the Reach of Thought,
And all's with wondrous Art, with wondrous Fancy wrought.

Line 513. **Dennis**: John Dennis (1657–1734), best known for his works of literary criticism, including *The Advancement and Reformation of Modern Poetry* (1701).

Line 515. **Vanbrook:** Sir John Vanbrugh (1664–1726), architect and dramatist, author of *Aesop: A Comedy* (1697) and *The Relapse* (1696).

Line 518. **Thersites:** Greek soldier in the Trojan war who railed against the vices of his superiors.

Line 519. **Garth**: Sir Samuel Garth (1661–1719), physician; member of the Kit-Cat Club; author of *The Dispensary* (1699) and translator of Ovid's *Metamorphoses* (1717).

Like him, methinks, I mighty Heroes view;
See fam'd *Camillus* flying *Gauls* pursue,
The prudent *Fabius* Rome from Danger shield,
And *Carthage* to victorious *Scipio* yield:
The great *Nassaw* unwith'ring Lawrels gain,
Unmov'd the Shock of *Gallick* Force sustain,
Fierce as the God of War on the *Phlegræan* Plain:
But he's no more: The Fair ascends Throne,
And we with Joy the lov'd *Minerva* own;
Pleas'd that we Heav'ns peculiar Care are grown.

Congreve to ev'ry Theme does Beauty give,
His fair *Almeria* will for ever live.
Homer looks great in his rich *English* Dress;
So well he *Priam's* Sorrow does express,
That I with him for valiant *Hector* grieve;
His Suff'rings on my Mind a deep Impression leave.
With sad *Andromache* a part I bear,
With her in all her Lamentations share:
With *Hecuba* bewail a darling Son,
Who for his Country glorious Things had done:

Line 528. **Camillus**: Camillus L. Furius (d. 365 B.C.), a famed Roman general who was banished for distributing the spoils of war but who came back to rescue Rome when it was besieged by the Gauls.

Line 529. **Fabius**: Quintus Favius Maximus (d. 203 B.C.) carried out a defensive strategy of delaying tactics against Hannibal.

Line 530. **Scipio**: Scipio (236–183 B.C.) conquered Hannibal and Spain.

Line 531. **Nassaw**: King William III of England.

Line 533. **Phlegræan Plain**: in classical myth, the site in Macedonia of the battle between the giants and the gods.

Line 535. **Minerva**: in Roman myth, goddess of wisdom.

Line 537. **Congreve**: William Congreve, dramatist (1670–1729), author of comedies, including *Love for Love* (1695) and *The Way of the World* (1700).

Line 538. **Almeria**: heroine of Congreve's tragedy *The Mourning Bride* (1697).

Line 539. **Homer ... Dress**: Congreve translated parts of Homer's *Iliad*, which Dryden published in *Examen Poeticum* (1693).

Line 545. **Hecuba**: Hector's mother; see her lament at the fall of Troy in Book XXII of the *Iliad*.

His Country, which its Prop thus snatch'd away,
She knew must to the *Græcians* fall a Prey;
And she with all her House must foreign Lords obey.

Rowe to the Skies does his great Hero raise;
His *Tamerlane* deserves immortal Praise:
No Pen but his cou'd ev'ry Feature trace,
No Pen but his describe each Martial Grace:
With noble Ardor to the War he goes,
And all around commanding Glances throws,
And fearless views Ten thousand thousand Foes:
Unwilling to destroy, he mourns their Fate,
Th'ensuing Slaughter does his Thirst of Fame abate:
When he from *Bajazet* has won the Field,
And all to his superior Virtue yield,
He's still the same; still humble, just, and kind;
In him we still the God-like *Scythian* find,
The same compassionate, forgiving, gen'rous Mind.

Who for *Arpasia* can from Tears abstain?
Or hear unmov'd, her much wrong'd Prince complain?
With melting Softness they their Woes express;
Their Sorrows charm in his attracting Dress.
Ovid himself could not with greater Art
Describe the tender Motions of the Heart,
The Grief they feel, who must for ever part.

Who beauteous *Selima* expos'd can see
To her inhuman Father's Cruelty

Line 550. **Rowe**: Nicholas Rowe (1674–1718), dramatist; he wrote tragedies, including *The Fair Penitent* (1703) and *Tamerlane* (1702), in which Tamerlane is presented as a heroic representation of William III and Bajazet as Louis XIV.

Line 559. **Bajazet**: brutal emperor of the Turks, defeated by Tamerlane.

Line 562. **God-like Scythian**: Tamerlane.

Line 564. **Arpasia**: bride of Mondesses, a Greek prince; both were captured by Bajazet.

Line 571. **Selima**: Bajazet's daughter, rescued by Axalla.

Without Concern? And when in such Distress
Not her *Axalla,* her Deliv'rer bless?

May he go on, still thus adorn the Stage,
Still show such bright Examples to our Age,
Till he to us lost Virtue shall restore,
And we see Honour flourish here once more:
Till Justice all her ancient Rights regains,
And in her once lov'd *Albion* unmolested reigns.

When these have for some time employ'd my Mind,
In other Authors I fresh Pleasures find,
And meet with various Scenes of Thoughts behind:
Lost *Montezuma* in *Accosta* view,
See what for Gold the barb'rous *Spaniards* do:
See the good *Inca's* bend beneath their Fate,
And dying mourn the downfal of their State:
Then with him lofty *Andes* Height ascend;
See the fam'd *Amazon* her Streams extend,
And to the Sea her wide-stretch'd Current bend.

Then view in others *Asiatick* Pride,
See a few Men the spacious East divide:
Whose hard Commands poor Wretches must obey,
Doom'd to the Mischiefs of Tyrannick Sway:
To Toil condemn'd, they pass their Time in Pain,
But dare not of their rig'rous Fate complain:
Nothing is theirs, their Lives are not their own,
To them no Pity, no Regard is shown:
Like Beasts they're us'd, and little more they know,
And ev'ry Place like them, does Signs of Slavery show:
Their Plains once fruitful, now neglected lie;

Line 574. **Axalla**: Tamerlane's favorite general, a Christian.

Line 584. **Montezuma**: in Dryden's two plays, *The Indian Queen* (1655) and *The Indian Emperor* (1667), he combined the Spanish conquests of the Aztec and Incan civilizations, bringing together Montezuma, Cortez, and Pizarro.

And glorious Structures which once brav'd the Skie,
Can hardly now their awful Relicks show,
We scarce can their majestick Ruins know,
While *China* govern'd by the wisest Rules,
And all her Nobles bred in great *Confutius* Schools,
Shews me what Art and Industry can do:
Pleas'd I their Morals and Politeness view:
Delighted see how happy they remain,
Who still the Love of Learning entertain,
And where, pure uncorrupted Reason still does Reign.

Then look on their Reverse, whom all deride,
Who seem design'd to pull down human Pride:
Those rude inhabitants of *Africk's* Shore,
Who seek no future Good, no God adore:
Whose Ornaments are nauseous to the Sight,
And who seem made with a Design to fright:
From such loath'd Objects I divert my Eyes,
And pity those I did at first despise,

Why, O ye Heav'nly Pow'rs, I sighing say,
Are Souls condemn'd to such vile Loads of Clay,
To Bodies which their Faculties confine,
Thro' which not one celestial Ray can shine?

We shou'd, alas! as despicable prove,
Were we not made the Care of unexhausted Love:
To That the diff'rence we must still assign,
And ev'ry proud aspiring Thought decline:
When we by Flatt'rers are rais'd too high,
And Man, vain Man, beyond his Sphere does fly,
Narcissus-like on's own Perfections gaze,
He ought to turn his Vanity to Praise,
And study to be grateful all his Days.

Line 606. **Confutius**: Confucius (551–479 B.C.), Chinese sage.

While thus employ'd, I no Misfortunes fear,
And can unmov'd the greatest Troubles bear:
Quiet, and pleas'd, on my own Stock I live,
And to my self Content, and Riches give.

A Pindarick Ode

1.

Pleasures, like Syrens, still invite,
And with delusive Charms,
Bewitching Baits of soft Delight,
Allure th'unwary to their Arms:
The thoughtless Many drawn away
By sweet inticing Lays,
Soon fall a voluntary Prey,
And meanly end their Days;
While the more manly, and the brave,
Themselves by Resolution save:
As on the boist'rous Sea of Life they sail,
With watchful Eyes,
A Vigilance which ne'er can fail,
They mark the Skies, the Rocks, the Sands:
Still at the Helm their Reason stands,
When she the fatal Isle descries,
And each Inchantress sees prepare
To tune her Voice, and lay her Snare.
She loudly cries, O my lov'd Charge, beware:
Fly, quickly fly that dang'rous Shore;
O see! with Bones 'tis cover'd o'er:
Let others Ruin make you wise;

Line 1. **Syrens:** in the *Odyssey,* mythical creatures, half woman, half bird, whose song enticed seamen to destruction; Odysseus escaped destruction by having his sailors block their ears with wax and by having himself bound to the mast of the ship to prevent his jumping overboard to follow their song.

Remote from them your Safety lies:
They none but thoughtless Fools surprize.

2.

They can't to you now wing their Way,
Their Plumes the Muses now adorn;
They only can by Wiles betray:
You their united Force may scorn.
Be like the wise *Ulysses* bound,
Pernicious freedom shun,
Be deaf to ev'ry flatt'ring Sound;
The most are by themselves undone:
How few like *Orpheus* dare depend
On their superior Skill,
How few with good Success attend
The fickle Motions of their Will!
None but exalted Souls who move
By the Direction of celestial Love:
Who soar aloft, and full of heav'nly Fire,
To the Perfection of their kind aspire,
Who with Contempt view ev'ry thing below,
And to the Source of Pleasure go,
That pure, unmix'd, eternal Spring,
From whence those muddy Rivers flow,
With which we strive to quench our Thirst;
To which we rav'nous Cravings bring;
And are with wish'd Repletion curst:
When we the largest Draughts obtain,
We but oppressing Burthens gain;
Which only swell the Mind,
And when they're gone, leave an uncomfortable Void behind.

Line 33. **Orpheus**: in Greek myth, a Thracian poet whose music was said to enchant even inanimate objects.

3.

Such Souls alone with Airs Divine
Always themselves delight:
In vain their Skill the Tempters try,
They both the Tempters, and their Skill defie;
Their Notes are lost in Strains more bold and high,
Asham'd they quit their vain Design,
And full of anxious Spight,
With drooping Heads repine;
While th' joyful Victors onward move,
And chaunt the Praise of him above,
Of him, who does their Art bestow,
From whom harmonious Numbers flow:
Thrice happy they who thus can live,
Can on the mounting Billows ride,
Can to themselves Contentment give,
And void of Fear, and void of Pride,
To lofty Heights themselves can raise,
And sweetly warble out their Days,
Regardless of designing, meaner Lays.

Icarus

Whilst *Icarus* his Wings prepar'd
His trembling Father for him fear'd:
And thus to him he sighing said,
O let paternal Love persuade:
With me, my dearest Son, comply,
And do not proudly soar too high:

Line 58. **Spight**: ill-will, malice.

Line 70. **designing . . . Lays**: carping attacks by lesser poets.

Title. **Icarus**: in Greek myth, the son of the inventor Dædalus who escaped with his father from Crete using artifical wings; he flew too close to the sun, which melted the wax holding the feathers on his wings, causing him to fall into the sea and drown.

For near, *Apollo's* scorching Heat,
Will on thy Wings too fiercely beat:
And soon dissolve the waxen Ties.
Nor loiter in the lower Skies,
Least Steams should from the Land arise,
And damp thy Plumes, and check thy Flight,
And plunge thee into gloomy Night.

Th' ambitious Youth led on by Pride,
Did all this good Advice deride;
And smiling, rashly soar'd on high;
Too near the Source of Light did fly;
A while, well pleas'd, he wanton'd there;
Rejoicing breath'd Æthereal Air:
But ah! the Pleasure soon was past,
The Transport was too great to last:
His Wings dropt off, and down he came
Into that Sea which keeps his Name.

His grieving Father saw him drown'd,
And sent loud moving Crys around:
Ah! wretched Youth, he weeping said,
Thou'rt now a dire Example made,
Of those who with ungovern'd Heat
Aspire to be supremely great;
Who from obscure Beginnings rise,
And swoln with Pride, Advice despise;
Mount up with hast above their Sphere,
And no superior Pow'rs revere.

O may thy Fall be useful made,
May it to humbler Thoughts persuade:
To Men th' avoidless Danger Show
Of those who fly too high, or low;
Who from the Paths of Virtue stray,

Line 23. **that Sea**: Aegean Sea, into which Icarus fell. Line 31. **swoln**: swollen.

And keep not in the middle Way:
Who singe their Wings with heav'nly Fire;
Amidst their glorious Hopes expire:
Or with a base and groveling Mind
Are to the Clods of Earth confin'd.

Song

1.

As vainly wishing, gazing, dying,
The fond *Narcissus* lay,
Kind Echo, to his Sighs replying,
These words was heard to say;
Ah! wretched Swain, by Pride betray'd:
That Pois'ner of the Mind;
That Voice by none but Fools obey'd,
That Test of Souls design'd:
That dang'rous Ill which ne'er is found,
In such as with *Minerva's* Gifts are crown'd.

2.

What will you do when Time decaying
That lovely beauteous Face,
And you the Laws of Fate obeying,
Must to old Age give place?
Old Age, which comes with Swiftness on:
Your hasty Minutes fly;
Some part of what you were is gone,
Deforming Death is nigh:
When Time and Pain your Charms abate,
How will you then this Chrystal Mirror hate?

Line 2. **Narcissus**: in Greek myth, he was condemned by Aphrodite to fall in love with his own image for spurning the love of one of her nymphs, Echo.

3.

The God of Love you're now offending,
He looks with Anger down;
And while you're on your self attending,
Regardless of his Frown,
He'll make you curse that fatal Hour
In which you hither came:
When he makes known his wondrous Pow'r,
You'll your indiff'rence blame:
And wish to me you'd kinder prov'd,
And less, much less, your own Perfections lov'd.

4.

Be gone, be gone, he still replying,
Felt an inward Anguish:
And still the wat'ry Image eying
For himself did languish:
The pitying Nymph stood grieving by
To see his vain Desire:
With out-stretch'd Arms she heard him cry,
O why dost thou retire?
Why does this dear attracting Shape,
From my Embrace with so much hast escape?

5.

While thus he was himself admiring,
The cruel Sportive Pow'r,
Who saw his Reason was expiring,
Transform'd him to a Flow'r:
The Nymph amaz'd, the Wonder view'd,
And wou'd not thence remove;
At length she by her Grief subdu'd,
An empty Voice did prove:
Both were to Folly Victims made,
She by her Fondness, he by Pride betray'd.

A Dialogue between *Virgil* and *Mævius*

Mævius. Where are those sacred Lawrels now
Which did above adorn thy Brow?
And where the mighty *Maro's* Fame?
Here *Mævius* is as great a Name.

Virgil. Tho' me the Ghosts will not obey,
Yet those Above due Honours pay:
There I'm by all the Wits rever'd,
And still by ev'ry *Mævius* fear'd.
Mine, and *Homer's* awful Shade,
By the learn'd World supreme are made;
There, like th' infernal Judges, we
Can punish, or Rewards decree.

Mævius. Can this a real Good bestow?
Or make you happier here below?
A starving Man may dream of Meat,
May in his Sleep choice Viands eat:
And Beggers, shivering with Cold,
May dream of Robes, of Fires, and Gold:
And Men, when tost on raging Seas,
May dream of Safety, Calms, and Ease:
But when they wake, are still the same,
Their Bliss from Sportive Fancy came.

Virgil. Immortal Praise does feed the Mind.

Mævius. You, that an airy Food will find.

Virgil. 'Tis what the Heroes still have sought,
What with their Blood and Lives they've bought:

Title. In Virgil's *Aeneid*, Mævius and his friend Bavius represent bad poets who are jealous of good ones.

Line 3. **Maro**: Virgil.

For This the Men of Sense contend;
In This their Toils of Thinking end:
'Tis This the Rich, the Proud, the Vain,
With so much Labour strive to gain:
For This the Fair their Charms employ,
In This they place their highest Joy:
In This all with one Voice combine;
All own it is a Gift Divine.

Mævius. How can a Puff of fleeting Air
Deserve to be a Wise Man's Care?
Or who'd be fond of empty Praise,
Of what the noisie Rabble says?
Men fickle as th' inconstant Wind,
Who but by Starts are Just, or Kind.
See those who when you were above
Did treat you with Respect and Love,
Do now by you regardless slide
With a stiff and sullen Pride,
Not one obliging Look will give:
Now all alone you here must live,
A poor forsaken wandring Shade,
By none desir'd, by none obey'd;
And to your self a Burthen made.

Virgil. The Man who is by *Phœbus* fir'd,
Can never with himself be tir'd:
He still within new Trophies raises,
Himself both entertains, and praises:
He ev'ry noisie Fool despises,
Good Sense and Learning only prizes:
And while he is of these possest,
When most alone is chiefly blest.

My Thoughts, the Springs of pure Delight,
Still to internal Views invite;

Scenes charming, gay, and ever new;
To me the Works of Nature shew,
And all the *Mimick* Art can do:
Me and my Muse they still employ,
To us are constant Funds of Joy:
We past and present Ages see,
And pry into Futurity;
Then thro' the glorious Fields of Light
We take a bold and towring Flight,
View all the happy Seats above,
The shining Court of thund'ring *Jove;*
Thence downward wing our easie Way,
And ev'ry Sea, and Land survey;
Then to these Realms descend again,
Where soft Delights for ever reign;
And where I something always find
Fit to divert and feast my Mind.

While thus employ'd, I here below
The Height of Bliss, and Pleasure know:
I neither need, nor value praise,
And scorn a with'ring Wreath of Bays.

To the Learn'd and Ingenious Dr. *Musgrave* of *Exeter*

1.

Those who like me their Gratitude would show,
Are griev'd to think they still must owe:
Be still oblig'd, and never know the way
The smallest part of the vast Sum to pay:
A Sum beyond th' Arithmetick of Thought,

Line 80. **Wreath of Bays**: in classical times, prize awarded for poetry.

And which does daily higher rise:
To be your Debtor is no more my Fault,
The whole that I can give, will not suffice:
I am too poor Returns to make,
Unless you'll Thanks as a Requital take:
Thanks are the whole that I can bring:
My Muse shall of Your wondrous Bounty sing;
Your gen'rous Temper to the World make known,
That gen'rous Temper you've so often shown,
And which I still must with the highest Praises own.

2.

But what, alas, is it I say!
Can I with Thanks for a lov'd Daughter pay?
Can her dear Life that's owing to your Care,
Any Proportion to such Trifles bear?
With weeping Eyes I saw her fainting lie,
Gasping for Breath,
But saw no Safety nigh.
As some poor Wretch who from the distant Shore,
And with insulting Waves quite cover'd o'er,
With piteous Crys does for Assistance pray,
And strives t' escape the liquid Death;
Thus almost lost your helpless Patient lay,
To the devouring Waters left a Prey,
Till she was rescu'd by your Hand:
By such amazing Skill, and Depth of Thought,
Once more into the Number of the Living brought:
Where she the Trophy of Your Art do's stand,
That pow'rful Art, which hitherto does save
A Life, which long since seem'd determin'd to the Grave.

Line 10. **Requital**: restitution, payment.

3.

Under Your Care while she remain'd,
Each Day she Strength and Spirits gain'd:
Her Health such quick Advances made,
That all with Wonder did its Progress view,
And when they look'd on her, applauded you:
But since she from your Care was snatch'd away
Like Plants which want reviving Rays,
She withers in the Shade,
And hourly does decay:
Had Heav'n design'd her Length of Days,
She ne'er had been from you remov'd,
But Fate to her has inauspicious prov'd:
Weak as she is, she still does Thanks repay,
Does still your former Favours own,
Those Kindnesses you've in her Sickness shown;
And in the fittest Words that she can frame,
She strives to pay her Homage to your Fame,
And add a worthless Mite to th'Glory of your Name.

4.

But by a Child, and one so young,
There can be no becoming Praises sung:
I'll undertake the Task, and try
If I can her Defect supply:
My Muse shall strive to make your Virtues known;
Those virtues which you modestly conceal,
She shall to th' applauding World reveal:
Your Prudence, Truth, and Justice shall rehearse,
Tho' each alone
Would prove a copious Subject for her Verse:
And you to all Mankind shall recommend,
For the sincerest, most obliging Friend,
For one in whom they may confide, on whom they
may depend:
For one who's blest with all they can desire,
With whatsoever can Esteem engage;

With all those Qualities in one combin'd,
Which singly they admire,
And can but seldom find:
Who to the Coolness of delib'rate Age,
Has added all that sprightly youthful Fire,
Which do's the noblest Thoughts inspire:
To solid Judgment, elevated Sense,
And all the Knowledge Learning can dispence,
Has join'd the Charms of pow'rful Eloquence.

5.

You like a second *Æsculapius* rise,
Before you *Fame*, that noisie Goddess, flies,
And *Musgrave's* Name is echo'd thro' the Skies:
Th' obsequious Mountains answer to the Sound,
And friendly Winds disperse the glorious Accents round.
Diseases yield; they to your Art submit,
And Health does on your Steps attend;
When you appear, Death must her Conquest quit;
She dares not touch what you defend:
Murm'ring she flies, griev'd at her Loss of Pow'r;
And finds she must not now with so much Ease devour.
Long may you live the Blessing of this Isle,
From ev'ry Pain, and ev'ry Ill secure;
On you may fortune ever smile,
And still your Happiness ensure.
O may we long your Conversation have,
And with the Sweets of Friendship blest,
For num'rous Years defeat the Grave,
And keep you back from everlasting Rest;
Till tir'd with Length of Days, and crown'd with Fame,
You the great Privilege of Dying claim,
Pleas'd to live only here in an immortal Name.

Line 77. **Æsculapius**: in Greek and Roman myth, god of healing and medicine.

The Observation

1.

No State of Life's from Troubles free,
Grief mixes with our vital Breath:
As soon as we begin to be,
From the first moment of our Birth,
We have some tast of Misery:
With Sighs and Tears our Fate we mourn,
As if our Infant Reason did presage
Th' approaching Ills of our maturer Age,
And wish'd a quick Return.
When Souls are first to their close Rooms confin'd,
Nothing of their Celestial Make is seen,
Obscuring Earth does interpose between:
Like Tapers hid in Urns they shine.
The Life of Sense and Growth we only see,
Which Beasts enjoy as well as we:
But th'active Mind
Which bears the Image of the Pow'r Divine,
Cannot exert its Energy:
The streiten'd Intellect immur'd does lie,
Shut up within a narrow place,
Till Nature does enlarge the Space,
And by degrees the Organs fit,
For those great Operations which are wrought by it.

2.

Thus for some Years we live by Sense,
Happy in nothing but in Innocence:
But when our feebler Age is past,
And we to sprightly Youth arrive,
The Race of Life we run so fast,
As if we thought our Strength would always last:

Hurry'd by Passion, and by Fancy led,
We all the various Paths of Folly tread:
Reason we slight, and her Commands despise,
    In vain she calls, in vain advise,
    And ev'ry gentle Method tries:
Against her kind Endeavours still we strive,
And run where ever Head-strong Passions drive:
Those Ills we court, which we as Plagues shou'd shun,
And are by ev'ry false Appearance won:
But wiser Thoughts when riper Years inspire,
We at the Follies of our Youth admire;
And wonder how such childish Things as these
    Cou'd Minds endu'd with Reason please;
Yet while we proudly our past Actions blame,
We do as foolish Things, tho' not the same;
Our Follies differ only in the Dress and Name.

3.

    Self-love so crouds the human Breast,
That there's no Room for any other Guest;
By it inspir'd we all Mankind despise,
And think our selves the only Good and Wise:
    Fond Thought! a Thought that only can
Become the vainest Part of the Creation, Man:
That haughty Creature, who puff'd up with Pride,
And fill'd with airy Notions soars on high,
And thinks himself the Glory of the Sky,
Where for a while in Fancy's flatt'ring Light
        Th'unkindl'd Vapour plays,
Much pleas'd with its imaginary Rays;
Till having wasted its small Stock of Flame,
The heavy Lump, the thing without a Name,
Falls headlong down from its exalted Height
Into Oblivion's everlasting Night.

Solitude

1.

Happy are they who when alone
Can with themselves converse;
Who to their Thoughts are so familiar grown,
That with Delight in some obscure Recess,
They cou'd with silent Joy think all their Hours away,
And still think on, till the confining Clay
Fall off, and nothing's left behind
Of drossy Earth, nothing to clog the Mind,
Or hinder its Ascent to those bright Forms above,
Those glorious Beings whose exalted Sense
Transcends the highest Flights of human Wit;
Who with *Seraphick* Ardor fir'd,
And with a Passion more intense
Than Mortal Beauty e'er inspir'd;
With all th'endearing Extasies of Love,
Will to their blest Society again
The long lost Wand'rers admit,
Where freed from all their former Pain,
And cleans'd from ev'ry Stain,
They bask with Pleasure in eternal Day,
And grow as pure, and as refin'd as they.

2.

But few, ah! few are for Retirement fit;
But few the Joys of Solitude can taste;
The most with Horror fly from it,
And rather chuse in Crouds their time to waste;
In busie Crouds, which a Resemblance bear
To th' unshap'd Embryo of the World,
That formless Mass where all things were
Without Distinction rudely hurl'd:
Tumult and Noise the Empire there had gain'd,

12. **Seraphick:** angelic.

Unrival'd there Disorder reign'd:
The thoughtless Atoms met by chance,
Without Design they mov'd, Confusion led the Dance:
Sometimes the earthly Particles aspir'd,
And upward forc'd their way,
While the spirituous Parts retir'd,
And near the Centre lay
Depress'd and sunk, till by the next Remove
They disengag'd, and got above,
But cou'd not long th' impelling Shock sustain,
By Turns they rise, by Turns they fell again.

3.

We in our selves a second *Chaos* find;
There is a Transcript of it in the human Mind:
Our restless Passions endless Wars maintain,
And with loud Clamors fill the Breast:
Love often there the Sov'reignty does gain,
As often is by Hatred dispossess'd:
Desire the Soul with anxious Thoughts does fill,
Insatiate boundless Thoughts instill:
Some distant Good we view,
Which we, by Hope push'd on, pursue,
Breathless, and faint, the toilsom Chase renew:
And when 'tis ours, tumultuous Joy does rise,
Ungovern'd Transport Sparkles in our Eyes;
And we all Extasie, all Fire,
The darling Prize admire,
And hug the Blessing till it does expire:
Then to despair our selves resign,
And sigh, and grieve, and still repine,
Curse Heav'n, our selves, our Friends, our Fate,
And new, more pungent, Woes create:
But if the Sportive Goddess lay
A bright Temptation in our way,
All is forgot, and full of Heat,
Our former Toils we soon repeat;

Again pursue the airy Game;
And fond of Grandeur, Fond of Fame,
Of Glory, Pow'r, and glitt'ring Clay,
We in laborious Nothings waste our short Remains of Day.

4.

When distant Ills we see,
The dismal Prospect us affrights,
The sad Futurity
Fear in our Minds excites:
And by a mean dishonourable Dread
Of Evils which may never be,
Our selves we fright, our Sprits waste,
And often our Misfortunes haste:
When they are present, then we rage,
Impatient, hot, and furious grow,
Nothing our Fury can aswage;
No Limits, no Restraints we know:
But by the Headlong Passion led,
Without the least Demur obey;
And like some mighty Torrent force our Way:
Some mighty Torrent which no Limit knows,
But with a rapid Course still onward goes,
Destroys the snowy Flocks, and lays Majestick Structures low:
But if a glimm'ring Hope arise,
If but a Gleam of Bliss appear,
Again we're easie, pleas'd, and gay:
Forgetful of what past before,
Above the Clouds we vainly soar:
Impending Dangers we despise,
And present Evils dread no more:
And while we proudly hover there,
Look down with Scorn upon the Phantom Fear.

5.

Thus they alternately do lose and win,
And all is Anarchy within:

Reason her native Right may claim,
And strive to re-ascend the Throne,
But few, alas! her Pow'r will own:
The most to Folly their Allegiance pay,
Pleas'd with her easie, and her childish Sway:
Their Passions rule, and they contentedly obey:
Slaves to themselves they without Murmurs prove,
And with the meanest, worst of Servitudes in Love,
By the strong Impulse of their Vices move:
Their Chains they hug, and Wisdom's Aid refuse,
And will not her for their Director chuse:
Her Paths they shun, her Yoke they will not bear,
And think her Precepts too severe:
Deaf to the Calls of Virtue and of Fame,
They madly wander thro' the Maze of Life,
Employ'd in Trifles, or engag'd in Strife:
Inslav'd by Interest, fond of glitt'ring Toys,
And much more pleas'd with Bubbles, than with solid Joys.

On the Death of my Honoured Mother Mrs. *Lee:* A Dialogue between *Lucinda* and *Marissa*

Lucinda. What, my *Marissa,* has *Lucinda* done,
That thus her once lov'd Company you shun?
Why is't from her you thus unkindly fly,
From her, who for your Sake cou'd freely die?
Who knows no Joy but what your Sight does give,
And in your Heart alone desires to live?
I beg you by that Zeal I've shewn for you,
That Tenderness which is to Friendship due,
By those dear sacred Bonds our Souls have ty'd,
Those Bonds, which Death it self shall ne'er divide;

Title: **Mrs. Lee**: Chudleigh's mother, Mary Lee, neé Sydenham (1632–1701).

By what so e'er you love, or I can name,
To let me know from whence this wond'rous
Strangeness came.
Remember by your Vows you're wholly mine,
And I to you did all my Thoughts resign:
My Joy was yours, and yours was all my Grief,
In your lov'd bosom still I sought Relief:
When you were chearful, I was truly blest,
And now your Sorrow deeply wounds my Breast:
I view it thro' the thin Disguise you wear,
And spite of all your Caution, all your Care,
Hear ev'ry rising Sigh, and view each falling Tear.

Marissa. Permit me, dear *Lucinda,* to complain,
That your Unkindness do's augment my Pain:
How could you think that one who lov'd like me
Would ever let you share her Misery?
To see you mourn would bring me no Relief,
No, that would rather double all my Grief:
For Love's a Passion of the noblest kind,
And when 'tis seated in a gen'rous Mind,
'Twill be from mean Designs and Interest free
Not interrupt a Friend's Felicity.
Had I been happy, with a smiling Face,
I long e'er now had run to your Embrace,
And in your Arms been eager to relate
The welcom Favours of propitious Fate:
But since ill Fortune do's me still pursue,
O let my Griefs remain unknown to you.
Free from sad Thoughts may you for ever live,
And all your Hours to Mirth and Pleasure give:
May no Concern for me your Peace molest;
O let me live a Stranger to your Breast:
No more, no more my worthless Name repeat,
Abandon me to this obscure Retreat;
Make haste from hence, my Sight will damp your Joy,
And the blest Calmness of your Soul destroy.

Lucinda. Think not I'll leave you to your Griefs a Prey:
No! here with you I will for ever stay,
And weep with you my coming Hours away:
Return each Sigh, and ev'ry moving Groan,
And to repeating Echo's make my Moan,
And tell them how unkind my lov'd *Marissa's* grown.

Marissa. To banish all Suspicions from your Mind,
And that you may not think me still unkind,
I'll let you know the Cause that makes me mourn,
The Cause that does my Joy to Sorrow turn:
But oh! a Loss so vast, so vastly great,
Who can without a Flood of Tears repeat!
It much too strong for my Resolves does prove,
And do's my tend'rest, softest Passions move:
Disturbs the Peace, the Quiet of my Mind,
And for some Minutes makes me less resign'd:
I to my Reason willingly would yield,
But strugling Nature keeps by Force the Field;
Compel'd, I stoop to her imperious Sway,
And thus each hour, methinks, I hear her say,
Wretched *Marissa!* all thy Comfort's fled,
And all thy Joy with thy lov'd Mother dead:
A Mother, who with ev'ry Grace was blest,
With all the Ornaments of Virtue dress'd;
With whatsoe'er Religion recommends;
The best of Wives, of Mothers, and of Friends.
And should not such a Loss Complaints inspire?
Their Apathy let Stoicks still admire,
And strict Obedience to their Rules require:
And on morose, ill-natur'd, thoughtless Fools,
Impose the rigid Notions of their Schools:
Insensibility were here a Fault,
And 'tis a Doctrine which I never taught:

Line 73. **Stoicks**: stoics; philosophical school emphasizing self-control and detachment from personal, worldly ties.

Tears are becoming, and a Tribute due
To one so worthy, and so dear to you.
By her thus urg'd, I gave my Sorrow way,
And did the Dictates of my Grief obey:
In this Recess, remote from Human Kind,
I thought I shou'd not Interruption find:
Most mind themselves, the Absent are forgot;
And this had doubtless been *Marissa's* Lot,
Had not the kind *Lucinda's* tender Care
Sought out this close Asylum of Despair,
And brought her hither all my Woes to share.

Lucinda. Such as have heard of good *Philinda's* Name,
Cannot with Justice sad *Marissa* blame:
A Mother's Loss, and such a Mother too,
Can't, my dear Friend, but be deplor'd by you.
All you cou'd wish she was; as Angels kind,
As Nature lib'ral, of a God-like Mind;
Steady as Fate, and constant in her Love;
One whom nor Wrongs, nor yet Affronts cou'd move
To mean Revenge, or a malicious Thought:
She liv'd those Truths her holy Faith had taught:
Joy cou'd not raise, nor Grief depress her Mind,
She still was calm, sedate, and still resign'd.

Marissa. Yes, she was more, much more than you can name,
Cheerful, obliging, gen'rous, still the same:
The Good she prais'd, the Absent did defend,
And was to the Distrest a constant Friend:
Full of Compassion, and from Censure free,
And of a most extensive Charity:
With winning Sweetness she did still persuade,
And her Reproofs were prudently convey'd:
In softest Language she'd the Vicious blame,
And none e'er lov'd with a more ardent Flame:
Her Friends Concerns she kindly made her own,
For them her greatest Care, her chief Regard was shown:

At no Misfortune she did e'er repine,
But still submitted to the Will Divine:
No discontented Thoughts disturb'd her Breast,
What ever happen'd, she still thought was best:
When her last Sickness came, that dire Disease
Which did on her with sudden Fury seize,
With utmost Rage the Fort of Life assail,
Resolv'd by racking Tortures to prevail;
O with what Patience did she bear her Pain,
And all th' Attacks of cruel Death sustain!
The dreadful Ill could not molest her Mind,
There she did still a happy Calmness find,
A well fixt Pleasure, a substantial Joy,
Serenity which nothing could destroy,
Sweet Antepast of what she finds above,
Where she's now blest with what she most did love;
That sov'reign Good which did her Soul inflame,
And whose Fruition was her utmost Aim;
And in whose Presence she do's now possess
A long desir'd, and endless Happiness.

Lucinda. Since she from all the Pains of Life is free,
And in Possession of Felicity,
'Tis unbecoming such a Grief to show,
As can from nothing but ungovern'd Passion flow.

Marissa. 'Tis, I confess, a Fault; but who can part
From one she loves, without a bleeding Heart?

Lucinda. 'Tis hard, I own, but yet it may be done;
Such glorious Victories are sometimes won:
Time will at length the greatest Grief subdue,
And shall not Reason do the same for you?
Reason, which shou'd our Actions always guide,

Line 128. **Antepast**: foretaste.

And o'er our Words, and o'er our Thoughts preside:
Passions should never that ascendant gain,
They were for Service made, and not to reign:
Yet do not think I your past Sorrow blame,
Were the Loss mine, sure, I shou'd do the same,
But having paid the Debt to Nature due,
No more the Dictates of my Grief pursue.
From that dark Grave where her lov'd Body lies,
Raise, my *Marissa*, your dejected Eyes,
And view her Soul ascending to the Skies,
By Angels guarded, who in charming Lays,
Sing as they mount, their great Creator's Praise;
And to celestial Seats their Charge convey,
To never ending Bliss, and never ending Day:
And is't not cruel, or at least unkind
To wish that she were still to Earth confin'd,
Still forc'd to bend beneath her Load of Clay?
Methinks I hear the glorious Vision say,
What is't, *Marissa*, makes you still complain,
Are you concern'd that I am void of Pain,
And wou'd you have me wretched once again?
Have me t'exchange this Bliss for Toil and Fear,
And all these Glories for a Life of Care?
Or is't th'Effect of a too fond Desire,
Do's Love, mistaken Love, these Thoughts inspire?
Is it my Absence you so much deplore,
And do you grieve because I'm yours no more,
Because with me you can no more Converse,
No more repeat your wrongs, or tell me your distress,
No more by my Advice your Actions steer,
And never more my kind Instructions hear?
If this do's cause your Grief, no more Complain;
'Twill not be long e'er we shall meet again;
Shall meet all Joy in these bright Realms of Love,
And never more the Pains of Absence prove:
Till that blest Time, with decent Calmness wait,
And bear unmov'd the Pressures of your Fate.

Marissa. Yes, my dear Friend, I your Advice will take,
Dry up my Tears, and these lov'd Shades forsake:
I can't resist, when Kindness leads the Way;
I'm wholly yours, and must your Call obey:
With you to hated Crouds and Noise I'll go,
And the best Proofs of my Affection show:
But where soe'er I am, my troubl'd Mind
Will still to my *Philinda* be confin'd;
Her Image is upon my Soul imprest,
She lives within, and governs in my Breast:
I'll strive to live those Virtues she has taught,
They shall employ my Pen, my Tongue, my Thought:
Where e'er I go her Name my Theme shall prove,
And what soe'er I say, shall loudly speak my Love.

On the Death of my dear Daughter *Eliza Maria Chudleigh:*

A Dialogue between *Lucinda* and *Marissa*

Marissa. O my *Lucinda!* O my dearest Friend!
Must my Afflictions never, never End!
Has Heav'n for me no Pity left in Store,
Must I! O must I ne'er be happy more,
Philinda's Loss had almost broke my Heart,
From her, Alas! I did but lately part:
And must there still be new Occasions found
To try my Patience, and my Soul to wound?
Must my lov'd Daughter too be snatch'd away,
Must she so soon the Call of Fate obey?
In her first Dawn, replete with youthful Charms,

Title. **Eliza Maria Chudleigh**: Chudleigh's daughter, who died in 1701/2; her illness is described in "To the Learn'd and Ingenious Dr. Musgrave of Exeter."

She's fled, she's fled from my deserted Arms.
Long did she struggle, long the War maintain,
But all th'Efforts of Life, alas! were vain.
Could Art have sav'd her she had still been mine,
Both Art and Care together did combine,
But what is Proof against the Will Divine!
  Methinks I still her dying Conflict view,
And the sad Sight does all my Grief renew:
Rack'd by Convulsive Pains she meekly lies,
And gazes on me with imploring Eyes,
With Eyes which beg Relief, but all in vain,
I see, but cannot, cannot ease her Pain:
She must the Burthen unassisted bear,
I cannot with her in her Tortures share:
Wou'd they were mine, and she stood easie by;
For what one loves, sure 'twere not hard to die.
  See, how she labours, how she pants for Breath,
She's lovely still, she's sweet, she's sweet in Death!
Pale as she is, she beauteous does remain,
Her closing Eyes their Lustre still retain:
Like setting Suns, with undiminish'd Light,
They hide themselves within the Verge of Night.
  She's gone! she's gone! she sigh'd her Soul away!
And can I! can I any longer stay!
My Life, alas! has ever tiresome been,
And I few happy, easie Days have seen;
But now it does a greater Burthen grow,
I'll throw it off and no more Sorrow know,
But with her to calm peaceful Regions go.
  Stay thou, dear Innocence, retard thy Flight,
O stop thy Journy to the Realms of Light,
Stay till I come: To thee I'll swiftly move,
Attracted by the strongest Passion, Love.

Lucinda. No more, no more let me such Language hear,
I can't, I can't the piercing Accents bear:
Each Word you utter stabs me to the Heart:

I cou'd from Life, not from *Marissa* part:
And were your Tenderness as great as mine,
While I were left, you would not thus repine.
My Friends are Riches, Health, and all to me,
And while they're mine, I cannot wretched be.

Marissa. If I on you cou'd Happiness bestow,
I still the Toils of Life wou'd undergo,
Wou'd still contentedly my Lot sustain,
And never more of my hard Fate complain:
But since my Life to you will useless prove,
O let me hasten to the Joys above:
Farewel, farewel, take, take my last adieu,
May Heav'n be more propitious still to you
May you live happy when I'm in my Grave,
And no Misfortunes, no Afflictions have:
If to sad Objects you'll some Pity lend,
And give a Sigh to an unhappy Friend,
Think of *Marissa*, and her wretched State,
How she's been us'd by her malicious Fate,
Recount those Storms which she has long sustain'd,
And then rejoice that she the Port has gain'd,
The welcome Haven of eternal Rest,
Where she shall be for ever, ever blest;
And in her Mother's, and her Daughter's Arms,
Shall meet with new, with unexperienc'd Charms.
O how I long those dear Delights to taste;
Farewel, farewel; my Soul is much in haste.
Come Death and give the kind releasing Blow;
I'm tir'd with Life, and over-charg'd with Woe:
In thy cool, silent, unmolested Shade,
O let me be by their dear Relicks laid;
And there with them from all my Troubles free,
Enjoy the Blessings of a long Tranquillity.

Line 78. **Relicks**: remains.

Lucinda. O thou dear Suff'rer, on my Breast recline
Thy drooping Head, and mix thy Tears with mine:
Here rest a while, and make a Truce with Grief,
Consider; Sorrow brings you no Relief.
In the great Play of Life we must not chuse,
Nor yet the meanest Character refuse
Like Soldiers we our Gen'ral must obey,
Must stand our Ground, and not to Fear give way,
But go undaunted on till we have won the Day.
Honour is ever the Reward of Pain,
A lazy Virtue no Applause will gain,
All such as to uncommon Heights would rise,
And on the Wings of Fame ascend the Skies,
Must learn the Gifts of Fortune to despise.
They to themselves their Bliss must still confine,
Must be unmov'd, and never once repine:
But few to this Perfection can attain,
Our Passions often will th'Ascendant gain,
And Reason but alternately does reign;
Disguis'd by Pride, we sometimes seem to bear
A haughty Port, and scorn to shed a Tear;
While Grief within still acts a tragick Part,
And plays the Tyrant in the bleeding Heart.
Your Sorrow is of the severest kind,
And can't be wholly to your Soul confin'd:
Losses like yours, may be allow'd to move
A gen'rous Mind, that knows what 'tis to love.
Who that her innnate Worth had understood,
Wou'd not lament a Mother so divinely good?
And who, alas! without a Flood of Tears,
Cou'd lose a Daughter in her blooming Years:
An only Daughter, such a Daughter too,
As did deserve to be belov'd by you;
Who'd all that cou'd her to the World commend,
A Wit that did her tender Age transcend,

Inviting Sweetness, and a sprightly Air,
Looks that had something pleasingly severe,
The Serious and the Gay were mingl'd there:
These merit all the Tears that you have shed,
And could Complaints recall them from the Dead,
Could Sorrow their dear Lives again restore,
I here with you for ever would deplore:
But since th'intensest Grief will prove in vain,
And these lost Blessings can't be yours again,
Recal your wand'ring Reason to your Aid,
And hear it calmly when it does persuade;
'Twill teach you Patience, and the useful Skill
To rule your Passions, and command your Will;
To bear Afflictions with a steady Mind,
Still to be easie, pleas'd, and still resign'd,
And look as if you did no inward Trouble find.

Marissa. I know, *Lucinda*, this I ought to do,
But oh! 'tis hard my Frailties to subdue:
My Head-strong Passions will Resistance make,
And all my firmest Resolutions shake:
I for my Daughter's Death did long prepare,
And hop'd I shou'd the Stroke with Temper bear,
But when it came, Grief quickly did prevail,
And I soon found my boasted Courage fail:
Yet still I strove, but 'twas, alas! in vain,
My Sorrow did at length th'Ascendant gain:
But I'm resolv'd I will no longer yield;
By Reason led, I'll once more take the Field,
And there from my insulting Passions try
To gain a full, a glorious Victory:
Which till I've done, I never will give o'er,
But still fight on, and think of Peace no more;
With an unweary'd Courage still contend,
Till Death, or Conquest, does my Labour end.

The Offering

1.

Accept, my God, the Praises which I bring,
The humble Tribute from a Creature due:
Permit me of thy Pow'r to sing,
That Pow'r which did stupendous Wonders do,
And whose Effects we still with awful Rev'rence view:
That mighty Pow'r which from thy boundless Store,
Out of thy self where all things lay,
This beauteous Universe did call,
This Great, this Glorious, this amazing All!
And fill'd with Matter that vast empty Space,
Where nothing all alone
Had long unrival'd sat on its triumphant Throne.
See! now in every place
The restless Atoms play:
Lo! high as Heav'n they proudly soar,
And fill the wide-stretch'd Regions there;
In Suns they shine Above, in Gems Below,
And roll in solid Masses thro' the yielding Air:
In Earth compacted, and diffus'd in Seas;
In Corn they nourish, and in Flow'rs they please:
In Beasts they walk, in Birds they fly,
And in gay painted Insects croud the Skie:
In Fish amid the Silver Waves they stray,
And ev'ry where the Laws of their first Cause obey:
Of them, compos'd with wondrous Art,
We are our selves a part:
And on us still they Nutriment bestow;
To us they kindly come, from us they swiftly go,
And thro' our Veins in Purple Torrents flow.
Vacuity is no where found,
Each Place is full: with bodies we're encompass'd round:

Line 14. **restless Atoms play**: reference to Dryden's translation of Lucretius's "atomic" theory.
Line 30. **Vacuity**: emptiness.

In Sounds they're to our Ears convey'd,
In fragrant Odors they our Smell delight,
And in Ten thousand curious Forms display'd,
They entertain our Sight:
In luscious Fruits our Tast they court,
And in cool balmy Breezes round us sport,
The friendly Zephyrs fan our vital Flame,
And give us Breath to praise his holy Name,
From whom our selves, and all these Blessings came.

2.

Receive my Thanks, 'tis all that I can pay,
The whole I can for num'rous Favours give;
Their Number does increase each Day,
I still on unexhausted Bounty live:
My Life, my Health, the Calmness of my Mind,
All those Delights I in my Reason find,
Those dear Delights which are from all the Dregs of
Sense refin'd,
Are Donatives of Love Divine,
The Benefactor in his Gifts does shine:
His boundless Goodness still it self displays,
Still warms with kind refulgent Rays:
In it the whole Creation share;
The whole Creation is his Care:
All Beings upon him depend;
To whatsoe'er he made, still his Regards extend:
Nothing's so high, nor yet so low,
As to escape his Sight,
He do's the Wants of all his Creatures know,
And to relieve them is his chief Delight,
A Pleasure worthy that Almighty Mind,
Whose Kindness like himself is unconfin'd.

Line 48. **Donatives:** donations, gifts.

3.

Ah! thankless Mortals, can't such wondrous Love,
   Inspire you with a grateful Sense?
   Can't such amazing Favours move?
Must he his Blessings unobserv'd dispence,
   Have no Return, no Tribute paid,
No Retributions for such Bounties made?
O think, and blushing at his Footstool fall,
   There beg his Pardon, prostrate lie,
And for Forgiveness to his Mercy fly:
Remember 'tis to him you owe your All,
He gives you Pow'r upon himself to call:
Should he from you his Aid withdraw,
   You quickly wou'd have cause to mourn,
   And sighing to your Dust return:
He is your Strength, your Life, your Light,
He to your jarring Principles gives Law,
   And the Destroyer Death does awe:
   His Angels compass you around,
And keep off Ills from the forbidden Ground:
By his Command you're ever in their Sight,
And made at once their Care, and their Delight:
O quickly then your Gratitude express,
And as becomes you, your Creator bless:
Before his Throne melodious Off'rings lay,
And in harmonious Strains your long neglected
      Homage pay.

4.

I'll strive with you my Zeal to show,
   With you I'll strive to pay
Some little Part of what I owe:
My self before his Throne I'll lay,

My self, and all he does on me bestow:
   My Reason for him I'll employ,
   And in his Favour place my Joy:
   His Favour which to me's more dear
   Than all the tempting Glories here:
My Tongue shall still extol his Name,
   Shall still his wondrous Works proclaim:
My Mem'ry shall his Kindnesses inrol,
   And fix them firmly in my Soul:
   From him my Thoughts no more shall stray,
   No more my Passions I'll obey,
No more to the rash Dictates of my Will give Way,
But still to him, and him alone, a glad Submission pay.

5.

   To Love I will my self resign;
   But it shall be to Love Divine:
   That o'er me ever shall preside,
Shall ev'ry Word, and ev'ry Action guide:
   To it I will my self unite,
   In it I'll place my sole Delight,
   And ev'ry meaner Object slight;
   Till one at last with it I grow,
And tir'd with treading this dull Round below,
To its blest Source with eager Swiftness go;
To its blest Source, where constant Joys are found,
And where ne'er ending Pleasures spread themselves
      around;
Where nothing's wanting that we can desire,
Where we to nothing greater can aspire,
And where e'en Thought it self can soar to nothing higher.

The Resolve

1.

For what the World admires I'll wish no more,
Nor court that airy nothing of a Name:
Such flitting Shadows let the Proud adore,
Let them be Suppliants for an empty Fame.

2.

If Reason rules within, and keeps the Throne,
While the inferior Faculties obey,
And all her Laws without Reluctance own,
Accounting none more fit, more just than they.

3.

If Virtue my free Soul unsully'd keeps,
Exempting it from Passion and from Stain:
If no black guilty Thoughts disturb my Sleeps,
And no past Crimes my vext Remembrance pain.

4.

If, tho' I Pleasure find in living here,
I yet can look on Death without Surprize:
If I've a Soul above the Reach of Fear,
And which will nothing mean or sordid prize.

5.

A Soul, which cannot be depress'd by Grief,
Nor too much rais'd by the sublimest Joy;
Which can, when troubled, give it self Relief,
And to Advantage all its Thoughts employ.

6.

Then am I happy in my humble State,
Altho' not crown'd with Glory nor with Bays:
A Mind, that triumphs over Vice and Fate,
Esteems it mean to court the World for Praise.

Song

Damon.

Cease, fair *Calistris*, cease disdaining;
'Tis time to leave that useless Art:
Your Shepherd's weary of complaining;
Be kind, or he'll resume his Heart.

Calistris.

Damon, be gone; I hate complying;
Go court some fond, believing Maid:
I take more Pleasure in denying,
Than in the Conquests I have made.

Damon.

Why, cruel Nymph, why, why so slighting?
Is this the Treatment I must have?
Were not your Beauty so inviting,
I wou'd no longer be your Slave.

Calistris.

Damon, begon, I hate complying,
Your Heart's not worth the having;
Were there Ten thousand Shepherds dying,
No one were worth the saving.

The Inquiry

A Dialogue between *Cleanthe* and *Marissa*

Cleanthe. Tell me, *Marissa*, by what Rule
May I judge who's the greatest Fool?
Is't he, that in pursuit of Wealth,
Neglects his Ease, neglects his Health,
And void of Rest, and full of Care,
Becomes a Slave to his next Heir;
To him, who does his Thrift despise,
And from him with Abhorrence flies:
And when he's dead, with eager haste
Will soon his ill-got Riches waste?
Or he, who seeks in bloody Wars,
For Fame, and honourable Scars?
For Fame, that idle, useless Toy,
Which Fools can give, and Fools destroy!
Or is't the Man, who dully grave,
Is to his Books a willing Slave?
Who, if he has the Classicks read,
And talk'd with all the mighty dead;
Knows the much fam'd Atomick Dance
And all the wondrous Works of Chance;
What Particles form th' active Fire,
And what the wat'ry Parts require;
Which constitute th'Earth, and which th'Air,
Which th' *Æsop's* Form, and which the Fair,
Which make the Fools, and which the Wise,
And where the grand Distinction lies:

Line 19. **Atomick Dance**: reference to the "atomic theory" of Democritus, Epicurus, and Lucretius, in which the random movement of atoms explains all phenomena.

Line 24. **Æsop's Form**: deformed.

Knows all the *Vortices* on High,
And all the Worlds that grace the Sky;
Can tell what Men, what Beasts are there,
And what gay Clothes the Ladies wear;
What their fine airy Heroes do,
And how they fight, and how they woo;
And whether like our Beaux below,
They're pleas'd with Trifles, Noise, and Show,
Full of a stiff pedantick Pride,
Does all besides himself deride:
If you some Syllables misplace,
And can't them to their Fountain trace;
Can't tell among the Words you speak,
Which are *Saxon*, *French*, or *Greek*,
Which to the *Roman* Tongue belong,
And which to th'ancient *Druid's* Song;
Why Names a diff'rent Sense have gain'd;
Why some are shun'd, and some retain'd;
And why, since Honesty's forgot,
The Title *Knave* shou'd prove a Blot;
Why Tyrant, which past Princes us'd,
Shou'd by crown'd Heads be now refus'd;
Those guiltess Names, which juster Times
That blush'd even at the Thought of Crimes,
And were too gen'rous to abuse,
Did without Scruple freely use:
He'll with a supercilious Air
His scornful Thoughts of you declare,
And gravely swear that you're unfit
For the Converse of Men of Wit.

Marissa. No, no, 'tis none, 'tis none of these;
But you, methinks, shou'd guess with Ease:

Line 27. **Vortices**: a whirl, or swirling mass. In Descartes it was the rotation of cosmic matter around an axis, which he believed accounted for the origin of all terrestrial systems.

Line 42. **Druid**: a priest of the ancient Celts.

Think, *Cleanthe*, think again,
And you'll find some yet much more vain.

Cleanthe. Is it that Ape in Masquerade,
The Gallant by the Tailor made?
The Man who hid with Snush and Hair,
And furnish'd with a modish Air;
Who's lately made the *Tour* of *France*,
And learnt to talk, to dress, and dance;
Who, if he can but neatly write,
And moving *Billets Doux* indite,
Cares nor for English, nor for Sense,
He knows we can with both dispence?
Or is't the worthy Country Squire,
Who does himself, and's Wealth admire,
Who hunts, and games, and swears, and drinks,
But seldom reads, and never thinks,
Who, if he can a Warrant write,
Or but a *Mittimus* indite,
Can in Law-terms harangue the Croud,
Call Names, insult, and talk aloud.
He struts about, and looks as great,
As if whole Armies he had beat?
Or is it he, who thinks he's able
To direct a Council Table,
To teach the Senate of the Nation,
And instruct the Convocation;
Presumes to judge what's fit and right,
And when we shou'd, and shou'd not fight;
Who can on *Machiavel* refine,

Line 63. **Snush**: snuff.

Line 75. **Warrant**: document issued by justice of the peace authorizing the arrest of a person.

Line 76. **Mittimus**: document issued by justice of the peace to the keeper of a prison ordering him to take a person into custody.

Line 84. **Convocation**: in the Church of England, an assembly of the clergy.

Line 87. **Machiavel**: Niccolo Machiavelli (1469–1527), Florentine statesman and author of *The Prince* (1513), who held that in the interest of the state, the ends justified the means.

And thinks his Policy Divine;
Who descants on the weekly News,
And can both *Dutch* and *French* accuse;
Find fault with *Italy* and *Spain*,
And dares the *Swede* and *Czar* arraign;
Th' *Emperor's* Conduct too dares blame,
And thinks the *German Diet* tame;
Censures each State, and full of Pride,
Thinks he the busie World could guide?
Or is't the Man who waking dreams
Of Nymphs, and Shades, and Hills, and Streams,
Makes Gods and Goddesses descend,
And on their Creature Man attend;
Who thro' th'infernal World dares go,
And does their griesly Monarch know;
Th'*Elysian* Fields distinctly view;
Knows what departed Heroes do;
Sees how the Beauties are employ'd,
And what Delights are there enjoy'd:
Then quick as Thought can upward fly,
And view the vast expanded Skie;
Sees the Celestial Monsters there,
The Crab, the Scorpion, and the Bear.
Hears *Canis* bark, and *Taurus* roar,
With many deaf'ning Noises more:
Then makes a *Tour* from Pole to Pole,
And sees the threatning Billows roll:
Sees Sea-Gods with their wat'ry Train
Riding in Triumph on the Main:
Thence sees the *Paphian* Goddess rise
With tempting Looks, and sparkling Eyes;
Amid the Waves she spreads her Fire,
And does each Breast with Love inspire;

Line 94. **German Diet**: the regular legislative meetings of the states of Germany.

Line 102. **griesly**: grisly, terrifying. Line 109. **Celestial Monsters**: constellations.

Line 117. **Paphian Goddess**: Aphrodite.

Fair *Amphitrite* feels the Heat,
And *Neptune* does his Vows repeat:
The *Nereids* sigh, the *Tritons* burn,
And each does Glance for Glance return:
Then like the glorious Source of Day,
He does both East and West survey,
Thro' ev'ry State, each Kingdom goes,
And all their Laws and Customs knows,
And which are Wits, and which are Fools,
Who bred in Wilds, and who in Schools;
Who with a courtly Neatness treat,
And who like Beasts devour their Meat:
And who of this vast Knowledge proud,
Looks with Disdain upon the Croud,
And thinks he has a just Pretence
To the Monopoly of Sense:
If's Thoughts he smoothly can express,
And put them in a florid Dress,
Can to a Poet's Name pretend,
And lash a Vice, or praise a Friend,
Thinks he's as happy and as great
As if he fill'd th'Imperial Seat;
And still averse to Gold and Cares,
The Badges of the Muses wears;
And is as fond of being poor,
As others of their boasted Store?

Marissa. I'll tell you, since you can't discover,
It is an awkard, whining Lover;
Who talks of Chains, of Flames and Passion,
And all the pretty Words in Fashion;
Words, which are still as true a Mark

Line 121. **Amphitrite**: in Greek myth, goddess of the sea, wife of Poseidon.

Line 122. **Neptune**: the Roman name for Poseidon, Greek god of the sea.

Line 123. **Nereids ... Tritons**: sea nymphs and sea gods, half human, half fish.

Of an accomplish'd modish Spark,
As a long Wig, or powder'd Coat:
Like A, B, C, they're learnt by rote;
And then with equal Ardor said,
Or to the Mistress, or the Maid:
An Animal for Sport design'd,
Both very tame, and very kind:
Who for a Smile his Soul would give,
And can whole Months on Glances live:
Who still a Slave is to your Will,
And whom you with a Frown may kill:
Who at your Feet whole Days will lie,
And watch the Motions of your Eye:
Will kiss your Hand, and fawn, and swear,
That you, and none but you, are fair;
And if he sees that you're inclin'd
At length his humble suit to mind,
He then all Exstasie will prove,
Is all Delight, and Joy, and Love:
But if you shou'd a Look misplace,
Or any favour'd Rival grace,
He full of Rage, and of Despair,
Nor him, nor you, nor Heav'n, will spare,
But challenges the happy Man,
Who whips him thro' the Lungs, and then
While he is bleeding, begs your pity,
In strains so moving, soft and witty;
That they your Heart at length must move
To some Remorse, if not to Love,
Which he soon guesses by your Eyes,
And in an amorous Rapture dies.

Line 152. **Spark**: a fashionable fop or dandy.

The Choice

A Dialogue between *Emilia* and *Marissa*

Marissa. Virtue sure's th' only Treasure,
Th' only solid lasting Pleasure:
It does our Souls, our Thoughts refine,
And gives us Joys almost Divine.
It may a while obscur'd remain,
But soon its Lustre will regain;
Like *Phœbus* chase the Shades away,
And bring again triumphant Day:
Censures like Clouds sometimes appear,
And keep its Rays from shining clear:
But having reach'd Meridian Height,
They fly before its conqu'ring Light;
Before that Light whose glorious Blaze
Does trembling guilty Souls amaze,
And from its dazling Seat on high
Disperses Splendor thro' the Skie:
Pale Envy sickens at the Sight,
And full of Shame, and full of Spite,
To the dark nether World returns,
And there, her Disappointment mourns:
But oh! my dearest Friend, I find
That Malice still is left behind:
Alas! that Fury never sleeps,
But thro' the World still slily creeps,
Each Day a new Disguise she takes,
Each Day some diff'rent Figure makes:
Like Zeal and Pity she appears,
And drown'd in false dissembling Tears,
Often the Mask of Friendship wears,
And with a Shew of Love insnares,
On me she's bent to wreak her Spite,
And with her dire Attacks affright:

From her to this Recess I fled,
And here my Life obscurely led;
Supposing She with Crouds wou'd stay,
Or with the Great, the Rich, the Gay,
With the Young, the Fair, the Wise,
And me, poor worthless me, despise;
But now too late, alas! I find
She will not, will not stay behind.

Emilia. Since Virtue's seated in her Breast,
Marissa ne'er can be distrest:
Malice may you perhaps assail,
But never, never can prevail:
Fortune too may take her part,
Exert her Strength, and shew her Art;
With these the Vicious may combine,
And favour their unjust Design;
But Virtue will the Shock sustain,
And you'll unvanquish'd still remain:
Your inward Joys will be secure,
And you'll no Loss, nor Ill endure.

Marissa. Virtue has, ever had my Love,
And still my Choice, my Guide shall prove;
To me shall still point out the Way,
Until I reach eternal Day,
That dear, that welcome, blissful Shore
Where I shall never suffer more;
No more the Toils of Life sustain,
But live secure from Sin and Pain.
Hark! hark! I'm call'd! I'm call'd away!
I cannot, will not, longer stay:
My Guardian Angel see appear,
See! see! he cuts the yielding Air:
Celestial Musick sweetly plays,
I hear! I hear Seraphick Lays!
O! the soft enchanting Sound!

Nothing here's so charming found!
Adieu, vain World, vain World, adieu:
I come, ye blest! I come to you!
Fortune's Gifts I ne'er could prize,
And now her Trifles I despise:
If at my Feet her Bounties lay,
And Crowns were scatter'd in my Way,
I'd scorn 'em all, and onward go;
There's nothing tempting here below.

Emilia. O! stay my Friend! O! stay for me,
I still will your Companion be:
My Love to Virtue, Love to you,
Was ever strong, and ever true;
And still the same shall ever prove;
Nothing my fixt Resolves shall move.
The Sun may sooner cease to shine,
And it may freeze beneath the Line;
Mountains may sink, and Plains may rise,
Beasts chuse the Seas, and Fish the Skies;
Birds their lov'd airy Region leave,
And flatt'ring Men no more deceive,
Than my *Marissa* shall e'er find
Emilia faithless, or unkind:
O! do not then her suit disdain,
O! let her not implore in vain:
She longs, she longs with you to die;
Thus, Hand in Hand we'll upward fly;
Thus, thus, my best, my dearest Friend,
Thus, thus embracing we'll ascend.

Marissa. No, thou lov'd Darling of my Heart,
We'll never, never, never part:
Those Virtues which our Souls combine,
Shall ever in our Union shine:
Together we'll lay down our Clay,
Together throw the Load away;

And bright as Fire, and light as Air,
To the superior World repair;
To glorious Seats, and Realms Divine,
Where Love do's in Perfection shine:
Love undisguis'd, without alloy,
Noble, pure, and full of Joy,
Sincere, and strong, and still the same,
One steady, bright, immortal Flame:
There, there our Friendship we'll improve,
Together tast the Sweets of Love;
Still in each other's Bliss rejoice,
And prove one Soul, one Thought, one Voice;
In nothing ever disagree,
Throughout a blest Eternity.

The Fifteenth Psalm Paraphras'd

Who on thy Holy Hill, my God, shall rest,
And be with everlasting Pleasures blest?
The Man who blameless is, and still sincere,
And who no Judge do's but his Conscience fear:
Whose Practice is a Transcript of thy Law,
And whom thy Omnipresence keeps in awe:
Who speaks the Truth, and wou'd much sooner die,
Than owe his Life to the loath'd Refuge of a Lie.
Whose Soul is free from Falshood and Design,
And in whose Words Integrity do's shine:
Who scorns to flatter, and by little Arts
To purchase Treasures, or inveagle Hearts:
Who to his Neighbour has no Mischief done,
Do's spiteful Actions with Abhorrence shun,
And cannot be to what's Inhuman won:

Title. **The Fifteenth Psalm**: describes a citizen of Zion.

Line 12. **inveagle**: inveigle, to wheedle or seduce.

Who thinks the best, and none will e'er defame,
But as his own, preserves another's Name:
Who's ever humble, and is still inclin'd
T'inspect himself, and his own Failings find:
Who loves Reproofs, and a Respect do's pay
To those who kindly guide him in his Way,
Who loves the Good, those who to Virtue true,
Its Dictates always cheerfully pursue;
And a Regard for Honour in their Actions shew:
Who when he swears, true to his Oath will prove,
And whom nor Fear, nor Int'rest e'er can move,
(No, not tho' it to's Prejudice should be,)
To disappoint his greatest Enemy:
Much less, tho' to his Ruin it should tend,
Once to deceive a kind confiding Friend:
Who bravely avaricious Thoughts disdains,
And is a Stranger to base sordid Gains:
Who'd rather starve, than th'Innocent betray,
Or to base undermining Thoughts give way:
He who lives thus, who this his Bus'ness makes,
And never once the Paths of Life forsakes,
Like some strong Tow'r unshaken shall remain,
And all the Batteries of Fate sustain.

Line 38. **Batteries**: blows.

One of *Lucian's* Dialogues of the Dead Paraphras'd

Diogenes. O *Pollux*, when thou next revisit'st Light,
Menippus to these nether Realms invite;
Tell him, if he's not tir'd with Fools above,
Where all that's said, and done, his Mirth does move,
He'll here fit Subjects for his Laughter find,
New Scenes of Madness to divert his Mind:
For tho' blind Mortals no Ideas have
Of any thing beyond the silent Grave,
But vainly fancy, as their Toil and Care,
So too their Souls find equal Periods there,
And all the dislodg'd Atoms mingle with the Air.
Yet here are no such impious Scepticks found,
Each Place does with complaining Ghosts abound:
He sure with me would full of Wonder gaze
On mighty Men whose glorious Acts amaze,
Who conquer'd Kingdoms, and who Thrones did grace,
And left their Sceptres to their God-like Race,
Here, undistinguish'd from the meanest Shade,
Depriv'd of Grandeur, and by none obey'd:
They by no other marks can now be known,
But Sighs, and Groans, and sad Complaints alone:
But bid him with him some Provisions bring,
A Crust were here a Present for a King:
He'll here find nothing Nature to sustain,
Throughout the vast Extent of this dark empty Plain.

Title. **Lucian**: (ca. A.D. 115–200), a Greek satirist whose satires such as *The Dialogues of the Dead* brought philosophers and different representatives of contemporary society together to discuss the human condition.

Line 1. **Diogenes ... Pollux**: Diogenes, a celebrated Cynic philosopher, who as a character in *The Dialogues* instructs Pollux, the son of Jupiter, brother of Castor, about the vanity of human wishes.

Line 2. **Menippus**: in *The Dialogues,* the chief satiric spokesman, who points out the vanity of human desires and ambitions.

Pollux. I'll readily perform what you desire;
But tell me where I shall for him inquire;
Describe his Person, Humor, and Attire.

Diogenes. He's old and jolly, and to *Bacchus* kind,
To Fools averse, to Satire still inclin'd:
A Cloak he wears the poorest Wretch wou'd scorn,
And which Ten thousand Patches wretchedly adorn:
At *Athens*, or at *Cornith* him you'll find,
Lampooning the whole Race of Human Kind:
He strikes at all, both th' Ugly and the Fair,
Nor Young, nor Old, nor yet the Great does spare,
But on Philosophers is most severe:
Their vain Pretences, and their towring Flights,
Their mystick Terms, and all those little Slights,
By which they strive their Ignorance to hide,
Those Cobweb Cov'rings for their nauseous Pride,
Are still the Subjects which his Laughter move
The chief Diversion that he finds above.

Pollux. By this Description he'll with ease be known:
But is your Message sent to him alone?
Can you not think of something that is fit
To be deliver'd to those Men of Wit,
Those high Pretenders to gigantick Sense,
To boundless Knowledge, matchless Eloquence?

Diogenes. Bid them lay all their vain Disputes aside,
No longer Truth from their Disciples hide:
No more thro' Nature's puzling Labyrinths stray,
No more of her mysterious Motions say:
No more with an affected haughty Air,
Their Thoughts of Things beyond their reach declare,
Things far remote from the most piercing Sight,
Beyond the Ken of intellectual Light.

Line 29. **Bacchus**: in classical myth, the god of wine. Line 57. **Ken**: knowledge.

Pollux. Such a Discourse as this wou'd not be born,
'Twou'd both expose me to their Hate, and Scorn:
They'll gravely tell me, I my Ign'rance show,
And rail at what I want the Sense to know.

Diogenes. Tell them from me th'important Message came;
'Tis I their Pride and Ignorance proclaim:
I bid them with Remorse past Follies view,
And their Repentance by their Blushes shew.

Pollux. I with exactest Care your Order will obey,
Without being mov'd at what the noisie Boasters say.

Diogenes. When this is done, then to the Great repair,
And speak to them with a commanding Air:
Say, What ye mad Men, makes you thus in vain,
To heap up Honours, and increase your Train,
As if you here for ever shou'd remain?
Riches and Grandeur do but load the Mind,
And they are Trifles you must leave behind:
Naked and poor, you to the Shades must go,
Only Despair will stay with you below:
The more you've now, the more you will lament,
When you from all your Pomp, and all your Joys are sent.
Next to th'Effeminate *Megilbus* go,
And let the brawny *Damoxenus* know
That none below are handsom, strong, or brave;
All are meer Phantoms when they're past the Grave:
None here their Youth and boasted Charms retain,
None here the fam'd *Olympick* Prizes gain:
No killing Eyes bewitching Glances dart,
No flowing Tresses win an amorous Heart:

Line 79. **Megilbus:** Megillus, a dandy known for his beauty.

Line 80. **Damoxenus:** a famous boxer of Syracuse, banished for killing his adversary.

No blushing Cheeks, not one inticing Smile,
Can here be seen th'unwary to beguile:
Nothing is lovely, nothing pleasing here,
Nothing but Dust and Ashes does appear.

Pollux. This I with Speed, and with Delight will do,
Since 'tis a Message worthy me, and you.

Diogenes. Inform the Poor, of whom vast Crouds you'll see,
That here they'll find a just Equality;
Tell 'em, they'll here unhappy Partners find,
Afflictions are not to one State confin'd:
Millions of Suff'rers throng the *Stygian* shore,
And there for ever will their Fate deplore,
Then bid them to complain and weep no more;
Since none will here their former Pomp retain,
But on a humble Level all remain:
None here will richer, greater, happier live,
No flatt'ring Titles to each other give:
No Room is left for Av'rice, or for Pride,
Where Poverty and Death, and dreadful Night reside.
And then from me, degen'rate *Sparta* blame,
Tell them they've tarnish'd their once glorious Fame;
They now no longer breath that Martial Heat,
Which made them once so formidably Great.

Pollux. Such Words as these, *Diogenes*, forbear,
I can't with Patience such Reproaches hear:
My Country's Honour, as my own, I prize,
And cou'd for it my Share of Life despise.
All your Commands, but this, without Delay
I'll e'er to morrow Night with Care obey.

Line 97. **Stygian**: referring to the river in Hades, the Styx, the river of Hate, characterized as black, infernal, gloomy.

Diogenes. 'Tis kindly said; I will no more desire:
May *Hermes* his persuasive Skill inspire,
And may your Voice be sweet as th' *Orphean* Lyre
That list'ning Mortals, by your Precepts taught,
May to the Knowledge of their Faults be brought,
Reclaim'd from Ill, and made themselves to know:
A Lesson they too late will learn below!

To the *Queen's* most Excellent *Majesty*

When Heav'n designs some wondrous Prince to raise,
Deserving Empire and eternal Praise;
It chuses one of an illustrious Line,
In whom Hereditary Graces shine:
Who good and great by his Descent is made,
And by the Rules of native Honour sway'd:
Him it exposes to th' Insults of Fate,
To all the Blows of Malice and of Hate,
Before it raises him to an exalted State.

The pious *Trojan*, its peculiar Care,
Did num'rous Hardships, num'rous Trials bear;
Ten thousand Toils with Patience he sustain'd,
Before he undisturb'd in *Latium* reign'd:
To pains inur'd, with Disappointments crost,
Wan'dring thro' Flames, on mounting Surges tost:
Suff'rings and War to Grandeur led the Way,
And fitted him for independent Sway.

Line 117. **Hermes**: in Greek myth, the messenger of the gods, a trickster figure.

Line 118. **Orphean Lyre**: in Greek myth, Orpheus's music was played on a lyre and enchanted all who heard it.

Line 10. **pious Trojan**: Aeneas. Line 13. **Latium**: Italy.

Happy that People whose blest Monarch owes
Unto himself the Wisdom which he shows,
Whose Prudence from his own Experience flows.
Who has in Shades seen dark'ning Vapors rise,
And gloomy Horrors over'cast the Skies:
Neglected liv'd in some obscure Retreat,
And learnt in secret to be truly great;
To rule within, his Passions to subdue,
And all his Souls most hidden Movements view:
Those Springs of Thought, which when they are refin'd
Bestow a dazling Brightness on the Mind:
Who disengag'd from Bus'ness and from Noise,
To noblest Purposes his Hours employs:
Searches past Records, and with vast Delight
Presents fam'd Heroes to his ravish'd Sight:
Sees them the shining Paths of Honour tread,
By Praise push'd on, and daring Courage led:
With eag'rest Hast to lofty Heights ascend,
And their Renown beyond the Grave extend:
Sees pious Kings with Joy and Zeal obey'd,
And cheerful Homage to wise Princes paid:
Who're still the Objects of a filial Love,
Whom all admire, whose Actions all approve.

Such was that Virgin Glory of our Isle,
On whom *Apollo* long was pleas'd to smile:
Who was with Wisdom and with Science bless'd,
By ev'ry Muse, and ev'ry Grace caress'd:
She knew Afflictions, felt a Sister's Hate,
And learnt to reign, while in a private State;
By adverse Fortune taught her self to know,
That Knowledge chiefly requisite below.

And such the Queen who now the Throne does grace,
The brightest Glory of her Royal Race:
In whose rich Veins the noblest Blood does flow
That God-like Kings, and Heroes could bestow:

Like her she bravely stood the Shock of Fate,
And liv'd serene in a dependent State:
Bore unconcern'd the Calumnies of those
Whom their Ill-nature only made her Foes:
Who thought her Merit too divinely bright,
And strove t'eclipse the overflowing Light:
Merit, in narrow Minds does Envy raise,
Large gen'rous Souls are most inclin'd to Praise.
Like her she stem'd the dang'rous swelling Tide,
And soar'd aloft with a becoming Pride:
Like her a gen'ral Approbation found,
And was with joyful Acclamations crown'd:
Ev'n Heav'n it self her Unction did approve,
And by auspicious Omens shew'd its Love:
Refreshing Breezes fan'd the balmy Air,
The fertile Earth a florid Green did wear:
No Clouds obscur'd the Sun's refulgent Light,
He never shone more eminently bright:
All things conspir'd her Welcom to proclaim,
Who the Protectress of her People came,
By Heav'n design'd, and her propitious Fate,
To be the Bulwark of a tott'ring State.

Britannia now all glorious does arise,
And shoots her Head above the starry Skies:
Her sacred Guardian, all the Sons of Light,
With Shouts of Joy behold the pleasing Sight:
The list'ning Goddess hears the cheerful Sound,
From Hill to Hill, from Vale to Vale rebound:
On all her Plumes at once, sublime she flies,
At once employs her num'rous Tongues and Eyes:
To distant Lands our Happiness makes known;
Tells them a Heroin fills the *British* Throne:
A Heroin greater than Romance can frame,
And worthy of the Line from whence she came;

Line 55. **Calumnies:** slanders. Line 74. **Bulwark:** support.

In whom the Great and Brave, the Soft and Kind,
In One are by the firmest Ties combin'd:
Where nothing's wanting that we can desire,
And where we see each Minute something to admire.

The trembling Nations aw'd by *Gallick* Arms,
Imploring come, drawn by resistless Charms:
To her they sue, and beg from her Relief;
She looks with God-like Pity on their Grief:
Exerts her Pow'r, and makes th' *Iberian* Shore;
The *Spaniards* hear her murth'ring Canon roar?
Her Fleet dilates a panick Terror round,
And *British* Valor's once more dreadful found:
Her Troops descend with noble Ardor fir'd,
By Heav'n, and their Heroick Queen inspir'd:
In vain they strive their darling Gold to save,
What can resist the Daring and the Brave?
Those Sons of War thro' Dangers force their Way,
And from the Dragons snatch the shining Prey:
Fame spreads the News thro' all th'incircling Air;
Aloud proclaims the Triumphs of the Fair:
The drooping Eagles prune their Wings and rise,
With joyful Haste they cut the sounding Skies;
Secure once more of that auspicious Fate
Which on them did so many Ages wait:
The *Belgick* Lion casts his Fear away,
And with new Strength pursues the destin'd Prey:
All the Distrest with Raptures of Delight,
In sweetest Songs of grateful Praise unite:
Blest *Albion's* Queen their only Theme does prove;

Line 95. **Iberian**: Spanish. Line 107. **prune their Wings**: preen, or groom the feathers.

Line 111. **Belgick Lion**: The lion was the heraldic symbol of the Duke of Flanders. In 1701, the "Grand Alliance" was made with the Netherlands, the Holy Roman Emperor, and England, to oppose France; after William's death in 1702, Queen Anne placed the Duke of Marlborough in charge of England's armies.

Like *Pallas* sprung from all-commanding *Jove*,
She comes, they sing, to give us timely Aid,
Is kind, and wise, as that celestial Maid:
As able to advise, and to defend,
And does her Care to ev'ry Part extend:
Like *Phœbus* darts reviving Beams of Light,
And dissipates the Horrors of the Night.

O that I cou'd the best of Queens attend;
Cou'd at your Feet my coming Moments end:
I past Misfortunes shou'd not then deplore,
And present Evils wou'd afflict no more:
But fill'd with Joy, with Transport, and with Love,
My Hours wou'd in a blissful Circle move:
And I the noblest Bus'ness still wou'd chuse,
Both for my self, and my ambitious Muse,
Be still employ'd in Service, and in Praise,
In glad Attendance, and in grateful Lays.

Line 116. **Pallas:** Athena. Line 132. **Lays:** songs.

The Song of the Three Children Paraphras'd

Thus wing'd with Praise, we penetrate the Skie,
Teach Clouds and Stars to praise him as we fly;
The whole Creation, by our Fall made groan,
His Praise to Echo, and suspend their Moan.
For, that he reigns all Creatures should rejoice,
And we with Songs supply their want of Voice.
The Church triumphant, and the Church below
In Songs of Praise their present Union show:
Their Joys are full, our Expectation long;
In Life we differ, tho' we join in Song.
Angels and we, assisted by this Art,
May sing together, tho' we dwell apart.

[Edmund] Waller.

Benedicite omnia Opera Domini Domino

Title. Also called "Song of the Three Young Men" or "Song of the Three Holy Children." It is the first of the apocryphal additions to Daniel inserted in 3:23–34; one of the young men cast into the fiery furnace by King Nebuchadnezzar for refusing to worship a golden idol praises the Lord for preserving them.

Epigraph. From "Of Divine Poesy: Occasioned upon the sight of the 53rd chapter of Isaiah turned into verse by Mrs. Wharton," canto I, ll. 37–48.

Benediction. "Praise all the works of the Lord of Lords."

THE PREFACE

The retir'd Life I live in the Country, affording me much Leisure, I thought I could not employ it more advantageously, or to better purpose, than in Paraphrasing the Hymn of the Three Children; which I think to be a very fit Subject for a Pindarick Ode, because it Comprehends all the Works of Nature, and excites not only Angels and Men, the noblest and most exalted Parts of the Creation, but also Brutes, Plants, and inanimate Beings, to pay a grateful Tribute of Praise to their bountiful Creator.

The Reason why I chuse this sort of Verse, is, because it allows me the Liberty of running into large Digressions, gives a great Scope to the Fancy, and frees me from the trouble of tying my self up to the stricter Rules of other Poetry.

How these Verses will please I know not, neither am I very solicitous about it. I writ 'em with no other design than that of exercising and enlarging my Thoughts, and of heightning and refining those Ideas which I had already fram'd, of the infinite Goodness, Wisdom, and Power of God, to whose Service I think my self oblig'd to devote my Time, my Faculties, and all that small Stock of Understanding which it has pleas'd his Divine Goodness to bestow upon me.

I have in this Poem taken the liberty to mention some Notions which are not generally receiv'd, but they being only Matters of Speculation, and not Articles of Faith, I thought I might be permitted to make use of them as often as I pleas'd. Among these, is the Doctrine of Pre-existence, which supposes, that all Souls were created in the beginning of Time, before any material Beings had their Existence, and that they being united to Ætherial Bodies, were made Possessors of as much Happiness as they were capable of enjoying. From their sublime Station, and Bliss unexpressibly great, being by the Solicitation of their lower Faculties, unhappily drawn to a Love of Pleasure, and by adhering too much to the Delights of the Body, enervating and lessening the Activity and Strength

---

Line 23. **Pre-existence:** the existence of the soul before its union with the body.

Line 26. **Ætherial:** etherial, celestial or heavenly; ether is the element more refined than air.

of their noblest and most perfect Powers, which proportionably abated, as the other increas'd, they sunk by degrees into an Aerial State, from whence, such as by repeated Acts of Disobedience, and the too eager Gratification of their sensitive Appetites, are render'd unfit for the Exercise of their more exalted Faculties (which by disuse, being almost laid asleep, and the Sensitive ones being quite tir'd by too long Exercises) fall lower yet, and lie in a State of Silence and Inactivity, till they are awaken'd into Life in such Bodies as by their previous Dispositions they are fitted for: So that no sooner is there any Matter of due vital Temper prepar'd, but presently a Soul that is suitable to such a Body, is sent into it. This is, according to the Notion I have of it, a true, tho' short Account of that Hypothesis, which has not only been asserted by *Plato* and his Disciples, by the *Pythagoreans,* the Jewish Rabbins, and some of the Fathers, but also by several modern Writers, Men of Wit and Learning, and by others as much decry'd. Its Advocates tell us, that 'tis contrary to the Idea we have of the Justice and Goodness of God, to believe that he would condemn innocent Spirits, such as had never committed any Sin, nor done any thing that could justly Occasion their forfeiting his Favour, to such Bodies as must unavoidably rob them of their Native Purity, and render them obnoxious to his Wrath, and its dreadful Consequence, eternal Punishment. Those who will not allow this Hypothesis to be probable, say among other things, that had we liv'd in a Preexistent State, 'tis very likely we should still have some Remembrance of our past Felicity, and retain a Consciousness of our past Actions, and that to believe that God will punish us for Faults which we have wholly forgotten, is not agreeable to those Sentiments it becomes us to entertain, of his infinite Justice and Goodness. The Sacred Scripture tells us, that at the great Day, when every one shall receive according to his Works, the Secrets of all Hearts shall be laid open, the Sentence shall be

---

Line 32. **Aerial State**: belonging to the air, rather than the purer ether.

Line 42. **Plato**: Greek philosopher (ca. 427–348 B.C.), author of numerous dialogues including *The Republic*, source of the doctrine of pre-existence; his disciples included neoplatonists such as Plotinus.

Line 43. **Pythagoreans**: philosophical school (fl. ca. 531 B.C.) characterized by the belief in metempsychosis: the soul as fallen divinity continued within the body as within a tomb, released through purification by study. They also believed in the transmigration of the soul from one body into a new one. **Rabbins**: rabbis, ordained teachers of Jewish law and usually the heads of congregations.

justified by the Consciousness all Persons shall have, that they themselves in whatsoever Bodies they appear, or what Substances soever that Consciousness adheres to, are the same that committed those Actions, and deserve that Punishment. And methinks 'tis highly rational to conclude, that, that way of proceeding which the infinitely Just and Merciful God will then make use of, has always been practis'd by him, as being most suitable to his adorable Perfections, and the unalterable Rectitude of his Divine Nature. But, yet I dare not rely so much on my own Judgment, as to presume to pass any Censure on an Opinion which has had the good Fortune to be espous'd by such a Crowd of ancient and modern Authors, Men of great depth of Thought, and solid Learning. To me 'tis indifferent which is true, as long as I know I am by the Laws of Poetry allow'd the Liberty of chusing that which I think will sound most gracefully in Verse.

In Paraphrasing that part of the Hymn which mentions the Stars, I have made use of the *Cartesian* Hypothesis, that the Fixt Stars are Suns, and each the Center of a *Vortex;* which I am willing to believe, because it gives me a noble and sublime Idea of the Universe, and makes it appear infinitely larger, fuller, more magnificent, and every way worthier of its great Artificer. We know very little of our selves, less of the World we inhabit: And of those few things with which we pretend to be fully acquainted, we have but very imperfect and confus'd Notions. This Earth on which we live, and which by being divided into so many mighty Empires, and spacious Kingdoms appears so vastly big to our imagination, is but a Point, a Nothing, if compar'd with the other Parts of the Universe: How numerous are those huge Globes which roll over our Heads! And how many more may there be in those boundless Spaces above us, which we cannot possibly discover! And yet some are so vain, or rather so arrogant, as to suppose, that those glorious Orbs were made wholly for our Use; doubtless the wise Author of Nature design'd them for nobler Purposes than to give us Light and Heat, to regulate and diversifie our Seasons, and render our Nights agreeable: 'Tis highly probable that as many of them are Suns, so others are habitable Worlds,

Line 75. **Cartesian Hypothesis:** René Descartes (1596–1650) rejected philosophical authority and tradition in favor of reason and developed a semi-mechanical theory of the universe that had space, matter, and motion governed by mathematical laws.

and fill'd with Beings infinitely superior to us; such as may have greater Perfections both of Soul and Body, and be by the Excellency of their Nature, fitted for much more rational and sublime Employments.

My Lord *Roscommon* tells us a great Truth in his excellent Essay on translated Verse, when he says, that,

> Pride, (of all others the most dangerous Fault,)
> Proceeds from want of Sense, and want of Thought.

For did we but accustom our selves to think, and employ our Time in endeavouring to pass a true and impartial Judgment on things, we should quickly have humbler thoughts of our selves, and be ready to own, that what we falsely call Knowledge, upon a strict and severe enquiry, proves to be nothing but Conjecture. We are very much in the Dark, and the greatest part of our time is spent in the pursuit of Shadows; but when Death draws up the Curtain, we shall have a full, clear, and distinct view of all those amazing Scenes, of which we can hardly now be truly said to have so much as a transient Glimps. The whole Oeconomy of Nature will then be visible to us, and we shall know the Truth of those things about which we now so eagerly and vainly dispute: In the mean time, it becomes us with profound Humility and an entire Submission to acquiesce in, and yield a full assent to all those Divine Truths which the infinitely Wise God hath vouchsaf'd to reveal to us; but in all other things to suspend our Belief, and make it our Business to avoid being impos'd on, either by our selves or others; which we cannot otherwise prevent, but by endeavouring to gain a generous Liberty of Mind, a large and universal Spirit, a Soul free from popular Prejudices, and a meek and teachable Temper.

I fear, what I have written of the Formation of the Earth will not please an Age so accurate, so inquisitive and knowing as this wherein we live: But 'tis not reasonable to expect that a Woman should be nicely skill'd in Physicks: We are kept Strangers to all ingenious and useful studies, and can have but a slight and superficial Knowledge of things: But if any thing in that Part of the Poem which mentions the Creation of the World, is thought to be contradictory to the receiv'd Principles of

---

Line 96. **My Lord Roscommon**: 4th earl of Roscommon (1633–85) who wrote a blank verse translation of Horace's *Ars Poetica* (1680) and an essay on translating verse (1684).

Philosophy, or the *Mosaick* Account of the Creation, I shall readily acknowledge my Errour, and take it as a Favour to be better inform'd: I know but one particular which relates to this Matter, that is liable to Exception, and that is, my supposing the Face of the Antediluvian Earth to be smooth, regular and uniform, without Mountains or Hills. This, I know, is with great appearance of Reason, deny'd by the learned Mr. *Ray,* but since 'tis asserted by both ancient and modern Writers, particularly by the ingenious Dr. *Burnet,* in his Theory of the Earth, and since Mountains are not mention'd in Scripture till the Water was risen to its utmost height, I thought in a Pindarick Ode, I might chuse which Opinion I wou'd, without troubling my self, nicely to examine all the Reasons that might be given for each. The like Apology I may make for my self, in reference to what I have said of a new habitable Earth, the Pleasures of a happy *Millennium,* and the Residence of separate Spirits before their reunion with their Bodies at the general Resurrection, and the Consummation of their Bliss in the Enjoyment of the Beatifick Vision; of each of which, learned Men have entertain'd very different Sentiments, and which of them are in the right God only knows; 'tis not becoming such weak-sighted Creatures as we are to be too positive, nor to rely too much on our own Judgment: These, and things of the like Nature, are part of the Divine *Arcana;* Mysteries which we should be contented to view at an awful Distance, and not presume to prophane by too near an Approach.

But I should quite tire my Reader, as well as my self, if I should make a Defence for every thing that needs it in this Poem: therefore to avoid giving either him, or my self any unecessary Trouble, I will only mention one Particular, and so conclude, and that is, the Freedom I take to advise the Clergy: I beg them to do me the Justice to believe, that I would not have assum'd so great a Boldness, had not my Subject led me to it: 'Tis impossible for any Person to have a greater Honour for them than I have; and I am ready to own to all the World, that I believe the

Line 132. **Mr. Ray:** John Ray (1627–1705) was considered Britain's preeminent naturalist and was the author of *Historica Plantarum* (1686–1704).

Line 133. **Dr. Burnet:** Dr. Thomas Burnet (1635?–1715), author of *The Sacred Theory of the Earth* (1684–90), a moralized cosmography.

Line 146. **Arcana:** secret or hidden knowledge.

Church of *England* was never bless'd with a more Learned, Orthodox, and Ingenious Clergy than now; Persons who make doing Good the Business of their Lives, who have no other Design, no other Aim, but that of imitating their great Master, and making themselves shining Examples of Piety and Virtue: Such among them as answer this Character, will not, I hope, misconstrue my Words, and take that ill, which I'm sure is well design'd. The pretending to be religious, the being bigotted to a Party, the placing Devotion either in a strict and nice Observance of the Punctilios of Publick Worship, or in a flying from, and an abhorrence of establish'd Forms, will not give us an Interest in the Divine Favour, or entitle us to a future Reward: All vicious Extremes must be avoided, all Violences and Heats, all uncharitable Censures, all Dependances on external Performances, all Disputes about trivial unnecessary Matters, about things in themselves indifferent, which being no Essentials of Worship, may be us'd, or not us'd without Sin, and are no longer Obligatory than they are made so by the Sanction of a Law, and the great, the indispensable Duties of Life made our Business. We should study to be really good, as well as to appear so; and be more concern'd to approve our selves to God, and our own Consciences, than to the World: We ought to consider, that the inward Applauses of the Mind, carry with them the truest, the highest Satisfaction, and that nothing can be more acceptable to the Deity, than a holy blameless Conversation, a spotless Innocency, a true substantial Integrity, a steady unshaken Honesty, a firm unbyass'd Justice, a constant unyielding Temperance, an humble, sincere, undesigning, compassionate, and forgiving Temper: In a word, a Life regulated by the Divine Precepts, and govern'd by an inward Principle, not by a slavish Fear, a Dread of Punishment, or the Prospect only of a future Recompence, but from an innate Love of Virtue, an ardent Desire of being united to the supreme Good, and of imitating all his communicable Perfections. From what I have said, I would not have it thought, that I am an Enemy to outward Observances, to publick Demonstrations of Reverence: I assure my Reader, I am so far from being guilty of a Fault of that kind, that I think I may truly say, none can be more conformable to the Ceremonies of the Church than I am: I look on them as decent Significations of Zeal, as necessary Helps

---

Line 165. **Punctilios**: niceties of behavior, trivial points of manners.

to raise our Devotion: All that I aim at is, to prove, that external Testimonies of Respect and Homage will be of little use, unless they are join'd with internal Honours, and an universal Obedience: unless the Mind is purify'd, the Will intirely subjected to the Divine Pleasure, and all our Passions, Affections, and Appetites devoted and consecrated to the Service of God: There must be an inseparable Union, an inviolable Agreement between them; and we may assure our selves, there will be so in all such as by a constant Contemplation of the Divine Nature, of his infinite, amazing, and adorable Excellencies, and of their own Imperfections, Weaknesses, and Defects, have fram'd in their Minds awful, noble, and reverential Ideas of him, and have by such sublime Exercises, rais'd their Souls above the little Concerns of Earth, the trifling Amusements of a worthless deceitful World. But it being a Truth too well known to be deny'd, that the generality of Mankind have false Notions of Religion, and are apt to fancy if they devote themselves to the Worship of God, and employ a considerable part of their Time in his Service, if they can talk plausibly, devoutly, and warmly for the Persuasion they espouse, and strongly calumniate, and abusively ridicule those whose Opinions are contrary to theirs, 'tis no matter what their Morals are; whether they are virtuous, honest, temperate, sincere, and charitable. 'Tis such as these I beg them to instruct: and I think they cannot do the Church a greater Service, or employ themselves in any thing more worthy their sacred Character, than in assuring these hypocritical Pretenders to Piety, that 'tis not Talking, but Living well, not the being of this or that Denomination, of this or that Sect or Party, that will make them eternally happy; but the being exactly conformable to those Divine Rules which are prescribed in the Holy Scriptures, those unerring Precepts, of which that sacred Volume is full.

The Song of the Three Children Paraphras'd

1.

Ascend my Soul, and in a speedy Flight
Haste to the Regions of eternal Light;
Look all around, each dazling Wonder view,
And thy Acquaintance with past Joys renew.
Thro' all th' Æthereal Plain extend thy Sight,
    On ev'ry pleasing Object gaze;
        On rolling Worlds below,
    On Orbs which Light and Heat bestow:
And thence to their first Cause thy Admiration raise
In sprightly Airs, and sweet harmonious Lays.
Assist me, all ye Works of Art Divine,
Ye wondrous Products of Almighty Pow'r,
    You who in lofty Stations shine,
And to your glorious Source by glad Approaches tow'r:
    In your bright Orders all appear;
    With me your grateful Tribute pay,
Before his Throne your joint Devotions lay.
Ye charming Off-springs of the Earth draw near,
And for your Beauties pay your Homage here,
    Let all above, and all below,
All that from unexhausted Bounty flow,
    To Heav'n their joyful Voices raise,
    In loud melodious Hymns of Praise.
When Time shall cease, and each revolving Year,
Lost in Eternity shall disappear,
The blest Employment ever shall remain,
And God be sung in each immortal Strain.

2.

O ye bright Ministers of Pow'r Divine,
In whom the Deity in Miniature does shine;
Ye first Essays of his creating Skill,
Who guard his Throne, and execute his Will,

Adore his Goodness, whose unweary'd Love
Call'd into Act that great Design,
That kind Idea to Perfection brought,
Which long had lain in his eternal Thought;
Who, when of all Felicity possest,
And in himself supremely blest,
To make his wondrous Bounty known,
Was pleas'd to raise
From nothing mighty Monuments of Praise:
Such as convincing Evidences prove
Of the Benignity Divine,
And in their blissful State above
With a resplendent Lustre shine:
Forms much more beautiful than Light,
And full of Charms to us unknown,
Of Charms peculiar to themselves alone:
Adorn'd with Glory not to be express'd;
With Glory much too bright,
To be the Object of a mortal Sight.
Active as Air, as *Æther* pure,
Exempt from Passions, and from Pain secure,
From cumb'rous Earth, and all its Frailties free,
Happy, and crown'd with Immortality,
And knowing as created Minds can be.
Blessings like yours, extatick *Euges* claim;
Thro' the celestial Courts your Thanks proclaim;
In highest Raptures, loudest Songs of Joy,
And Hallelujahs, your Eternity employ.

3.

Ye glorious Plains of pure unshaded Light,
Which far above the gloomy Verge of Night
Extended lie, beyond the sharpest Ken of Sight;
Whose Bounds exceed the utmost Stretch of Thought,

Line 51. **Æther**: element more refined than air, realm of the angels.

Line 56. **Euges**: exclamations of ecstatic praise.

Where vast unnumber'd Worlds in fluid *Æther* roll,
And round their radiant Centers move,
Making by Steps unequal, one continu'd Dance of Love:
Extol his Wisdom, who such Wonders wrought,
Who made, and like one individual Soul
Fills ev'ry Part, and still preserves the Mighty Whole.

4.

Ye Products of condensing Cold,
Ye Clouds, who liquid Treasures hold,
Who from your wat'ry Stores above,
(Where wafted by concurring Winds you move)
On the glad Earth your Bounties pour,
And make it rich with each prolifick Show'r:
Not so you fall, as when you were design'd
To punish the rebellious Race of human Kind:
Then, with impetuous haste stupendous Cataracts fell,
Descending Spouts, ascending Torrents met;
And mingled Horrors did the Vict'ry get:
Nature could not their mighty Force repel;
Beauty and Order from her Surface fled,
While o'er the Ball the liquid Ruin spread:
Now in mild Show'rs you make your kind Descent,
Refresh the Earth, and all our Wants prevent;
From lofty Mountains in *Meander's* slide,
And roll by grassy Banks your Silver Wealth along;
Let those celestial Springs from whence you are supply'd
Their silent Homage pay;
And till that fatal Hour the grateful Task prolong,
When fierce devouring Flames shall force their dreadful Way,
And make this beauteous Globe their Prey;

Line 78. **stupendous Cataracts**: reference to the Flood in Gen. 7.

Line 86. **Meander**: river in Phrygia, Greece, celebrated by Ovid and Virgil for its winding nature.

Line 90. **fatal Hour**: the Apocalypse.

From which sulphureous Steams shall rise
And chase the congregated Vapors from the Skies.

5.

Ye blest Inhabitants of Light,
Who from your shining Seats above,
Are often sent on Embassies of Love:
To distant Worlds you take your willing Flight,
And in the noblest Charity delight:
From the blest Source of Good, like Rays you flow,
And kindly spread your Influence below:
In vain the Great their mighty Deeds proclaim,
And think the highest Praise their Due,
And to themselves ascribe that Fame
Which wholly owing is to you:
In vain the grave considering Wise
Unto themselves Applauses give,
And think they by their own Endeavours rise,
And rich and honour'd live:
The whole unto your Care they owe,
From it each prosp'rous Turn, each blest Event doth flow:
That tender Care, which over all presides,
And for the common Good of Man provides.
Your high Prerogatives with Joy confess;
In lofty Strains your kind Creator bless:
In unforc'd, grateful, and exalted Lays:
You know him best, and ought him most to praise.

6.

Thou glorious Sun, bright Author of our Day,
Whose dazling Beams around themselves display,
And to the frozen Poles thy needful Heat convey.
From their long Night the shiv'ring Natives rise,
And see vast Trains of Light adorn their Skies.
Before thy Fire the vanquish'd Cold Retires,

Line 95. **Inhabitants of Light**: angels.

And Nature at the sudden Change admires:
Then their lost Verdure Woods and Fields regain,
And Seas and Rivers break their Icy Chain.
How blest are they who in Warm Climes are born!
Those happy Climes thy Rays do most adorn!
Where balmy Sweets their fragrant Off'rings pay,
And warbling Birds salute the rising Day:
Where vital Warmth does sprightly Thoughts inspire,
    Thoughts brisk, and active as thy Rays:
    Th'immortal *Homer* felt thy Fire,
That wondrous Bard! whom all succeeding Ages praise.
To the first Cause, the uncreated Light,
The radiant Source of everlasting Day,
    The Center whence thy Glories flow,
Those dazling Splendors we admire below,
    With us thy Adoration pay.
And thou, fair Orb, whose Beauties still invite;
Who with thy paler Beams of borrow'd Light,
Bring'st back the Solar Rays to bless our Night:
From thee reflected, on the Earth they shine,
And make the awful Prospect seem Divine:
Thy welcom Light the Northern Climates see,
Their tedious Night is pleasant made by thee:
    From that exalted Walk above,
Where round our Globe thou solemnly dost move,
Admire and laud thy mighty Maker's Love.

7.

Ye glitt'ring Stars, who float in liquid Air,
Both ye that round the Sun in diff'rent Circles move,
    And ye that shine like Suns above;
Whose Light and Heat attending Planets share:
In your high Stations your Creator praise,
    While we admire both him and you;

Line 135. **uncreated Light**: the eternal light emanating from God that created the sun.
Line 140. **fair Orb**: the moon.

Tho' vastly distant, yet our Eyes we raise,
   And wou'd your lofty Regions view;
Those immense Spaces which no Limits know,
Where purest *Æther* unconfin'd doth flow;
But our weak Sight cannot such Journies go:
'Tis Thought alone the Distance must explore;
Nothing but That to such a Height can soar,
Nothing but That can thither wing its Way,
   And there with boundless Freedom stray,
And at one View Ten thousand sparkling Orbs survey,
Innumerable Worlds and dazling Springs of Light.
O the vast Prospect! O the charming Sight!
   How full of Wonder, and Delight!
How mean, how little, does our Globe appear!
This Object of our Envy, Toil and Care,
Is hardly seen amidst the Croud above;
There, like some shining Point, do's scarce
      distinguish'd move.

8.

   Yet Man by his own Thoughts betray'd,
Curst with Self-love, not with Reflexion blest,
   If of a great Estate possest,
Is to his Vanity a Victim made;
   No longer he himself does know,
   And looks with Scorn on all below:
But if by chance a Kingdom is his Share,
   And he a Diadem does wear,
Full of himself, and heightned by his Pride,
   He to Divinity does tow'r,
And from his visionary Sphere of Pow'r
Commands his Subjects with imperious Sway,
And forces them his Passions to obey:
Humor, not Reason, is most times his Guide:
Too great to be advis'd, by Vice and Folly led,
He will the dang'rous Paths of slippery Grandeur tread,
And rashly mount that steep Ascent he ought to dread.

Mistaken Wretch! what is this worthless All
Which does thy heated Fancy move?
If thou the whole thy own couldst call,
'Twere but a Trifle if compar'd with those above;
Which may, perhaps, the happy Mansions be
Of Creatures much more noble, much more wise than we.

9.

Ye Exhalations that from Earth arise,
Whose minute Parts cannot be seen,
Till they're assembled in the lower Skies;
Where being condens'd, they fall again
In gentle Dews, or Show'rs of Rain.
To you we owe those Fruits our Gardens yield,
And all the rich Productions of the Field:
But Oh! how much are you by those desir'd,
Who are with scorching Sun-beams fir'd?
The swarthy Natives of the Torrid Zone,
Who live expos'd to the fierce burning Rays,
And wou'd in dazling Brightness waste their Days,
Did you not sometimes cast a Shade between,
And from their Sight th' excessive Glory skreen:
Your well tim'd Bounty they must ever own;
On them you annual Kindnesses bestow,
Their Air you cool, and all their Ground o'erflow.
As you descend, that God adore,
Unto whose Pow'r you owe your unexhausted Store.

10.

Ye blust'ring Winds, who spacious Regions sway,
As thro' your airy Realms you force your Way,
High as the starry Arch your Voices raise,
And with loud Sounds your great Creator praise,
Whose wondrous Pow'r your Motion does declare:
Strange! that such little Particles of Air,

Line 196. **Exhalations**: water vapor.

Such Nothings as escape our Sight,
With so much Strength, such wondrous Force shou'd move,
So pow'rful in their Operations prove!
Sometimes imprison'd in the Vaults below,
You all the dreadful Marks of Fury show;
The Earth you shake, make mighty Cities reel,
And ev'ry Part the dire Concussion feel.
Chasms you cause, and helpless Mortals fright,
Who trembling sink int' everlasting Night:
With dying Accents on their Friends they call,
They hear, and in one common Ruin fall:
The pale Survivors panting fly,
And with loud Screeches rend the Skie;
To neighbouring Hills they take their hasty Flight,
But Hills, alas! can no Protection yield,
They can't themselves from the devouring Mischief shield:
Pursu'd by Terrors, lost in wild Amaze,
They on surrounding Horrors gaze:
With Sighs and Groans, and with repeated Cries,
They prostrate fall, and with imploring Eyes,
All bath'd in Tears, from Heav'n they beg Relief,
From Heav'n which sees, and only can asswage their Grief.

11.

Sometimes disturb'd, they ruffle all the Air,
And neither Earth, nor Ocean spare:
The mounting Waves with loud Confusion roar,
And furious Surges dash against the Shore:
The stately Cedar bends her awful Head;
The meaner Trees can no Resistance make;
Their broken Branches all around are spread,
And all their leafy Honours shed:
The frighted Birds their shatter'd Nests forsake:
Their verdant Food the trembling Cattle shun,
And urg'd by Fear to gloomy Coverts run.

Line 242. **asswage:** assuage, lessen.

12.

Blest be that God who doth our Good design,
Whose Kindness do's in each Occurrence shine:
Who makes the boist'rous Winds declare his Love,
And from our Air the noxious Steams remove,
Those pois'nous Vapors which would fatal prove.
By him restrain'd, they gently blow,
And friendly Gales bestow:
To sultry Climes Relief convey,
Where Sun-burnt *Indians* faint away,
And curse th'excessive Heat of their tormenting Day.
To them the Greedy, and the Curious owe
A Part of what they have, and what they know.
By them assisted, they new Seas explore,
And visit ev'ry foreign Shore:
Their Sails they fill; the Ships make speedy way,
And to wish'd Ports their precious Freight convey.

13.

Thou kind inlivening Fire,
Which dost a needful Warmth inspire;
And Heat which does to all extend,
From Stars above, to Mines below:
Which does on Natures Works attend,
At once to cherish, and defend,
And make her tender Embryo's grow:
The whole Creation springs from thee,
Both what we are, and what we see,
Are owing to thy wondrous Energy.
Opprest with Cold, and void of Day,
The sluggish Matter stupid lay,
Till that propitious Hour,
When thy invigorating Pow'r
Did first its self display:
Then Life and Motion soon begun,
And fiery Atoms form'd the Sun.
How various are the Blessings you bestow!

    To that great God from whom they flow,
        With us your Praises send;
    Let them in purest Flames ascend;
    To your bright Centre swiftly move,
Th' eternal Fountain both of Heat and Love.

14.

Ye kind Vicissitudes of Heat and Cold,
Which thro' the Year a due Proportion hold;
As on the Wings of Time your Round you move,
    Extol that wise Almighty Mind,
    Who has your diff'rent Tasks assign'd;
    And from his lofty Throne above
Instructs you when to warm, and when to cool,
And does your Order with an undisputed Empire rule.
Your grateful Changes Health and Pleasure give;
Blest with the dear Variety we live:
    Variety which tempts us on
    The painful Ills of Life to bear,
    And when the cheating Vision's gone,
For us does new deluding Scenes prepare:
            From Place to Place,
        Fresh Pleasures we pursue,
    And the delightful Toil renew,
Till Death o'ertakes us in our thoughtless Chase,
And puts an End to our phantastick Race.

15.

Ye Frosts and Ice, and you descending Snow,
Adore that God to whom your Pow'r you owe,
While we, well-pleas'd, your chilling Cold endure,
And to the friendly Smart our selves inure;
And with the pure, the fresh, the salutif'rous Air,
The Mischiefs of the Summers Heat repair;
Then with new Pleasure wait th'approaching Spring,

Line 316. **salutif'rous**: salutiferous, bringing health.

And grasp those Blessings which th' increasing Year does
  bring.
But Oh! the Rigors of the Northern Air!
What Pains must those unhappy Mortals bear,
Who near the Pole, remote from *Phœbus* Rays
Wast in uncomfortable Darkness half their Days!
There, piercing Winds commence their stormy reigns,
  And Icy Cold th' Ascendant gains:
There, Seas congeal, and Rivers cease to flow,
Where harden'd Earth doth firm as Marble grow,
And where both Hills and Vales are ever hid with Snow.
Nature to them penuriously does give;
  They on a scant Allowance live:
Yet with contented Minds their Lot sustain,
Not knowing better, and inur'd to Pain.

16.

Ye silent Nights, who sacred are to Rest,
Wherein th' afflicted, by their Griefs opprest,
  Are with a short Cessation blest;
While in the downy Bands of Sleep they lie,
  Sorrow can no Impression make,
Slumbers the absent Joy supply;
  And they are happy till they wake.
Where you command, an awful Quiet reigns;
Ev'n Nature seems the Blessing to partake.
    On the smooth verdant Plains
  The weary Beasts recline their Heads,
And fall asleep upon their grassy Beds:
The drowsie Birds sit nodding on the Boughs;
To all her Works she soft Repose allows.
  E'er Darkness has her Veil withdrawn,
  Or Light unbarr'd her radiant Gate,
Before the cheerful Morn begins to dawn;
While you march slowly on in solemn State,
With gentlest Whispers, Accents soft as Air,
The Praises of your bounteous God declare.

17.

And ye bright Days, who from the East arise,
And with diffusive Glories gild the Skies,
With them your early Tribute pay;
While we by kindly Sleep refresh'd,
Rise gay and sprightly from our Rest,
And see, well-pleas'd, the Out-guards of the Night,
The gloomy Shades give way
To your victorious Light;
At whose Approach Joy spreads it self around,
Pleasures in ev'ry Place abound:
The busie Peasants their lov'd Toil renew,
And active Youths their noisie Sports pursue:
With loud-mouth'd Hounds the frighted Hare they chase,
And with his Spoils their Triumphs grace:
The harmless Flocks lie basking in your Beams,
And Birds awaken'd from their Dreams,
From their soft Wings shake off the pearly Dew,
And their melodious Strains, in tuneful Notes renew.

18.

Let Darkness, whom th' infernal Pow'rs obey,
And who e'er Time begun, with universal Sway
Thro' the wide Void its Empire did extend,
And still do's with its younger Sister Light
In its nocturnal Course contend,
And ancient Rights defend:
As round th' Almighty's Throne, with sable Wings display'd,
It forms a venerable Shade,
A Shade, which does from each celestial Sight
Such dazling Glories hide,
As did it not a needful Veil provide,
Wou'd with their prodigious Blaze
Attending Seraphims amaze;
For the high Honour thankful prove.

Line 358. **Out-guards**: remaining signs.

And thou, fair Off-spring of eternal Love,
    Thou brightest Gift of Pow'r Divine,
    Which thro' the happy Plains above
Didst with an undiminish'd Splendor shine:
    From whence thou kindly didst descend,
And thro' the mournful Gloom thy cheerful Beams extend;
(Then beauteous Nature from the *Chaos* rose,
    And did a thousand Charms disclose:
With wondrous Pleasure she receiv'd the Grace,
And blooming Joy sat smiling in her Face.)
To thy bright Fountain on retorted Rays
Send constant Tributes of unweary'd Praise.

19.

Ye transient Fires, who with tremendous Light
Rush thro' the dusky Horrors of the Night,
As with a dreadful Sound you force your way
Thro' those resisting Clouds where you imprison'd lay,
    To Heav'n your Adoration pay;
    While we your dang'rous Glories view
    Glories, whose pernicious Blaze
    Does the trembling World amaze:
    Both Birds and Beasts with Haste retire,
And Men the Dictates of their Fear pursue;
From open Fields, and from th' enkindled Air,
    They to the neighbouring Cliffs repair;
But who can shun your penetrating Fire?
The subtile Mischief spreads it self around,
And tumbles lofty Temples to the Ground;
Rocks feel its Pow'r, Marbles are forc'd to yield,
Nor can the Trees their shady Cov'rings shield:
Thro' closest Pores it makes its speedy Way,
    And on the vital Stock does prey.
Unhappy Mortals, thus expos'd by Fate

Line 395. **retorted Rays**: light thrown back on its source.

Line 397. **transient Fires**: lightning.

To the fierce Rage of each impending Ill,
  Find in their transitory State,
  That Death has many Ways to kill:
The Treasure, Life, is kept with Pains and Cost,
And sometimes hardly seen, before 'tis lost.

20.

O let the Earth her great Creator bless,
And all the Wonders of his Pow'r confess:
From Pole to Pole, let her resound his Praise;
Around her Globe let the glad Accents fly,
Till they are echo'd by the neighbouring Skie:
  To all the list'ning Worlds above
    Let her proclaim aloud
The blest Effects of his transcendent Love,
Who out of nothing did her beauteous Fabrick raise.
  O Prodigy of Art Divine!
The Deity did in the wondrous Structure shine!
Who can in fit Expressions the sublime Idea dress,
Or the stupendous Marvels of that Work express!
Angels themselves, whose Intellects are free
From those dark Mists which our weak Reason cloud,
Who things in their remotest Causes see,
Whose Knowledge like their Station's great and high,
Above the loftiest Flights of weak Mortality,
Astonish'd saw the rising World appear;
The new, the glorious, the transporting Sight,
  So full of Wonder, and Delight,
With rapt'rous Joys fill'd each celestial Breast,
  With Joys too vast to be exprest;
    Such Extasies as here
    We could not feel, and live;
They to our Beings wou'd a Period give:
The killing Pleasure wou'd be too intense,
  And quite o'erwhelm our feeble Sense;
But they who are all Intellect and Will,
    And what they please fulfil,

Whose Minds are pure, free from the least Allay,
Serene, and clear, as everlasting Day,
Imbibe the most extatick Joys with eager Haste,
Nor can th' immense Excess immortal Spirits waste.

21.

Zeal tun'd their Harps, by it inspir'd they sung;
The charming Sound thro' all th' *Empyrean* rung:
Their God they with unweary'd Ardor bless'd,
And in their sacred Hymns his Praise express'd:
His Wisdom, Pow'r, and Goodness they admire,
These were the constant Themes of all th'Angelick Quire:
All these they saw on his new Work Imprest:
They saw his pow'rful *Fiat* soon obey'd;
He spoke, and streight that mighty Mass was made,
  Where Earth and Water, Air and Fire,
Without Distinction, Order, or Design,
  Did in one common *Chaos* join:
Stupid, unactive, without Form, or Light,
They lay confus'dly huddl'd in their native Night;
Till on the gloomy Deep his Spirit mov'd;
Th' Emanations of the Power Divine,
Did all its Parts with vital Influence bless,
And scatter'd thro' the whole their motive Energies.
Th' active Warmth did ev'ry Part impell,
  The heaviest downward made their way,
  And to a new made Centre fell,
  Where, by their Weight together prest,
  They did in one firm Body rest,
  On which a Mass of Liquids lay:
The lucid Particles together came,
  And join'd in one propitious Flame,

Line 457. **Empyrean**: in ancient cosmography, the highest heaven composed of pure fire, used in Christian cosmography as the abode of God and the angels.

Line 461. **Quire**: choir. Line 463. **Fiat**: decree.

Which round the new-form'd Globe did Light and
Heat convey,
And blest it with the welcom Birth of Day:
But to one Sphere the Fire was not confin'd,
Still a sufficient Stock was left behind,
Which thro' the Whole in due proportion went,
And needful Warmth to ev'ry Part was sent.

22.

By Heat excited, Exhalations rose,
And did the Regions of the Air compose:
The thicker Parts our Atmosphere did frame,
While the more subtil took a nobler Flight,
And fill'd with purest *Æther* the celestial Height,
Then Land appear'd; th' obsequious Floods gave way,
And each within appointed Bounds did stay;
But rude and unadorn'd the new Concretion lay,
Till by a sudden Act of Pow'r Divine,
Th' unshap'd Mass a beauteous Earth became;
Charming it look'd in its gay Infant Dress;
Goodness and Art at once did shine,
And both the God confess.
Thrice blest that Pair, who in the Dawn of Time
Were made Possessors of that happy Clime:
But wretched they soon lost their blissful State,
Undone by their own Folly, not their Fate.

23.

Serene and Calm those early Regions were,
A constant Spring was always there,
And gentle Breezes cool'd the Air,
Rough Winds and Rains they never knew,
But unseen Showr's of pearly Dew,
(Aereal Streams) their Balmy Drops distill'd,

Line 493. **obsequious**: respectful.

Line 495. **Concretion**: a mass formed by the consolidation of separate particles.

And with prolifick moisture the smooth surface fill'd.
The beauteous Plains perpetual Verdure wore,
With lovely Flow'rs embroider'd o'er.
Flowers so wondrous sweet, so wondrous Fair,
Ne'er grac'd our Earth, never perfum'd our Air,
Peculiar to those happier Fields they were;
Thro' which the winding Rivers make their Way,
The clear unsullied Streams with wanton Play
In Thousand various Figures Stray;
Sometimes concurring Waters make
A little Sea, a Chrystal Lake,
Where for a while in their soft Bed they rest,
Till by succeeding Currents prest,
To distant Parts they gently flow,
And murmur as they go,
As if they wish'd a longer Stay,
And ran unwillingly away:
On their enamel'd banks were seen
Plants ever Beauteous, ever Green;
Plants, whose odoriferous Smell,
Did the since fam'd *Sabæan* sweets excell.
Nature profusely spread her Riches there,
The fertile Soil prov'd grateful to her Care,
The new unlabour'd Ground large stately Trees did bear,
Trees whose Majestick Tops aspir'd so high,
They almost seem'd to touch the Sky;
Loaden with Blossoms, and with Fruit at once they stood;
At once the Beauties of the Spring and Autumn crown'd the Wood:
At once they did the Bounties of both Seasons wear.

Line 531. **Sabæan sweets:** Saba, the largest city in Arabia Felix, was known for its perfumes and spices.

24.

Such was the Earth so Beauteous and so Gay,
Fresh as the Morn, delightful as the Day:
Not the *Hesperian* Gardens so much fam'd of old,
Where glorious Trees bare vegetable Gold;
Nor that whereof *Mæonides* has writ,
Alcinous Garden, which its Beauty ow'd
To that great Genius, that transcendent Wit,
   Who could the lowest Subject raise,
And make the meanest things deserve Eternal Praise:
Such was *Phæacia*, 'till with wondrous Art
      He 'mbelish'd ev'ry Part:
   His Fancy the rich Dress bestow'd:
To future Times it had been little known,
Having no native Lustre of its own,
   Had not his Muse enroll'd its Name,
And laid it up secure within th' Archives of Fame.
   Nor these, nor yet those happy Plains,
Virgil describes in his immortal Strains,
Could equal the Perfections of that charming Place,
Which Nature had adorn'd with her exactest Care,
   And furnish'd it with every Grace;
   Her Skill did every where appear:
All that was lovely, all that lov'd Delight,
Might there be seen in its exalted Height:
   In it conspicuously did shine
Th' inimitable Strokes of Art Divine,
The God was seen in every dazling Line.

Line 542. **Hesperian Gardens**: in classical myth, the location of the tree bearing golden apples.

Line 544. **Mæonides**: Homer's surname.

Line 545. **Alcinous**: in the *Odyssey*, king of Phæacia (which is an island in the Ionian Sea, known for its luxurious and dissolute population), who entertained Odysseus (Ulysses).

25.

Such it continu'd, till deform'd by Sin:
  Guilt call'd down Vengeance from above,
And quickly spoil'd the Workmanship of Love:
Guilt on the Earth a dreadful Deluge brought;
In vain th' offending Race Protection sought,
In vain they from the liquid Mischief fled,
  The fatal Cause was still within:
From Mountains Tops they saw the floating Dead:
Th' increasing Waters did their Steps pursue,
And none escap'd but the blest Fav'rite few:
Who rode in Triumph on the watry Waste,
Secure above the swelling Surges plac'd:
Amaz'd they saw the daring Billows rise,
They pass'd the Clouds, and mingl'd with the Skies:
High on th'exalted Waves they look'd around,
But no Remains of their dear Country found;
Th' insulting Floods had cover'd all the Ground:
With Pity they their Brethrens Fate deplore,
And then the Mercies of their God adore;
His Mercy, who such wondrous Diff'rence made,
And gave such pregnant Proofs how much he lov'd:
  Who, when no human Pow'r cou'd aid,
  Himself their kind Protector prov'd.
While thus employ'd, they saw the Sea subside,
Th' impetuous Waters gradually withdrew;
Nature for their Reception did provide;
And they cou'd once again their native Regions view.

26.

On some bleak Mountains Top they sighing stay'd,
And thence the Horrors of the Plains survey'd:
Those pleasant Plains, once fill'd with all Delight,
Afforded only now a melancholy Sight:

Line 570. **Deluge**: the biblical flood.

There Trees lay scatter'd, all defil'd with Mud,
And finny Monsters flounc'd where spacious Cities stood:
The Ground with Heaps of Bones was cover'd o'er,
They ev'ry where found something to deplore:
Long on the sad Catastrophe they gaz'd,
  At once afflicted, and amaz'd;
And the vindictive Justice of their God rever'd,
That Justice, which so dreadfully appear'd.
At length embolden'd, and the Earth grown dry,
They from th'inhospitable Heights descend;
Th' aerial Kind disperse themselves around,
  Their Steps the Flocks and Herds attend,
And seek their Food upon the slimy Ground,
The slimy Ground cou'd not their Wants supply;
Indulgent Nature pity'd their Distress,
And did the Fields with useful Herbage bless:
But Men, unhappy Men, were forc'd to toil,
To plough, to sow, and cultivate the Soil:
  The stubborn Earth without their Care,
Nor Fruits, nor Corn, nor the rich Vine would bear:
They to their Labour their Subsistance ow'd,
And all their Plenty on themselves bestow'd.

27.

We, the curst Off-spring of that wandring Race,
Are still condemn'd to this unhappy Place;
This Earth, where we with Tears are usher'd in,
And where our Griefs, do with our Years begin;
Where, without Labour, we can nothing gain,
And where the Purchase equals not the Pain;
Who wou'd with so much Toil th' Incumbrance
    Life maintain?
But we must live Probationers for Joy,
In noble Deeds our coming Hours employ;
That, when from this bad World releas'd by Fate,
We may be re-admitted to that glorious State,
Where our pure Souls possess'd supreme Delight,

And liv'd within the Verge of everlasting Light.
What, ye blest Spirits, what cou'd you excite
To leave your radiant Seats above?
Could mortal Bodies such Attractives prove?
Was Happiness grown your Disease?
Or were you surfeited with Ease?
O dreadful Lapse! O fatal Change!
Must you, who thro' the higher Orbs could range,
Survey the beauteous Worlds above,
And there adore the Source of Love,
Be here confin'd to Lumps of Clay,
To darksom Cells, remote from your Ætherial Day?
On this vain Theatre of Noise and Strife,
Must you be forc'd to act the Farce of Life:
Our Souls, Good God, to their first Bliss restore,
And let them actuate dull Flesh no more.

28.

'Tis granted; Hark! I hear the Trumpet sound,
The mighty Voice dilates it self around,
And in its Clangor ev'ry lesser Noise is drown'd.
He comes! he comes! with a refining Fire,
The Clouds before him awfully retire:
The parting Skies with haste give way
And show to trembling Men the bright eternal Day:
Lightning and Thunder on his Triumph wait,
With all the fiery Ministers of Fate:
Ten thousand Meteors roll along the Air;
Hot Exhalations waste their Fury there:
And burning Mountains send their Flames on high;
Swift as our Thoughts the scorching Mischiefs fly:
Mixt with thick Smoak the threatning Terrors rise,
And fill with sooty Atoms the dark gloomy Skies:
The Earth does shake, by fierce Convulsions rent,

Line 635. **Attractives**: attractions. Line 648. **Trumpet sound**: announcing the Apocalypse.
Line 650. **Clangor**: a loud, shrill sound.

And searching Fires to ev'ry Part are sent.
Hark! how the troubled Sea does roar!
Its scalding Waters beat against the Shore:
The Fishes leave their oozy Bed;
With Haste they swim to Land,
But find no Rest upon the burning Sand:
Both Land and Water equally they dread,
And on the glowing Beach in mighty Sholes lie dead.
The feather'd Kind forsake their lofty Heights,
And from the sultry Regions of the Air,
By speedy Flights
For Refuge to the Earth repair,
Where, with sing'd Wings they gasping lie;
The lowing Herds fall panting by,
And Beasts of Prey with strugling Fury die.
The brute Creation one great Holocaust is made,
And altogether on the burning Altar laid.

29.

By flaming Horrors ev'ry where pursu'd,
From Place to Place, poor frighted Mortals run;
Where e'er they go, their Danger is renew'd,
They can't the swift Destruction shun:
Tortur'd with Heat they fainting fall,
And cast despairing Glances round;
The Children on their Parents call;
The wretched Parents sighing lie,
And see their tender Off-spring die:
With loud Complaints they fill the Air;
The heav'nly Vault returns the Sound,
And spreads the mournful Accents round:
In vain they groan, in vain they cry,
In vain their Screeches pierce the Sky,
Alas! no Help, no Aid is nigh:
The common Vengeance all must share,
And with the Earth, the fiery Trial bear;
Both rich, and poor, must leave their mingl'd Ashes there.

30.

See! see! she's now a Sea of Fire,
A vast enormous Blaze!
The neighb'ring Worlds the Prodigy admire,
And on the new-form'd Glory gaze:
The Fire has all her Dross calcin'd,
Ev'ry Part is now refin'd:
Justice appeas'd, to Love gives way,
Love will once more its Pow'r display,
And the Foundations of a second Fabrick lay.
'Tis done! 'tis done! an Earth does rise,
Encompas'd round with purer Skies;
An Earth, much better than the first,
Than that, which for our sake was curst:
Much more beauteous, much more fine,
Much more of Skill Divine
Does in the charming Texture shine:
No inequalities of Air,
No noxious Vapors govern there;
The brighten'd Skies unclouded Lustre wear.

31.

There Plenty spreads her Wings around,
And broods upon the fertile Ground:
Without Expence, or Toil, or Care,
The fruitful Ground does all things bear:
It has an unexhausted Store;
The greedy cannot wish for more:
Sparkling Gems, and golden Oar,
Useful Corn, and gen'rous Wine,
Woods of Cedar, Oak, and Pine,
And lofty Groves for ever green,
With Beds of fragrant Flow'rs between;
Pure chrystal Springs, sweet cooling Streams,
Such as were once the Poets Themes.

Line 703. **calcin'd**: reduced to a powder through fire.

See! see! melodious Birds are there;
They please the Eye, and charm the Ear;
And inoffensive Beasts their Pleasure mind,
Neither for Labour, nor for Food design'd:
They do not on each other prey,
But new, and better Laws obey;
Both Lambs and Lions there together play.

32.

O ye celestial Race!
By Providence design'd,
The blest Possessors of this happy Place,
You who like us did earthy Bodies wear,
Like us did human Frailties share,
And all the painful Ills of ling'ring Life did bear:
But now to nobler Posts consign'd,
Have left your cumbrous Flesh behind;
And now are cloth'd with radiant Light,
With Bodies active, pure, and bright;
Admire and praise that wondrous Love
Which has for you such Joys in Store:
When landed on that glorious Shore,
You'll think of your past Griefs no more:
Divine Munificence will prove
The blest Employment of your happy Hours,
And still exert your most exalted Pow'rs.

33.

No more with Trifles you'll be then in Love,
No more your former vain Pursuits approve:
No more endeavour to be rich and great;
And to your Cares a Prey,
In anxious Thoughts employ the Night,
And in Fatigues the Day:
No more such needless Toils repeat;
No more in Luxury delight:
No more be wretched by your Passions made,

Nor by your Appetites betray'd:
From all your Follies you'll abstain,
No more penurious be, nor vain,
Nor will you ever more complain:
Your former Pleasures will insipid prove,
No more than Dreams your waken'd Reason move;
New Objects wholly will ingross your Love:
Objects of which we can't Ideas frame,
And Joys, for which we cannot find a Name.

34.

Such Joys as here from Contemplation spring;
That best, that noblest Pleasure of the Mind,
Which keeps the Soul upon the Wing,
And will not be to any Place confin'd;
But range at large, as unrestrain'd as Thought, or Wind.
To you Delights 'twill ever yield:
'Twill lead you into Nature's boundless Field;
To you her various Beauties shew,
And let you her *Arcanum* view:
The Scenes of Providence display,
Before you all the Machines lay;
The whole Oeconomy Divine,
Where Art does in Perfection shine,
And where amaz'd you'll find
Wisdom and Goodness, with Almighty Pow'r combin'd:
Shew you the past Occurrences of Time,
From Natures Birth, to her Decay,
From the rude *Chaos*, to that last concluding Day,
Which sweeps both Men and all their vast Designs away:
Sights such as these, so wondrous, and sublime,
Will highest Transports raise,
And prove fit Matter for eternal Praise.

Line 766. **penurious**: miserly. Line 781. **Arcanum**: hidden knowledge or secrets.

35.

There, with each other you'll with Joy converse,
And all the Warmth of sacred Love express:
Each Breast will with a holy Ardor flame,
Your Souls unite, and ever be the same:
Without Reserve, without Disguise you'll live,
No Artifice, no sep'rate Int'rest know;
You Heart for Heart will freely give,
And pay the Kindness which you owe.
That Friendship which from Virtue springs,
Immortal as its Cause does prove;
With it, Ten thousand Joys it brings,
Such Joys as Death cannot remove:
They will beyond the Grave remain,
And solace us above;
Where, for the Good we lov'd below,
We our Affection shall retain;
Which still to greater Heights shall rise,
Shall still more fervent grow,
And like the Glory of the Skies,
Shall no Decay, no Diminution know.

36.

Ye lofty Mountains whose aspiring Heights
Stop rising Vapors in their airy Flights;
Where when condens'd, from thence they flow,
And water all the Plains below.
To you, the mightiest Rivers owe their Birth,
And the most precious Treasures of the Earth:
Silver, and Gold, those Darlings of Mankind,
We in your wealthy Bowels find:
On us, you Copper, Iron, Lead and Tin bestow,
And there, both shining Gems, and useful Min'rals grow.
When from your airy Tops we look around,
On ev'ry side are pleasing Objects found,
Yonder, large Plains their verdant Beauties show,
And there, with noisie haste resistless Torrents flow:

Here, various Animals, and Herbs invite,
There, Towns we see, here Forests yield Delight,
And there, the mighty Ocean bounds our Sight.
As high above the Clouds your Heads you raise,
The wondrous Pow'r of your Creator praise;
Let thund'ring Blasts spread the loud Accents round,
And let each Hill return the joyful Sound.

37.

Ye lovely Greens, who cloath the Earth,
And to the Sun, and Moisture owe your Birth:
All you that are for use design'd,
The Pride of Meadows, where the bleating Cattle find
Enough their Hunger to suffice,
And still are blest with fresh Supplies:
Ye tender Herbs, who beauteous Flow'rs produce,
And ye, enrich'd with balmy Juice,
Who are with healing Virtues blest,
And you who for Delight were made,
For Ornament, or Shade,
With all th' odoriferous Kind:
To Heav'n from whence your Beauties came,
Your Thanks in pure *Effluviums* send;
Thither let all your Praises be addrest;
In plenteous Steams let them ascend,
And with an eager Swiftness fly
Thro' the soft yielding Skie.
Ye towring Trees, do you the same;
You, that with verdant Honours crown'd
Cast your wide spreading Branches round,
And from the Sun's too fervent Heat
Afford a welcom cool Retreat.
O ye lov'd Groves! my early dear Delight!
You to a thousand Joys invite:

Line 849. **Effluviums:** flowing streams of invisible particles.

Joys known but to a thoughtful Mind,
Which can within true Satisfaction find;
And needs no Foreign Help to make it blest,
But all-sufficient in its self can rest.

38.

Come all ye Fountains your due Tribute pay,
And let each River as it rolls along;
The universal Call obey,
And with the whole Creation join in one harmonious Song:
Thro' all the bright Expanse above,
The boundless Theatre of Love,
Let the melodious Noise resound,
And spread the grateful Transports round:
Let Nature too her Homage pay
In ev'ry charming Lay.
Hear, O ye Seas! th' inviting Sound,
Let all your boistrous Roarings cease,
And let your watry Subjects taste the Sweets of Peace.
See! they attend! a sacred Silence reigns,
And Quiet sits triumphant on the liquid Plains.
Ye list'ning Waves, with a low murm'ring Voice,
Express your Thanks, and with the rest rejoice:
With you we'll join, and the great Subject raise:
Almighty Goodness claims the highest Praise.

39.

Ye Monarchs of the finny Race,
Who in the Northern Seas delight;
Where your huge Bodies fill a mighty Space,
And show like living Islands to the wond'ring Sight;
As you your Heads above the Waters raise,
Speak by your Gestures your Creator's Praise:
With you let ev'ry lesser Fish combine;
Such as in scaly Armour shine,

Line 884. **Monarchs of the finny Race**: whales.

With those that near the Surface play,
And to the pleas'd Spectator's Sight,
Their beauteous Forms, and glitt'ring Finns display;
All such as in the Depths delight,
And thro' the weedy Lab'rinths stray;
Those who themselves in muddy Coverts hide,
And such as in strong pearly Shells reside;
With those that in the Rivers live,
Far distant from th' incroaching Tide;
Let all by Signs their Plaudits give;
Before his Throne their mute Devotion lay,
And, as they can, their silent Adoration pay.

40.

Ye pretty Rangers of the Air,
Who, unconfin'd, can at your Pleasure fly
Thro' the wide Regions of the lower Sky:
And in pursuit of fresh Delight,
Or weary'd with your towring Flight,
Can to the Earth with Ease repair,
And feed on tempting Viands there;
And thence to silent Groves retire,
Where, undisturb'd, you sit and sing,
And welcom back the flow'ry Spring;
Or at the Summer's Warmth rejoice;
That Warmth, to which you owe the Fire
Which does harmonious Strains inspire.
Well-pleas'd with your delightful Choice,
From Bough to Bough you warbling fly;
While neighb'ring Hills return the Voice,
And to each charming Note reply.
As thus your happy Minutes glide along,
To Heav'n melodious Off'rings pay:
With you an equal Share
Let the whole Species bear;

Line 910. **Viands**: foods.

The wild and tame, the beauteous, swift and strong;
Let all contribute to the Song:
And each in his peculiar way
To Heav'ns eternal King,
With cheerful Haste his vocal Tribute bring.

41.

Come all ye Beasts, your Homage pay,
You of the fierce devouring Kind,
Who chiefly live on Prey;
And all the Night intent on Spoil,
Range up and down with restless Toil,
Where if by chance you wretched Trav'lers find,
Who are by Fate your Prey design'd,
On them without Remorse you seize,
And with their Blood your craving Stomachs please;
But when returning Day
Has chas'd the dusky Shades away,
Back to your Dens with Fear you run,
At once pursuing Men, and hated Light to shun:
And you, whose Innocence, and Use,
Keep you secure from all Abuse;
Ye harmless Flocks, who grace the Field,
And you, that milky Treasures yield:
All you that on the Mountains breed,
And you, that in the Vallies feed:
You, who on craggy Rocks reside,
And you, that in the Earth abide:
Let ev'ry individual Beast,
As well the largest, as the least,
Before their bounteous God rejoice,
And pay their Thanks with an united Voice.

42.

Ye Sons of Men, ye chosen Race
Whom God does with transcendent Favours grace:
You, who depend on his Almighty Pow'r,

And taste his Bounty ev'ry Hour;
Return those Thanks which are his Due,
And let the brutal Kind be all out-done by you:
Exert your Reason, ev'ry Thought improve,
And let your Faculties be all employ'd on Love:
That Love, to which our all we owe,
And which takes Pleasure freely to bestow.
When first this beauteous World was wrought,
While we existed but in Thought,
Love, even then our Good design'd,
Even then in ev'ry Part it shin'd:
Each Place had something to invite,
The whole was crouded with Delight.
The Air was calm, the balmy Spring
Did all its fragrant Treasures bring:
The Beasts rejoyc'd, and void of Strife,
Enjoy'd a pleasant, easie Life:
Sung the glad Birds, and all conspir'd
To make the Earth a Place desir'd,
A Paradise, that cou'd not be enough admir'd!

43.

When thus prepar'd, Love smiling came,
And did our happy Parents frame:
Beauteous they were as dawning Light,
Their Understandings clear and bright.
To you, said he, this Earth I give;
Amidst unnumber'd Pleasures live.
Prove but obedient, and your Bliss shall be
As lasting as my own Eternity.
He spoke; they listen'd to the joyful Sound,
Then cast their ravish'd Eyes around,
Where e'er they gaz'd, they some new Wonder found.
Ah! thoughtless Pair! how soon were you undone!
O cou'd you not the fatal Tempter shun!
Accursed Pride! thou Ruin of our Race,
Thou black Inhabitant of Hell,

How durst thou enter that forbidden Place,
And prompt them to rebel?
O 'twas the vain Desire of knowing more,
Of adding to your intellectual Store,
Which made both you, and all your wretched
Off-spring poor.

44.

Too late, alas! they their sad Change lament,
And to the Woods their fruitless Sorrows vent.
Its dire Effects their Guilt displays,
For Innocence once lost, Content no longer stays:
Pursu'd by Vengeance, of themselves afraid,
They were a Prey to ev'ry Terror made:
The Fear of Death, that unknown worst of Ills,
Their sad desponding Souls with black Ideas fills:
Where e'er they look'd, a dismal Horror reign'd,
And ev'ry Creature in its turn complain'd:
Full of Despair, they shun the hated Day,
And in dark Shades sigh their sad Hours away:
But they, alas! in vain retire;
Shades cannot hide from Wrath divine;
That all-consuming Fire
Will thro' the thickest Covert shine:
Nor subterranean Vaults, nor an *Egyptian* Night
Are Proof against the searching Rays of pure
Æthereal light.

45.

Offended Justice comes to try their Cause,
And from their close Recess the trembling Wretches draws.
Struck pale with Horror, self-condemn'd they stood,
And for themselves some vain Excuses made:
Deceiv'd they were by a pretended Good,
And all the Blame on the false Tempter laid:
The Judge incens'd, their Follies wou'd not hear,

The weak Results of Shame and Fear.
Their Wills were free, and they had Pow'r to chuse;
The Good they knew, and might the Ill refuse:
Felicity was theirs; and if they'd pleas'd
The glorious Treasure had been still their own;
They cou'd not be by Fraud, or Force disseiz'd:
Their Loss was owing to themselves alone:
Their Disobedience to the Law divine
Made Death, eternal Death, their Due:
In vain they at their Punishment repine,
Th' impartial Judge will no Compassion shew.
Their future Race with them must bear a Part,
Involv'd both in the Guilt, and in the Smart.

46.

Love look'd with Pity on their lost Estate,
And strove to mitigate their rig'rous Fate:
But its Attempts all unsuccessful prove.
Relentless Justice nought could move:
'Twas deaf to all the soft Remonstrances of Love.
When it in vain all other Ways had try'd,
It put on Flesh, and for the Guilty dy'd:
Offer'd it self in Sacrifice for All,
And did a willing Victim fall.
O wondrous Goodness! Kindness all Divine!
The God does in the bounteous Action shine!

47.

See, he appears! he leaves his glorious Throne!
Puts off his Robes of dazling Light
And all alone
He downward takes his Way
To Realms remote from his eternal Day!
Where all those splendors which our Eyes invite,
Are if compar'd to those above,

Line 1028. **disseiz'd**: wrongfully dispossessed.

Like Lunar Beams, or wandring Fires,
And all as mean, as transient Pleasures prove.
He comes! he comes! our Nature wears!
And all our sinless Frailties shares,
And all our Sorrows, all our Suff'rings bears!
Each Angel at the Sight admires,
And stooping low, with wondring Eyes,
Into th' awful Myst'ry pries.
Gaze on, gaze on, O holy Quire!
And as you gaze, his Praises sing;
Such wondrous Love you can't enough admire,
A Love which only cou'd from boundless Pity spring.

48.

But stay a while, your heav'nly Musick cease,
Behold a Scene your Wonder will increase:
A Scene, that wou'd, cou'd you be touch'd with Grief,
The deepest Sorrow in your Breasts excite,
A melancholy, an amazing Sight,
A Prodigy beyond Belief!
A God surrounded by insulting Foes,
And meekly yielding to their barb'rous Rage,
Condemn'd, despis'd, and scourg'd by those
For whose lov'd sakes he this hard Treatment chose!
With cruel Men, infernal Pow'rs engage,
And the Variety of Torments try:
No common Suff'rings can their Wrath asswage,
He must with complicated Tortures die.
View him! O view him on th' accursed Wood,
His tender Hands and Feet all stain'd with Blood,
Bending beneath an ignominious Fate,
The dire Result both of their Guilt and Hate.

49.

See, by his Cross, the Virgin Mother stands
With streaming Eyes, and lifted Hands:
Fixt on the mournful Object she appears,

And only speaks by Sighs and Tears.
Thou wondrous Pattern of maternal Love!
Cou'd Grief like thine no Pity move?
Such Sorrow might ev'n hungry Tigers charm,
And fierce *Barbarians* of their Wrath disarm:
But the more savage *Jews* were Strangers grown
To those soft Dictates Nature does inspire;
They did all tender Sentiments disown,
And were by Hellish Malice set on Fire:
But oh! our Sins strike deeper than their Rage,
And in their Cause, celestial Wrath ingage:
They pierc'd his Soul with Sorrows more intense,
Than ever since were felt by human Sense.
While thus he suffer'd, the condoling Sun
Withdrew his Light,
That he the dismal sight might shun;
Darkness, great as their Crimes, the World o'erspread,
And ev'ry Ray back to its Center fled.
While they are wondring at the sudden Night,
His dreadful Agonies increase,
Our Sins disturb'd his inward Peace:
With loud Complaints, and strong pathetick Cries,
He tow'rds his Father's Throne cast his expiring Eyes,
To him resigns his Soul, and full of Anguish dies.

50.

See! O thou holy Mourner! see!
Commiserating Nature joins with thee!
The trembling Earth resounds thy Moans,
And answers ev'ry Sigh with loud redoubl'd Groans:
The Beasts refuse their Meat, the Birds complain,
And with sad Notes fill each adjoining Plain;
The neighb'ring Hills return the mournful Sound,
And spread the melancholy Musick round:
The Rivers with condoling Murmurs flow,
And crystal Fountains Signs of Sadness show:
The Rocks are rent,

And the rough Soldiers wear
Th' unusual Badge of Sorrow and of Fear:
Full of Compassion each retires;
The moving Sight so vast Concern inspires.
All, but the cruel *Jews* relent;
Their harden'd Hearts cannot of Ill repent.

51.

The kind Redeemer in his Grave is laid;
For us he has a mighty Ransom paid,
And for our Sins full Satisfaction made.
With liveliest Colours in our Thoughts we'll paint
The buried Son, and the lamenting Saint;
By him she sits, with num'rous Woes opprest,
And wrings her Hands, and beats her snowy Breast:
With Sorrows, such as she ne'er felt before,
And Floods of Tears, she does her Loss deplore;
Fain wou'd she speak, but Words can find no way,
She must the Motions of her Grief obey,
And only by her Sighs her Thoughts convey.
Those thronging Dolors which her Soul molest,
Are much too great to be exprest;
They can't in sad Complaints a Passage find;
By their Excess, unhappily confin'd,
They still remain within, the Burthen of her Mind.

52.

Oh! who can see the holiest of her Kind,
With humble Duty to her God resign'd,
Bear such Afflictions with a Patient Mind,
And not with conscious Shame
Their own ungovern'd Tempers blame?
Ah! blessed Virgin, let us learn from thee
To live from all our sinful Passions free:
Let us no more at Providence repine,

Line 1140. **Dolors:** sorrows.

But yield a calm Submission to the Will Divine:
Like thee all Injuries, all Losses bear,
And be contented when they're most severe.
Thy pious Grief succeding Times shall praise,
And to thy Honour lasting Trophies raise:
Where e'er thy Son extends his Heav'nly Laws,
And with his saving Precepts vicious Mortals awes;
Thy dear Remembrance ever shall remain,
And thou a mighty Veneration gain:
Thy blest Example shall our Pattern be,
We'll strive to live, to love, to grieve, like thee.

53.

Now cease to weep, thy Task of Grief is done;
Attend the Triumphs of thy conqu'ring Son:
He shall no longer in the Grave remain,
With Ease he breaks Death's adamantine Chain;
O'er it, and Hell, see him victorious rise,
And once again
Restore himself to thy desiring Eyes;
Make hake, make haste, with eager Raptures meet
Th' ascending God, and breath thy Transports at his Feet:
Make known thy Troubles, there thy Griefs repeat,
And let thy Joys, be like thy Sorrows, great.

54.

The holy Dead re-visit Earth again;
Those who whole Ages in their Graves had lain,
Awake from their long silent Night,
And croud to see the joyful Sight:
With them, the faithful Few on their dear Saviour gaze,
And lose their Reason in the blest Amaze:
With doubting Minds on his lov'd Face they look;
The welcom Vision strikes them with Surprize;
At once with Joy and Wonder strook,

Line 1167. **adamantine**: unyielding, made of the hardest substance.

They trembling stand, and disbelieve their Eyes;
Till his known Voice dispels their Fear,
That Voice, with Transports they were wont to hear
Go, my lov'd Followers, graciously he said,
Go, and the sinful World persuade;
I will my self your kind Endeavours aid:
First to the *Jews* my righteous Doctrines preach,
And then the Heathen Nation teach;
To them my sacred Laws make known,
I will by Miracles your Mission own:
Go, fearless on, and my Commands obey,
And slight those Dangers which obstruct your way.
Pursue those Paths which I have trod,
And boldly share the Suff'rings of your God:
Eternal Glory your Reward shall prove,
The dear-bought Purchase of your Master's Love.

55.

These charming Accents their glad Souls elate,
And reconcile them to their coming Fate;
To honour him who for their sakes had dy'd,
They Death, and its preceding Ills, defy'd:
Resolv'd they wou'd the cruel *Jews* oppose,
And preach Repentance to his barb'rous Foes:
They to remotest Countries dauntless go,
Thro' burning Sand, and chilling Snow:
No Pain, no Labour spare,
But ev'ry where
His sacred Truths declare:
Those sacred Truths which Souls refine,
And if they his Assistance have,
The most obdurate Sinners save.
While fill'd with Pleasure all Divine,
They gaz'd on the transporting Sight,
He his Blessing to them gave;
And then before their wond'ring Eyes
Return'd to his deserted Skies,

And re-assum'd his Regal State.
They saw him mount cloth'd with refulgent Light:
Th' incircling Air, made by Reflexion bright,
They saw with dazling Splendor shine.
And now above the Reach of Fate,
Beyond the narrow Verge of Time,
By his pleas'd Father's side he sits sublime;
With him ador'd, encompass'd round
With num'rous Crouds, who his due Praise resound:
There, he for ever will his Merits plead,
And with unweary'd Kindness intercede,
For such as here his just Commands obey,
And at his Feet their darling Int'rests lay.

56.

While the Disciples with attentive Eyes
Fixt their Regards on the resplendent Skies,
And view'd those distant Tracts of Light
Which their dear Lord had left behind,
Two glorious Forms appear'd before their Sight,
And with fresh Wonder fill'd each Mind:
Beauteous they were as new created Day,
And did resistless Charms display:
Ætherial Splendors compass'd them around,
And they with glitt'ring Beams were crown'd:
With wondrous Grace, and a majestick Air,
They to th'astonish'd List'ners said,
Why, O ye *Galileans*, stand ye gazing here,
By too much Love betray'd
To groundless Fear?
He is not lost, for whom you mourn;
You shall once more see him return:
From Heav'n he shall descend again
Attended by a pompous Train:
Myriads of Angels, than the Sun more bright,

Line 1220. **refulgent**: shining brightly, glittering.

Clad all in Robes of shining white,
Shall on his radiant Chariot wait,
Resounding trumpets shall proclaim his coming State,
While bending Clouds their glorious Weight disclose,
And show th'avenging God to his despairing Foes.

57.

That God whom they did once despise,
Shall then become the Terror of their Eyes:
With swiftest Haste they'll his dread Presence shun,
And to dark Caves, and closest Caverns run:
With deaf'ning Clamors to the Hills they'll call,
And wish the Mountains on their Heads wou'd fall;
Beneath the mighty Ruins they wou'd hide,
Or in unfathomable Depths abide:
As They with Horror, so the Good with Joy,
Shall on the bright Appearance gaze,
And meet their God with cheerful Songs of Praise:
He comes! he comes! exultingly they'll sing,
He comes the wicked to destroy!
Those long since dead, and those that yet remain,
He dooms! he dooms! to everlasting Pain:
But from each Land his suff'ring Saints will bring:
From their long Sleep his injur'd Servants wake;
They shall a Part of the resplendent Triumph make:
In pure, immortal Bodies they shall rise,
And mount, all-glorious mount the Skies:
Where free from Sin, from Pain, from Fear,
They shall the welcom *Euge* hear;
Well done, well done, shall their pleas'd Saviour say;
Come, and receive a Recompence from me;
You've been my Follo'wers in the rugged Way,
And now shall taste of my Felicity.
Go, these important Truths make known;
His Resurrection joyfully declare;
Not to the *Jews* alone;
Let the whole World in the glad Tidings share.

They said; and as a transient Flash of Light,
With Swiftness glances on Spectators Sight,
And in a moment mingles with the Air,
   And loses all its Splendor there;
Such was the quick Appearance, such the quick Remove,
Of those bright Forms, those Ministers of Love.

58.

Replete with Joy, by flaming Ardor sway'd,
The pleas'd Disciples their lov 'd Lord obey'd:
With prosp'rous Haste his holy Faith they spread,
And his Name restor'd the Sick, and raisd'd the Dead;
That awful Name from which the trembling Devils fled!
Th'opposing World they for his sake defy'd,
For him they liv'd, and in his Service dy'd.
Thrice blest are you who still obey his Voice,
And make this dang'rous Proof of Zeal your Choice:
Who, by a Love for your dear Lord inspir'd,
   And by diffusive Goodness fir'd,
Cross Seas unknown, thro' pathless Deserts go,
And no Concern for your own Safety show;
Intrepid, and untir'd, no Toils decline
   That may advance your great Design:
Contemning Dangers, still pursue your Way,
And far as the remotest Bounds of Day,
The glorious Ensign of your Suff'ring God display.

59.

   Let *Israel,* that distinguish'd Race,
   Those Darlings of almighty Love,
Whom Heav'n has bless'd with his peculiar Grace,
To their great Benefactor thankful prove:
   To him, who in their infant State,
   When they, expos'd and helpless, lay,
   To ev'ry threatning Ill a Prey:
   Obnoxious to the Storms of Fate,
   And their insulting Neighbours Hate,

Kept them from all approaching Harms
Secure, in his all-pow'rful Arms:
And who in their mature Estate,
When they *Egyptian* Fetters wore,
And cruel Pressures bore,
Then, even then, their Good design'd,
Midst all their Streights his Kindness shin'd,
And when resolv'd to set them free
By Methods All-divine,
He brought about his great Design;
And let the haughty Tyrant see,
That while he multiply'd their Pains,
And faster strove to tie their Chains,
He but his own Destruction wrought,
And on his Land a speedy Ruin brought.

60.

The fav'rite People safe remain'd,
While Plagues among his Subjects reign'd;
Such Plagues as with amazing Haste
Laid all his fruitful Country waste:
His fertile *Nile* with Blood made flow,
The sanguin Mischief thro' its Channels spread;
While from th' infectious Stench the poison'd Fishes fled,
And on the putrid Mud in noisom Heaps lay dead:
The Crocodiles their watry Haunts forsake,
And to the Land for Shelter go;
Where, all defil'd with Gore, they wall'wing lie,
And stretch'd at length, the bulky Monsters die:
The wretched Natives of these Ills partake;
Quite parch'd with Thirst, they all the Land survey'd,
Thro' ev'ry Field, and ev'ry Desart stray'd;
With wishing Eyes they search'd around,
But wholesom Streams they no where found:

Line 1323. **Egyptian Fetters**: reference to the Egyptian bondage of the Israelites.

Line 1340. **sanguin**: sanguine; bloody. Line 1342. **noisom**: noisome; fetid, disgusting.

In this Distress, upon their Gods they call;
Before their Shrines the fainting Suppliants fall:
They to their *Isis,* and *Osiris* cry'd,
But all in vain; their Wants were not supply'd.

61.

Frogs in vast Numbers from the Rivers came,
And with loud Crokings their Ascent proclaim:
With hideous Clamors they the Land invade,
The Temples fill'd, and in the Royal Chambers stay'd:
While on their loathsom Guests the People gaze,
Succeeding Wonders heighten their Amaze:
Dry earthy Particles prolifick prove,
Each animated Dust does move:
On Men and Beasts the eager Insects seise,
And with a bloody Feast their hungry Stomachs please:
These soon were follow'd by vast Swarms of Flies,
Which fill'd the Earth, and darken'd all the Skies;
In Triumph rode the Circuit of the Air,
And play'd, and wanton'd there,
And neither *Pharaoh,* nor his Gods revere.

62.

A deadly Ill does on their Cattle seise;
They faint, they sink, they yield to the Disease:
From th' unerring Shaft 'twere vain to fly,
They in the Fields, and at the Altars die:
The small Remain with grievous Boils were seis'd:
Nor were the harmless Beasts alone diseas'd;
With them th' infectious Ill their Masters share,
With them, the noisom Sickness bear:
As they were murm'ring at their Fate,
And cursing their abhorr'd Estate,
They saw new Plagues preparing in the Air,
Black dreadful Clouds were gath'ring there;

Line 1354. **Isis ... Osiris**: ancient Egyptian deities.

Loud Thunders roar, and forky Lightnings fly
With glaring Terror cross the darken'd Sky,
Vapors congeal'd, in mighty Hail descend,
And certain Ruin did its Fall attend:
Nor Men, nor Beasts its Fury cou'd avoid;
The Fields it spoil'd, and ev'ry Herb destroy'd;
The Trees it rob'd of all their native Green,
And nothing round their Roots but scatter'd Boughs
  were seen:
The frighted Peasants with Amazement strook,
With trembling Haste their rural Cares forsook,
To closest Caves, and sacred Vaults they fled,
And there, remain'd secure, among the happier dead.

63.

At all their Ills *Pharaoh* remain'd unmov'd,
His flinty Heart more hard than Marble prov'd:
He still resolv'd the *Hebrews* to detain;
  And for their sakes was plagu'd again:
With fatal Haste vast Flights of Locusts came.
  Their Prince, the suff'ring People blame;
And see with Grief, the quick Devourers shar'd,
That little which the Hail had spar'd.
Thick darkning Vapors from the Earth arise,
And with their clammy Atoms fill all th' ambient Skies;
So vast their Numbers, not one Ray of Light
Cou'd penetrate the Shades of that black horrid Night:
Three Days they sate hid from each other's view,
And all their Sighs, their Tears, their sad Complaints renew.
Highly provok'd by their obdurate King,
God did on them a greater Judgment bring:
While with soft Sleep they strove to calm their Grief,
And hop'd to find in Slumbers some Relief,
To ev'ry House he the Destroyer sent,
  And bid him all the First-born kill;
With Haste he on the dreadful Errand went,
  And did the dire Command fulfil:

Amaz'd, and griev'd the sad *Egyptians* rise,
And with shrill Screeches, and loud dismal Cries,
Proclaim their Loss, and to their King repair,
And beg he wou'd his mourning Subjects spare:
They saw impending Dangers threaten from on high,
And fear'd they shou'd like their dear Off-spring die:
With Horror struck, they their sad suit renew'd:
Mov'd by their Prayers he did at length relent;
And by their Sighs and Tears subdu'd,
From *Egypt* he the joyful *Hebrews* sent.

64.

Their great Preserver now their Guide became;
By Night he led them with a bright auspicious Flame;
By Day a Cloud did their Conductor prove,
Thus were they still the Care of his unweary'd Love.
Th' *Egyptian* Tyrant soon his Rage renew'd,
And with a num'rous Host the frighted *Jews* pursu'd:
On th' *Erythræan* Shore they trembling stay'd,
And thence the Sea, and their approaching Foes survey'd:
Inclos'd with Dangers, to their God they cry'd,
To him, who never yet his Aid deny'd:
When thus distrest, he bid the Sea retire;
Th' obsequious Sea with Haste obey'd,
And at an awful Distance stay'd,
While they were thro' its Depths from all their
Fears convey'd:
With joyful Speed amid the Shades of Night,
They follow'd their directing Fire,
And by its glorious Light,
View'd all the Wonders of the new-form'd Way,
And saw their God his mighty Pow'r display.
The rash *Egyptians* still their Steps pursu'd,
And thought they might be now with Ease subdu'd;

Line 1433. **Erythræan Shore**: the shore of the Red Sea, named after Hercules' son, Erythræum, who drowned there.

Onward they went, push'd forward by their Fate,
And saw no Danger till it was too late.

65.

When the safe Shore the *Israelites* had gain'd,
The Sea no longer was restrain'd,
But with tumultuous Haste its ancient Ground regain'd.
From Place to Place the lost Pursuers fled,
And vainly strove th' impetuous Waves to shun,
Each Path to some new Danger led,
They could not from surrounding Waters run:
Strugling and weary to their Gods they cry'd,
And full of Horror, and Confusion dy'd:
The joyful People, when returning Day
Had chas'd the melancholy Shades away,
Saw on the Shore the dead *Egyptians* lie,
With Arms and Horses scatter'd by;
Thick as Autumnal Leaves they lay,
To ev'ry rav'nous Bird, and ev'ry Beast a Prey.

66.

Those mighty Men, whom they so lately fear'd,
Now Objects of Contempt appear'd:
With Joy they gaz'd, and as they gaz'd, they sung;
The Heav'nly Arch with cheerful Accents rung:
With thankful Hearts they their Protector bless'd,
And in sweet moving Strains their Gratitude express'd.
Then forward march'd, by the same Kindness led,
Secur'd from Dangers, and divinely fed
With Angels Food, with pure celestial Bread:
Thus favour'd, they thro' trackless Desarts went,
Where from hard Rocks reviving Streams were sent:
Continu'd Mercies fill'd each circling Hour,
The rich Productions of unbounded Pow'r!
In vain against them warlike Nations rose,
In vain 'gainst them combine,
In vain their conqu'ring Arms oppose;

In vain was ev'ry deep Design:
Without Success, their Stratagems they try,
Without Success, to lawless Arts they fly:
In vain did *Moab* Altars raise,
In vain desir'd the Prophet's Aid,
In vain that he wou'd curse them pray'd:
In vain the Seer to curse the Blest essay'd:
An inward Force, a Pow'r Divine,
Turn'd his intended Curses into Praise:
Compell'd, their Triumphs he foretels,
Long on the hated Subject dwells.
Thus blest, and prosper'd by Almighty Love,
In sacred Pomp their Forces onward move;
And full of Glory, reach'd the happy Soil,
The kind Reward of their obedient Toil,
The promis'd *Canaan;* where, the fruitful Ground
Did with rich Nature's choicest Gifts abound,
And where, their Wishes were with full Fruition crown'd.

67.

Ye sacred Priests, who at the Altar wait,
And there, well-skill'd in Rites Divine,
His wondrous Passion celebrate,
In whom unprecedented Love did shine:
Extol his Name, enlarge upon his Praise,
And as it merits, the great Subject raise:
With Zeal, and Clearness, holy Truths relate;
And strive by Reason to convince the Mind:
Let useless Subtilties, those Tricks of Pride,
Those Masks that Ignorance does chuse
Her Sloth, and her Deformity to hide,
No Place in your Discourses find:
For solid Notions, banish empty Shews,
And in the noblest Cause your Rhet'rick use:

Line 1484. **Moab**: enemy of the Israelites, see 2 Kings 3.

No more in vain Disputes engage;
No more a War with diff'rent Parties wage,
But make it your whole Bus'ness to reform the Age:
With Vice alone the Combat try,
To vanquish that your Skill apply;
And with a Courage dauntless and sublime,
A Courage, worthy of your Faith, and you,
Exert your utmost Strength the *Hydra* to subdue.
Preach Justice to the Great, to such as climb
With guilty Haste the dang'rous Heights of Fame,
And wade thro' Blood to Grandeur and a Name.
Tell them a *Nemesis* Divine,
Does all the Actions of Mankind survey,
Sees each ambitious, each unjust Design;
And tho' Oppressors prosper for a while,
And Fortune seems on their Attempts to smile,
Yet in the last impartial Day,
God with eternal Vengeance will their Crimes repay.

68.

Tell those whose Bliss is to their Wealth confin'd,
Virtue's the greatest Treasure they can gain,
A Treasure which for ever will remain.
Persuade them with a bounteous Mind
To be to the deserving Needy Kind,
And like that God to whom they all things owe,
Their Riches freely to bestow.
Th' unthinking Proud unto themselves make known;
Tell them they've nothing they can call their own:
Those things they boast, may soon be snatch'd away,
They can't insure their Bliss for one short Moment's stay.
Wealth may be lost, and beauty will decay:
Titles are vain, and what they Honour call,

Line 1520. **Hydra**: many-headed monster killed by Hercules.

Line 1524. **Nemesis**: infernal deity, goddess of vengeance, rewarder of good and virtue.

Does often to the Share of the unworthy fall:
Inconstant Fortune blindly does bestow
Promiscuous Favours with a careless Hand;
  Sometimes she lifts the Mean on high,
And Sons of Earth again insult the Sky;
On the bright airy Heights of Pow'r they stand,
  Prais'd and ador'd by all below;
While such as merit Empires, live obscure,
And all th' Indignities of Fate endure.

69.

Persuade all such as of their Knowledge proud,
Cast scornful Glances on th' illiterate Croud,
To look within, and let each haughty Thought
Be to the Test of sober Reason brought:
  Tell them their Pride from Ign'rance flows,
  He's ever humblest who most knows:
  Those whose rich Souls are always bright,
Who live encompass'd round with intellectual Light,
Do in their Minds a thousand Errors see,
And seldom are from their own Censures free:
  Their Wisdom adds but to their Pain,
  And they by their Researches gain
Only uncertain Notices of Truth:
When they to outward Objects turn their Sight,
  They find them all involv'd in Night;
Like fleeting Shadows they escape their view:
If at th' Expence of Health, of Ease, and Youth,
  They the thin airy Forms pursue,
Themselves they tire with the long toilsom Race,
And lose at last the Phantoms which they chase:
The World of Learning none could yet explore;
The most laborious only coast it round the Shore;
View Creeks, and Bays, and distant Mountains see,
The rest is hid from Human Industry.

70.

Teach the luxurious with a noble Scorn
To look on all the glitt'ring Trifles here below:
Tell them they were for higher Bus'ness born,
And on their Minds should all their Thoughts bestow;
There all their Care, and all their Skill should show.
Tell them the Pomp of Life is but a Snare,
Riches, Temptations which they ought to fear,
Empire, a burthen few have Strength enough to bear.
The true, substantial Wealth is lodg'd within;
  'Tis there the brightest Gems are found:
Such as wou'd great and glorious Treasures win,
Treasures which theirs for ever will remain,
Must Piety and Wisdom strive to gain:
Those shining Ornaments which always prove
  Incentives to Respect and Love.
Virtue its Splendor ever will retain,
And Wisdom still an inward State maintain;
Still in the Soul with a Majestick Grandeur reign.
In vicious Minds they Admiration raise,
What they won't practice, they are forc'd to praise:
With gnawing Envy they their Triumphs view,
But dare not their malignant Rancor shew,
Nor undisguis'd the Dictates of their Spite pursue:
Like Birds obscene they shun th' offensive Light,
And hide themselves beneath the gloomy Veil of Night.
Thrice blest are they who're with interior Graces crown'd,
Whose Minds with rational Delights abound,
With Pleasures more delicious, more refin'd,
Than the voluptous can in their Enjoyments find;
Such Pleasures as ne'er yet regal'd their Sense,
Which Earth can't give, nor mightiest Kings dispence,
And whose Description far exceeds the Pow'r of Eloquence.

71.

To th' Intemperate, Abstinence commend,
Tell them what Mischiefs vicious Lives attend:
How soon Excesses will their Health destroy,
That chiefest Blessing here below;
That unexhausted Spring of Joy,
Without which, all things else inspid grow.
Tell them tho' now they kind Instructions slight,
And their unhappy Conduct praise;
Yet when they're to Diseases made a Prey,
They'll then for their retrieveless Follies mourn,
And in Repentance languish out each painful Day.
To please the Taste is but a mean Delight;
The Bliss of Beasts, and not of Men:
And all those Arts by which their Appetites they raise,
Are only finer, more compendious Ways
Destructive Poisons to convey.
How happy shou'd we be, if we agen
To the first rules of Living cou'd return,
By Nature, the best Tut'ress taught,
Her just and easie Laws obey,
Like those she on th' early Stage of Action brought?
Who to few Things their Wishes could confine,
On Herbs and Fruits contentedly cou'd dine;
To quench their Thirst of crystal Springs cou'd drink;
Pure crystal Springs the want of Wine supply'd:
No harmless Beast t'appease their Hunger dy'd.
From Bough to Bough Birds unmolested flew.
They sought no Pomp, no Delicacies knew
Nor Wealth admir'd,
That greatest Plague of Life;
Nor glorious Palaces desir'd;
But underneath some pleasant Shade,
Strangers to Toil, to Care and Strife,
Did sweetly sleep, or calmly think;

Line 1627. **Tut'ress**: female instructor.

To one another kind Discourses made,
With Cheerfulness their Consciences obey'd,
And to their God a joyful Homage paid.

72.

Temp'rance is still Companion of the Wise;
They only can those Snares avoid,
By which th' Imprudent are with so much Ease destroy'd:
They only taste those Pleasures which from Abstinence arise;
Those pure Delights, those Banquets of the Mind,
Which from enlighten'd Reason spring:
Reason, when from the Dregs of Sense refin'd,
From all those Steams, those darkning Vapors freed,
Which from Excess proceed;
When no thick Damps of Earth retard its Flight,
Or make it flag the Wing,
Will boldly soar on high,
Above the Atmosphere,
Where all is calm, and all is clear,
And there, at Pleasure fly,
Bless'd with a free, distinct, unclouded Sight
Of all those Glories which adorn the happy Realms of Light.
Our Faculties will all awake,
And each will sprightly grow,
Exert its Pow'r, and its whole Force will show:
Th' Imagination quick and active prove,
Thro' the whole Compass of created Nature rove:
Collect bright Images, from them Ideas make,
From ev'ry Object some new Hint will take,
And with them entertain the Mind,
And Bus'ness for the Understanding find:
The Understanding more sublime will grow,
We shall more accurately think, and much more fully know.

73.

To the Revengeful teach the gen'rous Way,
With Kindness, Inj'ries to repay:
Tell them 'tis great, and shews a noble Mind,
To pass Affronts regardless by,
And look on Contumelies with a careless Eye:
The brave an inward Firmness find;
They will not from their State descend:
Like Rocks they dare the Tide and Wind,
Themselves from ev'ry Storm defend.
Reproaches from the Earth like Vapors rise,
And fill with Noise the lower Skies.
But cannot to superior Regions fly:
They are above the Sphere of their Activity.
What we call Wrongs would not be so,
Nor the least Impression make,
Did we our selves not aid each Blow.
'Tis from Opinion we our Measures take;
And often rage, complain and weep
For things, which of themselves would no Offences prove,
Wou'd not our Indignation move,
If we but judg'd aright,
And view'd them in their true and proper Light.
Reason, did we its help desire,
Wou'd its Assistance lend;
Wou'd us impassive keep,
Or from Attacks defend:
With pious Sentiments wou'd us inspire,
Tell us 'tis glorious to forgive;
Bid us all angry Thoughts expel,
And by the best of Patterns live;
The suff'ring JESUS, who lov'd those so well,
From whom he did the utmost Scorn sustain,

Line 1678. **Contumelies**: disgraces, insolent rebukes.

By whom revil'd he liv'd, and was unpity'd slain,
That in th' extremest Agonies of Death,
He pray'd for them with his departing Breath.

74.

Thou blest Example of transcendent Love!
O may we in thy shining Footsteps move!
By thee instructed, to our Foes be kind;
With their Mistakes, their Frailties bear;
And with a mild commiserating Mind,
The guilty Sallies of their Passions see,
Yet keep our selves from the Contagion free:
Good, for their Evil let us still return,
And for their Sins, and Follies mourn:
Our selves to them by friendly Acts endear;
Not only make our Patience to appear,
But them with gen'rous Tenderness pursue,
To them repeated Favors shew,
With their Aversion thus a War maintain,
And not leave off, till we the Conquest gain;
Till all their Enmities and Quarrels cease,
And we enjoy the *Halcyon* Calms of Peace.

75.

Sincerity and Truth to this bad Age
With all your Rhet'rick recommend;
You cannot in a nobler Cause engage,
Nor more the Word befriend:
Tell false designing Men, 'tis much below
Th' exalted Creature Man, such little Tricks to show:
To fawn, deceive, and cringe, for sordid Ends,
For worthless Gold, or for the Bubble Fame,
For Grandeur, Pow'r, or for the Trifle call'd a Name.
Heroick Souls such Meannesses despise,

Line 1725. **Halcyon Calms**: a perfectly still and motionless state; dead still water, named for the myth of Alcyone and Ceyx.

They scorn to circumvent their greatest Enemies,
And wou'd much sooner die than once delude their Friend;
Honour and Conscience are to them more dear,
Than all the Gifts which Fortune can bestow,
Themselves they more than all the World revere,
Still to themselves the highest Def'rence pay,
And Reason as their Lord obey:
Unworthy Actions they disdain to do,
Are just to others, to themselves are true;
One uniform, direct, and steady Course pursue;
Intrepid and unmov'd still onward go,
And no concern for Censures, or Applauses show;
Desire no Gain, but what from Virtue springs,
Nor wish for any higher Praise, than what she brings.

76.

Thus to your Auditors their Duty shew,
Teach them their Passions to subdue,
To shun each Vice, and ev'ry Good pursue:
And that your Precepts may successful prove,
Practice those Virtues you wou'd have them love:
Strict blameless Lives, will more than Words, persuade;
We're by Examples chiefly sway'd:
Like beauteous Pictures they invite;
At once they fix, and entertain the Sight,
And yield us both Instruction and Delight.
Happy! O happy they
Who like the lucid Spring of Day,
At once both Life and Warmth convey;
Who to Mankind such pious Lessons give,
And universal Blessings live:
Their holy Labours due Rewards shall find,
And Wreaths of Glory their immortal Temples bind.

77.

Ye Servants of the Lord your Homage pay;
To your great Master thankful prove,
Before his Throne th' expected Tribute lay
Of Gratitude and Love:
Observe his Laws, and let each stubborn Thought
Be a Submission to his Precepts taught:
In your Discourses praise his holy Name,
And let your Actions at his Glory aim:
Since all that's yours you to his Bounty owe,
Be grateful, and your selves on him bestow,
No other Good, no other Joy, no other Bus'ness know.

78.

Ye holy Souls, who from your Bondage free,
Have reach'd th' inmost Mansions of the Skie,
And there, those dazling Glories see,
Which lie
Beyond the utmost Ken of a weak mortal Eye:
Adore his Goodness who has broke your Chains,
And put a Period to your Pains;
And gives you leave in Vehicles more fine,
More active, more divine,
To live at large in the soft balmy Air,
And feast on ev'ry Pleasure there;
Pleasures adapted to your nobler Taste,
And such as will not in th' Enjoyment waste,
How vastly diff'rent is your present State,
From that which you once liv'd below!
Here, Sickness did your Joys abate,
And Disappointments, Injuries and Fears,
Render'd uneasie your long tedious Years;
With Toil you gain'd that little you did know;
Laborious was the Task, and your Advances slow:
But now your Understandings are refin'd;
Your Reason strong, your Knowledge unconfin'd;

Vast is your Prospect, and enlarg'd your Sight,
At once you view this Earth, and all the Worlds of Light.

79.

But yet your Happiness is not compleat;
There are reserv'd for you Joys much more great;
Felicities proportion'd to a higher State:
To that blest State to which you shall ascend,
To that blest State which shall your Wandrings end:
Where you no more shall Revolutions see,
But live from Dangers, and Temptations free:
Whither in glorious Bodies you shall go;
Not such as you inform'd below;
But in immortal Bodies, which shall ever be
From Pains, from Death, and all Disorders free:
Which shall be Proof against th' Attacks of Fate,
Against th' Assaults of Envy and of Rage,
And all th' Efforts of dull deforming Age:
Whose Beauty still shall in its Bloom appear,
Which still Ten thousand Charms shall wear;
Like Suns shall ever, ever shine,
But be than Suns more bright, their Lustre all Divine:
With these lov'd Part'ners you shall ever stay,
And with the beatifick Vision blest,
Employ your everlasting Day
In Transports much too vast to be exprest;
In Pleasures which from boundless Goodness flow;
Which boundless Goodness only can bestow,
And which none but the blest Possessors of those
Regions know.

80.

Those happy Seats, where Love Divine
Does with refulgent Brightness shine:
Where, the great Suff'rer sits inthron'd,
And is with universal Plaudits own'd:

Where his blest Mother her Reward has found,
And by him stands, with beamy Glories crown'd:
Where, on their golden Harps rejoicing Angels play,
And in melodious Strains their pleasing Homage pay:
Where, ev'ry Object Extasies do's raise,
And where, with them, you'll sing your bounteous
Maker's Praise.
O blest Employment! O supreme Delight!
O wondrous Place! and O more wondrous Sight!

81.

Look, dearest Saviour, with a pitying Eye,
On those for whom thou didst with so much
Kindness die:
Raise our dull Souls above the Joys of Sense,
Above those Trifles Earth can give:
And when by Death we're summon'd hence,
Let us for ever in thy Presence live;
In thy lov'd Presence, where is all Delight,
All that can charm the Mind, or please the Sight,
All, all that can the most aspiring Soul invite:
And ye blest Spirits who have liv'd below,
And who our Miseries by your own Experience know,
Add your Requests, and beg that we may share
Your Pleasures, and with you immortal Glories wear;
Then we'll together join in Hymns of Praise,
Together Trophies to our dear Deliv'rer raise,
Together at his Feet our Joys make known,
And with one Voice his unexampl'd Kindness own.

82.

Ye holy Men, whose humble Hearts are free
From swelling Pride, and childish Vanity:
Who know your selves, and all those Arts despise,
Which others use, to make themselves thought wise:
Who own your Faults, and without Anger bear
Reproofs, and never think them too severe:

Who judge your selves, and still employ'd within,
Have neither Leisure, nor Desire,
To censure those with whom you live:
Their Failures, Pity in your Breasts inspire,
And you Allowances for human Frailties give:
The vicious you with Kindness strive to win,
And in the softest Language tell them of their Sin;
But while you their immoral Actions blame,
You with the nicest Care conceal their Shame,
Their Persons you esteem, and still preserve their Fame:
O praise that God from whom these Virtues flow;
Him, for your heav'nly Tempers bless;
Discharge some Part of that vast Debt you owe,
In fervent, and unweary'd Thankfulness.

83.

Ye *Jewish* Heroes, whose unshaken Zeal
Was Proof aginst the strong Efforts of Pow'r;
Who in that trying Hour,
When the *Assyrian* Monarch menac'd high,
And Death stood threatning by,
Would not your holy Faith conceal:
Before the Idol you refus'd to fall,
And wou'd not on the glorious Nothing call.
With noble Scorn you to the Tyrant spoke,
And did his utmost Rage provoke:
Seize them he cry'd, and let them feel that Pain,
And meet that Fate which they so much disdain:
Heat hotter yet the Furnace they despise,
And let its Flames with frightening Horror rise:
You dauntless saw the dire Command obey'd,
And by his mightiest Men were to the Fire convey'd,
By those, who with their Lives, for their Obedience pay'd.

Line 1876. **Jewish Heroes:** (Dan. 3:8–30) Shadrach, Meshach, and Abednego, the three young men who refused to worship a golden image of King Nebuchadnezzar, the king of Assyria.

84.

Safe in the burning Furnace you remain'd,
And walk'd unmov'd, and calmly there:
The Fire on your impassive Bodies gain'd
No more Advantage than on fluid Air:
The lambent Flames incircling Glories prov'd,
Round you the waving Splendors play'd;
And that th' admiring Croud might see
How much you were belov'd,
The God you serv'd, whose Laws you still obey'd,
Did to your Aid a glorious Angel send,
And bid him your Companion be:
Th' obsequious Minister of Light
Did from superior Joys descend,
And hither came your Triumphs to attend:
Th' astonish'd King beheld the dazling Sight,
And wonder'd at a Form so bright:
With eager'st Haste he call'd you from the Fire,
And did th' amazing Pow'r of your great God admire.

85.

O bless, for ever bless his holy Name,
From whom your wondrous Courage came:
That Courage, which was your Support
Amid the tempting Glories of a vicious Court:
Which kept you firm, when both the Great, and Wise,
Were by their Fear, to mean Submissions led;
You did ev'n then the Tyrant's Threats despise,
And brav'd those Dangers they so much did dread:
Life, on vile impious Terms you did refuse,
And, unconcern'd, did all your Honours lose:
Inclos'd with Terrors, you intrepid stood,
And durst amidst a guilty Croud be good.
Now you the Purchase of your Faith enjoy,
And in a State Divine,

Line 1897. **lambent**: flickering.

Among the blest Confessors shine,
In grateful Retributions all your Time employ:
Recount with Joy the Wonders wrought for you,
And with continu'd Zeal the pleasing Theme pursue;
His Favours to admiring Saints rehearse,
And cloth your Raptures in harmonious Verse;
With charming Numbers their Attention move,
And loudly sing the Triumphs of his Love.

86.

To God the Father let us Glory give,
Unto th' immortal King,
The great Original of all,
In whom we center, and in whom we live,
With never ceasing Ardor sing:
The Benefits which he bestows,
For constant Praises call,
A gen'rous Soul no higher Pleasure knows,
Than paying what he owes.
Let narrow Minds, let grov'ling Sons of Earth,
Stick to that Dirt from whence they have their Birth;
On glitt'ring Dust let them with Transports gaze,
And never their dull Eyes to nobler Objects raise:
While we by better Principles inspir'd,
Will learn to think aright;
And having a due Sense of things acquir'd,
To the all-bounteous Giver turn our Sight:
The distant Streams we'll pass regardless by,
And to the Source of Blessings swiftly fly,
There quench our Thirst, and then replete with Joy,
In Hallelujahs all our Hours employ.

87.

Th' eternal Son let all the World revere,
With his great Father let him equal Glory share:
And let us still, with thankful Hearts, retain
A grateful Sense of Favours past,
Long as our Lives, may the Remembrance last.
O Love, thou sweetest Passion of the Mind,
Thou gentlest Calmer of the Storms within,
Where didst thou ever find,
A kinder welcom, a more noble Seat,
Than in his Breast, who by Compassion led,
And by the tender'st Sentiments possest,
Left undesir'd, his everlasting Rest,
Left that bright Place, where Light Divine has spread
Its glitt'ring Beams around,
Where all that's charming, all that's good is found,
And where unutterable Joys abound:
Left it for us, when all deform'd with Sin,
And for our sakes with Patience did sustain
Th' intensest Sorrow, and the sharpest Pain.
O who, unmov'd, such Goodness can repeat!
Or who enough the dear Obliger praise!
Such wondrous Kindness a Return does claim,
And in us equal Flames should raise.
Of all the Virtues we can boast,
'Tis Gratitude becomes us most,
It gives a Grace, a Varnish to our Fame,
And adds a Splendor to the brightest Name.
But where, O where, can it a Subject find!
Like this among the Race of human Kind:
Who ever did such Obligations lay!
O let us strive the mighty Debt to pay:
Let meaner Objects now no more delight,
Nor lesser Favours entertain the Mind,
For to our Love he has a double Right,
Both by his Merit, and by being kind.

88.

To that blest Spirit who does us inspire
With every grateful, every good Desire,
Let us due Honour pay,
And with attentive Heed, and reverential Fear,
His holy Motions entertain,
And all his gentle Whispers hear:
Now he his Gifts in secret does convey;
On Minds prepar'd, like Morning Dews they fall;
Thro' unresisting Air they make their silent Way,
And unobserv'd, Admittance gain:
Not so of old th' Inspirer did descend;
Then wondrous Pomp his coming did attend;
With a loud rushing Sound amidst the faithful Few
The God his bright Appearance made,
And on each sacred Head the glorious Vision stay'd:
The num'rous Gazers trembl'd at the Sight,
An awful Horror seiz'd on all,
But 'twas a Horror mingl'd with Delight;
At once their Pleasure, and their fear they shew'd,
And with fixt Eyes the dazling Wonders view'd.

89.

But O, how great was their Surprize,
To what a Height did their Amazement rise,
When by the blest Apostles they were told
Important Truths till then unknown,
In Languages peculiarly their own!
Parthians and *Medes*, and those whose fruitful Land
Betwixt *Euphrates* and swift *Tygris* lies;
With those who heard the stormy *Euxine* roar;

Line 2014. **Parthians**: a race that lived south of the Caspian Sea and fought with the Romans; noted for their skill as archers. **Medes**: earliest inhabitants of Persia. **fruitful Land**: Babylonia.

Line 2016. **Euxine:** the Black Sea, the sea between Asia and Europe.

Natives of *Asia,* and *Pamphylia's* fertile Soil,
With such as dwelt nigh the *Ægean* Shore,
Near that fam'd Place, where *Ilium* stood of old,
And where, by flow'ry Banks, divine *Scamander* roll'd:
Egyptians, Cretans, and that warlike Race
Who liv'd in Tents amid the barren Sand;
With those who breath'd scorch'd *Lybia's* sultry Air,
Where fond of Toil,
And pleas'd with rural Care,
They dwelt secure; of Ease and Peace possest,
Envy'd by none, and with Contentment blest:
Inhabitants of *Rome,* that august Place,
That glorious Seat of independent Sway,
Which to the prostrate World gave Law,
And still does Sovereign Princes awe,
And the most haughty makes obey:
All these they taught; to each themselves addrest;
And with a sudden Elocution blest,
In ev'ry diff'rent Tongue, their flowing Notions drest.

90.

O let such glory still be given
To these eternal THREE,
This great united ONE,
By the Possessors both of Earth and Heav'n,
As was by Infant Nature pay'd
As soon as Time begun to be,
And God, no longer pleas'd to live alone,
His mighty Pow'r had shown,
And for his Honour noble Creatures made;
Creatures, design'd to celebrate his Fame,
To build immortal Trophies to his Name,
And make his Service their immediate Aim:
And such as is by all the grateful here,

Line 2017. **Pamphylia**: province of Asia Minor. Line 2019. **Ilium**: citadel of Troy.
Line 2020. **Scamander**: celebrated river of Troy, east of Mt. Ida.

And by the num'rous Hosts above,
Who think they never can enough revere
Amazing Goodness, and unbounded Love,
With Ardor pay'd in Strains Divine:
And such as shall, when Time shall be no more,
But vast Eternity, like some high swelling Flood,
Shall pass its long confining Shore,
Pass all those Banks which its Insults withstood;
And o'er the whole extend its mighty Sway,
And sweep both us, and all our towring Thoughts away,
The joyful Bus'ness prove
Of those blest Souls, who in the Realms of Light
Shall on the beatifick Vision gaze,
And then with Transports of Delight,
In one harmonious Song combine,
And in the noblest Flights of Love and Praise,
Employ with an unweary'd Zeal, their everlasting Days.

Line 2061. **beatifick:** blessed, holy.

Essays upon Several Subjects in Prose and Verse

{ 1710 }

TO HER ROYAL HIGHNESS THE PRINCESS SOPHIA,

Electress and Dutchess Dowager Of Brunswick

Madam,

The Greatness of your Birth, the Sublimity of your Station, the vast Extent of your Knowledge, and all those other shining Qualities which have rais'd you to an elevated Height, and given you an undisputed Title to the Respect and Wonder of Mankind; all this stops every Approach to your Royal Highness, and makes you to be view'd only at an awful Distance: But just Reflections on the inviting Sweetness of your Temper, the charming Humility of your Mind, and that condescending Goodness you are pleas'd to express on all Occasions, puts a pleasing Force on all to whom your Fame has reach'd, (and to whom has it not?) powerfully attracts them, and throws your Admirers with a delightful Trembling at your Royal Highness's Feet; where, together with my self, I beg Leave to lay the following Essays. Pardon the Presumption of this Address, and suffer your great Name to be their Protection from the Assaults of Malice and Envy, and a secure Refuge for their Author; who is, with the profoundest Veneration, and faithfullest Duty,

Madam, Your Royal Highness's most Humble and Devoted Servant,

Mary Chudleigh.

Title. **Her Royal Highness The Princess Sophia**: Sophia, electress of Hanover (1630–1714), the granddaughter of James I and mother of George I; she came from a family of extremely well educated women.

TO THE READER

That the Pleasures of the Mind are infinitely preferable to those of Sense, intellectual Delights, the Joys of Thought, and the Complacencies arising from a bright and inlarg'd Understanding, transcendently greater and more satisfactory than those of the Body, than those that owe their Original to the Animal Life, has, through all Ages, been an acknowledg'd Truth, a Truth that comes attended with all the convincing Evidences that can be desired, and will soon be found to be undeniably so by all such as will be at the Pains of making the Experiment.

Such as have been so happy as to have had a Taste of these Delights, a pleasing Relish of these internal Joys, have always been blest with an inward Satisfaction, an unexpressible Felicity; their Minds have been calm, easy, and intrepid, amidst the greatest Storms, the most deafning Hurricanes of Life, never ruffled by Passions, nor disturbed by the most threatning, the melancholiest Circumstances of Fortune. They have been long the dear, the favourite Companions of my solitary Hours, and while they are mine, I cannot only be contentedly, but even chearfully alone; they fill up all the Spaces, all the Intervals of Time, and make my Days slide joyfully along.

O what Pleasures, what transporting Joys do rational instructive Thoughts afford! What rich Treasures do they yield the Mind! What unexhausted Stores of Knowledge may be drawn from them! They leave no Vacancies, no room for dull insipid Trifles, debasing Impertinencies, nor any of those troublesome Reflexions which generally proceed from narrow groveling Souls, from Souls that have not learn'd to use their Faculties aright. Though I cannot boast of having mine improv'd, and must with Blushes own my Thoughts are infinitely inferior to multitudes of others; yet, mean as they are, to Me they prove delightful, are always welcome, they present me with new and useful Hints, with something that agreeably, as well as advantageously, entertains my Mind; the Notices they give me, I strive to improve by Writing; that firmly fixes what I know, deeply imprints the Truths I've learn'd.

The following *Essays* were the Products of my Retirement, some of the pleasing Opiates I made use of to lull my Mind to a delightful Rest, the ravishing Amusements of my leisure Hours, of my lonely Moments.

'Tis only to the *Ladies* I presume to present them; I am not so vain as to believe any thing of mine deserves the Notice of the *Men;* but perhaps some of my own Sex may have occasion for such Considerations as these; to them they may prove beneficial; they'll in 'em be perswaded to cultivate their Minds, to brighten and refine their Reason, and to render all their Passions subservient to its Dictates; they'll there be instructed by great Examples, read of several Men, and some Ladies, that have struggled with Pain, Poverty, Infamy, Death, and whatsoever else has been accounted dreadful among the Sufferings incident to Humanity, without being overcome, without losing their Resolution, or lessening their Patience; see them chearful and smiling amidst Misfortunes, submitting themselves with a decent Contentedness, with a becoming Resignation to the Allwise Disposal of their merciful Creator; they will there learn to be easy and Mistresses of themselves amidst Sicknesses, the Loss of Friends, Indignities, Calumnies, and all the other Accidents that attend Mortality; will there be told, that the greater the Difficulties are with which they encounter, the greater will be the Glory of the Conquest; and that when Death has put an end to their Conflicts, Virtue will remain victorious, and the Rewards of a Future-state abundantly compensate for all the Miseries of this.

I hope they will pardon the Incorrectness of my Stile: The Subjects of which I write are worthy of their Attention; 'tis those I recommend to them: Truth is valuable though she appears in a plain Dress; and I hope they will not slight her because she wants the Ornaments of Language: Politeness is not my Talent; it ought not to be expected from a Person who has liv'd almost wholly to her self, who has but seldom had the Opportunity of conversing with ingenious Company, which I remember Mr. *Dryden*, in the Preface to one of his *Miscellanies*, thinks to be necessary toward the gaining a Fineness of Stile; this being a Qualification I want, it cannot be suppos'd I should understand the Delicacies of Language, the Niceties of good writing; those things I leave to happier, more accurate Pens: My whole Design is to recommend Virtue, to perswade my Sex to improve their Understandings, to

---

Line 49. **Calumnies**: lies, slander.

Line 62. **Miscellanies**: collections of verse compiled by Dryden between 1684 and 1704 that included many of his translations of the classics.

prefer Wisdom before Beauty, good Sense before Wealth, and the Sovereignty of their Passions before the Empire of the World: I beg them to do me the Favour to believe one that speaks it from a long Experience, That a greater Delight, a more transporting Satisfaction, results from a pure well-regulated Soul, from a Consciousness of having done Things agreeable to Reason, suitable to the Dignity of ones Nature, than from the highest Gratifications of Sense, the most entertaining Gayeties of an unthinking Life.

Mr. *Lintott,* some time since, intending to Reprint my *Poems,* desir'd me to permit him to add to 'em a *Dialogue* I had in the Year 1700, written on a *Sermon* preach'd by Mr. *Sprint,* a Non-Conformist, at *Sherbourn* in *Dorsetshire:* I refusing, for several Reasons, to grant his Request, he, without my Knowledge, bought the Copy of the *Bookseller* who formerly Printed it, and, without my Consent, or once acquainting me with his Resolution, added it to the Second Edition of my *Poems:* and that which makes the Injury the greater, is, his having omitted both the *Epistle Dedicatory* and the *Preface;* by which means, he has left the *Reader* wholly in the Dark, and expos'd me to Censure. When 'twas first Printed I had Reason to complain, but not so much as now; then the *Dedication* was left intire, as I had written it; but the *Preface* so mangl'd, alter'd, and considerably shortned, that I hardly knew it to be my own: but it being then publish'd without a Name, I was the less concern'd: but since, notwithstanding the great Care I took to conceal it, 'tis known to be mine, I think my self obliged, in my own Defence, to take some notice of it. I had once Thoughts of Printing it again, together with the *Dedication* and *Preface;* but not being willing to trouble the World any further with what I always thought an inconsiderable Trifle, I judg'd it advisable to take this Opportunity to justify my self, that it may appear I am not so blame-worthy as I've been represented: 'Twas written with no other Design, but that innocent one of diverting some of my Friends; who, when they read it, were pleas'd to tell me they lik'd it, and desir'd me to Print it, which I should never have had the Vanity to have done, but in a Compliment to them. Sir *John Brute,* one of the chief Characters, was a Name borrow'd from a Play of Mr.

Line 76. **Mr. Lintott**: Bernard Lintot (1675–1736), well-known publisher of Pope, Steele, Gay, and Chudleigh.

Vanbrugh's, call'd *The Provok'd Wife*, and design'd as a Representative not only of all ill Husbands, but of all vicious Men in general. I would beg the Favour of all such as are willing to understand my *Poem*, to give themselves the Trouble of reading the *Sermon* which occasion'd it; part of it was answer'd in the *Preface*, and the whole paraphras'd in the *Dialogue:* Some Expressions I thought too harsh to be spoken by a Divine; for which Reason they are repeated by Sir *John Brute*, who, as I've already observ'd, is a complicated Character, a Person in whom are sum'd up all the disagreeable Qualities that are to be found among Mankind. I assure my Readers, there are no Reflections in it levell'd at any particular Persons besides the Author of the *Sermon;* him I only blame for his being too angry, for his not telling us our Duty in a softer, more engaging way: Address and good Manners render Reproofs a Kindness; but where they are wanting, Admonitions are always taken ill: As Truths of this sort ought never to be conceal'd from us, so they ought never to be told us with an indecent Warmth; a respectful Tenderness would be more becoming a Messenger of Peace, the Disciple of a humble, patient, meek, commiserating Saviour. The whole was design'd as a Satyr on Vice, and not, as some have maliciously reported, for an Invective on Marriage: None can have a higher Veneration for that sacred Union than my self; but give me leave to say, I think it ought to be a Union of Minds as well as of Persons and Fortunes; where it does not happen to be so, there is the greater Trial of Virtue, but never the less Obligation to Duty and Respect: We ought on all Occasions to do what becomes us, to have a Regard to the Dignity of our Nature, and the Rules of right Reason; and having govern'd our selves by the Dictates of Religion and Honour, to be contented with the secret Approbation of our own Consciences, without being made uneasy at the ill-grounded Reproaches of the talkative part of Mankind, who by their being for the generality unavoidably ignorant of our Circumstances, cannot be capacitated to become proper Judges of our Actions, and consequently their Censures are too often not only highly uncharitable, but false and injurious. I can with Truth affirm, that in whatever I have writ, I have had no other View, but the promoting of Virtue; I would perswade all my Acquaintance, particularly those of my own Sex, to be obedient to its Commands, and always to do such things as they may be able to reflect on with a rational Pleasure. If in any thing I've written, I've been so happy as in the least to contribute to the more regular Conduct of their Lives, I am satisfied, and shall the less regret the unkind Reflections of an ill-natur'd Age.

I fear the Clergy will accuse me of Irreligion for making Sir *John Brute* talk so irreverently of them: but, before they condemn me, I desire them to be so just as to consider, that 'tis not my own Thoughts I speak, but what it might be rationally suppos'd a Man of his vicious Character would say on such Occasions. The Poets are full of Examples of this kind, particularly *Milton;* he makes some of his Apostate Angels say blasphemous things of God, and yet the judicious part of Mankind have never blam'd him for it, because what they spoke was agreeable to their Nature, and expressive of their implacable Malice: 'Twould have been absurd in him to have made his Devils personate Saints: Characters ought to be exactly suited to the Persons they are design'd to represent; they are the Images of the Mind, and ought to be drawn to the Life.

In the latter part of the *Dialogue* I have spoken of such of the Clergy as are Persons of Learning, Good Sense, and Virtue, with all imaginable Respect; the same I've done in the Essay writ on *Avarice;* for which Reason I think it needless to make any farther Apology.

OF KNOWLEDGE
To the Ladies

When I look abroad into the World, and take a Survey of the Rational Nature, it grieves me to see what a vast Disproportion there is as to intellectual Endowments between the Men and Us: 'Tis a mortifying Prospect to see them exalted to such a tow'ring Height, rais'd so infinitely above the generality of our Sex. Some few indeed may vie with them, may shine bright in the Firmament of *Knowledge:* But what are they to the surrounding Splendors, to the Multitude of Lights? they are lost in the glorious Crowd, and cannot be retriev'd without a narrow Inspection, an attentive View! I wish I could perswade all, at least the greatest part of my Sex, those whose Circumstances do not necessarily oblige them to lower Cares, to put in for a Share, to enter their Claims, and not permit the Men any longer to monopolize the Perfections of the Mind, to ingross the Goods of the Understanding: I would not have them suffer themselves to be willingly dispossess'd of their Reason, and shut out of the Commonwealth of Learning: Neither would I have them so far impos'd on, as to be made to believe, that they are incapable of great Attainments. We have already given noble and undeniable Instances of the contrary, and can produce a long Catalogue of illustrious Names, can boast of *Ladies,* who have been as famous for their *Knowledge* as their *Vertue.*

When ancient *Greece* was for her Arts renown'd,
Was for her Learning and her Honour crown'd;
The *Men* alone did not the Glory share,
The *Muses* had their Female Votaries there.
Some *Women* all the Depths of *Knowledge* trac'd,
And were with ev'ry Science, ev'ry Virtue grac'd,
Their Understanding, like a Light Divine,
Did thro' their Lives with pleasing Splendor shine.
From thence the *Roman* Emulation grew,
Some *Ladies* there did the bright Tract pursue,

Line 13. **ingross:** engross, totally occupy, monopolize.

Made great Advances in the Paths of *Fame*,
And, rich in Learning, to her Temple came.
There a *Cornelia* did her Father grace,
The worthy Daughter of a Conqu'ring Race:
Not he more Glory cou'd from *Carthage* bring,
Than from her Pen, and from her Tongue did spring.
In other Countries we have Trophies rais'd;
The wise *Zenobia* can't enough be prais'd;
She famous, as her August *Tadmor,* grew,
Almost as much as its first Founder knew.
No guilty Passion e're her Glory stain'd,
She still with Justice and with Mildness reign'd,
And when inslav'd, she never once complain'd.
Still was the same in each Extreme of Fate,
Humble when high, and when depress'd sedate.
In latter Times a great Example's found,
A Cottage-Virtue for her Merit crown'd;
An *Athenais,* by her Learning led
To the bright Honours of a Royal Bed!
Admir'd, tho' poor, both for her Mind and Face,
In both you might surprizing Beauties trace:
But 'twas the First wise *Theodosius* gain'd,
Such Charms he lik'd, as still the same remain'd,
Which neither Age, nor Sickness, cou'd remove,
Which still would shine, still would attract his Love.
Italian Shores with Female Praise resound,
Amalasuntha there was suff'ring found;
A Lady blest by Nature and by Art:

Line 33. **Cornelia**: mother of the Gracchi, daughter of Scipio Africanus.

Line 38. **Zenobia**: Queen of Palmyra in Syria; she fought against the Romans and invaded Asia Minor and Egypt.

Line 39. **Tadmor**: also called Palmyra, Zenobia's stronghold.

Line 48. **Athenais**: another name for Eudocia (A.D. 400–460), the learned daughter of the philosopher Leontius. She married the Roman emperor Theodosius and left behind several literary works.

Line 52. **Theodosius**: Theodosius II (A.D. 401–50), emperor of Rome.

Line 57. **Amalasuntha**: Queen of the Ostrogoths in the 6th century A.D., who was celebrated for her learning; the man she elevated to rule with her, Theodahad, in some accounts her second husband, ordered her exiled and then killed because of her alliance with the Roman emperor Justinian.

She'd all the Treasures *Knowledge* could impart,
A Mind well furnish'd, and a gen'rous Heart.
But these, alas! could not a Husband move,
Could not perswade his barbarous Soul to love.
Her shining Qualities glar'd much too bright,
They shew'd those Vices he had hid in Night.
Provok'd, and blushing at the shameful View,
He at the guiltless Cause invenom'd Arrows threw.
Love fled, affrighted, from his Savage Breast,
A Place too cruel for so kind a Guest.
The gentle God to *Paphian* Shrines retir'd,
And there his Goddess Mother's Aid requir'd:
They join'd their Skill, their utmost Pow'r they try'd;
But he both them, and all their Arts defy'd,
Stood unconcern'd while his fair Princess dy'd,
By him destroy'd, who shou'd have sav'd her Life:
O Wretch! unworthy of so good a Wife:
Inhuman Prince, her Charms had Tygers mov'd,
She'd been for them, by fiercest Lions lov'd;
Thro' wildest Desarts might have safely stray'd,
And there been by the bestial World obey'd,
By none, but treacherous Man, have ever been betray'd.
Virtue's no Shield, it rather does expose;
The Bad are still the Good's inveterate Foes.
Merit in them does always Envy raise,
They hate the Persons they are forc'd to praise.

I could name several others, were I not afraid of tiring you; as *Anna Commena*, the Daughter of *Alexis*, Emperor of *Constantinople; Margaret* of *Valois; Jane*, Queen of *Navarre, Katherine* of *Portugal*, Dutchess of *Braganza,* and the famous *Anna-Maria Schuerman:* But I

Line 69. **The gentle God**: Cupid or Eros. **Paphian**: belonging to Venus.

Line 86. **Anna Commena**: (1083–1153), daughter of the Byzantine emperor Alexius I; she wrote the history of his reign in the *Alexiad*.

Line 87. **Margaret of Valois**: (1492–1549), queen of Navarre and author of the *Heptameron* (1558) and *Les marguerites* (1547). **Jane of Navarre**: Jeanne (d. 1304), wife of Philip IV of France, founded the college at Navarre. **Katherine ... Portugal**: Duchess Catherine of Braganza, wife of Charles II (1638–1705).

Line 88. **Anna–Maria Schuerman**: Anna Maria von Schurman (1607–78), pupil of Descartes and celebrated for her skill in languages; she wrote among other works *The Learned Maid* (1659).

think my self obliged to take notice, that our own Island has afforded us some great Examples; we have had a Queen *Jane*, a Queen *Elizabeth*, and a Queen *Mary*, besides some others of an inferior Degree, who have been admir'd for their Wit and Learning; and are now so happy as to be bless'd with a QUEEN, in whom the Graces of the former shine with an united Lustre. I cou'd name others, who move in a lower Sphere, and are, by all who have the Honour to know them, accounted the Living Ornaments of their Country; but I dare not do it, for fear of disobliging them, and offending that Modesty which compleats their Character, and adds a heightning Lustre to their other Virtues, all they desire is to approve themselves to their own Consciences, and the Good and Wise, the fewest, but the best Judges. As for Popular Applauses, they shun them as troublesome Vanities, and chuse rather to live to themselves, their Books, and their Thoughts, than to be fatigued with the nauseous Flatteries and insipid Impertinences of the Age.

Germany has now the Happiness of being bless'd with an Excellent Branch of the *Brittish* Line: *Hanover* can boast of a Princess who far outshines the most celebrated *Grecian* or *Roman* Ladies, and is Mistress of more Learning, more admirable Qualities, than all the *Zenobia's*, *Athenais's*, and *Amalasuntha's* of Antiquity.

In *France*, the Glory of our Sex displays it self afresh; we see our Honour revive in the famous Madam *d'Acier:* The Ladies there begin to assert their Rights, and are resolv'd the Salic Law shall not extend to their Minds, shall not obtrude it self on their Intellectuals.

Let us endeavour to improve those Faculties our kind Creator has given us, awaken our Understanding, and employ it about Subjects worthy of it. Would we but for some time withdraw our Eyes from out-

---

Line 90. **Queen Jane**: Lady Jane Gray (1537–54) was renowned for her skill in Greek and Latin and was queen for nine days. **Queen Elizabeth**: Elizabeth I (1553–1602).

Line 91. **Queen Mary**: Mary II (1662–94). Line 93. **QUEEN**: Queen Anne (1665–1714).

Line 105. **Hanover ... Princess**: Elizabeth, Princess Palatine (1618–80), sister of Sophia, a student of Descartes, to whom he dedicated his *Principles of Philosophy* (1637).

Line 110. **Madam d'Acier:** Anne Dacier (1651–1720), a classical scholar, translated numerous volumes including works of Sappho, Anacreon, Terence, and Homer's *Iliad* (1711) into French.

Line 111. **Salic Law**: fundamental law of France, by which females were excluded from succession to the crown.

ward Objects, and turn them inward, reflect seriously on our selves, pry into the secret Labyrinths, the shady, the obscure Recesses of our Souls, we should there find the *Embrio's* of Science, the first Rudiments of Virtue, the Beginnings of all useful *Knowledge;* and should hear the soft and gentle Whispers of Truth, which to every attentive List'ner, every humble Enquirer, will prove a happy Guide, a kind Director; and upon a nice Scrutiny, an exact Review, should find a Stock of our own sufficient to begin with, which, if well managed, will not fail of yielding us plentiful Returns. If to these Riches of our own we add Foreign Manufactures; if we chuse the best Books, the most instructive Conversations, and, by a due Recollection, digest and make our own, both what we read and what we hear, we shall make wonderful Progresses, and prodigiously encrease our Wealth. 'Tis commendable to be greedy of such Treasures: Avarice is here a Virtue: It becomes us to be covetous of every Minute, to employ every Moment to Advantage, and not permit our selves to be robb'd of any part of a short Life.

If at any time we happen to be unavoidably ingag'd in idle, trifling, unprofitable Company, among such as can talk of nothing but what is not worth the knowing, of the little mean concerns of the Animal Life, their Domestick Affairs, their Remarks upon others, their Extolling themselves, their Complaints, their Murmurs, and all their restless Inquietudes, or in other Words, with the various Efforts of their Passions, the Triumphs of their Vanity, and the numerous Instances of their Folly: Let us instead of censuring and despising them, retire into our own Breasts, and seriously ask our selves whether we are so Ignorant, so Partial, so full of Faults, so void of Judgment, and so deeply immers'd in Sense? And let us carefully endeavour to avoid those Rocks on which we see them split: Let their Complaints make us calm and resign'd, their Murmurs teach us to acquiese in the disposal of Providence, and their uneasinesses make us resolve at any rate to purchase an inward Serenity and Tranquility of Mind; their expressing so great a concern about their Houses, their Dresses, their Diversions, and all other merciless devourers of their Time, make us look back with Blushes on our own Remissness, on the sloathfulness of our Tempers, and the deplorable emptiness of our Minds, on those small Improvements we've made in Virtue, our slow advances in Knowledge, our inconsiderable progress in Learning, and the weak Attacks we have made on our Passions: and then with a hearty Sollicitude, a serious desire of being rightly inform'd, inquire of our selves and of our Friends, Whether we are not as troublesome to others as they are to us? Whether our Discourses are not as irrational as insignificant, and to as little purpose as those we blame? This is the Use we ought to make of what we see amiss in others. By doing thus, there will accrue some Advantage to us from every Occurence of Life; we shall be the better for every one we converse with, and extract Wisdom out of the greatest Instances of Folly. It will enable us to pass right Judgments on Things, show us the vast Difference there is between Opinion and Reason, give us a wonderful Strength and Liberty of Mind, a Vivacity and Clearness of Thought, and keep us continually on our Guard.

What I would advise my self and others in relation to a course of Study, should be to indeavour to get an insight into the useful Parts of Learning, and to attend more to Things, than Words. Let Languages be left to the Grammarians, and let the Rhetoricians contend about the niceties of Style; and while they are quarrelling about the Husk, the Shell, the superficial worthless Part, let us be sollicitous only for the Substance; be industriously striving to make such Things ours, as will prove real Accomplishments to our Minds, true and lasting Ornaments to our Souls. And such are the Knowledge of God, and our Selves: These are large and comprehensive Subjects: The First takes in the whole Creation, the full extent of Being; and by contemplating the Effects, we shall rise to the Cause, and as by considering that wonderful, that amazing Power, that inimitable Wisdom, that admirable Beauty, that transporting Harmony, and that immutable Order, which at first discover'd themselves in the formation of the Universe, and are still every where visible in it, we shall be led to their Divine Original, to the unexhausted Source, the Foundation of all Perfections. So by making a due Reflection on the Operations of our Minds, on the large extent of our intellectual Faculties, their several Offices, their distinct Employments, and their Superiority to each other; the activity of our Souls, the several Methods by which they move and exert themselves, and exercise their Dominion over our Bodies, we may attain to some competent Knowledge of what we are, and by degrees grow acquainted with our selves.

In order to the raising our Thoughts to such sublime Speculations, 'tis necessary that we should be able to form to our selves clear Ideas, should have right conceptions of those Things on which we contemplate, to the Attainment of which Logick will be requisite; 'twill teach us to think regularly, to reason justly, to distinguish between Truth and Falshood, Things that are Simple, and such as are Compounded; Things that are Contingent, from such as are Necessary. And something of Geometry will be useful to qualifie and prepare our Minds for the Contemplation of Truth, and for the profitable Reading of any Books: 'Twill enable us to fix our Thoughts, and give a check to that quickness of Imagination, which is seldom consistent with solidity of Judgment. Physicks ought to be our next Study, that will show us Nature, as she variously displays her self, as she manifests her self in material Objects, explains to us her surprizing *Phænomena*, instruct us heedfully to consider all her wonderful Productions, and trace infinite Wisdom and Power thro' the immense Space, from the Heights Above, to the Depths Below; from the glorious Orbs which roll over our Heads, to the minutest Insect that crawls under our Feet; discover to us Beauties which Art can never imitate, and which common Spectators do not observe. From the Consideration of those Divine Attributes which conspicuously shine in the visible Creation, we may ascend to the Metaphysicks, which is the Noblest, the most elevated Part of Science, that on which all the rest depend; it raises us above sensible Objects, advances us to Things purely Intellectual, and treats of Being, as abstracted from Matter: 'Twill perfect our Knowledge, and brighten our Reason; enable us to proceed in our researches after Truth, on steady and unerring Principles, and give us clearer and more distinct views of the adorable Excellencies of the Divine Nature. Geography will make us acquainted with the Earth we inhabit, will mark out its several Regions, and show us how one Part is divided from another either by Seas, Rivers, or Mountains; 'twill also be of use to abate our Pride, by representing to us how little and inconsiderable a Part our Globe is of the mighty Whole, and yet as despicably small as 'tis, it appears unmeasurably Great, if compar'd with that Point, that nothing on which we live.

To these let us joyn Moral Philosophy: That will in some measure teach us what we owe to God and our selves, will inform us how we

---

Line 192. **Things . . . Simple**: reference to Locke's distinction between "simple" and "complex" ideas, between ideas formed solely through sensory perception and those formed through reflection and combination.

may reduce our Knowledge into Practice, and live those Truths we have been learning: But these things we shall be best taught from the Sacred Volumes; our Blessed Saviour has exalted *Ethicks* to the sublimest height, and his admirable Sermon on the Mount, is the noblest, the exactest Model of Perfection. When we are tir'd with more intricate Studies, we may apply our selves to History, which that we may read with Advantage, we ought to have some insight in Chronology, and to render what we read the more Intelligible, 'as well as in order to its making a deeper Impression on our Memories, twill be best to understand something of Geography, and to have both the Ancient and Modern Maps before us of those Places to which our Books refer. History is a large Field, we shall there see wonderful turns of Fortune, surprizing Occurrences, and an amazing variety of Accidents, foolish Mortals labouring for Trifles, contending eagerly for things they would be much happier without; some curst in having their own Wishes, rais'd to the utmost height of Power and Grandeur, only to be thrown thence with the greater Obloquy and Contempt; others pleasing themselves with their Obscurity, and laughing at the Noise and Bustle that surrounds them. With such Amusements as these Poetry may claim a Place, and we may at our leasure Hours, be allow'd to entertain our selves with those Masters of Wit and Eloquence. There's something charming in Verse, something that strikes the Ear, moves the Soul, and ingages the Affection: 'Twas the first way of Writing, and in some Countries even older than Letters; It seems to be the voice of Infant Nature, of Nature in her early Bloom, in her first Native Sweetness: In it the Ancients spoke their Thoughts, convey'd their Laws, and deliver'd the severest Precepts of Morality: The People lik'd the Instructions which came attended with Delight, and as they heard them with Pleasure, so they retain'd them with Ease.

Such Sciences as I've been recommending to you, I know only so much as to make me bewail the want of them, they are like the Glories of the Sky, things I admire, but cannot reach: Were I to live over my Life again, I would make them my early Study; but I would have you exact in that wherein I'm deficient, Mistresses of those Excellencies to which I han't so much as a Pretence.

Line 239. **Obloquy**: abuse, derision, detraction.

I can this *Canaan* only view,
The Conquest is reserv'd for you:
From thence I've Samples only brought;
By you the Wonders must be wrought.
I'm much too weak for such a Toil,
Your's be the Glory, your's the Spoil:
Whilst I to *Pisgah's* Height retire,
See your Success, and pleas'd, expire.

But, notwithstanding my Ignorance, I will presume to say, that the Studies I've been mentioning, are all useful in their several kinds, and will so entirely take up our Time, that we shall have no idle Moments to throw away on Romances and Trifles of that Nature, which serve only to stuff the Memory, to fill it with extravagant Fancies, with false Notions of Love and Honour, to excite the Passions, soften and emasculate the Soul, and render it at once both vain and effeminate. Believe me, the reading of ingenious Books, and the accustoming your selves to reflect on what you read, will in a short time recompence all your Pains: Thinking will give you a brightness of Thought, a clearness and distinctness of Conception: You'll find your Minds fill'd with great, noble and delightful *Ideas*, with such rational and agreeable Sentiments, as will make you easie with your selves, pleas'd with your own Conversation, and chearful in the most retir'd Confinement, at the greatest distance from your Friends and Acquaintance, and render Solitude preferable to the most diverting Company. When you are alone, how transportingly pleasant will it be to take a view of the Universe, of the vast extent of created Nature, the not-to-be-number'd Emanations of exuberant Goodness? To contemplate the Superiour Regions, and their blest Inhabitants, those bright Intelligences who make the nearest approach to absolute Perfection, and are at once the most exalted, and the happiest Parts of the Creation; to survey all those solid Globes which swim in the fluid *Æther*, see vast Masses of fiery Matter whirl'd round their *Axis* with an amazing, an inconceivable Rapidity, and at the same time moving with them their respective Vortices, and attending Planets, to consider their Distances, and the several Circles they describe; and when dazl'd with an almost infinity of glorious Objects, to turn your Thoughts to Prospects no less wonderful, but

Line 264. **Pisgah**: the mountain from which Moses was permitted to see the Promised Land.

nearer to you, and more adequate to your Capacities, to the World you inhabit, and revolve in your Minds what you've read of it in General, and what of each Country in Particular, in reference to its Situation, People, Religion, Laws, Customs, Cities, Animals and Plants, whatever is remarkable in it, and peculiar to it: In a Word, all the admirable Productions of Nature, and the delightful Curiosities of Art.

What can be more diverting than this, what more entertaining to Rational Beings? And if 'tis so desirable, so improving, so unexpressibly delectable, why should it be conceal'd, made only the Entertainment of our Thoughts, the Companion of our Solitary Hours? why should it not be introduc'd into general Conversation? why should not an ingenious Discourse be more acceptable, than a tedious account of the Fashions? And why may we not speak with as good a grace of the Pyramids, as of a fine Manteau; of the Mausoleum, as the trimming of a Petticoat? And why should we be any more laugh'd at for talking of Pagods, than Head-dresses; or of the Hottantots, than of the Beaux? And would it not be to better purpose, to give an account of the ceremonious Behaviour of the *Chineses*, and the exact Civility of the *Italians*, than to entertain the Present, at the expence of the Absent, with the ill Shape of one Lady, the awkard Mien of another, the ungenteel Tone of a Third? And would it not be more Instructive, as well as more Innocent, to talk of the Victories of an *Alexander*, and of a *Cæsar*, of the Bravery and Courage of a *Boadicia*, or a *Zenobia*, than of the mean, pitiful Conquests of a Coquet, or the Amours of a Fop? Of the uncorrupted Manners of the Ancient *Romans*, of the admirable Government of the *Spartans*, of that happy Equality which was establish'd amongst them; their wonderful Temperance, Wisdom, contempt of Riches, and all the pompous vanities of Life; their universal love of Virtue, and solid Knowledge, than all the trifling Concerns of our Neighbours, the Management of their Families, the Faultiness of their Conduct, their Want of Sense, with a thousand other little Impertinences, which perhaps none of the Company are concern'd to know, and which, 'tis probable, are as far remov'd from Truth, as they are from Charity?

Line 306. **Manteau**: a woman's robe. Line 307. **Pagods**: pagodas, Chinese temples.

Line 308. **Hottantots**: South African natives. **Beaux**: dandies, fops.

Line 315. **Boadicia**: legendary queen of the Britains who led a revolt against the Romans.

Would not Time thus employ'd turn to a much better Account, than if it were parcell'd out between the *Glass* and the *Table*, the *Park* and the *Playhouse*, unnecessary *Visits* and expensive *Games*, those merciless Wasters of our little Stock, our small Pittance of Leisure? From what I've said, I would not have it thought I am an Enemy to any of those things; no, 'tis their Abuse only I wou'd prevent. Decency requires that we should take some Care of our Dress, and the Necessities of Nature oblige us to eat and drink; but then we must do it without a studied Luxury, without an unbecoming Application of Mind, without being Slaves to our Palates, and valuing our selves on the number and variety of our Dishes: Neither do I think it a Fault to go sometimes to the Play-house, or divert our selves at Cards, provided they do not engross too much of our Time, which is one of the chief Reasons of my cautioning you against the last; not but that I think there are others of almost an equal Weight, as their augmenting an avaritious Humour, and exciting our Passions, which we find by Experience they do in Persons that are not govern'd by their Reason: such as are, will not need to be advised by me, they being too fond of their Time to throw it away on Trifles; they know its Worth, and how to employ every Minute to Advantage. I expect to be censur'd for using this Freedom; but if I am, I shall not be concern'd at it any otherwise, than as I am misunderstood: I would have my Sex as Wise, as Knowing, and as Virtuous, as they are by Nature capable of being; and if I can, by my Advice, be so fortunate, as in the least to contribute to it, I shall think my self happy. To endeavour this is some degree of Service, and may deserve a favourable Interpretation.

OF PRIDE

Among the numerous Vices incident to Mankind, and in which they are unhappily immers'd, there is none they have a stronger Propensity to, and which they more willingly indulge, than *Pride*, and none for which they have a less Appearance of Reason. 'Tis strange that depending

---

Line 340. **avaritious:** avaricious, greedy.

Creatures, such as owe whatever they are Masters of to another, should be so vain, as to be proud of what they cannot call their own, and of which 'tis in the Power of Ten thousand Accidents to deprive them; and (which is yet more considerable) of that, which, supposing they could have a long and full Enjoyment of, yet it would neither add to their Happiness, nor their Merit, nor entitle them to the Esteem of Persons, whose Approbation is worth the desiring.

Beauty cannot bestow Desert, nor a great Estate Wisdom. A Man may be born to Honour, and yet a Fool; may be able to boast of his being sprung from illustrious Progenitors, from a long Race of Heroes, and yet prove the Disgrace of his Family; may have the Knack of getting Riches, of amassing vast Treasures, and yet be hardly able to speak common Sense; may be Master of several Languages, well read in ancient and modern Authors, and yet be a ridiculous Pedant; a great Politician, and not an honest Man; a polite Courtier, and yet a Stranger to Virtue; an accomplish'd Beau, without having so much Understanding as his Tailor, or *Valet-de-Chambre*.

Ladies may be nicely skill'd in Dressing, and admirable Managers of their Families, and yet despicably impertinent; neither able to speak nor think regularly, and as much unacquainted with the World as with themselves: They may indeed know the little Arts of Pleasing, the way of carrying on Intrigues; may be Mistresses of a modish Set of Compliments, of the nauseous Jargon of the Town; may be able to rail with a good Grace, be exactly well instructed in all that may tend to the Defamation of those they converse with, every way qualified for the momentous Business of a visiting Day, for making a Tour from one Drawing-Room to another, and yet wretchedly ignorant in all the necessary Parts of *Knowledge*, destitute of all the real Ornaments of the Mind, the true Imbellishments of the Understanding, of all that's either improving or instructing, of all that can render them amiable in the Sight of judicious and discerning Judges, of such as are too wise to be led by exterior Appearances, who pay no Respect to empty Pretenders, and will be so far from mistaking Clouds for *Juno's*, that instead of proving their Admirers, they will despise them for their Folly.

Line 37. **mistaking Clouds for Juno's**: in Roman myth, Juno was the queen of the gods and often used clouds as a vantage point from which to spy on her unfaithful husband, Jupiter.

For what can be more childish, what a greater Argument of Stupidity, than to be proud of a Face, of that which a Disease may quickly spoil, and over which Time must unavoidably triumph? Or, which is much worse, only perhaps of an adventitious Beauty of borrow'd Charms, a well-dress'd Head, and gaudy Cloaths; of Things which, allowing them to be praiseworthy, yet the Commendation belongs wholly to the Tirewoman, the Mercer, the Lace-man, and the Manteau-maker; or of having got into the Road of saying pretty taking Things, which pass for Wit with those who are on the same Level with themselves, and for which they expect to be applauded, tho' perhaps, on a strict Examination, there is nothing in it that deserves that Name, nothing in which a Parrot might not in a short time be as good a Proficient.

But were Mankind what they vainly fancy themselves to be, had they all those Perfections in reality, which they only possess in Dreams, as large Shares of the Goods of Fortune as they could desire, or their Avarice grasp, and as much Honour and Power as the most aspiring Ambition could wish for, yet they ought not on this account to set a higher Value on themselves, or be so weak as to expect it from others, nothing of this kind being in it self really estimable.

Would not that Man deserve to be laugh'd at, who should be proud of the Beauty of his Horse, of the Gilding of his Coach, or the Trimming of his Liveries? And are not all other external Things as foreign to him as these? If any thing would justify our Vanity, it would be the Indowments of the Mind, our having larger Shares than others of those Perfections which are the Glory of the rational Nature, more adequate Conceptions of Things, clearer and brighter Idea's, quicker and more penetrating Apprehensions, truer and more solid Judgments, more orderly and better regulated Thoughts. But if, instead of admiring our selves for being above others in intellectual Accomplishments, we did with a serious Attention reflect on the Narrowness of our Faculties, the small, the inconsiderable Proportions we have of those Abilities which are requisite towards the Attainment of those Sciences which enrich and enoble the Soul, how little (by reason of the Shortness of our Views) 'tis that we are capable of knowing, and of that little, that almost nothing, which lies within our Kenn; how ignorant we are, as being either too

Line 45. **Mercer:** one who sells fabrics. Line 73. **Kenn:** ken, knowledge, understanding.

slothful, or too much clogg'd with Earth, to raise our Eyes, and make farther Discoveries, methinks it should give a Check to our tow'ring Imaginations, damp the Wings of our *Pride*, and much lessen that good Opinion we are too apt to entertain of our selves.

But if, after having made these Reflections, we farther consider, that there being a Scale of Beings, which reaches from the first Cause to the most imperceptible Effect, from the infinite Creator to the smallest of his Productions, we have reason to believe, that as we see an innumerable Company of Beings below us, and each Species to be less perfect in its Kind, till they end in a Point, an indivisible Solid: so there are almost an infinite Number of Beings above us, who as much exceed us, as we do the minutest Insect, or the smallest Plant, and, in comparison of whom, the most elevated Genius's, the greatest Masters of Reason, the most illuminated and unweary'd Enquirers after Knowledge, are but Children, such as hardly deserve to be of the lowest Form in the School of Wisdom, we cannot but have contemptible Thoughts of our selves, cannot but blush at our own Arrogance, and look back with Shame on the several Instances of our Folly.

Methinks I see those bright Intelligences, those exalted Understandings, who by the Dignity of their Nature, are raised to sublime Stations, to the most intimate Union that created Minds can have with the Supream Good, viewing us with a scornful Smile, but with a Scorn that is mix'd with Pity. It moves them to Compassion to see poor wretched Mortals chusing Servitude, and hugging Chains; proud of Toys, and fond of Bubbles; drawing Fairy-Rounds, and courting Shaddows; boasting of Sight, yet blindly stumbling on, and tumbling headlong down from Precipice to Precipice, till they are lost in a retrieveless Depth; they, and their vain Designs, for ever hid in endless Night. Such is the Farce of Life, and such is the last concluding Scene: And can there be anything in Moments thus employ'd to authorize our *Pride?*

O let us rather sink into the Earth,
  Into that Dust from whence we came,
  And, mindful of our humble Birth,
  All unbecoming Thoughts disclaim.
As well may Flies their Exaltation boast,
    Because they in the Sun-beams play;
Because they feel the Warmth of each reviving Day,

Extend their Silken Wings, and o'er the flo'wry Meadows stray.
As well may Ants with a prepost'rous *Pride*
Their fellow Worms deride,
And fancy they, of all the Reptile Host,
Are the most diligent and wise;
Because with Toil and Care
They for contingent Wants prepare;
As Man be proud, whom nobler Forms despise
For that in which his greatest Glory lies;
His Fame, his Riches, and his pompous Train,
With all those Things which make th' aspiring Wretch so vain,
They view with Scorn, as being not design'd
To constitute the Bliss of humane Kind,
Or satisfie the impetuous Cravings of the Mind.

2.

Sure we should much more humble be,
If we our selves could see:
But few, alas! but few,
Can bear the sad, the melancholy View,
They with Disgust avoid the Sight,
And turn 'em from the searching Rays of Light,
More pleas'd to wander in the dusky Shades of Night:
Where only seen by Lunar Beams,
Which weakly glimmer on the Streams,
And but a faint Reflection yield
To ev'ry Grove, and ev'ry Field.
By that pale, that feeble Flame,
Which has of Light no more but Name;
They but like fleeting Phantoms show,
And nor themselves, nor others know;
In Ignorance immers'd, and pleas'd with being so.

3.

If Lambent Fires around their Temples blaze,
In Fancy's flatt'ring Glass they gaze,
And, fond of the transporting Sight,
Give way to Raptures of Delight.
Too fierce their Joys, too quick their Sense,
They cannot bear what's so intense:
No more they Reason's Laws obey,

No more regard what Truth does say:
But when th'enkindled Vapours cease to shine,
Then they sigh, and then repine;
As much they grieve, as they rejoyc'd before,
With Tears their vanish'd Splendors they deplore;
Till some false Fire again they view,
Till Hope bids them some distant Light pursue.
By it urg'd on, from Place to Place they run;
But still the nimble Flame do's its Pursuers shun:
Yet they th'unequal Chase renew,
Till tir'd and panting by delusive Streams,
They fainting sink, and only quench their Thirst in Dreams.

'Tis a great Truth which the Son of *Syrach* tells us, when he says, *That Pride was not made for Man.* Sure nothing can be more unbecoming a Creature, a Creature that had his Original from nothing, and who is every Moment sustain'd by an Almighty Power, and who as at first he could not give himself Life, nor any of the Enjoyments that attend it; so neither can he continue them one Minute: His Being, and all he falsly calls his own, depends on God, as the Light does on the Sun; and should he withdraw the Irradiations of his infinite Goodness, withhold his Divine Influence but for one single Now, he would necessarily and immediately sink into his first Nothing; and who, as he has a precarious Being, so he has a short and limited Prospect, is condemn'd to *Plato's* Cave, sees nothing but Shadows, takes Phantoms for Realities, and empty Sounds, reverberated Eccho's for rational Discourses: The Light is at a vast Distance behind him, and he is so stak'd to the Earth, so fasten'd down to the animal Life, that he cannot turn to it, can make no Discoveries, till he is releas'd by Death, freed by that happy Dissolvent from the Clog of Mortality, from those thick Mists in which he's invelop'd, from every thing that obscures his View, retards his Flight, and keeps him from ascending to the Region of Spirits, the intellectual World, the bright Field of Truth and Light.

Dart, O thou eternal Wisdom, some Rays of thy Divine Splendour

Line 160. **Son of Syrach**: one of the books of the Apocrypha, also known as Ecclesiasticus, which presents proverbial wisdom.

Lines 170–71. **Plato's Cave**: reference to the allegory of the cave found in Plato's *Republic*.

into my Soul, illuminate my Understanding, give me a Sight of my self, of my Imperfections, of all my Frailties, of the Dulness of my Apprehension, which, by its being too closely united to the Body, is fill'd with sensible Images, crowded with imaginary Appearances, like the first Matter, dark and full of Confusion, and hardly receptive of pure Idea's, of simple intellectual Truths; discover to me the Errors of my Judgment, the false Notions I have of Things, and the early Prejudices with which 'tis fetter'd, the Obscurity and Weakness of my Reason, the Incoherence and Disorder of my Thoughts, the Depravity of my Will, the Strength of my Passions, and my too close Adhesion to the Delights of Sense.

O that thou would'st be pleased to purifie and brighten my Imagination, make it strong and regular, fit to contemplate thy Divine Essence, and form becoming Idea's of thy adorable Attributes; Pardon the Failures of my Judgment, and give me a clearer View of Things; Inspire me with a Rectitude of Will, a Love of Order; strengthen my Reason, and give it the entire Sovereignty over my Passions: Take off my Affections from sensible Objects; let me have no Desires but for thy Self, no Aims but for thy Glory.

O let thy Goodness fill the whole Capacity of my Nature, let thy infinite Perfections employ my Thoughts, and exclude the little Concerns of Life, the momentary Pleasures of a deceitful World; but, above all things, imprint in me a reverential Awe of thy Divine Majesty, of the vast Disproportion that there is between Being it self and Nothing, between the Incomprehensible Creator and a poor weak finite Creature, between Wisdom and Ignorance.

O make me humble, and when I find any Temptation to Vanity, any Inclination to despise others, and put too high a Value on my self, to be proud of external Advantages, teach me to retire into my own Breast, to set a Guard on my Thoughts, to be very careful of my Words, nicely circumspect in my Actions, that nothing may be seen in the remaining Moments of my Life that's either derogatory to thy Honour, or unbecoming thy Creature.

Accursed *Pride* taught Angels to rebel,
Govern'd by That, immortal Spirits fell
From Heav'nly Seats, and Mansions all Divine,
Where they did with a spotless Brightness shine;

Where Light, as glorious as Meridian Day,
Did all around its lustrous Beams display,
And where Delights, for Mortals much too high,
Did them with unexhausted Joys supply,
They sunk to Realms of Darkness and Despair.
No Light but that of livid Flames was there;
A pale, a dismal, melancholy Sight:
All there was Horror, all did there affright,
And there they still must live, excluded from Delight.
This dang'rous Mischief I with Care will shun,
Will never be by haughty Thoughts undone.
My self I know, and by that Knowledge taught,
My Soul have to a humble Temper wrought.
Nothing that's mine shall proud Idea's raise;
Weak little Minds still fondest are of Praise.
'Tis want of Sense that does Mankind elate,
The Wise consider their dependant State;
How short their Views, how little 'tis they know,
By what slow steps thro' Nature's Labyrinth go,
Where, like mean worthless Worms, they to superior Beings show.

OF HUMILITY

Of all the Virtues which adorn the humane Nature, there is none more amiable than *Humility:* 'Tis the most charming Ornament of the Mind, that which gives the finishing Stroke to all its other Perfections; it invites the admiring Spectator, and joins Love with Veneration; while *Pride*, like the fiery Guardian of *Paradise*, keeps us at a Distance, and mixes Fear and Aversion with the Honours we pay the Great.

But 'tis highly advantageous to us on several other Accounts, besides that of the Service it does us in giving us a Title to the Affection of those we converse with: It makes us watchful over our selves, fences us against Flattery, furnishes us with a necessary Diffidence, a needful Circumspection, keeps us reserv'd and silent, modest and respectful, attentive to what is said, and willing to be instructed, makes us easie in Conversation, not apt to be passionate, dogmatical, or imposing, ever ready to submit to the Decision of Reason, and never better pleas'd, than when we make a Part of the Triumphs of Truth.

The humble Mind is still improving, always employ'd in discovering its Defects, and in filling up Vacancies; it sees its own Worthlesness, and blushes at it, feels every Malady, and endeavours to cure it; while the Proud are despising and censuring others, this is finding fault with it self. While they are rediculing Mankind, making uncharitable Reflections, malicious Remarks, ruining Reputations, misconstruing innocent Actions, making wrong Comments on Words, and magisterially dictating to all about them: This is nicely examining it self, making a narrow Scrutiny into every Intention, following the Soul into her most hidden Recesses, tracing her through all the Labyrinths of Thought, through all the intricate Mazes of the Understanding; and then passing an impartial Judgment on whatever it finds amiss: 'Tis always ready to acknowledge its Errors, to beg Pardon for its Faults, and still places Reproofs among the greatest Favours; is never tempted to envy the more Deserving, nor concern'd to see others more valued; is neither to be provok'd by Contradictions, nor inrag'd by Affronts; the first it can bear with Ease, because the Knowledge it has of its own Ignorance keeps it from being tenacious of its Sentiments, or too much bigotted to its own Notions; and the other it can sustain with Patience, support with a becoming Temper, because it assumes nothing to it self, lays no Claim to Praise. Now such a Disposition cannot but be infinitely desirable, as being the Source of an uninterrupted Serenity, and the Foundation on which the noblest and most beautiful Superstructures imaginable may be raised.

The tow'ring self-sufficient Mind
Hastily leaves the World behind;
Like *Icarus*, does soar too high,
Too near the melting Heat does fly:
It tempts the Dangers it should shun,
And by Presumption is undone:
While such as with a prudent Care,
By small Essays for Flight prepare;
Who raise themselves by slow Degrees,

First only perch upon the Trees,
Or on the Summit of some Hill,
E're they their great Designs fulfil,
There prune their Wings, and thence with Fear
Explore the dusky Atmosphere;
Which having done, they higher rise,
And trembling mount the upper Skies:
Then, more embolden'd, take their Way
Thro' purest Air to brightest Day,
May roam at large in Fields of Light,
And safely leave both Earth and Night.

Those who rise by such secure Steps, who mount gradually, who frequently try their Strength, often use and extend their Wings, and for some considerable time fly near the Ground, (where should they fail, their Fall would not be very hazardous) before they venture to soar aloft, will, by their Prudence and necessary Caution, be able to maintain their Station, to live in the Heights to which their Industry and Merit have elevated them, and will be so happy as to see themselves out of danger of being involv'd in the Misfortunes of the *Phaetons* of the World, who think themselves capable of driving the Chariot of the Sun, of ordering the Affairs of the Universe, of managing the great Machine of Nature, and were the admirable Frame now to be set together, wou'd, with the audacious *Alphonsus*, be so arrogant, as to presume to advise the Almighty Architect, and think themselves wise enough to assist him in the Government of the World. 'Tis wonderful that Men should be so little acquainted with themselves, be such Strangers to the Narrowness of their Faculties, to the Limitedness of their Understandings! But that which is most amazing is, that such as have the smallest Share of Sense, who are but one Remove from Idiots, should have a high Opinion of their Reason; that Blockheads should take themselves to be Wits, and Fools set up for Teachers of Wisdom.

Line 67. **Phaetons**: those who resemble Phaeton, the mythological son of Phœbus, the sun; Phaeton demanded to be allowed to drive his father's chariot.

Line 71. **Alphonsus**: Alphonso X of Castile (1221–84), known as "the Wise" for his contributions in law, science, and literature.

They whose Fire does dimly shine,
    In Smoke hid from themselves remain;
Their Heat cannot their Dross refine,
    Nor chase thick Vapours from their Brain:
They think they see, yet still are blind,
    Think they alone are blest with Sight.
This, for their Good, has Heav'n design'd,
    That they may still enjoy Delight:
For if it should the Vail remove,
    They quickly would themselves despise;
From Ignorance proceeds their Love,
    In that alone their Dotage lies.

Self-love and Ignorance please the generality of Mankind; they make the bitter Draught of Life go down; they not only quicken and exhilerate their Spirits, give a Relish to all their Enjoyments, but make them easie in every State, under every Circumstance: They support the poor Man, and comfort the Miserable, make the Great Man exult amidst ten thousand Cares, the haughty Courtier fawn and wheedle, the proud affected Fop, the empty tawdry Beau, the fantastick noisy Woman, pleas'd and satisfy'd with themselves; they keep the greatest part of the World in Humour, and are of as much Use to Fools, as Wisdom is to Men of Sense: For were their Eyes open, their Understandings enlighten'd, could they see themselves distinctly, view their Faces in Mirrours that would not flatter, they would blush at the comical Representation, and fancy they rather saw Monkeys playing Tricks, than Men acting rational Parts; rather a Company of Buffoons diverting a sensless Mob, than intelligent Beings, than Pretenders to Wisdom. Thus they appear to us, and thus we appear to them: Those we laugh at this Day, perhaps will laugh at us to Morrow; and those very Qualities we admire in our selves may render us despicable to others. Thus the Frolick goes round, and we scorn, and are scorn'd by Turns.

Now, should any body be so generous, as to endeavour to undeceive us, so kind as to tell us, that we have no reason to be so childishly fond of our selves, that we foolishly view our selves at the magnifying End of the Perspective, that we set too high a Value on our Possessions, on our Persons, our Acquirements, and the Endowments of our Minds, exalt Molehills into Mountains, think our selves Giants in Understanding, when we are but Pygmies in Sense; *Narcissus's* for Beauty, when perhaps we have no more Pretence to it than the *Thersites's* or the *Esops* of the Age, we should grow angry, so little are we able to bear the Language of Truth. Such obliging Reprovers would meet with *Socrates's* Fate they would make Enemies, engage the greatest part of Mankind against them. *Humility* is a solitary Virtue, few desire her Society, she palls their Joy, abates their Tumor, lowers their tow'ring Imagination, and gives them a mortifying Prospect of themselves: They praise her because they think it decent to do so, because 'tis for their Reputation; but they keep her at a Distance, will not make her an Inmate, will not treat her as a Friend, lest she should grow too familiar, should presume to unmask them, and by discovering them to themselves, rob them of the Satisfaction of fancying they have some Pretence for their Pride.

Had *Socrates* been unsollicitous about the Reason why *Apollo* pronounc'd him the wisest of Men, he had remain'd secure; had he acquiesced in the humble Thoughts he had of himself, he had been exempted from the Persecution of his ungrateful Countrymen; but when he resolv'd to try if he could find any wiser than himself, when he begun the allarming Search, when he pull'd his *Athenians* out of their belov'd *Asylum,* endeavour'd to convince them of their Ignorance, to perswade them they were not the Persons they took themselves to be; that in pretending to know Things, they only render'd their Folly the more conspicuous; and that they fell infinitely short of him, to whom the God gave so desirable a Title, on no other Account but because he humbly disclaim'd all Knowledge, all Pretences to Wisdom, he made them his implacable Enemies: Not only the Politicians, the Masters of Eloquence, and the Poets, but also the Tradesmen, those whose Enquiries ought to have been confin'd to their Shops, to the Business of their respective Callings; both the Wits and the Fools, the Nobles and the Peasants, the Boasters of Sense and the brutish Multitude, were all inraged against him, and he fell the glorious Martyr of Truth. Who would not envy such a Fate? and much rather chuse to be the humble, patient, dying *Socrates*, than the haughty, passionate, vainglorious

---

Line 118. **Thersites:** deformed Greek warrior in the *Iliad*. **Esop**: author of Aesop's *Fables,* known for his ugly deformity.

Line 123. **Tumor**: swelling pride.

Alexander? Methinks, I see him take the Cup, and with a meek, forgiving, chearful Air, a Look that speaks Content, and shows a modest, a submissive Temper, drink off the welcome Draught. O how much happier was he, than his Accusers!

Give me a lowly Mind, a Mind like his, and take who will the Trifles of the Earth; from them my Soul has long been wean'd. Where-e'er I look, there's nothing tempting; nothing without deserves my Notice, and within my self I cannot see enough to merit my Regard; my Thoughts are dark, confus'd, and full of Error, and there's not any thing that I can truly say I know; with him I freely own my Ignorance: But O! I fear I have not yet attain'd his Firmness, his calm unalter'd Temper: I could not, like him, without Emotion, bear Reproaches, hear unconcern'd my self expos'd, and made the publick Jest: Calumnies like his would grate upon my Spirits, make my Life uneasie, and prove much worse to be endur'd, than Poverty, or Pain, or Death it self. But what's the Source of this? From whence proceeds this Tenderness? This Sense of Ills which have their Being but in Fancy, are Creatures of Opinion: Alas! it must proceed from Pride. Were I as humble, my Apprehensions sure would be the same with his, and I should be as little mov'd at Censure as Applause, which, till I am, I have no Pretence to Happiness; my Satisfaction will not be my own, but in the Power of every envious Wretch, of every base Detractor; which to prevent, I will strive to learn this needful Lesson, prepare my self for what may happen, will still encourage depreciating Thoughts, accustom my self to Reprehension, to be told my Faults; and if it be in Anger, yet to bear it with a mild and gentle Temper.

Reproaches often useful prove,
Malice may be as kind as Love;
No matter what the Bad intend,
If I'm the better, I've my End:
If that I to my self propose,
I shall defeat my greatest Foes.

OF LIFE

Would we accustom our selves to speak the strict Language of Truth, to fix Idea's to our Words, we should not talk so improperly as generally we do, should give Things their true Appellations, call them by their right Names, learn to distinguish between our selves and our Instruments of Action, betwixt immortal Souls and perishing Bodies, betwixt Life and Death, and appropriate each to its proper Subject. We should then know, that to live is essential to a rational Soul; and that when we speak of Dying, we do not understand what we mean.

Socrates was much in the right, when he derided *Crito* for asking him how he would be buried? What can be more pleasant than to hear him answer, *Just as you please, if you can but catch me, and if I do not give you the Slip;* and then to see him turn to his lamenting Friends, and, smiling, tell them, *He fancies this* Socrates, *who now discourses with you, is the Thing that shall see Death by and by; he confounds me with my Corps.*

Life is still the same, still adheres to its Subject, is not liable to any Alteration: What once truly lives, will live for ever.

Beasts, and all the sensitive Creation, are but Matter variously modify'd; the same may be affirm'd of Vegetables, of Humane Bodies, and of all corporeal Substances in general; and what we call *Dying*, is only an assuming a new Form, an appearing in a new Shape. Matter is in a perpetual Fluctuation; some Parts fly off, and others are added: We are not entirely the same we were Yesterday, and we shall not have, some few Years hence, one of those Particles which are now constituent Parts of our Bodies; the Matter remains, but the accidental Figurations alter: The restless Attoms shift Places, and there is nothing perfectly solid in corporeal Nature.

None but immaterial Substances are fix'd, they are not extended, and therefore not divisable, and consequently not capable of being made greater, or render'd less, of having any thing added to them, or taken from them; they must be still what they are, still possess the Perfection essential to their Nature, still enjoy that Degree of Being, which they

Line 9. **Crito**: in his dialogue *Kriton*, Plato urges Socrates to escape death as a duty to his children.

derive from Being it self, those Degrees of *Life* which they at first imbib'd from its inexhaustible Fountain.

Upon the whole, if our Souls are immortal, if by the Purity and Simplicity of their Nature, they are not liable to the least Mutation, and may as soon cease to be, as to be what they now are, and shall be for ever, as to their essential Properties: And if these are our selves, if to these alone we owe the distinguishing Denomination of Rational Creatures, 'tis absurd for us to talk of Dying, the Body being but the Habit of the Soul, I will not say the Ornament, that being too Poetical, too good an Epithet for a Lump of Dirt.

'Tis the House she dwells in during her Probation, in which she continues while it is Tenantable; but when it ceases to be so, she takes another Lodging; sometimes, before it decays, she is call'd off by the Great Master of the Family, and commanded to go to some other Room, to take up her Residence in some other Apartment.

Would any Person in his Wits be afraid of leaving a dismal melancholy Prison, for a glorious delightful Palace; a close gloomy Cell for the open balmy Air, the chearful Light and wide Expanse of Heaven; a corruptible State for the World of Life; and a few walking Shadows, fleeting Dreams, Phantoms, as little known to themselves as others, for real Substances, for spiritual Beings, exalted Understandings, Divine Forms of the first Rank, the sublimest Order?

Let us be no more concern'd for our Bodies, than for our Cloaths; no more troubled at the wearing out of the one than the other, as looking upon them to be almost equally foreign to us, there being indeed this only Difference between them, That our Bodies are the Garments we first put on, those that are nearest to us; the other superadded Habits, Things owing to Decency, to Custom, and too often to Effeminacy, Luxury, and Pride. On both these we are allow'd to bestow some Regard; to nourish our Bodies, to defend them from Injuries, to keep them as long as tis possible in the same Degree of Strength and Beauty, in which we receiv'd them from our bounteous Maker, and to prevent their being dishonour'd and polluted by immoral Actions, to observe a *Decorum*, a Neatness in our Dress, a Conformity to establish'd Modes.

But 'tis our selves we ought chiefly to mind; to our Souls we ought to confine our intentest Care; those it becomes us to cultivate, to improve and adorn.

The Pains we bestow on the two first are lost, they turn to no Account; but the Labour we are at about the last will bring us in a wonderful Return; those Ornaments they acquire here, will continue their's for ever; and those necessary Truths they learn now will be eternally their's in that future State, where Knowledge, in all Probability, will be everlastingly progressive; and the greater Advances they make in Virtue here, the happier will they be there, where none but the Good, the Just, the Wise, the considering Part of Mankind shall find Admittance.

Such only those Delights shall share,
Which in Perfection still are there;
Delights too great for us to know,
While we're thus hood-wink'd here below;
While we to Flesh are thus confin'd,
To Flesh, that Darkner of the Mind;
That *Medium*, which obscures the Light,
That worse than an *Egyptian* Night:
But when we've thrown this Veil aside,
Dispell'd those Shades, which Day does hide;
When from the Cells in which we lie,
All Thought, to glorious Heights we fly:
We then shall Truths with Clearness see,
Shall then as wise as knowing be;
As finite Intellects can prove,
As much possess, as much shall love,
And all our rapt'rous Hours employ
In highest Extacies of Joy.

OF DEATH

Since I've a long time thought, that the Fear of Death is the occasional Cause of the greatest part of those mean dishonourable Actions which are done in the World; none will, I believe, think it a Misemployment of my time, seriously to consider, what 'tis renders it so formidable, makes it so dreadful not only to the Vicious, but also to the

Pretenders to Virtue, not only to those who by their immoral Lives have consign'd themselves over to eternal Punishments, but to those who promise themselves glorious Rewards, and talk of Heaven, as of a Place, where they hope to be everlastingly happy.

'Tis not to be wonder'd at, that such as are immers'd in the Delights of the Animal Life, who lie wallowing in sensual Pleasures, whose Understandings are so darkned by the Interposition of their Passions, that they cannot see one Ray of intellectual Light, can discover nothing beautiful beyond the Kenn of their Senses, should be unwilling to leave a World they are acquainted with, for an unknown Futurity; a State fitted to their deprav'd Faculties, to their brutish Inclinations, for a place of Horror and unexpressible Misery, or at least where they shall cease to Be, and at once lose both themselves and their Pleasures, themselves and their Hopes, all their Happiness, all their Expectations: But I cannot see how such as have nobler Views, who boast of being above sensible Allurements, of having their Affections not only disengag'd from terrene Objects, but fix'd on such as they acknowledge to be transcendently, infinitely better, both as to their Magnitude and Duration, can answer it to their Reason; how can they be sollicitous for Life, can shrink back, grow pale, and tremble, when Death makes its Attack: 'Twould be more consonant to their Principles to meet it with Smiles, to welcome it with Joy; for if they are really what they are willing to be thought, if they have lov'd Virtue for her self, have seen the Charms that are in Truth, endeavour'd to live up to the Dignity of their Nature, to make as near Approaches as 'tis possible to the divine Perfections, 'tis contradicting themselves, making their Actions give the lye to their Words; for their Unwillingness to Die cannot then be suppos'd to proceed from Fear, there can be no room for that debasing Passion in a purify'd Mind, in a Soul transported with the ravishing Prospect of approaching Felicity, neither can it be the Result of their Fondness for present Enjoyments, as being things too mean, too despicable, to be much esteem'd, or parted from with reluctance; therefore may I not be allow'd, without breach of Charity, to suspect that there's some darling Vice within, some conceal'd Passion, which disturbs their Consciences, or ties them, nails them to

Line 6. **Pretenders:** those who lay claim. Line 21. **terrene:** earthly.

the World, or that they have not such well-grounded Hopes, such clear distinct Views as they would be thought to have?

I know we are told by those who are willing to excuse themselves, as being asham'd to own their Weakness, that Death is what Nature abhors, and Self-preservation cogenial with our Being, a Principle implanted in us by our Creator; from whence they draw this Conclusion, that 'tis their Duty to be tenderly concern'd for their Lives, anxiously careful of them, and that they ought to use their utmost Industry to ward off every Blow: Now such a Solicitude as this, I think, betrays an unmanly Imbecility, and plainly discovers a Truth they are willing to hide; and that is, that their Passions are too strong for their Reason, and they more fond of Earth than Heaven, more pleas'd with the Delights they are actually possess'd of, than those of which they think there is only a remote Possibility: Besides too many, especially those of my own Sex, have from their Infancy imbib'd wrong Notions of Life and Death, have been taught to think the one a real Good, and the other an essential Evil; and to these false Idea's all the Disorders we see in the World owe their Original: For what can be more natural, than for such as believe Life to be a necessary Good, to endeavour to preserve it, and render it pleasant, by shunning with the greatest Abhorrence whatever is disgustful and destructive to it? This occasions an effeminate way of Living, an indulging their Humours, a Fear of every little Accident, every slight Indisposition, and subjects them to the basest, vilest Actions; there is nothing they will stick at, to assure themselves the Continuance of what they are so childishly fond of: Now the Fear of Death cannot but be the unavoidable Consequence of such an immoderate Love of Life: They look upon it as the Grave of all their Hopes, the Extinguisher of all their Joys, as an Outlet into a dismal melancholy State, a dark unknown Somewhere, a World of Spirits, of Beings they've been taught to dread; and therefore 'tis no wonder to see them dress it up with all the Circumstances of Horror, and then fly from the frightful Monster they have made, and shun it, tho' with the Loss of their Innocency, their Honour, and all they ought to esteem valuable. This I take to be the true Source of that Treachery, that Covetousness, that Cowardice, and, in a word, of all that Swarm of Vices which overspread the

Line 44. **cogenial**: congenial, agreeable.

World, and, like an epidemical Contagion, infest all Mankind: But wou'd they with unprejudic'd Minds, and an unclouded Reason, view both the one and the other in a proper Light, they would see that they are in themselves neither good nor evil; for were they either necessary Goods, or necessary Evils, they would be unalterably and eternally so, not only to this or that individual Man, but to the whole Species, which Experience tells us they are not; for what one flies from, another courts; and while some are sedulously, scandalously labouring to prolong a precarious Being, others are pleasing themselves with the Hopes of a speedy Dismission, and impatiently wishing for a sudden Exit.

Now, I think both the Extremes are equally faulty: Life ought to be look'd on as a thing indifferent, to be devoted to Virtue, made subservient to the Soul, and carefully employ'd to the noblest Purposes; enjoy'd without Anxiety while 'tis permitted to be ours, and when the Almighty Donor thinks fit to resume it, to be parted with without a Murmur, but by no means to be despis'd or thrown away; that would be a Reflection on infinite Wisdom, an unbecoming Return to divine Bounty; as 'tis his Gift, we ought to receive it with Reverence, and restore it with Submission, to maintain the Post in which he sets us with Honour, and when he calls us to another Station, we ought to go to it chearfully, but not think of quitting the first till he gives us leave.

Such a Temper of Mind as this is, I think to be indispensably necessary in order to both our Living and Dying well; 'twill make us our own, and wholly independent on things without us; keep us calm amidst Storms, easy amidst Disappointments, and happy in all the Emergencies of Life.

To get a just Concern for things that do not belong to me, such a Concern as they deserve, and no more, has been the Business of several Years; and I hope I have at last attain'd, I will not be so vain as to say the whole of what I've been striving for, but some few Degrees, some small Beginnings of that Fortitude, that equal and uniform Steadiness of Mind which is so necessary an Ingredient of Happiness, and without which we should be continually worry'd with dismal Apprehensions, discompos'd by every Accident, frighted by every little Pain, every Harbinger of Death, and should stand shivering on the Bank of that vast Abyss into which we must plunge, thro' which we must all pass.

To Die, is no more than to Sleep; 'tis but a going from one Place to another, a leaving the Round we have been a long time treading, an enlarging our Views, and pleasing ourselves with newer, nobler, and more entertaining Prospects.

These were the Thoughts I lately had of it, these my Reasonings about it, when I had Cause to believe my Fate inevitable, when nothing but a wonderful over-ruling Providence, nothing but the peculiar Care of my Guardian Angel, could have secur'd my Life. When I saw the Precipice, and at the same View saw my self falling from its Top, tumbling to the Bottom with an impetuous Motion, an amazing Violence, I then found the Advantage of a strong, a firm Resolution, and of being disengag'd from the World; I had nothing to pull me back again to the Earth, to make me unwilling to leave it; I cou'd with Joy have taken my Flight to the Upper Regions, there have assum'd an Ætherial Vehicle, and made a Tour, thro' all the shining Fields of Light.

Thro' the pure *Æther* wing'd my way,
    And view'd the Works of Art Divine;
Seen boundless Love it self display,
    And Wisdom in Perfection shine:
With the bright Natives of the Sky,
    And such as once frail Mortals were,
Had rang'd thro' all the Realms on High,
    And trod the liquid Plains of Air,
Where something new would still delight,
    Something my Knowledge still improve;
Would me to Songs of Praise invite,
    To soft harmonious Hymns of Love.

But since 'tis the Will of God I should live longer, let me exercise the same Act of Resignation, be willing to wait a while for those Pleasures which I then had in view, and to which I pleas'd myself with the Hopes of my being swiftly hast'ning; and as it becomes me chearfully to devote to his Service that Life he thinks fit to prolong, and be very thankful for escaping those Mischiefs which are generally the unhappy Consequences of such dangerous Falls; so let me resolve to employ all my coming Moments in gratefully acknowledging his Favours, and in endeavouring to advance his Glory, and next to that, in the Improvement of my own Mind; in the diligent and unwearied Pursuit of Truth, the Exaltation of my intellectual Powers, and assuring to myself such

Goods as are accommodated to Rational Beings, and perfective of their Nature: such as will contribute to my present Happiness and future Felicity, to my unspeakable Satisfaction here, and the transporting Delights of a blessed Eternity:

Where Night her sable Wings shall ne'er display,
Nor rising Vapours hide refulgent Day;
Where Health, and Peace, and Pleasures all divine,
Shall mix their Charms, shall all in one combine,
Then dart themselves into each happy Breast,
And give them Raptures not to be exprest;
Inebriating Joys, too great for Sense,
Which heav'nly Forms can only bear, and God dispense;
Where Hopes shall cease, and Wishes have an end,
And our Fruitions our Desires transcend;
Where no Disgusts, no Griefs, shall Entrance find,
Nothing disturb the Quiet of the Mind;
Where Death's unknown, and Life is only found,
Where with immortal Wreaths the Good are crown'd,
And all together join in Songs of Praise,
Together tune their sweet melodious Lays;
The grateful Tribute of their Voices bring,
And find no other Business, but to Love and Sing.

OF FEAR

Fear is a Passion which strangely disorders and weakens the Mind, breaks all its Measures, and unavoidably subjects it to a thousand Inconveniences: 'Tis generally the Effect of a too tender and effeminate Education, of those fatal Impressions which are made on us in our Infancy, in the first Dawnings of our Reason, by the Folly and Mismanagement of Servants, of such as are unhappily intrusted with us, either by the Laziness or Imprudence of our ill-advis'd Parents.

Line 153. **refulgent**: shining brightly, glittering.

'Tis to These poor Children owe their false Notions of Things; they stuff their Memories with dreadful Stories of Apparitions, are still frightning them from Evil, when they should be encouraging them to do well, representing Death to them in the most hideous Shape that their Imagination can form, making them tremble to be alone, and afraid of being one Minute in the Dark: 'Tis by such Methods as these, that they sink their Spirits, and render them Cowards from their Cradles. And is it to be wonder'd at, that Children thus us'd should have a Meanness in their Tempers? These Beginnings, these unregarded Embrio's of Baseness and Pusillanimity, have too often deplorable Effects, and in their riper Years precipitate them into vile and unworthy Actions: Whereas they ought to make them familiar with Death, should tell them 'tis no more than they do every Night: 'Tis but an undressing themselves, and lying down to Sleep; the only Difference is, that 'tis a longer, sweeter Rest; but a Cessation from the Hurry and Toil of Life; no more than walking from one Room to another; only changing Places and Company, and looking on new Objects; and assure them, that their Graves will prove no more uneasy to them than their Beds: And to make them the more intimately acquainted with the Truths they would inculcate, they should by degrees accustom them to the Sight of the Dead, make them conversant with Objects of Mortality, which they'll find will in a short time harden them, and make them no more afraid of seeing dead human Bodies, than they are of looking on those of brute Animals in that state; it being nothing but Use, that renders the one less shocking than the other: And instead of terrifying them with idle Tales of Spirits in horrid Shapes, Spectres delighting in Mischief, haunting Houses, and doing a thousand improbable ridiculous things, and telling them of Witches metamorphos'd into more Shapes than *Proteus* ever assum'd, or *Ovid* dream'd of; they should make it their Business to possess them with rational and becoming Idea's, pleasant and entertaining Notions of separate Beings; tell them such as are good, are blest with Beauty, Wisdom, and Happiness, are full of Kindness and Compassion, and ever ready to do friendly Offices to Mankind, and that those which are bad, are by the infinite Goodness of God restrain'd from doing Mischief, and not permitted to act according

Line 36. **Proteus:** in classical myth, a minor sea-god who had the power to take any shape.

to the Malignity of their Nature; that they are govern'd by Laws peculiar to them, and cannot move beyond their assign'd Bounds; and they may assure themselves, that almost all those dreadful Stories of Ghosts, with which the World has been so long impos'd on, are Fables, the Creatures of Imagination, Chimera's form'd in the Brain, and nothing else but the Effects of a disorder'd Fancy; and to convince them that they are really so, that they are only the Result of Fear, use them to be by themselves, to be as chearful, as easy, and well pleas'd in the Night as in the Day, to think themselves as safe in the greatest Darkness as in the clearest Light.

Of this we have an Instance among the *Spartans*, who always went from their publick Halls without Lights, the Use of them being forbidden by *Lycurgus*, to the end that they might accustom themselves to walk boldly in the Dark.

To prevent their doing mean and dishonourable Actions, let them be taught to reverence Truth, to abhor a Lye, to abhor it for it self, from a Sense of the Baseness and Deformity of it, and not from a slavish Dread of Punishment; perswade them, that their abstaining from what is evil ought to proceed from innate Principles of Virtue, from a noble Disdain, a native Bravery of Spirit, and a commendable Scorn of being outdone by others; carefully cherish every Seed of Honour, blow up every little Spark of Courage into a Flame; inure them to Pain, make them in love with Labour; teach them to slight Sickness, to laugh at little Uneasinesses, at trivial Indispositions; blame them when they complain; use them to Hunger and Thirst, to bear Heat and Cold; and, as their Reason grows stronger, and their Judgments more solid, inspire them with contemptible Thoughts of those who sink beneath the Dignity of their Nature, who forget what is owing to their Character, what it becomes them to do as they are Men, the noblest Part of the visible Creation; give them right Idea's of Things, instruct them in the Method of giving everything its proper Place, its just Value in their Esteem; endeavour to raise their Thoughts above Riches, Grandeur, the Favour of the Great, nay Life it self; at least, strive to bring them to an Indifference, to a

---

Line 47. **Chimera's**: mythical monsters.

Line 55. **Lycurgus**: founder of the Spartan system of laws and social values, stressing self-reliance and fortitude, who banished luxury and restored the state.

being unconcern'd whether they enjoy them or not: and when you've brought them to a state of Independency, they will have nothing to fear, no Temptation to be Cowards.

This Method which I've propos'd, would be of wonderful Use towards the Regulation of Manners, and would have an universal Influence on the Morals of Mankind: For whatever the World may think to the contrary, 'tis impossible to be Good and not Magnanimous: Virtue and Cowardice are incompatible; they cannot subsist in the same Subject. A Man who has a just Value for himself, will scorn to cringe and fawn, or by a Word, an Action, or a Look, belye his Conscience, or deviate from his Character; he will still be steady to himself, firm to his Principles, and neither to be shaken by Menaces, discourag'd by Difficulties, frighted by Dangers, nor yet discompos'd by the impending Horrors of an approaching Fate, and at the same time equally Proof against the more hazardous Attacks of Vice, the inviting Allurements of Sense, and the importunate Sollicitations of Pleasure; as great a Stock of Courage, as great a Strength of Resolution, being requisite to resist the one as the other, or rather more; the last being not to be conquer'd by less than an *Herculean* Strength. *Ulysses* found it much more difficult to escape the *Syrens*, than all the rest of his Enemies; those fatal Charmers were more powerful, more formidable, than *Polyphemus*, or the *Lestrigones;* and more carefully to be avoided than *Scylla* and *Charybdis:* but the good Man passes them by with an equal Assurance, an equal Fortitude; his Courage is still the same; 'tis universal; it meets every Danger, and bravely makes a Stand against every Difficulty, against whatever dares oppose it: He carries all his Treasure within himself; 'tis securely lodg'd within his own Breast; he has nothing that another can take from him: And he that has nothing to lose, has nothing to fear, nothing to shake him, or in the least imbitter his Enjoyments: He maintains his Station with Honour; he's not afraid of Poverty, he can be chearful in a Prison, pleas'd in Exile; and so far from dreading Death, that he dares meet it, dares look it in the Face without a change of Colour, and is so far from

Line 96. **Polyphemus**: in the *Odyssey,* the one-eyed giant defeated by Ulysses. **Lestrigones**: Laestrygones, in the *Odyssey,* a race of giants who destroyed ships and ate sailors.

Line 97. **Scylla and Charybdis**: Odysseus had to navigate between the deadly whirlpool Charybdis on one side and the monster Scylla on the other.

shunning it, that he welcomes it with Smiles, and dies as he liv'd, consistent with himself, full of Serenity and Peace.

O how happy shou'd I be, could I attain such an unshaken Steadiness of Mind, such a firm fearless Temper! I see its Beauty, feel the Truths I write, have struggled long to disingage my self from every Clog, from every thing that ties me fast to Life: I never yet could find a Fondness in my Nature for any of those Trifles to which the Most confine their Happiness, for which they labour, sweat, and toil, condemn themselves to anxious Days and restless Nights, and which too many are content to purchase at the Expence of Innocence, of Honour, of all they ought to value. Riches to me were never tempting, nor did I ever covet Grandeur; my Wishes were contracted to a narrow Space, and my Desires but few; and now, with Joy, I find, that this Indifferency does every Day encrease; my inward View extends, and every outward Object lessens; and, if I know my self, I could, without a Murmur, relinquish my Right to every thing besides my Friends and Books; they are the whole I value, to me the Joys of Life; and yet even these I can give up at my great Master's Call, and all alone enjoy my Solitude, and feast upon the sweet Repast of Thoughts, that delicious Banquet of a Mind at Peace and easy with it self. This being the present Temper of my Soul, the resign'd and chearful Frame in which I find my self, may I not be allow'd to hope I shall in time obtain the Conquest I so much desire, see every Passion subject to my Reason, and this among the rest, which I shall find the easier to subdue, because it never yet had much Dominion over me.

Let such as value Life be full of Fear,
It is a Trifle much below my Care:
To distant Objects I direct my Sight,
To Prospects pleasant, permanent, and bright:
Celestial Glories I still keep in view,
With eagerest Haste the dear Delights pursue.
The Virtuous, cloath'd with Rags, I'll dare to praise,
And make the Poor, if Good, the Subject of my Lays;
But will not be to servile Flatt'ry brought:
My Tongue shall speak the Language of my Thought.
The Great, if vicious, with Contempt I'll shun,
And will not be to base Compliance won
By Bribes, or Threats; nor wealthy Fools caress,

Nor a Respect for gawdy Fops express:
True to my Self, and unsubdu'd by Fear,
I'll meet each Storm, and every Pressure bear;
Maintain my Post until I'm call'd away,
And then the Summons with a chearful Look obey.

OF GRIEF

Grief is a Passion, which most People believe it becomes them to indulge: They tell us, 'Tis what the Miseries incident to the human Nature exacts from us; and that, as not to be concern'd for their own Misfortunes, would be Stupidity; so to be unmov'd at the Afflictions of others would be the Height of Barbarity. The greatest part of Mankind are led by Opinion, and what they have once taken for Truth, they will never be at the Labour of examining. They are almost as much afraid of Innovations in Matters of Reason, as in those of Faith. Besides, 'tis painful to form a new Set of Thoughts, to deviate from the beaten Road, to run counter to establish'd Maxims, to wander in unknown Paths, and follow Reason to her solitary Recess. They are every Day regal'd by their Senses, and so encompass'd by the Pleasures that attend them, so totally absorb'd in the Delights of the animal Life, that they cannot disengage themselves, cannot so much as dart one single Glance beyond their thick Atmosphere, beyond that Region of Vapours, to which they are fatally confin'd. That which afords them a present Satisfaction, they fancy to be good, and by Consequence that which deprives them of it to be evil. On this *Hypothesis* they ground all their Arguments, and from hence draw all their Conclusions. Health, Riches, Relations, Fame, Honours, *&c.* they take to be constituent Parts of Happiness, and therefore their Contraries must necessarily bring Misery. These Mistakes run them into innumerable Absurdities, involve them in inextricable Errors, and render them obnoxious to the Insult of every prevailing Passion, liable to the Shock of every cross Accident, every unexpected Disappointment; and 'tis no wonder, while they are govern'd by such wrong Notions, to see them excessively griev'd for the Death of Relations, lamenting the Loss of Wealth, sad and dejected when in Disgrace, and impatient when depriv'd of their Health. This being the natural Result of such Principles as their's, and while they adhere to them, they may as well cease to be, as cease to be unhappy.

Nothing but viewing Things in a due Light, looking on them as they really are, learning to distinguish between what is and what is not ours; what we may bestow upon our selves, and what is given us by another, and to put a Value on them according to their true Estimate; to make a Difference between what will be always our own, and what we must part with, will exempt us from Uneasinesses, and make us Masters of our selves. Now, that we may do this effectually, we ought to consider, with all imaginable Accuracy and Circumspection, with all the Nicety and Exactness we are capable of, the particular Advantages that will accrue to us from the Possession of those Blessings which are generally known by the Name of Temporal or Contingent Goods; and that we may be the better acquainted with their Nature, let us strip them from all their artificial Coverings, wash off their glaring Colours, and view them as they are in themselves, and then see if they will appear the same to us as they did to the ancient Philosophers.

To begin with those that are accounted the most valuable, what is that Life, of which we take so much Care, for which we are so childishly solicitous? And what real Good does it prove to us? Is it not a vain Repetition of the same Acts, a constant Combat betwixt *Reason* and *Folly,* a walking blindfold, and a conversing with Shadows, a dark melancholy Passage into a better State, a World of Light and Joy? Is it rational to be fond of our Road, to be willing to continue in our Inn, to think our selves wrong'd when we are call'd into the Port, commanded to quit the Ship, and assign'd to another, a more honourable Post? Is it not ridiculous to call that a Good which is so precarious, and which, if it were in it self estimable, would be so to all Mankind? But that 'tis not so, is evident: *Socrates* would not save his Life when 'twas in his Power to do it; he preferr'd Obedience to the Law, before his own Safety; *Regulus* had no Concern for it; several of the ancient Heroes and Heroines despised

Line 58. **Regulus:** Marcus Atilius Regulus, Roman consul in 267 and 256 B.C.; captured by the Carthaginians, he was sent as a hostage to urge peace terms with the Roman senate, but instead he convinced the Romans to reject them, whereupon he was severely tortured by his captors.

it, and the Martyrs took their Leaves of it not only willingly, but with Transports. Let us then blush at our own Weakness, and no longer give it a Name it does not deserve. Let us put it to that Use for which it was given us, employ it to the best Advantage while 'tis ours, and, when 'tis call'd for, give it back chearfully; while we have it, strive to possess it with Indifferency, express neither a Weariness of it, nor a Fear to lose it; neither a Desire, nor an Unwillingness to die.

And let us, in reference to our Friends and Kindred, manage our selves with the same Equality of Temper: If when we have lost any of those dear Relatives, we find our selves discomposed, if the natural Tenderness of our Souls inclines us to melancholy Reflections, let us resist the first Beginnings of Sorrow, and reason our selves into a calm Resignation: Let us consider, that they were only lent us, and are not wholly lost, have but changed their Place, are only gone before us, and it will not be long before we shall enjoy them again: Besides, how can we be thought to love them, if we do not rejoice at their Happiness? 'Tis a Contradiction to talk of our Affection, and at the same time to grieve at their being in Possession of an unchangeable Felicity. What Construction would any considering Person put on such a Sorrow? Would he not be tempted to think it proceeded from a mean narrow Principle, from Self-Interest; and that, to gratifie a foolish Fondness, we would be contented to have them once more Partners with us in the Uneasinesses and Impertinences of Life?

Some will perhaps readily grant, that if our Friends and Relations are good, it will be a Fault to mourn immoderately for their Death; But, supposing they are not so, 'twill be barbarous not to grieve for them, because we should then have too much Reason to doubt of their eternal Happiness. To this I answer, in the First place, That we cannot, without giving an ill Character of our selves, call such Friends as are not virtuous; and, in the Second place, if our Relations are ill, they have no Right to our Affection. Our Pity they may claim, but not our Love; for that we ought not to bestow on Persons we have any just Cause to fear are hated by God. While they are living we must use our utmost Endeavours to reclaim them, must tell them of their Faults, represent to them the Dangers into which they are precipitating themselves, the inexpressible Miseries to which they are hastening; but if they still continue vicious, and die loaded with Crimes, to grieve much for them would be unbecoming us: We may at their Exit give them a few Sighs, may commiserate their Condition, and express a Concern for their having made themselves so deplorably unhappy; but, I think, neither Reason nor Religion will allow of any more.

Health is another thing from which they cannot part without infinite Regret: 'Tis, I own, a very valuable Blessing, and that which gives a Relish to the other Enjoyments of Life; but yet I can by no means allow its Deprivation to be a real Evil, since it does not impede the Operations of the Mind, nor put the Will under any Confinement, it cannot hinder us from being virtuous, from acting according to the Principles of Honour, nor from proceeding in our Search after Truth; Our Thoughts may be well employ'd amidst the sharpest Pains, and we may in time overcome them by a Strength of Resolution: Of the Truth of this, the *Lacedæmonian* Boys were an undeniable Proof: To what inhuman Discipline did they submit! What cruel Scourgings did they endure! What Barbarities did they inflict on each other! And yet with what Constancy did they bear them! and all to purchase a little Vain-glory, to have the empty Satisfaction of being applauded, of being thought courageous and undaunted. With what a wonderful Patience did *Anaxarchus* bear his Tortures! With what a Composure of Spirits, what a Sedateness of Mind, did *Possidonius* talk to *Pompey!* The Extremity of his Pain occasion'd no Pauses in his Discourse, no Alteration in his Face, extorted no Complaints from his Tongue! Now, had Pain been an Evil, it would have been so to these, as well as the rest of Mankind; but 'tis evident it was not so to them, and therefore is not so in its own Nature. 'Tis our Effeminacy makes us dread it, 'tis that renders it so insupportable, and makes us yield to every Attack, makes us shew an indecent Feebleness of Mind: The way not to be guilty of such Follies, not to be surpriz'd, is, in the midst of our Health to prepare for Sickness; when we are perfectly easie, to resolve not to be shock'd by Pain, to observe every Approach it

---

Lines 109–10. **Lacedæmonian Boys**: Spartan youth were raised under an extremely severe regimen intended to create hardened warriors.

Line 115. **Anaxarchus**: companion of Alexander the Great; when he was being pounded to death by the tyrant Nicocreon in a stone mortar, he announced that pounding his body could not touch his soul.

Line 117. **Possidonius**: Posidonius (ca. 135–51 B.C.) friend and advisor of Cicero and Pompey.

makes, and contend with it, meet it with Courage, consider that it cannot be avoided, that Lamentations are childish, Groans can give no Relief, that Tears and Sighs are Arguments of Weakness; and that, as Pity can do us no Good, so it is below us to desire it; and that, if our Pain is violent, 'twill quickly put an End to our Lives, free our Souls from their cumbersome Loads, and restore them to their primitive Activity, to that Vivacity and Purity of which they were originally possess'd. If they are moderate, they are an Exercise of Patience, and will not only teach us Temperance, but be of use to disengage us from the World, will make us attend to the Bettering of our Minds, the subduing of our Passions, and the preparing our selves for that State, where, in Bodies compos'd of the purest Particles of Matter, and adapted to the noblest Purposes of Life, we shall be blessed with perfect Indolence, with everlasting Ease.

Next to these, Fame and Riches claim a Share, and 'tis difficult to determine which Mankind are fondest of; Indeed some sordid Souls, some Sons of Earth, who, like the Brutes, are always looking downward, who love Gold for it self, and have no farther Aims, but those of being rich, may terminate their Happiness in their Bags, and be capable of grieving for nothing else but the Loss of their idoliz'd Treasures; But the generality of Men value Wealth for the Reputation that attends it, and are pleas'd with having it said, that they are Owners of great Estates, and if they happen to lose them, they are almost as much troubled at their being thought poor, as at their being really so: The Contempt which usually attends Poverty is what they are concern'd at; they cannot bear the Thoughts of being slighted and neglected; their Pride is rouz'd, their Self-love alarm'd, and they are touch'd in the most sensible, the tenderest part of their Souls; That which makes them so eager for Fame in general, is their being so full of themselves; they wou'd ingross Respect, would be look'd on with Honour and Veneration: Now, whatever lessens them, whatever darkens their Splendor, they think insupportable; every Aspersion grieves them, every Slander stabs them to the Heart; they are not proof against the slightest Reflection, the weakest Attacks of Envy: And what can be vainer, what more irrational than this? What real Good can accrue to us from the Praises of others? Or what real Evil can their Censures bring on us? Why should we be Slaves to Opinion, and govern our selves by the capricious Humours of Persons as fallable as our selves, of Persons who perhaps will be one Day our Friends, and the next our Enemies; this Day will admire and court us, to Morrow decry and shun us? But suppose they were constant, steady in their Applauses, assiduous in their Addresses, and firm in their Friendship, of what Advantage would it be? Would it make us either the better as to our Morals, or the wiser as to our Intellectuals, add any thing to what is truly ours, augment our Virtue, or give us a surer Title to a blissful Eternity? And may we not be as easie, as happy without it? As well pleas'd with the Approbations we give our selves, with the Plaudits of our own Consciences, as with the united Acclamations of a Multitude? And is it not infinitely more eligible to approve our selves to God, and those glorious Spirits, to whom we are going, and whose Society we hope to enjoy for ever, than to leave the World with the vain Hopes of a posthumous Fame, of a Reputation which can do us no Service, and which we shall be either ignorant of, or despise.

Wealth, if seriously consider'd, is of as little Moment: We know a *Zeno*, a *Crates,* a *Stilpho,* a *Fabricius,* and many others, have been happy without it; nay, they have contemn'd it, look'd on it as a Clog, an Impediment to Virtue; And shall we be griev'd for the Loss of that, which some of the best, as well as the wisest Men of the Age in which they liv'd, thought a Burden? *Epictetus* was more throughly easie, possess'd a higher Satisfaction, and tasted more of the true Delights of Life in his little mean Cottage, than his cruel Master could boast of, tho' honour'd with the Favour of an Emperor, and enjoying the Effects of his Bounty in the greatest, the most magnificent Court in the World; And are there any amongst us expos'd to greater Hardships than those he chearfully underwent? And after he had his Freedom, and was esteem'd by Princes, did he not make the same Poverty his Choice? Suppose we were stripp'd of all the Conveniences of Life, must we therefore

---

Line 180. **Zeno:** (335–263 B.C.) founder of the Stoic school of philosophy, which taught that the only real good is virtue and the only real evil moral weakness, so that riches, pain, or death are merely incidental. **Crates:** Cynic philosopher (c. 365–285 B.C.) who lived in poverty by choice and who was horribly deformed. **Stilpho:** (fl. 336 B.C.), founded the Megarian school of philosophy, teacher of Zeno. **Fabricius:** Fabricius Luscinus (fl. 280–270 B.C.), Roman consul celebrated for austerity and simplicity of life.

Line 184. **Epictetus:** (A.D. 60–ca. 140) a Stoic philosopher, born a slave of Epaphroditus and freed by Nero; his thoughts on austerity, humility, patience, and contempt of riches were collected by a student under the title of *Enchiridion.*

be necessarily miserable? Will not Nature be easily satisfy'd? Do not the Springs afford us Liquor, the Earth Roots and Herbs, the Trees and Bushes Fruit? Is there not something shocking in eating Flesh, something barbarous in the taking away the Lives of harmless Creatures? And are there not People that live without it? Don't the *Indian Faquirs* and *Brahmens* live as poorly as the meanest of our Beggars, or rather more meanly, they never eating any Flesh, and drinking nothing but Water; their Houses are the Galleries of their Temples, and their Beds (as Monsieur *Bernier* tells us) are three Inches thick of Ashes, and yet are not they contented? Do not they live as pleasant Lives as any of their rich *Mahometan* Neighbours? The same may be said in all other Instances; and it may with Ease be demonstrated, that Poverty, tho' in the greatest Extreme, can be no Evil, can do no real Injury to the Soul, and therefore is not to be dreaded; and if it is our Lot to be expos'd to it, we ought to resolve not only to bear it with a decent Resignation, but with Courage, and such an unshaken Greatness of Mind as may make it evident to the World that we are above being disturb'd at what they think so formidable, and deprecate as an Evil.

After these things I know nothing that deserves Consideration, unless it be Banishment, or the being confin'd to a Prison: As for the first, it has not, in my Opinion, so much as the Shadow of an Affliction; and such as complain of it are rather to be laugh'd at than pity'd: What can be more pleasant than Liberty? What more desirable than an Opportunity of enlarging one's Prospect? What more delightful than a new Scene of Things, than to gaze on Variety of Objects, to have fresh Subjects of Contemplation, and to be introduced into a different Set of Company? Virtue will every where procure Friends; but if it should not, yet the Good cannot fail of being agreeable to themselves, and every Place they are in, every thing they see will afford them Entertainment, and render even Solitude diverting. Imprisonment, I cannot but own, has a much juster Pretence to be the Object of Grief: 'Tis uneasie to be confin'd, to be abridg'd of one's Freedom, to have one's View shorten'd,

---

Lines 197–98. **Indian Faquirs and Brahmens**: a fakir is a Hindu or Muslim holy man who lives as a beggar; a Brahmin is a member of the Hindu priestly caste.

Line 201. **Monsieur Bernier**: François Bernier (1620–88), author of *The History of the late revolution of the empire of the Great Mogol* (1671).

and to be deny'd the Conversation of one's Friends: But even this, as uncomfortable as it is, may be supported; the Thoughts cannot be immur'd, they enjoy an entire Liberty: All that have the Use of their Reason may, if they please, make themselves easie; but such as have the good Fortune to lay in beforehand a large Stock of Knowledge and useful Learning, will not only be easie, but happy; their Minds will expand themselves, and reach from the Beginning of Time to the final Consummation of all things; they'll take a Survey of the Past, the Present, and the Future, view Nature in all her Changes, and please themselves with the Variety of her Productions, and will consider, with an attentive Regard, all the Transactions of Mankind, what Figures they have made, what mighty Empires they have rais'd, what dreadful Devastations they have caus'd, what Mischiefs their Passions have involv'd them in, and what Enemies their Vices have made them to themselves and the rest of their Species: And can such as have so large a Field to range in be properly said to be Prisoners? Can they want any thing to make them pleasant? And can there be any room left for Complaints? The Body is but the Instrument of the Soul; while the last has its Freedom, 'tis no matter for the Confinement of the first; its Murmurings are below its Notice. 'Tis not in the Power of our greatest Enemies to exclude our Virtues; they cannot deprive us of the Pleasures of a good Conscience, of the inward Satisfactions of the Mind; and while these are ours, 'tis impossible to be wretched.

Besides the things I have mention'd, I know none that deserve a Place in the Catalogue of Troubles, none of that ought to be rank'd among the Occasions of *Grief*, and amidst them all, I know none so powerful, but that they may be conquer'd; Reason is given us for that purpose, and we have none to blame but our selves, if we do not make that Use of it for which it was design'd. Let us then resolve to trouble the World no more with tedious Accounts of our Sufferings, nor indulge our selves in making dismal Reflections on the disagreeable Circumstances of our Lives; let us not put it in the Power of every trifling Accident to ruffle our Minds, and disturb our Peace; let us accustom our selves to make little Experiments of our Strength, to use our selves to little Trials, to consider beforehand what may happen, and then prepare for it. Premeditation will keep our Minds sedate and cool, firm, and ready for an Assault, prevent Surprizes, put us in possession of a pleasing Serenity, a delightful

Calmness of Soul, and such a Chearfulness of Temper, as will discover it self in our Faces, and manifest it self in all our Actions.

I would not have my Readers think I perswade 'em to what's impracticable, to Flights beyond the reach of Nature: The Advice I give, I assure them I've follow'd; I've had Troubles to struggle with, Difficulties to conquer; have met with Uneasinesses enough to extort Complaints; a great many of those things which are call'd Afflictions; have past a considerable part of my Time in Solitude, and divided my Hours between my Thoughts and my Books: At first I repin'd at my Fate, thought my self hardly dealt with, could not forbear finding fault with the unequal Distributions of Providence, the Unkindness of Relations, and the too little Regard they often have for the Happiness of such as it becomes them to be tenderly concern'd for: and when I found my self dispirited, and sinking under the Pressure, good God! with what Pleasure did I think on that which most believe to be the greatest of temporal Evils! How amiable did Death appear to me! With what Delight could I have retir'd into a dark silent Grave, and in that welcome Recess, that quiet desirable State, have taken an everlasting Leave of all my Misfortunes! But O it was thy Will that I should Live: Without thy Permission I durst not quit my Post; the awful Deference that I bore to thee calm'd all my Passions, allay'd my Discontent, reduc'd me to some degree of Acquiescence, to some faint Resolutions, some weak Endeavours; but my Reason was not yet strong enough to assist me; Without thy divine Aid, I'd still been groveling in my melancholy Shades, been sighing out my Hours, condemn'd to all the Tyrannies of Grief, and left a Prey to my own Thoughts; thou wert pleas'd to illuminate my Mind, to dissipate its Clouds, to spread a chearful, a reviving Warmth, through every part of my desponding Soul, to bid my Passions be still, and subject to the Laws of Reason.

From that auspicious Moment I begun to get new Strength, my Understanding grew brighter, and I'd a clearer View of Things: I found I'd magnify'd Objects, had swell'd my Afflictions to a larger size than really they were, had created Phantoms of Grief, frighted my self with Monsters of my own forming, and given the Name of Evil to Things which my enlightned Reason told me were not so; This made me resolve to make a narrow Scrutiny into my self, to examine by what Principles I was govern'd, what my Sentiments of Good and Evil were;

how agreeable to the Dictates of Truth; what those Things were which deserv'd my Concern, and for the Loss of which I could justify my Complaints; of what kind those Evils were whose Presence made me uneasy; and whether I could defend my Conduct before the Bar of impartial Reason. At length, on a severe Enquiry, I found I had proceeded on wrong Grounds, had gone in the common Road, taken up the Notions of the ignorant unthinking Vulgar; had call'd Things by those false Names they give them; then acknowledging my Errors, and asham'd of my Folly, I resolved to be no longer influenc'd by my Passions, no longer discontented about Trifles, Things wholly foreign to me, such as were no Appendages of my Happiness; to keep a constant Guard over my Thoughts; and as soon as I found any Disturbance within, any Tendency to Sorrow, Anger, Fear, or any other Disquieters of my Repose, I made a timely Resistance, never left contending till I'd vanquish'd my Opposers, and argu'd my self into a patient Submission, a calm Acquiescence of Temper.

I quickly found this Method to be highly advantageous; the more I made use of it, the more Ground I got; every Step was an Advance, a pressing nearer to that Tranquillity of Mind at which I aim'd. O how beneficial was it to me, when I saw the best of Mothers, best of Friends, rack'd with tormenting Pains, all pale and full of Anguish, meekly giving up her Soul, and taking her last, her dying Farewel! and at the same time an only Daughter, a Daughter worthy of my Love, threatned with impending Death, a Death which swiftly came to end the dismal Tragedy! Had I not then been arm'd with Resolution, how wretched had I been, how much a Slave to Grief! I consider'd they were not lost, were still the same to me, full of the same Tenderness, the same affectionate Concern, and would perhaps 'ere long meet me with Ecstacies of Joy, and be my kind Conductors to those peaceful Seats, those Mansions of Delight, where they are now possessing everlasting Pleasures, and joining with the Celestial Choir in grateful Songs of Love and Praise.

I'm now fully convinc'd, that the All-wise Disposer of Events knows what is fittest for me, and has been pleas'd to order all Things for the best; Whatever has been disgustful, whatever has given me Trouble, has been most afflicting among the melancholy Circumstances of my Life, has had its Use, has tended to the Improvement of my Mind, the Exercise of Virtue, and the fortifying of my Soul. Prosperity enervates, but

Adversity gives a manly Firmness, fences us against the Allurements of Sense, the tempting Blandishments of Life, makes us retire into our selves, and seek Satisfaction where 'tis only to be found.

From what I've said, I would not have it thought that 'tis a Stoical Apathy I've been recommending, and that in order to the being happy, I would have Persons insensible; no, I design no such thing: I allow them to delight in what they possess, to be thankful for Life, careful of Health, to enjoy Riches, to endeavour to get and preserve Reputation, to be pleas'd with Honours, to love their Friends and Kindred, and to be sollicitous for them; but then I would have all this done without disturbing their Minds, and without grieving for such Disappointments as they may probably meet with in reference to each of them: in a word, I would have them keep them without Anxiety, and part with them without Murmurs, still remembring, that it becomes them to prefer the Serenity of their own Minds before all other Concerns.

OF RICHES

Were we to form Judgments only from outward Appearances, from the general Practice of the World, should we not be inclin'd to think Riches the *Summum Bonum,* the chief, the only Good of Mankind, that without which 'twere impossible for them to enjoy the Felicity appropriated to their Nature? What else could be a Temptation strong enough to make them sacrifice their Ease, their Quiet, their Health, their Liberty, their Fame, and what ought to be infinitely more dear, their Virtue, their Honour, their Conscience, and all their future Hopes, to their Avarice? What prevalent enough to make them prize a great Estate more than an unspotted Innocence, a glittering Treasure more than a bright Understanding, and the Reputation of being richer than their Neighbours, more than that of being better and more rational? By what can they demonstrate a greater degeneracy of Soul, a higher pitch of Frenzy,

Lines 339–40. **Stoical Apathy**: detachment or disdain for worldly things.

than in making it the Business of their Lives, the chief Employment of their few flying Hours, of that short Portion of Time which was given them for much nobler, much more important Purposes, to add Acre to Acre, Field to Field, and by all the little, mean, sordid Arts of Saving, the base unworthy Methods of Gain, to accumulate Wealth, and add one heap of Dirt to another.

Such are much more cruel to themselves than the Poets feign the *Harpies* were to *Phineus;* they deny themselves the Conveniences of Life, languish for what's their own, and starve while they're surrounded with Plenty: Like *Midas,* they turn all things into Gold, and then, like him, are curs'd with the Fruition of what they passionately coveted, and as much unsatisfied with Plenitude, as they were with Want, as voracious and as craving as when they had nothing; always contriving how to get more, and as anxiously studious how to keep what they have gotten; restlesly busy by Day, watchful and fearful by Night, ever envying the Rich, and harassing the Poor, suspicious of being wrong'd, distrustful of their Neighbours, tyrannical to their Servants, niggardly to their Children, and wretchedly penurious to their Wives, a Curse to themselves, and a Plague to all that have the Misfortune to be near them, who lose all the Pleasures of Life, entail Infamy on their Names, and run the hazard of being everlastingly miserable only for the Vanity of having it said after their Death, that they have left a great Estate, have aggrandiz'd their Family, without considering that they must not only be answerable for the Injustice they've been guilty of in gaining their Riches, and for the little Good they've done with them, but for all the Mischiefs they may do those to whom they leave them; every Crime they occasion, every Vice they cherish, every Passion they raise, will be charg'd on them, and not only add to the Terrors of their awaken'd Consciences, but, like a mighty Weight, press them down, and sink them full of dreadful Apprehensions, of tormenting Remorses, and unconceivable Horrors, to the lowest, blackest, and more direful part of their infernal Prison.

And they are equally blame-worthy who employ their Wealth in the Service of their Ambition, their Pride, their Luxury, and their other Vices; who value themselves upon their Money and what it procures,

---

Line 21. **Phineus:** the Thracian king who was tormented by the Harpies, who stole or fouled all his food; he was rescued by the Argonauts.

big sounding Titles, glorious Equipages, magnificent Houses, rich Cloaths, and that Train of cumbersom Vanities which a large Estate draws after it; or who waste it in Intemperance, in gratifying their Palats, who place their Happiness in making the nearest Approaches they can to the brutal part of the Creation, and are never better pleas'd than when their Understandings are clouded, and their Reason thrown into a kind of Stupor, who divide their Time between Eating, Drinking, and Sleeping, and are more delighted with a fine-made Dish than with a wise Discourse, with the dear Relish of their delicious Wines than with the most ingenious entertaining Company; and who, were it put to their choice, would rather be the *Sardanapalus's,* the *Apicius's*, or *Vitellius's* of the Age, than the *Epaminondas's, Aristides's,* or *Antoninus's;* that is, had rather be the very Dregs of Mankind, than some of the most exalted Parts of the Rational Nature.

Unhappy Wretches! How are they tost from one Extreme to the other! forc'd to be avaricious in order to be wastful, extravagant and stingy by turns; now flattering, soothing, prostituting their Consciences, stooping to the basest, vilest, most unbecoming Actions, guilty of Perjuries, dip'd in Blood, and loaden with the Imprecations of the Oppressed; at other times, scornful, insulting, Pretenders to the highest Generosity, the greatest Liberality, and the most diffusive Charity, still inconsistent with themselves, a Prey to every ruling Vice, to every domineering Passion.

Now all this proceeds from having a wrong Notion of Things, from thinking that to be valuable which really is not so, from not knowing how to distinguish between those Things which contribute to our Happiness, and such as are no essential Parts of it; that is, betwixt what we may call our own, and what does not belong to us: Among which, I

Line 58. **Sardanapalus:** 4th-century king of Assyria known for decadence, luxury, and debauchery. **Apicius:** the name of three different Romans noted for being decadent gourmets.

Line 59. **Vitellius:** Emperor of Rome (A.D. 15–69) known for his extravagant feast of exotic foods; his reign lasted less than one year. **Epaminondas:** the celebrated Theban soldier (418–362 B.C.) who refused luxurious gifts offered by Artaxerxes, the king of Persia. **Aristides:** celebrated Athenian soldier and judge (fl. 484 B.C.), called "Aristides the Just," who died in poverty. **Antoninus:** Roman emperor (A.D. 137–61) surnamed "Pius" for his integrity and concern for the welfare of the people; known for his modest, simple lifestyle.

Line 66. **loaden:** laden, weighted down.

reckon Dignities and Riches, together with that Honour, Respect, and Reputation, which result from them; Things which, upon a due and serious Reflection, all must own we may be without, and yet be happy. Felicity consisting in the inward Peace and Satisfaction of the Mind, and is the Product of those internal Joys which spring from an inlightned Understanding, a well-regulated Judgment, a rectified Will, and an unpolluted Conscience, and not from any thing that is external, what we can neither bestow on our selves, nor keep when 'tis ours.

Of the Truth of this I would, if 'twere possible, convince the World, especially those of my own Sex; I would not have them fond of Wealth, or afraid of Poverty, neither look on the one as a real Good, nor on the other as a real Evil; but learn to put a right Estimate on Things, to prize them only according to their true Value, to think the Riches of the Mind the only desirable Possession, Virtue and Wisdom to be more inestimable Treasures than the brightest Jewels, Knowledge much better than Gold, and the Government of their Passions infinitely preferable to the most ambition'd Empire: They would not then be so busy about Trifles, so much concern'd about their Dresses, the Ornaments of their Houses, the making a splendid Appearance, and raising the Envy of each other: Neither would they be under the Temptation of selling their Liberty; they would, in their Marriages, prefer Virtue before a Title, good Sense before an Estate, and chuse a Man of Honour in Rags, rather than a vicious Prince, though he were Master of the World. If all would imbibe these Principles, what Order, what Beauty would there be! what an universal Harmony! All would be guided by the noblest Maxims, by the unerring Dictates of Truth: Riches, when in such Hands, would be a Blessing, and never be bestow'd but on such as deserv'd 'em, and knew how to employ 'em to the best Advantage: Parents would not then sacrifice their wretched Children to their Interest, and rather chuse to see them live miserably than poorly, as being more sollicitous for their being rich than happy: We should see no more unsuitable Matches; no Force would be put on Inclinations, Virtue and Vice would not be join'd, the Meek would not then be constrain'd to sigh out their Hours with the Passionate, the Humble subjected to the insupportable Humours of the Proud, nor the Liberal chain'd to the Covetous, confin'd to their Reverse, to what is diametrically opposite to their Temper; the Golden Age would be renew'd, and we should fancy our selves among the first happy Mortals, the innocent Inhabitants of the Anti-Diluvian Earth, the ancient Patriarchs, whom the Holy Scripture stiles the Sons of God.

O that 'twere in my power to reduce that into practice which I so much wish! Wou'd I had Eloquence enough to perswade my Readers to encourage Virtue, by making their Wealth the Reward of just, brave, and laudable Actions! If my Heart does not deceive me, I would readily do what I earnestly recommend; and were I Mistress of a great Estate, would much sooner leave it to a pious Servant than avicious Son: I own no Relations but what are founded on Virtue, no Friendships but what spring from a joint Love of Truth; and would rather, were I left to my Choice, live with a *Socrates* in his Prison, than be the Companion of an *Antony* amidst the Excesses of a luxurious Court, much rather have been the Wife of a *Crates,* or an *Epictetus;* of a Husband poor as the first, and deform'd as the last, than the Partner of a Throne with a *Tiberius*, a *Caligula,* a *Nero,* or a *Heliogabalus.*

Me sacred Virtue moves alone;
I will no Rival Passion own:
Begone, begone, in vain ye sue,
I'll to my firm Resolves be true:
No more shall Riches tempt my Sight
With their false, their glaring Light:
Before me when the Phantoms play,
From them, with Scorn, I'll turn away;
Defy their Power, and slight their Art,
And still be Mistress of my Heart.

Line 125. **Antony**: Mark Antony (83–31 B.C.), the Roman general and lover of Cleopatra.

Line 126. **Crates**: Cynic philosopher (ca. 365–285 B.C.) who lived in poverty by choice and who was horribly deformed. **Epictetus**: (A.D. 60–ca. 140) a Stoic philosopher, born a slave of Epaphroditus and freed by Nero; his thoughts on austerity, humility, patience, and contempt of riches were collected by a student under the title of *Enchiridion*.

Line 127. **Tiberius**: Roman emperor (42 B.C.–A.D. 37) known for his patronage of learning and for his debauched life.

Line 128. **Caligula**: Roman emperor (A.D. 12–41) whose reign was characterized by madness and tyranny. **Nero**: Roman emperor (A.D. 36–68) noted for barbaric cruelty; he ordered the executions of his mother, Seneca, Lucan, and Petronius. **Heliogabalus**: (A.D. 204–22), Roman emperor whose reign was noted for its cruel capriciousness and debauchery; he made his horse a consul.

The only Use I know Riches are of, is the having it in one's Power to help the Needy, to do Good to the Indigent. I assure the Reader, were they given to me on condition, I should wholly keep them to my self; I would not accept of a Gift so clog'd: But such a Supposition ought not to be made; 'tis unfit to imagine so much as a remote possibility of such a Narrowness of Mind in God; in him who is Goodness it self, and gives to all his Creatures with an unbounded Munificence, and whom we cannot in any thing please better, than in imitating the Benignity of his Nature, and in endeavouring to be Bountiful as he is Bountiful; which tho' we cannot be in effect, yet we may be in desire; we may wish well to all; and those we cannot make Rich, we may by our Advice endeavour to make Easie, Patient and Resign'd; tho' we cannot give them Gold, yet we may teach them Wisdom, and by inspiring them with a Love of Virtue, Probity, and Truth, put them in possession of the most valuable Treasures, Treasures without which all others would be Curses instead of Blessings, and consequently should deserve to be plac'd among their chiefest Benefactors, as having made them the greatest, the most inestimable Present.

OF SELF-LOVE

We are born with a strong Desire of being happy; 'tis a Principle coæval with our Souls, it grows with us, and will prove as lasting as our Beings; 'tis the Centre to which all our Motions tend, it gives a Byass to our Actions, a sort of Fermentation to our Spirits, makes us press forward, keeps our Thoughts bent, and always ready, with a precipitous Eagerness, a violent Impetuosity to rush on every Appearance of Good, to grasp whatever has but the Resemblance of Happiness, or, what is infinitely more deplorable, too often obtrudes upon us real Evils for seeming Goods: But this is wholly owing to the Depravity of our Judgments, and the Darkness of our Understandings; for none, no not the most

Line 1. **coæval:** coeval, of the same date of origin.

profligate Wretches, chuse Evil, as Evil: Were it unmask'd, did it appear as it is, they would shun it with the greatest Abhorrency, fly from it with the utmost Detestation; 'tis the specious Vizard that deludes them, the tempting Case that allures them: The beautiful Cover conceals the ugly Face, hides the natural Deformity, and proves pernicious to the unwary Spectators, makes them mistake that for their Interest, which is not so, and, with the fond *Narcissus,* place their Affection on a wrong Object; makes them, like him, pine for Trifles, and foolishly address themselves to charming Nothings, Shadows of Felicity, to Things much below the Notice of Pretenders to Reason.

Such as endeavour, by darkening other People's Reputations, to make their own shine the brighter; who basely cringe and flatter to get Favour, lye and perjure themselves to serve a Cause, to strengthen a Party, or promote what they call an Interest, who without Scruple make use of all the little mean Arts of raising an Estate, all the vile cheating ways of getting Money, fancy they love themselves; 'tis that mistaken Imagination which involves them in all the Injustice and Folly with which they are chargeable: First, it blinds their Judgment, and then corrupts their Reason; and when that's done, hurries them impetuously on, and on a sudden plunges them into an Abyss of Crimes, a Fathomless Depth of Guilt: Whereas, were they but so happy as to have right Notions of Good and Evil; did they but know wherein their true Interest consisted, what would give them lasting Reputations, intitle them to the highest Honours, and put them in Possession of the most valuable Treasures, they would soon make use of different Methods, fix their Esteem on nobler Objects, and love themselves with a more rational Affection, an Affection which would exert it self in the most generous Acts of Kindness; they would then be sensible that they cannot be Enemies to others, as to themselves, that every Breach of Justice, every Violation of Truth, and every Infringement of Charity, is a Wrong to themselves; that 'tis impossible for them to calumniate, or deceive their Neighbours, without injuring their own Souls; can't amass Treasures, purchase Titles, or raise themselves to Honours by undue Ways, without deeply wounding their own Consciences, drawing on themselves unavoidable Mischiefs, and running the Risque of being everlastingly miserable. Such Considerations as these would have a vital Influence on their Lives, and soon make them universal Blessings; the more they lov'd themselves, the more they would love others, would endeavour to make them feel the same Truths, and see the same Beauties. That glorious Reward, which is always the Recompence of virtuous Actions, would be still in view, and that secret Satisfaction, that internal Pleasure, which arises from the Sense of having done what they ought, would sweetly lead them on, and make them take an inexpressible Delight, an inconceivable Complacency in doing Good. O how happy should we be, were we all equally convinced of this important Truth! how securely should we then live, in how much Innocence and Peace! The World would then be one continued Scene of Pleasure, one great Family of Love.

Love quickly would the World unite,
 In ev'ry Breast erect its Throne,
Mankind to solid Joys invite,
 Joys to poor Mortals now unknown.
Friendship would then no Traffick prove;
 But, by much nobler Precepts taught,
All like th' Angelick Forms above,
 Would be one Soul, one Mind, one Thought:
To them 'twould then uneasie grow,
 To them a *Self-denial* be,
The smallest Disrespect to show,
 Where they superior Merit see.
Then, influenc'd by a Law Divine,
 They would become each other's Care,
The general Good would still design,
 And seek their own Advantage there.

But this will never be, while they are impos'd on by their Senses, while they look on their Passions as part of themselves, and fancy to resist them is to offer Violence to their Nature: If they are blam'd for their Folly, so far are they from owning that they are culpable, that they plead for their Faults, turn Advocates for their Crimes, call in their Senses as Auxilaries to assist them, and would, if it were possible, suborn their Reason to give Evidence for them; they make use of all the Artifice and Industry imaginable to hide them from themselves; they put on them the Appearances of Virtue, and represent them to their Imagination under wrong Figures, under false Names. Avarice they call a Love of Temperance, Moderation, Prudence, and a laudable Concern for Posterity: Prodigality, a being careful of their Reputation, Generosity, Liberality and Magnificence: Pride, a setting a due Value on themselves: Fear, a becoming Caution, a putting a true Estimate on Life. Thus they turn to themselves only the wrong Sides of Objects, contribute to their own Delusion, are accessary to their own Captivity, and do as much as in them lies to reduce their Souls to the worst Slavery. If at any time they seem averse to one Passion, 'tis either because it is not agreeable to their Constitution, or suitable to their present Circumstances, or else they abandon it, in order to the indulging some other; and if they happen to be allur'd by some transient Glimpse of hope of a future Reward (which the worst of Men have one time or other experimented) or be deterr'd by the terrifying Dread of a future Vengeance from gratifying a Vice, they think it a great piece of *Self-denial,* a very meritorious Action; Whereas, according to the strict Language of Truth, to act contrary to the Dictates of Reason, to subject the Soul to the Body, the Intelectual Faculties to the Senses, and the Understanding to the Passions, is, properly speaking, the greatest, the only *Self-denial,* the most convincing Proof of their being their own Enemies. Could they quiet these internal Disturbers, allay the Storms they raise in their Breasts, and reduce their Minds to a peaceful Silence, they would in that happy Calm, that Cessation of their Passions, be at leisure to attend to the Calls of their Consciences, and the Perswasions of Reason; they would hear the soft Whispers of Truth, and be no longer deaf to its Remonstrances; the Divine Light would dart it self into their Understandings, give a new Turn to their Thoughts, inform their Judgments, rectify their Wills, and make a through, a wonderful Change, an advantageous Alteration, transform them into something so beautiful, so worthy of Esteem, as would at once justifie their having a Kindness for themselves, and entitle them to the Love and Veneration of Mankind.

Line 110. **through**: thorough, complete.

OF JUSTICE

There is no Virtue more talk'd of, and pretended to than *Justice,* and yet perhaps none less understood, and worse practised.

The greatest part of Mankind are chain'd to what they call their Interest, incessantly tugging at the Oar, imploy'd in the tiresome Service of their Vices, or in the no less troublesome Gratification of their Humours: Reason has no Superiority over them; her Voice is too soft, her Whispers too low to be heard amidst so much Hurry and Noise. She delights in a calm Mind, chuses to reside in the inmost Recess of a silent compos'd Soul; such unhappy Wretches, such unthinking Creatures, cannot bear her Reproofs, cannot endure her gentlest Admonitions, her kindest, most endearing Perswasions. Whatever runs counter to their Vices, gives a Check to their rapacious Desires, sets Bounds to their Avarice, or attempts to stop them in their impetuous Career, offends them. They think it an Injury to be kept from committing Crimes, from doing Wrong; and, what is most to be wonder'd at, so much are they govern'd by their Passions, that what they are apt to censure in others, to load with the highest Imputations, and place in the blackest Catalogue of Sins, they not only wink at in themselves, but are so audacious, as to own them publickly, and plead for them as equitable Actions.

The sordid starving Miser exclaims against Covetousness in others, though at the same time he cruelly oppresses the Poor, encroaches upon his Neighbours, robs them of their Rights, cheats them in Buying and Selling, injures the Orphan, makes his Children miserable, his Wife a Servant, and his Servants Slaves; yet he pretends to abhor these things, fancies himself to be at the remotest Distance from them, and would be believ'd to have the highest Detestation for them; none complains more of the Injustice of others, tells you longer Stories of the hard Usage he has met with, the Law-Suits he is unhappily involv'd in, the Trespasses that are done him, the Damages he sustains from ill Men; In short, all the Misfortunes that surround him, all the Troubles that break in upon him, like an overflowing Torrent.

Now, this would never be, if Men had right Notions of Justice, if they knew how to distinguish between Good and Evil, were attentive to Reason, and willing to hearken to the Voice of Truth, ready to permit it, to set them Rules of Living, and then make it the Judge, not only of their Words and Actions, but of their very Thoughts, they being the vital Principles, the Springs, the Master-wheels that put the rest in Motion; and, that being done, submit to its decisive Sentence, and resolve, after having once chosen it for their Director, to pay it a constant uniform Obedience, to give themselves up entirely to its Conduct, and to do nothing without its Approbation; and whenever they are contriving a Design, or about to perform any Action, I would desire them to view it in the clearest Light, to bring it to the severest Test, to examine it before the Bar of Conscience, and seriously ask themselves this necessary Question: Is what we are now going to do, what we would willingly have done to our selves? Would we be so used, so spoken of? And if they find they would not, then they ought carefully to avoid it.

This Method would entitle them to Treasures infinitely greater, infinitely more valuable than those transient ones which they are in pursuit of, would give them the Possession of an internal Tranquility, of an inexpressible Satisfaction, of those pure and lasting Pleasures which result from Innocence, from the Sense of having done what they ought. O how happy, how delightful will it render their Days, how easie and undisturb'd their Nights! They will hear nothing but Praise, nothing but Repetitions of their just, generous, and honourable Actions; they will have no melancholy upbraiding Thoughts, no black Idea's obtruded on their Imagination, nothing to interrupt their Rest, to render their Sleep less pleasant. The same may be said of all others; there are none but will find a strict Adherence to the immutable Laws of Truth and Justice, very advantageous; they will make them easie to themselves, as well as to those they converse with, render them universal Blessings, and bestow on them the Honour of being Conservators of the Order of the World, of that admirable, that beautiful Order, which owes its Origin to the Almighty Creator, to that infinite Wisdom which made the Universe.

The Rich will then perceive, that they are under an Obligation of doing all the Good they can with their Wealth; that they are but Stewards, Persons intrusted by another, by the Proprietor of all things, and by him employ'd to be the Distributers of his Bounty, the Bestowers of his Gifts on the Needy, and the Rewarders of Merit; that the Great, those that are rais'd above the rest of Mankind, that are incircled with Honours, and possess'd of Grandeur, are made more powerful than their

Fellow-Mortals, with no other Design, but that they may protect the Innocent, right the Injur'd, encourage the Virtuous, punish the Ill, and by their Menaces fright the Vicious from their execrable Practices. The Lovers of Pleasure will, by these Laws, be taught to regulate their Conduct, to keep within the Bounds of Honour, to do nothing that may deserve a Reproof, or occasion a Blush, nothing that they can be justly reproach'd for, either by their own Consciences, or the World, will be deterr'd from the barbarous, the ungenteel Custom of diverting themselves at the Expence of their Neighbours Reputations, will scorn to do them Wrong only to make themselves Sport: They will be acted by better, by nobler Principles, proceed on more becoming Motives, and place their Delight in something much more innocent, as well as more exalted.

How happy would the World be, were Mankind influenc'd by these Rules! They would then be induc'd to do good Actions from the Beauty they see in them, from their Agreeableness to Reason, to that Truth which speaks within them, from that Justice which dictates to their Souls, because they tend to the Honour of God, and are universal Blessings, Blessings not only to those to whom they are done, but to those who do them; and they would not then be so vain, so childishly proud, as to expect Applauses for doing what they ought, or be angry for not being thank'd for performing Actions, which if they had left undone, they would have deserv'd to have been punish'd.

When we talk of Gratitude, of Generosity, of Retributions, of making Returns for Favours, we do but complement the Persons to whom we speak, do but sooth their Vanity, humour their Pride, treat them as we do froward Children, give them Rattles to keep them quiet, our Discourse is not according to the strict Language of Truth. Did we tye our selves to that, we should tell People, That such as boast of their being highly generous, of their showing a more than ordinary Liberality, are either performing Acts of Justice, or giving the World Specimens of their Imprudence. Charities ill bestow'd are real Mischiefs to Persons that receive them, and to those that give them; and if they are conferr'd on the Good, on the Deserving, they are what they may challenge, Things to which they have a legal Claim, Kindness being a Debt due to Humanity; and that they have no other Business here but to be useful and serviceable to each other; that they are all parts of one great Community, and obliged by the Laws of their Creation to be assistant to each other, to do all the friendly Offices they can for every one they are acquainted with, nay, they ought to extend their Regard to the whole Species; some they may relieve, others advise; to some may be beneficial by vindicating their Fame, to others by defending them from Dangers; to their Inferiours by Acts of Charity, by endeavouring to make them easie, to render them as happy as their Condition will bear, as they can be here, and by instructing them in necessary Truths, to put them in the Way of being so for ever; to their Equals, by all the endearing Instances of Kindness, all the Demonstrations of a sincere and hearty Affection, of a zealous and active Esteem; to their Superiors by paying them all imaginable Services, giving them all the convincing Testimonies of a dutiful Concern, of a real and disinteress'd Respect; and as for such as are not within the Verge of their Acquaintance, the Sphere of their Knowledge, they may wish them well, and afford them a Room in their Prayers. If these things were universally observ'd, there would be no Place for Complaints.

If all did what became them in their respective Stations, were just from an inward Principle, from that internal Delight and Complacency they take in doing good and commendable Actions, a Delight which terminates in it self, has no regard to Praise, to sordid Gain, or to any little base Design, how great would be our Felicity! how much would Earth resemble Heaven!

'Twould like the blest *Millennium* prove,
That Prototype of Joys above,
Where Truth th'Ascendant still shall gain,
Justice shall triumph, Virtue reign:
Where having view'd each other's Heart,
And found them void of Fraud and Art,
Free from Avarice, free from Hate,
Sincerely good, and firm as Fate,
We shall our Souls in one combine,
Shall join them with a Knot Divine,
A Knot so closely, strongly ty'd,
That nothing shall the Bond divide;
And that it may be sure to last,
Love, with a Smile, shall bind it fast:

Line 130. **Millennium**: period of one thousand years after the Resurrection in which Christ will reign on earth with the faithful.

Where we shall equal Plenty have,
None be poor, nor none a Slave;
None shall wrong, nor none complain,
A peaceful Temper there shall reign.
The tender Lamb and Wolf shall play,
The Kids among the Lions stray;
The lowing Herds with Bears shall feed,
No Guardians no Protectors need;
So mild, so gentle shall they prove,
They at a Child's Command shall move;
Their little Leader, pleas'd, obey,
And follow where he leads the Way.
Weak Infants shall with Serpents sport,
Unhurt, shall to their Dens resort.
None there shall any Mischief do,
None there their native Fierceness shew.
Goodness Divine shall there abound,
And Mercy spread it self around,
Shall every where it self display,
Into each Breast it self convey:
Delights so pure, intense, and strong,
Shall fill their Minds, and swell their Song,
That they'll their Thousand Years employ,
In one Extatick Now of Joy.

O thou, who art Justice it self, make me, I humbly beseech thee, like thee in this, and all thy other communicable Attributes. Let my whole Life be conformble to that immutable Order which thou hast establish'd in the World, to that universal Reason which ought to govern all intelligent Beings: Let that Divine Pleasure it affords imprint it self sweetly on my Thoughts, display it self in my Words, and powerfully influence all my Actions; Let my Understanding clearly see that Amiableness, that Train of Beauties, that Concatenation of Charms there is in what it loves; and enable my Judgment to form strong and convincing Conclusions of that Truth it embraces, that my Affection may become the Result of a deliberate and rational Choice, not the Product only of Chance, or a warm Imagination. Let me act from the highest, the most exalted Principles, endeavour to be exactly just in all my Transactions,

Line 175. **Concatenation:** combination.

my Discourses, and all the various Circumstances of Life, and this without having a Regard either to Applauses here, or Recompences hereafter, without being brib'd by Secular Advantages, or frighted by the Threatning of an eternal Vengeance, as much doubting were I sway'd only by such Motives, I should (supposing there were no such Inducements) desist from doing what I ought, and become negligent in the Pursuit of Virtue, deficient in Matters of the most important Moment: Assist me in banishing from my Mind all false Notions, whatever may serve to heighten my Pride, encrease my Vanity, raise my Anger, or augment any uneasie Resentment: When I have done good Offices, been kind to the Distress'd, liberal to the Needy, affectionately concern'd for those with whom I converse, and ready to serve them to the utmost Extent of my Power, let me not expect Retributions, nor be troubled if I am not thank'd, nor upbraid those to whom I have been friendly with their Forgetfulness, but contentedly retire into my self, and there seek that Satisfaction which accrues from having done what becomes me: And on the contrary, if I have done any thing to which the World thinks fit to affix the Epithet of *Generous,* any thing that attracts Regard, and looks like an Act of uncommon Bounty, let me consider, that all I have is thine, that it was given me to be laid out for thy Glory, and that while I detain it from the Indigent, I am incurring thy Displeasure, drawing Guilt on my self, and robbing my Soul of those Joys, which are the inseparable Companions of a just and innocent Life, a benificent and chearful Temper, and depriving my self of those transporting *Euge's,* those ravishing Benedictions, which at the final Judgment, the great Day of Retribution, shall consummate the Bliss of the Righteous.

That Bliss to which I longing haste,
Those Joys I even faint to taste.
Say, ye bright Forms, who once were Men,
Would you assume your Flesh agen,
And leave your Beatifick Sight,
For all the World can call Delight?
O no! You'd all things here decline
But for a Glimpse of what's Divine;
And if one Glance so dear wou'd prove,
How much must full Fruition move?

Line 201. **Indigent**: needy.

OF ANGER

Anger in the moral World, is the same that a Hurricane is in the natural; it raises a violent Tempest in the Soul, clouds the Judgment, overturns the Reason, shatters the Understanding, puts a resistless Force on the Will, crouds the Memory with black Idea's, with infernal Images, Thunders from the Tongue, Darts pointed Lightning from the Eyes, sometimes breaks forth into Flouds of Tears, and too often vents its Fury in Deluges of Blood: It throws the Thoughts into the utmost Confusion; they appear like a troubled Sea, where Billow meets with Billow, one Wave with deafning Horrour breaks upon another; sometimes the mounting Surges almost reach the Sky, and then are on a sudden thrown low as the Center of the Earth: The Mind is furiously agitated, the whole Body disorder'd; there is nothing within but Hurry and Tumult, nothing to be seen without but Fierceness and Rage, Convulsive Motions, staring Eyes, broken Sentences, frightful Looks, Faces pale as Death, or red as Blood: In a word, a Mixture of Folly and Madness, Man and Beast blended together, or rather something more savage; something crueller than hungry Lions, than provok'd Tigers.

Would you represent the angry Man to your self, would you form lively Idea of him in your Imagination, fancy you heard *Cerberus* barking, and at the same time saw the Furies with their Torches flaming, their Eyes casting forth malignant Flashes, the nauseous Froth forcing a Passage thro' their distorted Lips, and the dreadful Vipers hissing round their ghastly Heads; yet this, and whatsoever the most pregnant Invention can add, to render it more hideous, will not come up to the ugly, the monstrous, the horrid Original. Could he see himself, he would be so far from falling in Love with his own Resemblance, that he would do the World a Kindness, and at once free Mankind and himself of one of the greatest Plagues, their most insupportable Burdens: But he is too much blinded by his Passion, to be able to discern his own Deformity,

Line 19. **Cerberus:** in classical myth, a dog with three heads that guards the entrance of hell to prevent the dead from escaping and the living from entering.

Line 20. **Furies:** ministers of the vengeance of the gods, on Earth and in Hades, typically represented as having serpents rather than hair.

or the Devil that possesses him. *Lucifer* himself had not more Pride, nor a larger Share of Envy and Malice; and were his Power as great, the Effects would be as deplorably pernicious; he would soon spoil the beautiful Order of Things, destroy the Harmony of Nature, and reduce the World to its original Confusion, its primitive Chaos, to an Anarchy like that which he has in his own Breast.

How unhappy! how unexpressibly miserable are they who condemn themselves to so rigorous, so shameful a Slavery, who put it in the Power of every trivial Accident, of every little Disappointment, to harrass and torture their Minds; and whom, if you would be spiteful, if you would give your self the Liberty of gratifying an ill-natur'd Pleasure, you might with a Glance, a Word, or an Action in it self innocent and well intended, but dexterously manag'd, blow into a Flame, and deprive of all their Peace, all their Satisfaction, and make 'em as ragingly impatient as a blind *Polyphemus*, or a disappointed *Ajax*. While the Frenzy lasts, you might have the Diversion to see them, like that *Grecian* Hero, exercising their Valour on Brutes, and mistaking Hogs for *Agamemnons*, or, like *Don Quixote*, fighting with Windmills, and doing things more ridiculously extravagant than any that are to be found in Romances. What greater Punishment could their most implacable Enemies wish them? And what Objects are there in the World that more deserve our Compassion? And what would be more generous, more becoming Christians, the Followers of a meek, tender, patient, and commiserating Master, than to endeavour to restore them to the Use of their Reason, resettle them in the Possession of themselves, reinstate them in those Privileges, to which their Humanity gives them an indisputable Right, and of which 'twas impossible for them to have been disseiz'd, without their own Consent.

In order to the compassing a Design, which will prove so universal a Good to Mankind, so unexpressibly beneficial to the whole Community, it will, in the First place, be best to enquire, what those things are which generally excite *Anger?* And when we have exactly weigh'd them, and heedfully consider'd all their Circumstances, we will put into the opposite Scale that Calmness, Easiness, Sedateness, Firmness, and

---

Line 44. **Polyphemus**: single-eyed monster blinded by Ulysses. **Ajax**: Greek warrior who, in Horace's *Satires* 2.3, in a fit of rage slaughtered a flock of sheep believing them to be sons of Atreus, who had given Achilles' armor to Ulysses.

Tranquility, that inward Complacency and Joy, together with those outward Demonstrations of Love and Veneration, which are the inseparable Attendants of a humble, quiet and dispassionate Temper, and see which will preponderate.

Anger proceeds from an Opinion of our being injur'd either in our Persons, Reputations, or Possessions: Now though all Evils of this kind are imaginary, as having no Existence in Nature, yet to a disturb'd Fancy they appear real, and will sensibly afflict, till we free our selves from them by the Use of proper Remedies, by having Recourse to Philosophy, the Physick of the Soul, that Catholicon which will cure all its Maladies, enable it to throw off all its peccant Humours, strengthen and invigorate its Constitution, give a Clearness and Vivacity to its visive Faculty, and render it capable of taking a thorough View of Things, of seeing them as they are, of rightly distinguishing between what is truly ours, and what is anothers; between what has its Dependancy on us, is free, and cannot be hinder'd from being ours, and what has not its Dependance on us, but is subject to another, and may be denied us at pleasure; of discerning the Difference betwixt the Things we ought to wish for, and those we ought to shun; the Objects of our Desire, and those of our Aversion.

Of the first kind are our Inclinations, our Opinions, and all the Operations of our Mind, all that comes within the Verge of our Will, whatever we can give our selves, and continue in our own Power: The second are such Things as are without us, such as we receive from another; I mean, all such as are vulgarly known by the Name of the Goods of Fortune, Things which are not within the Sphere of our Activity, within our Reach, or at our Disposal, which no more belong to us than they do to separate Beings, or inanimate Lumps of Matter: Till we can thus revolve them in our Minds, assign them their proper Stations, place them in opposite Ranks, and are intimately acquainted with their specifick Discrimination, we can never be easy, never be happy, never be Masters of our selves; cannot know what to have a Repugnance against, or on what to fix our Desires.

Now such as know that their Bodies, their Reputation, their Kindred,

---

Line 72. **Catholicon**: a universal remedy. Line 73. **peccant**: morbid, inducing illness.
Line 74. **visive**: visual; concerning the power of vision.

their Friends, their Acquaintance, their Servants, their Wealth, their Honours, their Places, or whatever else serves to swell the Catalogue of contingent Goods, are Things foreign to them, Things that do not in the least concern them; some of them such as they cannot get without indefatigable Toil, without little mean Compliances, without hazarding their Liberty, their Integrity, their Sincerity, all that ought to be dear to the Lovers of Virtue, to all such as make Truth the Standard of their Actions, the Criterion by which they desire to be try'd; and that for others, they must be obliged to the favourable Concurrence of several Things to compass them, to a propitious Conjunction of lucky Hits, to make them theirs; and if they at the same time consider, that there are as many Ways of losing them as there are of gaining them, and that they cannot assure themselves of them for the short Duration of a Moment, they will look on them with Indifference, as Things infinitely below the attentive Regard of a rational Soul, much less of an affectionate Tenderness.

The deeper Impression such Thoughts as these make upon them, the farther will they withdraw themselves from them, the more they will be upon their Guard, the better prepar'd to encounter every cross Accident; nothing will be surprizing, nothing new, or unexpected; they will, as *Epictetus* says, when they remove an earthen Cup, consider, that 'tis Brittle, and may easily be broken; and they will from such inconsiderable Instances, from Things which have the lowest place in their Esteem, rise to such as are higher and more valuable, to such as have a nearer Relation to them: If their Parents, their Kindred, their Friends, those that are oblig'd by the Ties of Blood, of Honour, of all that's estimable among Men, to treat them with Affection and Respect, should prove unkind, treacherous, and malicious, they will quiet themselves by reflecting on the Fickleness of Human Nature, by considering that Inconstancy is the Characteristick of both Sexes, and 'tis as easy to find a Phoenix as a Person that is always the same: The Philosopher who made a narrow Scrutiny for an honest Man, might with as little hopes of Success have search'd for a faithful Friend, they being equally difficult to be found.

If their Children prove disobedient, they'll remember 'tis natural for Youth to be rash, headstrong, fond of themselves, impatient of Restraint, and violently hurried on by their Passions, and therefore the Follies they are guilty of are not to be wonder'd at, and that 'tis more disagreeable to Reason for them to be moved at them, than for the others to do them.

If such as are making their Approaches to the Grave, who are taking their Leave of Life, and all its Enjoyments, prove their Enemies, if they oppress them, detain their Rights from them, and treat them inhumanly, they will be so far from being enrag'd, that they will look with pity on the Infirmities of their Age, and be ready to impute their Failures to their true Cause, to the Decays of their Understanding, their repeated Acts of Injustice, to the mistaken Love of themselves, and their insatiable Thirst after Riches, which unhappily encreases proportionately to their Incapacity to use them, to the Boundlesness of their Desires, and the making Wealth the Center to which they direct all their Aims, and for which they hope to be valu'd when they've nothing else left to recommend them.

If the Great endeavour to injure them, if they insult over them, they will look with Scorn on their Attempts, will consider them on the same Level with themselves in respect of their Souls, and of those Materials whereof their Bodies are jointly compos'd, as Parts of the same Community, of the same Order of Beings, and distinguish'd from one another only by a few adventitious Advantages, Things that have no intrinsick Worth in them, and consequently can confer none on their Possessors, but derive all their Value from the Opinion of others; they will likewise reflect on the Limitedness of their Power, that after all their Threatnings, they can extend it to nothing that is truly their own, that they can't rob them of their Virtue, their Constancy, their inward Serenity, the unspeakable Delights of a well-satisfied Conscience, of a regular, calm, and intrepid Mind.

If their Equals abuse them, if they make it their Business to defraud them of their Legal Rights, to injure them either in their Persons or their Fame, they will, if 'tis possible, secure themselves from Violence and Contumelies, will endeavour to justify themselves, will avouch their Innocency, and strive to undeceive those they converse with; but if the World will still think them culpable, they will despise the invidious Censurers, and quiet themselves with the Plaudits of their own Breast, with the Knowledge of their own Innocency, without once condescending to any thing so mean, as to express a Dissatisfaction; no, they will still make a brave Defence, a noble Resistance, will stand firm against every Attack, and if they must lose the Day, they'll fall with Honour, die without Complaints, or so much as a Change of Countenance, without making indecent Reflections, doing or saying any thing that might give the nicest Observer occasion to call their Conduct in question.

If they are their Inferiors that displease them, they'll look on them as Persons below their Anger; and 'twill be alike to them whether the Provocation proceeds from Insolence or Carelessness, from Contempt or Inadvertency, from Dullness or Obstinacy, from Want of Sense or Malice: Let the Motive be what it will, they are resolv'd not to give 'em so great an Advantage over them, as to put it in their Power to discompose their Minds: They know Injuries consist only in Opinion, and that they can't be wrong'd, can't be affronted, unless they themselves contribute to it; there must be the Concurrence of their own Will to make it an Evil; therefore they prudently fence against the first Impressions, the first Ebullitions of Passion, and think themselves sufficient Gainers if at any Rate they can purchase so great a Blessing as Constancy.

And as for Riches, they will consider, that they are not essentially necessary, that Nature is contented with a little; that the way to enjoy them, is to keep the Heart loose from them, to be unconcern'd whether we have them or not, and by little Trials to prepare for greater, to bear small Losses unmov'd, always remembring, that Poverty with Contentment, is much more desirable than a plentiful Estate with Uneasiness and an anxious Sollicitude, it being better to suffer all the Extremities of Hunger, Thirst, and Cold, and preserve a compos'd, chearful, and resigning Temper, a steddy, firm, and undaunted Greatness of Mind to the last Gasp, than to live amidst the greatest Affluence of Wealth, with a Soul full of Disturbance and insatiable Desires, a Soul which neither knows how to keep, nor how to part with what it has, which pierces it self with what it grasps, turns its Blessings into Punishments, its Joys into Fears, and the Bounties of Heaven into Occasions of Mischief both to it self and others.

They farther consider, That Titles and Places of Trust, their being advanc'd to honorable Posts, to dazling Heights, to Stations above the Kenn of vulgar Eyes, will not justify their being Proud, Imperious, Passionate, Cruel, and Revengeful; no, they'll rather make them more watchful over themselves, more vigilant Inspectors of their own

Line 185. **Ebullitions:** bubblings.

Actions; they will check every peevish Humour, suppress every arrogant Thought, every malicious Suggestion, every furious Motion, will arm themselves with Patience, put favourable Constructions on every Occurrence, mild and charitable Interpretations on whatever they see or hear, will strive to sweeten their Minds, to free them from Perturbations, from the dangerous Sallies of an ungovern'd Anger, of an unmanageable Rage, and all the other ill Effects of a brutish forbidding Temper; and in order to the rendring themselves fit to be belov'd, will assume a soft engaging Air, a humble and inviting Mein, and, as far as they are able, endeavour to imitate that Goodness to which they owe their Exaltation, and make it their Care to become universal Blessings, as knowing they have no other way of making themselves valu'd by the rational, the thinking part of Mankind.

None but the Mob, the Dregs of the Creation, will prize the Beast for its Trappings, or honour it the more because it carries a Goddess; others will know how to distinguish between the poor worthless Bird and its gay borrow'd Plumes; betwixt the gawdy Outside, and the contemptible Wretch that owns it; will laugh behind the Scenes, to see a Pigmy strut in Buskins, now act the fiery Son of *Peleus*, the mad *Orestes,* the greedy *Midas*, the enrag'd *Cambyses*, the revengeful *Coriolanus*, the cruel *Marius,* the bloody *Sylla*, and the inhumane *Nero*, personating by turns all the Monsters of Antiquity; Such become *Phalaris's* and *Procrustes's* to themselves and others; they share in the Torments they inflict; their Passions exercising the same Barbarities on them, they do on such as have the hard Fate to be subjected to their Tyranny.

'Tis unaccountably strange, that while the Bears, the Wolves, the

---

Lines 221–22. **Bird and its gay borrow'd Plumes**: Aesop's fable of the jay who dressed up in peacock feathers.

Line 224. **Buskins**: thick-soled laced half-boot worn by actors of Greek and Roman tragedies. **Son of Peleus**: Achilles. **Orestes**: avenged his father's (Agamemnon's) death and was driven mad by the Furies.

Line 225. **Cambyses**: King of Persia, son of Cyrus the Great; he killed his brother, Smerdis. **Coriolanus**: Caius Marcius, celebrated soldier who turned against Rome.

Line 226. **Marius**: Roman military dictator (157–86 B.C.) who rose from the peasantry to become a cruel tyrant.

Line 227. **Phalaris**: (ca. 570–49 B.C.) tyrant of Agrigentum; he was known as a torturer who was killed by his own people using his same methods. **Procrustes**: the robber of Attica who attacked travelers and tortured them by tying them on a bed and either stretching or chopping them up to fit it.

Foxes, the Apes, and all the numerous Individuals of the Bestial Kingdom, are kind to their own Species, never quarrel among themselves, nor break the Union made by Nature, when press'd by Hunger they fall on different Kinds, or on Man, the Common Enemy, but are never known, though urged by Famine, or the most voracious Appetite, to feed upon themselves, or any of the same Denomination; That Men should become fond of ruining each other, should thirst for each other's Blood; that a Glance, a Word, a Mistake, a seeming Neglect, a few useless Trifles, Toys fit only for Children and Fools to fight and cry for, should set them together by the Ears, and make them prove Beasts of Prey to one another: How will they worry each other for a little Dirt! with what Eagerness snatch the half-chew'd Morsels from each others Mouths! The Shadow of an Injury, the bare Opinion of a Wrong, is enough to make them bite and scratch, and murder Reputations, do the vilest, most execrable Actions.

Now if, upon the whole, we would consult our Reason, would with a cool, a silent, calm Attention, listen to the Director that is within us, we should quickly be convinc'd of the Deformity of this Vice, of its Contrariety to the immutable Order of Things, of its fatal Consequences, the innumerable Mischiefs it produces, the Irrationality of its Conduct, and the Impetuosity of its Motions, we should then, with the highest Detestation, behold all those deplorable Effects of Rage with which Histories are crowded, gaze on the angry Man with an instructive Horror, view him in every outrageous Transport, in every terrifying Fit of Madness, and having well consider'd every monstrous Feature, turn us from the frightful, the tremendous Image, to its charming Opposite, the chearful, patient, mild, forgiving Man; see him still constant to himself, still easy, gentle, bountiful, and kind, pleas'd with a little, and still contented, even when that little's lost: Unmov'd he stands the Shock of Malice and of Envy, by Innocence and Virtue made invulnerable, slights the invenom'd Darts of spightful Tongues, and goes unalter'd on in the same steady Course.

Such was the good, the much-wrong'd *Socrates;* at Home a peevish and ill-humour'd Wife disturb'd his Peace, Abroad the mercenary *Aristophanes*

Line 265. **Aristophanes:** writer of comedies (455–385 B.C.) who attacked Socrates in *The Clouds.*

expos'd him to the Hatred and Derision of his ungrateful Country-men: He saw himself made a publick Jest, despis'd, scorn'd, and pointed-at by every mean *Athenian,* charg'd with Impiety, accus'd of Crimes to which he was a Stranger, and at length unjustly sentenc'd; yet all this he bore without a Murmur; his Defence was meek, sedate, unmix'd with sharp Invectives, yet there was nothing low or whining in it, nothing that look'd like Fear, or an unmanly Love of Life; no, he talk'd of Death as of a Thing he wish'd for; and when he might have liv'd, when his Friends had made it easy for him to escape, he refus'd to owe his Life to what might look like Guilt, and would not break those Chains the Laws had bound him with: When the fatal Cup was given him, he took it with a calm untroubled Look, with such a Look as spoke the inward Quiet of his Mind, and drank it with a Soul resign'd; no Sighs, no Groans, were heard; no indecent Struggles seen; all was of a piece, all beautiful, and all instructive. His firm Belief of Immortality, of that eternal Joy to which his Soul was hastning, of that Reward which injur'd Virtue meets with in a Future state, was his Support, and made his Passage easy.

Another Instance we have in *Epictetus,* that last and best of all the *Stoicks,* who, though diseas'd and lame, and born a Slave, a Slave to an imperious, vicious, humorous Master, yet still retain'd his Evenness of Temper. When his cruel Lord, to try his Patience, made it his Diversion to bend his Leg, he calmly bore the Pain, and only told him smiling, *He would break it;* which when the inhuman Beast had done, he only meekly said, *I told you, you would do it.* What a Philosophick Strength of Mind was here! Methinks I see him in his little House, that mean, that despicable Cell, that something below a Cottage, that had not so much as the weak Defence of a Door, and could boast of no other Ornament, but a poor Earthen Lamp, instructing his admiring Pupils, and teaching them at once by Precept and Example; they saw him still the same when bound and free, when a Slave to *Epaphroditus,* and when the Favourite of Emperors; Poverty was still his Choice, Virtue his only Treasure, and to do Good his sole Delight: How does he combate every Vice, contend with every Passion! How admirable are those Rules he has prescrib'd us! As never any knew better how to

---

Line 293. **Earthen Lamp**: ironically sold for 3000 drachmas after Epictetus's death.

Line 295. **Epaphroditus**: master of the philosopher Epictetus while he was a slave.

suffer, so it must be own'd, that never any Philosopher taught it better: *Socrates* was the Man he propos'd to himself for an Example; and certainly none was ever a more exact Imitator of his Life: He renounc'd all other Pleasures, but those of the Mind, and preferr'd Tranquility and Indolency of Soul, before all other Possessions: In order to the attaining of which, he gives his Disciples very useful Lessons, of which these following ones are some.

"If having consider'd what things have their Dependance on you, and what have not, you resolve to look on nothing as yours, but what is truly and really so, it will not be in the Power of any Accident to disturb you, or divert you from what you have propos'd to your self; no body shall check or disappoint you; you shall accuse no body, shall complain of nothing, receive no Harm, have no Enemy; for no Man will be able to do you any Prejudice; and certainly a Life so totally exempt from all Perturbation, must needs be above Anger, Grief, or Fear, absolutely free, and unexpressibly happy."

He farther bids them, in every Action they undertake, consider first with themselves, and weigh well the Nature and Circumstances of the Thing; nay, though it be so slight an one as going to Bathe, he bids them represent to themselves, what Accidents 'tis probable they may meet with; That in a Bath is often rude Behaviour, dashing of Water, justling for Passage, scurrillous Language and Stealing, and having done this, he says, They may the more securely do the thing; and he tells them, after such prudent Preparations as these, should any thing that's disgustful intervene, this Reflection will presently rise upon it; Well, but this was not the only thing I propos'd; that which I principally intend, is to keep my Mind and my Reason undisturb'd; and this, I'm sure, can never be effected, if I suffer every Accident to discompose me: He adds, That which gives Men Disquiet, and makes their Lives miserable, is not the Nature of the Things as they really are, but the Notions and Opinions which they form to themselves concerning them; Therefore whenever we meet with Hinderances and Perplexities, or fall into Troubles and Disorders, let us be just, and not lay the Blame where it is not due, but impute it wholly to our selves and our prejudicate Opinions.

Next, in order to their keeping themselves easie, he bids them not to trouble themselves with wishing that Things may be just as they would have 'em, but be well pleas'd that they should be exactly as they are:

Again, on every fresh Accident, he advises them to turn their Eyes inward, and examine how they are qualified to encounter it: If Labour and Difficulty come in their Way, they will find a Remedy in Hardiness and Resolution; if they lie under the Obloquy of ill Tongues, Patience and Meekness are a proper Fence against it: And he says, If they accustom themselves always to act after this manner, occurrent Objects will have no Prevalence over them.

In the next place, he tells them, They must never use themselves to say they have lost any thing, but only restor'd it: As for Instance, If they lose their Estates, they are not to say, They are taken from them, but paid back to the Giver; then he supposes them to make this Objection, but they were Knaves who defrauded us; to which he replies, What's that to the purpose? Or, how does it concern you by what means, or what Hand, he that gave it, resumes it to himself? Trouble not your selves therefore about these Matters; but while he permits the Enjoyment, use it as a thing that's not your own, but another's, and let your Concern and Affection for it be just such as Travellers have for an Inn upon the Road.

If you indeed, says he, are willing to improve in Virtue, you must never allow your self in such mean Thoughts as these; I must solicitously follow the Business of my Calling, or else I and my Family shall starve; I must take pains with this Son of mine, must chide and chastise him, or he'll be ruin'd. These are the Misgivings of an anxious Mind, and unworthy a Philosopher, whose first Care should be the Quiet of his own Breast. Perhaps some will say, this has too much of the Stoick in it to be propos'd for an Example; but I think such as disaprove of it will injure *Epictetus,* if they suppose he would not have People follow the Business of their Calling, or correct their Children; he does not blame the thing, but the manner of doing it; a convenient Provision may be made for a Family, and all due Care taken of a Son, and yet the Mind kept quiet and undisturb'd. In order to the gaining such a calm easie Temper, he advises us to use our selves to little Trials; if a Cruse of Oil be broken, or a Pint of Wine stollen, he bids us reflect immediately, that this is the Purchase of Constancy and a compos'd Mind; and since nothing can be had *Gratis,* he that buys these so cheap has a good Bargain: So again, he says, When you call your Servant, consider 'tis possible he may not attend; or if he does, he may not obey your Command; however it be, have a care you do not give him so great an Advantage over you, as to put it in his Power to ruffle and unsettle your Mind.

Again, that Person is properly my Lord and Master, who hath it in his Power to gratify my Wishes, or make me afraid; to give me what I desire to have, or to take from me what I'm unwilling to part with: The only way then to preserve one's Liberty, is to restrain one's Passion, and to have neither Desire nor Aversion for any thing in the Power of others; for he that does not so, is sure to be a Slave as long as he lives.

Again, let it be your constant Care to behave your self in all the Affairs of Humane Life with the same Decency that you would at a publick Entertainment; If any thing be offer'd you, receive it with Modesty; if it pass by you, and be sent to another, do not with-hold it from him, or keep what was not intended for you; if it be not yet come down so low, show not your self impatient, nor snatch at it greedily, but wait contentedly till it comes to your Turn.

Again, remember, that when any Man reviles or strikes you, 'tis not the Tongue that gives you the opprobrious Language, or the Hand that deals the Blow, that injures or affronts you; but 'tis your own Resentment of it that makes it such to you; When therefore you are provok'd, 'tis owing entirely to your Apprehensions of Things; therefore you ought to be very careful that you are not transported with Rage; for if you can but so far subdue your Passion, as to get time for cooler Thoughts, you will with Ease attain to a good Government of your self.

Again, if you happen to be told, that another Person hath spoken ill of you, never give your self the Trouble of refuting the Report, or excusing the thing; but rather put up all with this Reply, That you have several other Faults; and that if he had known you better, perhaps he would have believ'd he had reason to have spoken worse.

If we can chearfully permit each Observer to be a Censurer of our Actions, can, without the least Emotion, bear Reproof, bear it not only from a Friend, but from an Enemy, can satisfie our selves with an Appeal to Heaven; and if we have Failures, can be content to have them known, and, full of humble Sorrow, be thankful to such as blame us for 'em, we have got above the World, above the Earth's magnetick Force, the Whirls of grosser Matter, and are securely settled in that calm, that peaceful Region, where all is bright, serene and quiet: Vainglory then will vanish, Ambition be no more, nor will there be room for Ostentation left; Anger will be depriv'd of its most powerful Aids, its Foundation will be struck at, and when that fails, the Superstructure soon will sink.

Thus I have epitomiz'd this good Man's Rules, at least such as concern this Subject. There are others I might recommend for their excellent Precepts on this Topick, as *Seneca, Plutarch,* and *Marcus Aurelius;* but I think neither of them equall'd those great Masters of Morality, *Socrates* and *Epictetus:* Their Writings and their Lives had something more agreeable, were more of a Piece; there were no darkening Shadows in their Characters, no Incoherencies or Contradictions, and, if I am not mistaken, fewer Errors in their Doctrines: As for *Seneca,* when I read him, I cannot but admire his Flights of Fancy, the Delicacy of his Wit, and the Sharpness of his Stile; Satyr seems to be his Province, and he, like another *Hercules,* destin'd to encounter Monsters: Who ever reprehended Vice with greater Severity? How much does he blame Avarice, Pride, Ambition, Ingratitude, Cruelty, *&c.* how pathetically recommend Continency, Temperance, Justice, Poverty and every thing that it becomes a good Man to approve of? He carries me away with the Stream of his Eloquence; but when I reflect on the Character that's given him by some Historians, I'm shock'd, I stem the Tide, and strive to swim against the Torrent: I am strangely startled to find him revenging himself on *Claudius,* by ridiculing him in the Panegyrick his Royal Pupil spoke at his *Apotheosis*, amaz'd to see so strict a Pretender to Virtue, suspected to be a Consenter to *Nero's* Matricide, and a Defender of that horrid Villany, one who too plainly show'd his Approbation, by seeking plausible Reasons to give it a Colour: To hear him praise Poverty, one wou'd have thought he had chosen, with *Diogenes,* to have liv'd in a Tub, had been a Stranger to the Luxury of Courts, to the Pomps of Life, at least had known them only by Report, and not Experience, and had been so great

---

Line 415. **Seneca**: Stoic philosopher (d. A.D. 65) who educated Nero and wrote *De Ira* (*On Anger*). **Plutarch**: celebrated Roman historian (A.D. 46–120) and author of *Moralia* and *De cohibenda ira*. **Marcus Aurelius**: Roman emperor and philosopher (A.D. 121–80) author of *Meditations*.

Line 431. **Claudius**: (10 B.C.–A.D. 54) Roman emperor and object of Seneca's satire *Apocolocyntosis* on Claudius being deified. **Royal Pupil**: Nero.

Line 432. **Apotheosis**: elevation to the status of a god.

Line 433. **Nero's Matricide**: in 59 A.D., Nero ordered his mother, Agrippina, murdered.

Line 436. **Diogenes**: (ca. 400–325 B.C.) Greek philosopher who lived in the greatest simplicity.

a Despiser of Riches, that he would rather, with *Crates,* have thrown his Wealth into the Sea, than have been, by his Extortion, the Occasion of an Insurrection in *Britain:* But when I read the Apology *Causin* has made for him, I please my self with Hopes, that what has been said to his Prejudice is false: I consider, that the Good have been always malign'd, and that Merit has been ever the Object of Envy.

And as for *Plutarch,* I acknowledge him to have been a great Man; his Lives of illustrious Men, is a useful and noble Work: but, in my Opinion, he does not seem to have a right Notion of Good and Evil; he praises several Things that are in themselves blame-worthy, as 'twill be easy for any Person to observe who reads him attentively, and of which there are numerous Instances in his Treatise of famous Women, where several Ladies are applauded for Actions which I should have judg'd to be criminal, and where many things which to me appear Faults, are by him esteem'd Virtues: When he gives an Account of the *Spartan* Institutions, how many shocking Things are there in them, which he tacitly commends? Now such a Procedure as this may prove of ill Consequence to an unwary injudicious Reader, who may be apt to be too much sway'd by so great an Authority.

As for the Emperor *Marcus Aurelius Antoninus,* he was a Prince who liv'd in the constant Practice of all sorts of Virtues; nothing can be finer than his Writings, nothing more instructive; but his leaving such a Successor as *Commodus,* left an irreparable Blemish on his Life, and tarnish'd a Fame, that would have been otherwise eternally glorious: He was not ignorant of the vicious Disposition of his Son; he cou'd not but know that he was unfit for so great a Charge: If he had been true to his Principles, he ought to have been led by nothing but Truth, to have own'd no Relation, no Kindred, but what was founded on Virtue; not to have valu'd *Commodus* the more for being his, but to have look'd on him with the same Indifference that he would have done on a Stranger; and, without having the least regard to the Character of a Son, look'd with an impartial Eye on the Qualities of his Mind, the natural Propensities of

Line 441. **Insurrection in Britain**: during his preceptorship under Nero, Seneca was frequently accused of accumulating great wealth for himself. **Causin**: Nicolas Causin (1583–1651), author of *The Holy Court in Five Tomes* (1650).

Line 461. **Commodus**: (A.D. 161–92), Roman emperor, son of Marcus Aurelius, naturally cruel and licentious.

his Soul; and if, after all the Care he had taken of his Education, he had discover'd in him an Inclination to Evil, he ought, in spight of all the Reluctancies of Nature, the importuning Tendernesses of a Father, to have disinherited him, and adopted a worthier Man, one of a consummate Virtue, one in whom he had reason to believe the *Roman* People would be happy: This it became a Philosopher to have done, as 'tis what all others, in parallel Cases, ought to do. And I think I may boldly venture to affirm, that nothing would more effectually tend to the Reformation of Manners: Men would then find it their Interest to be good, at least to appear so; and though it might have no inward Force, might not affect the Heart, yet it would influence the Practice, and prove more prevalent than either Sermons or Laws.

There are in History several other shining Examples of Patience and Moderation, of Calmness and Evenness of Temper: Who can enough commend *Lycurgus,* for not only pardoning *Alcander* when he was given up to him by the People, and he had it in his Power fully to revenge himself for the Loss of his Eye, by taking away his Life, but making it his Business to cultivate and meliorate his savage cholerick Temper, to make him hate those Vices he had formerly indulg'd, and of a wild, debauch'd Young man, to render him one of the soberest and most prudent Citizens of *Sparta.*

Augustus was a great Master of his Passion, of which he gave a memorable Instance in his pardoning *Cinna,* who was engag'd in a Conspiracy against him; as the Action was noble, so his manner of doing it had something in it peculiarly brave; for after he had convinc'd him that he knew the whole Plot, together with the Certainty he had of his being in it, he reminded him of his Obligation to him, bid him remember, that when he found him in Arms against him, he gave him both his Life and Fortune, and then told him, notwithstanding his Ingratitude, he freely forgave him; adding, that the Life he once bestow'd on him as an Enemy, he would now give him as a Traitor and a Parricide, and then generously promis'd him this should be the last Reproach he would ever

Line 485. **Lycurgus:** founder of the Spartan system of laws and social values, stressing self-reliance and fortitude, who banished luxury and reformed the state. **Alcander:** in Plutarch's account, he accidentally put out Lycurgus's eye but was forgiven by him.

Line 492. **Augustus:** (63 B.C.–A.D. 14), first Roman emperor.

Line 493. **Cinna:** grandson of Pompey; he plotted against Augustus but was pardoned.

give him, and that for the future there should be no other Contest between them, but which should exceed the other in point of Friendship; and to assure him of his Sincerity, he made him Consul: This gentle, kind, and generous Usage, made him, of an inveterate Foe, become a faithful and an affectionate Friend.

'Twere easy to give many more Instances of this kind; Histories are full of them; and some may be found in our own Annals, as well as in those of foreign Kingdoms: We can boast of a Royal Martyr, who calmly bore ten thousand Indignities, who without repining, endur'd a long Imprisonment, saw himself treated by some of his insolent Subjects, as if he had been one of the meanest of his People, or the vilest of Malefactors, heard himself reproach'd and wrongfully accus'd, and at last sentenc'd to Die by those to whom he stood doubly Related, both as a Father and a Soveraign; and yet all this he saw, and heard, without Emotion, was still Master of his Temper, still meek, patient, and forgiving; no passionate Expressions, no opprobrious Language, once escap'd him; he lost his Crown and Life without a Murmur, dy'd the same he liv'd, the same submissive, gentle, mild, Religious Prince.

And now, as if the Doctrine of a Metemphychosis were true, we seem to see him animate another Body, to live once more in one of his immortal Line, in that unequal'd Queen who fills his Throne, and is the Glory of her Sex, the Joy of all her Subjects, all they could wish to make them happy: She inherits every shining Quality that was admir'd in him; like him, she had Misfortunes to contest with, was made the common Theme, the Sport of envious Tongues, was blacken'd by invenom'd curst Detractors, by vicious Wretches, who, like the Birds of Night, cou'd not endure the Lustre of her Virtue; but she, like some firm Rock, bore all the dashing Surges, they roar'd in vain, in vain they broke themselves against her; she undaunted saw each rising Billow, and stood collected in her Self, safe in her Innocence, and kept unmov'd by the innate Greatness of her Mind: Her Enemies she pitied, but knew not how to

Line 510. **Royal Martyr**: Charles I.

Line 521. **Metemphychosis**: Metempsychosis, the Pythagorean belief that the soul as fallen divinity continued within the body as within a tomb, and was released through purification by study. Pythagoreans also believed in the transmigration of the soul from one body into a new one.

Line 523. **unequal'd Queen**: Anne.

hate; that was a Passion foreign to her Soul; not one revengeful, discontented, one uncharitable Thought, was ever harbour'd there: And when from her Retirement, from her obscure and humble State, Heav'n call'd her to a Throne, she unalter'd mounted to the height of Power; was still the same; obliging, humble, merciful, and ready to forgive; so far from reflecting on the Indignities she had suffer'd that, like a kind indulgent Parent, that looks with a commiserating Eye upon the Follies of his Children, she freely pardons every past Offence, and, like that infinite Goodness whose Representative she is, to all extends her Kindness, and with a Maternal Tenderness, an endearing Sweetness, caresses all her Subjects, and takes them into her Protection: For them are all her Cares, her Toils, while they enjoy their Rights, and Plenty pours her Blessings on them: 'Tis her whole Study to keep them safe, and make 'em happy, and to defend them from those affrighting Ills which ravage all the neighbouring Nations: They see no bloody Fields, nor hear the murdering Cannons roar, a sacred Quiet fills her happy Land.

Our Days are crown'd with soft Delights,
With undisturb'd Repose our Nights:
The Golden Age revives again,
Bears Date from her auspicious Reign:
The Wicked from her Court are fled,
And drooping Truth erects her Head:
See! See! she rises dazling bright!
The Clouds are fled that hid her Light!
Lo! Justice does with Pomp descend,
On her each Virtue does attend;
From her, their Rays themselves disperse,
And all the wide Circumference bless:
With Joy Religion now appears,
And void of Doubts, and void of Fears,
Does all her native Charms display,
Is pure as Light, and bright as Day:
Such as she was, when first she rose,
When first she did her Beams disclose;
When Conscience was supreme within,
And happy Man was free from Sin:
When Goodness for it self was lov'd,
And none by servile Fear were mov'd:

When Nature govern'd void of Art,
And Love was regnant in each Heart:
When Merit was esteem'd alone,
And spightful Censures were unknown:
Those Times she will again restore,
And add new Joys unknown before:
She comes! she comes! ordain'd by Fate,
Both to Reform and Shield her State!
Like favour'd *Israel's* Guardian Light,
She leads us through the Shades of Night:
In vain *Egyptian* Foes pursue;
She fearless does the Troublers view;
Their Chariots move but slowly on,
Their Wheels are off, their Strength is gone:
Surrounding Waves their Fury show,
And they no Place of Safety know:
Aurora does with Pomp arise,
Returning Day adorns the Skies:
When it has reach'd Meridian Height,
We from the Shore shall please our Sight
With the fam'd Trophies of the Fair,
And say, these who our Terror were,
By whom we've been so long opprest,
Depriv'd of Peace, depriv'd of Rest,
Who did for our Destruction wait,
Are made themselves the Prey of Fate.

But the greatest, the most amazing Instance is yet behind, the Original which she has copy'd, and of which her Life has been a beautiful Transcript; I mean our kind compassionate Redeemer, who as far surpasses the most celebrated Patterns of Antiquity, as the Sun in his Noon-day Glory does the little Glow-worms, that adorn the Night; who, when in the highest Exaltation, when encompass'd by adoring Angels, when sitting at the Right-hand of the Paternal Glory, and rais'd by his Union with the Deity to a Station inconceivably sublime, infinitely above the brightest Intelligences, the first and noblest Orders of created Beings, left those glorious Regions, those blissful

Line 573. **regnant**: ruling.

Seats of pure unclouded Light, where Peace, and Joy, and Harmony Divine for ever dwell, and in a mean Disguise, a despicable Form, a mortal Shape, came humbly down, by wondrous Pity led, to save a sinking World, a World which knew not how to prize so vast a Favour, which barbarously abus'd its Benefactor, return'd Neglect and Scorn for boundless Love, with Obloquies repay'd his Kindness, and made him suffer all the Indignities that Malice could invent, or Rage inflict. Though all was his, the whole Creation the Product of his Word, the Efflux of his All-commanding *Fiat,* yet he was poorer than the meanest of his Vassals, had nothing he wou'd call his own; no, not so much as Birds or Beasts possess: Poverty he made his Choice, Humility and Meekness the constant Practice of his Life: Yes, He, in whom was every Virtue, every Excellence, all Perfections in the Abstract, was pleas'd to make these his darling Attributes, and they are those he chiefly recommends to us, as being highly useful, indispensably necessary for Creatures plac'd in a dependent State, a State of Trial, becoming Creatures which at first were rais'd from nothing, and are every Moment tending to the Grave.

O let us heedfully observe each Step he made, and keep exactly in the unerring Track. Teach me, O my Saviour, to be lowly, as thou wert; when tow'ring Thoughts arise, and swell my Soul, remind me of the humbling Wonders of thy Life: O let me view Thee in each condescending Act, in each debasing Circumstance, attend thee from the Stable to the Prison, from the Manger to the Cross, see thee reproach'd, revil'd, and spit upon; scourg'd, crown'd with Thorns, and crucify'd between two Malefactors; and, to compleat thy Sufferings, rail'd on and mock'd by the insulting Croud, mock'd in thy greatest, thy most poinant Agonies, the last and sharpest Pangs of Death; yet still replete with Patience, meek, and full of Love, still offering up thy Self a willing Sacrifice for base ungrateful Men, for Enemies, for those who triumph'd in thy Shame, and look'd with Pleasure on thy Pain. From this stupendous Sight! this Miracle of Kindness! this unequall'd Instance of Forgivenness, Mildness, and endearing Goodness! O let me inward turn my Eyes, and view my self, inspect the secret Movements of my Soul, the hidden

---

Line 616. **Efflux:** flowing out, issuing in a stream, emanation.

Springs of Thought, and see, concern'd, each Deviation, how much I vary from thy Precepts, how far I am from following thy Example.

Alas! small Disappointments shock me, Reproaches damp my Spirits, or stir up angry Thoughts; Fame is what I'm too fond of; the secret Plaudits of my Conscience, the Pleasures of a Mind averse to Vice, and passionately loving Virtue, are not enough to yield me an untroubled Satisfaction; I would by all be thought to be what really I am; but this I fear, my Saviour, is the Effect of Pride. O let me be contented with thy Approbation, delighted with the internal *Euge's* of thy Spirit, and wholly unconcern'd for popular Applauses, the injudicious Praises of the Multitude.

Give me, I humbly pray thee, that Poverty of Soul, to which thou hast annex'd a Blessing, a State of Mind remote from Avarice, from eagerly desiring such things as most believe to be constituent parts of Bliss: Whatever I possess, let me esteem it but as 'tis thy Gift, value it no more than it deserves, enjoy it without a childish Fondness, and be ever ready to part with it without Reluctance, without an unbecoming Murmur; let me be still the same, contented with my Lot, sedate and calm in every Circumstance of Life; let not my small Attainments, those things which Vanity is but too apt to magnifie, stir up indecent Thoughts, make me greedy of Respect, and angry when I'm disappointed. Alas! that little which I know, I owe to thee; my self, and all I am, are thine; I'm wholly owing to thy Goodness, and kept in Being by thy Power; What then have I to boast of? to be acquainted with thy Excellencies shall be my Study, and to conform my Will to thine the Business of my Life: Like thee, I'll strive to bear Indignities and Wrongs, to bear them meekly, to support them with a chearful, free, untroubled Look, to be unmov'd at Calumnies, dispassionate and mild, when treated ill; so far from Anger and Revenge, as not to countenance one unkind recriminating Thought: Like thee, I'll labour to do good, to be compassionate and pitiful to all; Cruelty shall have no Harbour in my Breast; Tenderness is connatural to my Soul, it I'll extend unto my greatest Enemies; for them I'll pray, and, if 'tis in my Power, will freely serve: None will I purposely offend or grieve, no not the poorest, meanest of Mankind, for them, as well as me, thy Blood was shed; Riches and Honours make no

---

Line 646. **Plaudits**: applause, acclaim. Line 673. **connatural**: innate, belonging naturally.

essential Difference, our Bodies are the same, our Souls are equal, and in the future State the virtuous Beggar shall be possess'd of Glories greater far than all the Monarchs of the Earth do now enjoy: Nor shall my Mercy be confin'd unto the Humane Race, but be extended to the brutal Kind; they sure are more than Machines, are sensible of Pain, and I cannot, without a sort of Horrour, without some Sentiments of Pity, see them tortur'd; they are part of thy Creation, and may claim the Good adapted to their Nature, and ought not to be treated cruelly to gratify a savage Inclination, or divert a sanguinary Temper; I could with Pleasure let them live, and satisfy my self with Roots and Herbs, and Fruits, the cheap and wholsome Viands Nature does provide, those, with the milky Treasure of the Flocks and Herds, would yield me a delicious Feast, and more regale my Taste, than all the study'd Luxury of Courts.

O let me aim at nothing but doing Good, at imitating, as far as a frail Creature can, thy great Example; give me a comprehensive Charity, an universal Love, a peaceful, quiet, and well-order'd Mind, a Soul not fetter'd with mean, narrow Principles, not tainted with corroding Envy, but gentle, placid, easie to forgive, inclin'd to think the best, and ever ready to pay a chearful Deference to superior Worth, never more pleas'd than when I can oblige, desirous where'er I come to encrease those mutual Kindnesses, which are the Bands that knit Mankind, those sacred Ties which should endear us to each other; and when by these previous Dispositions, these faint Resemblances of thy Perfections, I'm fitted for a happier Life, O take me to thy self, and in that State where nothing is disturbing, where Anger is unknown, and black Detraction dares not enter, where all past Troubles are forgot, are swallow'd up in Joy and endless Bliss, let me for ever, ever dwell, and sing thy Praise.

Then I no more shall grieve, no more complain,
No more th' Attacks of angry Tongues sustain:
But with the Wise, the Good, Sincere, and Kind,
Shall undisturb'd enjoy the Pleasures of the Mind.

Line 685. **sanguinary**: bloodthirsty.

OF CALUMNY

'Tis a great, but melancholy Truth, that as this Age encreases in Politeness, in Finenesses of Learning, in Niceties of good Breeding, and in the Punctilio's of an exact Civility; so it proportionbly decreases in Justice, Sincerity, that affectionate Concern it becomes us to have for each other; and in all those commendable Qualities, those antiquated Virtues, which were the Ornaments of earlier Times. Alas! there are not so much as the Footsteps left of that noble Simplicity, native Plainness, unartificial Kindness, and uncorrupted Integrity, which appear'd in the Infant World, and from thence, as from a pure uncorrupted Fountain, ran for some Ages unmix'd with foreign Streams, till an overflowing Deluge of Vice broke down the Banks, and by pouring in its muddy and polluted Waters, robb'd them of their natural Purity. We may trace them in the first Histories, see them meliorating the *Egyptian* Soil, affording rich Production in the ancient *Persia,* diffusing themselves thro' *Greece,* and plentifully watering the *Roman* Commonwealth, till, like the Rivers of Paradise, they were lost in the Abyss, and, after the fatal Inundation, remain'd undistinguish'd from the great Mass of Liquids, from whence, I fear, nothing less than the general Conflagration, the last refining Fire, will be able to extract them: We see nothing amongst us but the very Dregs, the nauseous Sediment of that universal Corruption; there's hardly any thing left that looks like the Work of God, that has the Impress of Divine Goodness, the Stamp of infinite Justice, or any Participation of the Eternal Truth. The generality of Men seem to have Treachery interwoven with their Nature, something that's Diabolical in their Temper: Malice, Pride, Envy, and Uncharitableness seem to make up the Composition of Humanity; they fill their Thoughts, influence their Actions, and discover themselves in their Discourses.

Should any of the Natives of the superior Regions look through our thick Atmosphere, and take a Survey of Humane Affairs, would they not think this Globe to be rather a Den of insociable Monsters, than a well regulated World, inhabited by rational Creatures? Wou'd they not be amaz'd to see Persons courting those, whose Ruin they are meditating; entertaining those with all the indearing Expressions of an engaging Tenderness, to whom they are at the same time, privately resolving to do all the ill Offices imaginable, and bestowing the highest *Encomium's*, the most luscious Praises, the most dawbing nauseous Flatteries on such as they despise, not only scorn, but hate? 'Twould make them wonder, or rather smile, to see 'em with a respectful Air, a humble Mien, an obliging inviting Aspect, fawn on the present, and even tire them with their Caresses, and as soon as absent, say a thousand scandalous Things of them, and prove busier than Fame, with all her Tongues, and Eyes, and Ears: If any has a shining Character, is remarkably eminent, either for Wit, Virtue, or Learning, such an one is a Butt, against which they shoot all their Arrows; his Virtues are represented as counterfeit, his Wit as borrow'd, and his Learning as Pedantry: Envy comes into their Assistance, and brings the Furies with her, who, glad of the Employment, convey their favourite Vipers, the dreadful restless Mischiefs, into each invenom'd Breast; then, possess'd with hellish Fury, fraught with more than an infernal Rage, like greedy Bloodhounds, they incessantly pursue the Good, and strive to extinguish Merit: Virtue is their Aversion, they hate it as the Birds of Night do Day; and since by Vice weigh'd down, they cannot rise to others Excellencies, they strive to sink them to their own mean despicable Level, and by invidious Falshoods, sly Insinuations, closely-manag'd Whispers, all the subtle Arts of dexterous Malice, hope to raise darkening Mists, and cloud their Lustre, and would if it were feasable, draw an *Egyptian* Veil, a thick impenetrable Night, over their dazling Fames.

'Tis strange that they should hate what calls for Love, be made Enemies by that which should excite Respect, and kindle Admiration: Methinks, that Pride, to which they owe their base detracting Temper, should spur them on to generous Emulation; instead of railing on them, they shou'd endeavour to outvy them, to exceed them in every praiseworthy Quality, in every intellectual Grace: This would be a commendable Ambition, a noble glorious Pride; but, alas! they are too lazy to attempt it: To calumniate strongly they think the easier Way, and if it does not make them equal, (which is what they aim at) at least it gratifies their Envy. But, as malicious as they are, they dare not tell them, that they hate them; Virtue commands an outward Veneration, extorts an awful Reverence; this makes them flatter, and promise

Line 36. **Encomium's:** praises.

everlasting Friendship to those whom they detest, cringe to those that they would trample on, and hug the Men that they would stab. Thus the Vicious have not only Pride and Folly in their Composition, but also Sloth and Cowardize: They are a Medly of all that's ill, of all that's detestable in the whole Creation; and 'tis no wonder they abhor the Good, since they are so diametrically opposite; Light and Darkness might as well subsist together.

With as much Ease may Fire and Ice combine,
Together in one Subject meet;
As well may Heat condense, and Cold refine;
Things be at once both soure and sweet;
As well may *Cinthia's* Beams adorn the Day,
Or *Phœbus* gild the dusky Night,
Weak Babes with hungry Lions play,
Or Lambs in ravenous Wolves delight.

Tho' I have a great many Follies to blush at, numerous Faults to correct, yet I can, with a safe Conscience, say, Envy is none of the Number: I can, with a great deal of Pleasure and Satisfaction, behold superior Merit, and give it the Applause it deserves: I abhor Detraction in others, and will never practise it my self. That Golden-Rule, of *doing to others, as I would have others do to me,* is ever present to my Thoughts, and I resolve to make it the governing Principle of my Life. If our Enemies abuse us, if they strive to sully our Reputation, we ought to endeavour to do our selves right, by representing Matters as they really are, by shewing them in a true Light; but this must be done calmly, without an anxious Concern, an indecent Solicitude, without retaliating the Injury, returning Calumny for Calumny, or giving ourselves the liberty of using abusive Language, such mean, base, ungenerous Revenges being things we ought to abominate; nothing of that kind being on any account allowable.

We are commanded to forgive the greatest, the most provoking Offences, and to do good to our most implacable Enemies; but were it not a Duty, yet methinks it should be agreeable to our Inclinations, to those natural Propensities we find in our selves to Kindness: Methinks

---

Line 81. **Cinthia:** Diana, goddess of the moon. Line 82. **Phœbus**: god of the sun.

our Souls should shrink at any thing that looks but like Inhumanity: There is a secret Pleasure in doing friendly Offices; we gratify our selves in it, and cannot, without delight, look back on all Instances of that nature. If at any time, through Inadvertency, we have reported any thing to the Prejudice or Disreputation of others, we ought to reflect on it with Trouble, and endeavour to make them all imaginable Reparation; and this, not only if we were the first Reporters, but if we receiv'd it from others, and were only their Eccho's; and we should have just Cause to think our selves chargeable both with Injustice and Pusillanimity, if we should hear any slander'd in our Presence, without taking their part, and endeavouring to clear their Innocency; and this it becomes us to do, without considering whether they are our Friends or our Enemies, our Kindred or Strangers, it being a Debt we owe to the whole Rational Nature.

'Tis upon the same Account I think it highly criminal, or, to give it the softest Epithet it will bear, very blame-worthy, to speak Ill of the Dead: For Heaven's sake let 'em lie quiet in their sacred Repository; the Grave is an Asylum none ought to violate; let their Ashes remain undisturb'd. There is not a Possibility of their vindicating themselves, and therefore it is unjust, as well as cowardly and base, to accuse them: Were it done with a good Design, as 'twas among the ancient *Egyptians*, 'twere not faulty: There, as soon as any Person was dead, he was brought into publick Judgment; the publick Accuser was heard, and if he prov'd that his Conduct had been ill, his Memory was condemn'd, and he was depriv'd of Sepulture; this was of admirable Use, because it made the People have a Veneration for their Laws, and kept them in perpetual Awe, by letting them see that they were capable of reaching them even after Death; and they being a serious, considering People, had a great Concern for their Reputation, and dreaded nothing more, than the Thoughts of intailing Infamy on their Memories and Families: But if the Deceas'd was not convicted of any Crime, he was then allow'd an honourable Interrment, and they joyfully gave him the Praises due to his Merit: This Way to them appear'd highly equitable; and it could not but please the Virtuous, to be assur'd that their Names would be transmitted with Honour to Posterity: By this Means the Vicious were aw'd, and the Good secur'd from having their Actions misrepresented; their Fame continu'd bright, there being none that durst attempt to obscure it. But among us they find no Respect; with a savage Barbarity we pull them out of their silent Sanctuary, tear them in pieces, and make them suffer a sort of second Death.

Next to this, nothing can be more inhuman, than to Rail at the Absent, nothing more ungenerous, ungenteel, and indeed more imprudent: The speaking the Truth to the Disadvantage of others, can (I think) never be excus'd but in one single Instance; and that is, when 'tis done in order to the preventing any of our Acquaintance from confiding in 'em by reason of their being Strangers to their Tempers, their Inclinations, and the particular Designs they may be carrying on; for it would be very cruel, as well as highly unjust, to permit an innocent Person to be impos'd on by the Perswasions and Insinuations of another to their prejudice; but this ought to be done in private, and with due Respect to their Weakness, that is, Care ought to be taken, that it be not divulg'd to their Disgrace: but in most 'tis, I fear, either the Effect of Envy, of Malice, or of Folly, a childish inconsiderate Talkativeness, an Emptiness of Mind, Barrenness of Invention, and a not knowing how else to entertain Persons as ignorant, as ill-natur'd, and as impertinent as themselves.

After they have talk'd of their Cloaths, of the Affairs of their Kitchen, of the Faults of their Servants, and all their other Domestick Trifles, what can the poor dull Creatures say next, if they are not permitted to abuse and ridicule their Neighbours, to make Reflexions on their Conduct, to enquire into their Concerns, the minutest Circumstances of their Families? And provided it keeps up the languishing Conversation, 'tis no matter whether what they hear, or what they report, be true or false; the one pleases 'em as well as the other, or rather, the last is more agreeable to their Taste. O how will they hug a calumniating Story! How dear to them are the Spreaders of Reproaches! After the first Compliments are over, they must sacrifice somebody's Reputation to the Lady they visit, or she will think her Entertainment lost, her Tea cast away.

Nor are the Men wholly excusable; tho' I must own we ought to bear the greatest part of the Blame, and that they do not wrong us in fixing an Odium on us on this account; yet they are not altogether guiltless: Such among 'em as are Studious, who divide their Time between Books and Contemplation, cannot find Leisure for any thing so idle, so mean, so much below the Dignity of their Nature; their Thoughts are employ'd on sublimer Subjects, and they cannot, without pain, stoop to any thing that's trifling, much less to any thing that's contradictory to their Reason, to the immutable Laws of Truth, and those Rules which every intelligent Being prescribes to it self: But for others, either those who devote themselves to the Pleasures and Gayeties of the Town, who know no Happiness besides that of Dressing, of Sweating beneath a Load of Hair, of Lolling in a fine gilt Coach, eating at a *French* Ordinary, taking some Turns in the *Park,* and concluding the Farce in a Tavern; or their *Antipodes*, the plain, frugal, Country Gentlemen, who are too wise to value themselves upon fine Cloaths, nice Breeding, exact Sense, and polite Language; they take a better, a more discreet Method, they leave their ancient venerable Houses, their long worm-eaten Pedigrees, their Demeans, and their Mannors, together with their noble Coats of Arms, to speak for them, and while they are doing them Right, they strut about among their cringing Tenants, insult over their trembling Servants, hector their Wives, and pay Visits to their Sheep and Oxen, or make a Noise with their Dogs, and are as much pleas'd with running down a timerous Hare, as the General of an Army would be with winning a Battle; and as proud of bringing back the poor vanquish'd Creature, as *Emilius* was of leading *Perseus* in Triumph: They love their Money too well, are too fond of their Mammon, to throw it away in Ragou's, in hard-nam'd Dishes; they are for the old *English* way of living, for eating such Meat as will prevent their Spirits from being too volatile, their Imaginations too sprightly, and their Apprehensions too quick; they prudently consider, that the momentous Business of the Country requires Solidity, that the administring Justice among their noisy litigious Neighbours, makes it necessary for them to have the Wisdom of *Solomon,* and the Patience of *Job,* and they know

---

Line 186. **Ordinary**: an eating establishment with a fixed price menu.

Line 187. **Antipodes**: the other side of the globe, complete opposite.

Line 191. **Demeans**: an estate, goods that one owns outright.

Line 198. **Emilius ... Perseus**: Lucius Aemilius Paullus Macedonius, Roman consul, defeated King Perseus of Macedonia in 168 B.C.; according to Plutarch, Perseus and his sons were taken to Rome and dragged through the streets in front of Aemilius's chariot.

Line 200. **Ragou's**: a fashionable method of French cooking.

not where to find either of them, unless it be in a Bottle; to that they have Recourse, with that they solace themselves; and 'tis in those dear Hours which they consecrate to *Bacchus,* that they give themselves the liberty to be witty at the Expence of their Neighbours; then it is they play with Reputations as well as Words, and spare neither our Sex, nor their own; but they are the less culpable of the Two, because what they say is more to divert themselves, than design'd to vent either their Vanity or their Malice, and is rather owing to the Liquor than the Men; whereas the First have nothing else in their view: 'Tis to gratify their Pride, their Spight, their Ill-humour, that they make a Jest of all Mankind: They look upon themselves as the finest, the wittiest, the beautiful'st, the most accomplish'd Part of the Creation, and are so vain as to fancy, that every one that sees 'em cannot avoid having the same Opinion of them that they have of themselves; they are their own Idols, and pay Adoration to nothing but themselves: From such, Justice is not to be expected, neither are their Censures to be much deprecated.

But these are Practices which are not consistent with the Order of Things, and which we must by no means allow ourselves in; the Dead ought to be safe where we are, and so should the Absent, whom we are never to make the Subject of our Diversion: To ridicule them for personal Defects, is highly barbarous as well as profane; 'tis not only an abusing them, but a reflecting on their Maker, who being Almighty as well as Omniscient, not only sees, but is able to revenge the Affront: If they are accidental Imperfections, ill Habits, contracted Indecencies, or Failures in the ceremonious Parts of good Breeding, it becomes us not only to pity them, but to consider, that we may sometimes do Things as absurd, Things that as much deserve to be laugh'd at; besides, we ought to remember, that our Ridiculing them intimates that we weakly think them necessary, when indeed they are so intirely accidental, that they have been reckon'd good Breeding, not only in our Climate, but in other Parts of the World; and the variable Humour of Mankind may in a short time make them so again. What is thought to be a Civility in one Country, is accounted a Rudeness in another: Custom bestows a Beauty, a Decorum, on outward Forms, and renders that graceful and becoming in one Place, which is ungenteel and shocking in another: 'Tis our Ignorance, and the Narrowness of our Minds, makes us apt to be disgusted at whatever appears strange or unusual to us.

If any of our Acquaintance have real Faults, we ought in the softest Language, and the most engaging Manner imaginable, to tell them of 'em, and be sure so to manage the Matter, that they may be convinc'd, that what we say is the Effect of Kindness, of the Affection we have for them; and at the same time we make known our Dislike, let us earnestly beg them to do us the same Favour; for there are none but want Advice, as much as any of those to whom they presume to give it. If they are Strangers to us, 'tis fit for us to be silent, and not seem to take notice of what we cannot mend; but we must always carefully avoid joining with others in exposing them, and never, out of a Vanity of Talking, mention what we have heard to their Disgrace, nor let it make an Impression on our Minds to their Prejudice; for 'tis highly unjust to believe the ill Things we hear of others, till we are well assur'd of their being true, till we have undeniable Proofs of it from their own Mouths, or by ocular Demonstration.

All these Things we ought religiously and constantly to observe, without having an Eye either to Applause, or private Interest; no, they are Things below our Regard, Things too inconsiderable to be made the Motives of our Actions: We should never say we love but where we really do so; never shew Respect, but where we think 'tis due; never commend, but where we suppose they merit it; in a word, our Hearts should still join with our Tongues, and always dictate to 'em, our Faces declare our Thoughts, and every Action prove the Voice of Truth.

How admirably well were these Rules practis'd in *Sparta!* She was never happier, than when there was an Equality among her Citizens, than when Luxury and all effeminate Pleasures were banish'd, when all were oblig'd to live frugally, to eat publickly, to practise an universal Temperance; they had no Temptation to do or say ill Things, nothing to covet, none to envy: Riches, if they had had 'em, would have been of no Use, where there was nothing to purchase, no Reputation to gain by them, and where all were upon a Level, the Noblemen no wealthier than the meanest of the People, the Kings than the most inconsiderable of the Citizens; where all were imbark'd in one common Interest, all intent on the same Design, concern'd for nothing but the Honour and Safety of their Country, and their mutual Improvement in Virtue; there could be no room left for Hatred, Malice, Envy, Pride, Ambition, Injustice, or any other Vice; no, the wise *Lycurgus* in extirpating Riches, and introducing a happy Equality among his *Lacedæmonians*, gave them at once all the Virtues: There Love might have been seen triumphant; Love, pure, disinteress'd, and constant; all were Friends, all were for bettering each other, for making one another not only wiser, but more virtuous, for advancing each other's Fame, and so far from repining at the growing Reputation of their Neighbours, that they were pleas'd with it, and generously strove to encrease it; and so far were they from being angry when others were preferr'd before them, that they rejoyc'd at it; of which we have a memorable Instance in *Pædaretus*, who not being admitted into the List of the Three Hundred, who were chosen to make good the Pass at *Thermopyle* in *Thessaly*, against *Xerxes*, return'd home full of Joy and Satisfaction, telling his Fellow-Citizens, *That he was very glad to find, that there were in* Sparta *Three Hundred better Men than himself.* The Saying of *Argilconide* was as remarkably brave, who asking some Strangers who came from *Amphipolis*, If her Son *Brasidas* dy'd as it became a *Spartan*? They gave him the Praises due to his Merit; and, to make her the greater Complement, added, That he had not left his Equal in *Lacedæmon;* She, instead of being pleas'd with so high an *Encomium,* interrupted them, and, willing to do Justice to her Countrymen, told them, *That indeed* Brasidas *was a valiant Man, but there were in* Sparta *many more valiant than he.* Where there was so much Kindness, so true, so affectionate a Concern for each other, where they would as soon wrong themselves, as their Friends, as soon be false to their own Souls, as to those to whom they'd promis'd to be faithful, there could be no such thing as Detraction, as ridiculing the Absent, and endeavouring to lessen them in the Opinion of others. The Men at their publick Tables both taught and practis'd the Art of Conversation: There was to be learn'd the way of being witty, without reflecting; of being facetious, without injuring Reputations, and of taking a Jest, with the same Innocence and Temper with which it was given: And they were also instructed in that prudential necessary Les-

---

Line 281. **Lacedæmonians**: Spartans.

Line 289. **Pædaretus**: in Plutarch, a Spartan soldier who, on not being elected to the list of 300 to go on an expedition, declared his joy that there were 300 Spartans more worthy than himself.

Line 296. **Brasidas**: a famous Spartan general who died bravely at Amphipolis (422 B.C.) as described by Thucydides; Argilconide was his mother.

son, of not divulging what was talk'd of there; by this means they were accustom'd to Secrecy; a childish Inquisitiveness was discourag'd, and their Discourses kept from being misrepresented: The old Men put the Young in Mind of their Duty, and were as much concern'd for them, and as careful of their Education, as if they had been their Fathers, or Tutors: Each had his Lover, who was an Observer of his Actions, a faithful Monitor, an Encourager of him in Virtue and every laudable Quality, and an equal Sharer with him in his Honours and Disgraces, his Rewards and Punishments: The Women took the same Care of those of their own Sex, and made it their Business to make the young Beauties, for whom they had a Kindness, as good, as ingenious, and as judicious as they were capable of being: And if several happen'd to love the same Person, so far was it from creating any Reservedness or Jealousie among them, that it rather strengthen'd their Friendship, and made them use their utmost Endeavours to render the happy Favourite Possessor of all imaginable Perfections.

How unexpressibly great would be our Felicity, did we follow their Example! there would then be no Animosities, no Slanderings, no ill Offices render'd to those with whom we converse; a pure and chaste Passion would be predominant in every Breast, a Heavenly Flame warm every Mind, and a diffusive Charity impregnate every Soul; we should then be ever ready to think the best, to put the most candid Interpretation on Actions, should be always kind, always just, ever ready to pay a Deference to Merit, and constantly, industriously careful either to hide, or at least extenuate the Faults of those with whom we converse.

Would I could exactly practise those Rules I presume to prescribe to others, and be my self an Example of those Precepts I would inculcate: If my Heart deceives me not, 'tis what I earnestly desire; and though, through the Frailties incident to Humanity, and the want of keeping a strict Guard over my Passions, I may sometimes do those things I blame, may be too easily provok'd, too apt to resent Injuries, to take Appearances for Realities, to censure such as my Imagination represents to me as Enemies, too much inclin'd to listen to the disadvantageous Characters I have heard given of others; yet I can truly say, I do not approve of them, they are things for which my Reason severely checks me, Nusances of which I am every hour endeavouring to cleanse my Soul: I see something infinitely amiable in those things I recommend, something superlatively excellent, something that ingrosses my Affection, and claims the Preference in my Heart.

1.

Sincerity's my chief Delight,
The darling Pleasure of my Mind:
O that I cou'd to her invite
All the whole Race of Humane Kind:
This Beauty, full of tempting Charms,
I freely tender to their Arms.

2.

Take her Mortals, she's worth more,
Than all your Glory, all your Fame,
Than all your glitt'ring boasted Store,
Than all the things that you can name:
She'll with her bring a Joy Divine,
All that's good, and all that's fine.

3.

Will soon your Hearts in one unite,
No disagreeing Interest leave;
Love shall to all things give a Right,
And Men shall never more deceive:
Slander and Envy then shall cease,
And Friendship every where encrease.

4.

The World shall then as happy be,
As 'twas in *Saturn's* blissful Reign,
All who the wondrous Change shall see,
Will think that Age restor'd again,
And bless their Fate for being born,
Where Truth does ev'ry Breast adorn.

OF FRIENDSHIP

Among the numerous Blessings which our bountiful Creator has bestow'd on Humane Kind, there's none in which a pious and well-regulated Soul takes a greater Complacency, than in the Union she has with such as by their acquir'd Excellencies approach nearest to Perfection; that is, such as by a constant Contemplation of Truth, a steady Adherence to the Dictates of Reason, and a chearful and unweary'd Exercise of Virtue, have enlarg'd their Views, enlighten'd their Understandings, freed their Minds from Prejudices, from mean, narrow, and unbecoming Sentiments, from false Notions of Things, and who by submitting their Passions to the Government of their nobler and more exalted Faculties, have obtain'd a happy, an unshaken Serenity, an inward Purity, a great, firm and well-grounded Satisfaction, and who, without being byass'd by Interest, elated by Pride, made restless by Ambition, cramp'd by Avarice, or sour'd by Envy, are sweetly and gently led on to a Degree of Eminence, resembling, as near as may be, that of the Divine Nature.

To such as these, she seems to be drawn by a magnetick Force, a pleasing Violence, by irresistable Charms. At first she feels a secret Veneration, perceives an awful Respect, a growing Esteem; but the nearer she advances, the more intimately she's acquainted with the Virtue she admires, the more her Esteem encreases, the more her Affection augments, and the more ardent is her Love; she then incessantly presses forward, and never rests till she becomes one with the dear Object of her Choice; one by the holiest, firmest, and most indissoluble Union; a Union not cemented by Wealth, not founded on Greatness, not the Result of a fickle Humour, a childish Tenderness, nor an indecent Fondness, nor yet the Product of external Beauty, the Embellishments of Art, the Delicacies of Wit, or any of those other Accomplishments, which make so many Votaries among the many, the unthinking part of Mankind, but owing its Original to much nobler Causes, springing from sublimer Motives, more rational Inducements, from the Resemblance they bear to the eternal Truth, the infinite Wisdom, the great Examplar of all Perfection.

But, alas! such a Union as this can hardly be hop'd for, till we are freed from our Bodies, from these heavy Lumps of Matter, which depress the Mind, and hinder its Operations, not only sink it to the Earth, but fasten it there; till our Souls are fully at Liberty, and can act with their native Vivacity and Fervour, till we are disengag'd from our Passions, and all little ungenerous Designs, mean Suspicions, unkind Reflections, and all the other Frailties of Humanity, and nothing shall be left that can hide us from each other's View, nothing that can hinder our Thoughts from being visible, our Integrity from being fully known, or keep the Sincerity of our Intentions from being as manifest as the Light. Then shall we have a Regard for Virtue, abstracted from all other Considerations, and an Affection for each other much greater than Imagination can form, or Words express; such an Affection, as none but the blest Possessors of the Celestial Regions have yet experimented.

Such wondrous Friendship, wondrous Love,
As constitutes their Bliss Above;
And such a strong refining Fire,
As melts them into one Desire,
Makes both their Aims, their Thoughts the same,
And leaves them different but in Name.

O how happy should we be, could we thus mingle Souls, thus anticipate the State of Bliss, and taste a Part of those Pleasures here, which are to consummate our Felicity hereafter, and to be the delightful, the ravishing Entertainment of a joyful Eternity!

But most have wrong Notions of the Blessings I am recommending, they prostitute the sacred Name, and call that Friendship, which is rather a Confederacy in Evil. Whoever espouses their Quarrels, flatters them in their Vices, or sooth them in their Pride, they think deserve the Title of Friends; and they also fancy the Appellation due to all such as 'tis their Fortune to be related to, either by Affinity, or the closer Ties of Blood, without considering their Merit, or being concern'd whether they are virtuous, Lovers of Justice, and such as act from an internal Principle or not; these are things they can dispense with, and which they look on as unnecessary Qualifications.

As these widen the Inclosure, throw down the Mounds, and lay the sacred Ground in common, so some on the other Side too much streighten it, confine it to too narrow a Compass, are avaricious in their Kindness; and while they say 'tis impossible, according to the strict

Sense of the Word, to be a Friend to several at once, they betray a Littleness of Mind, a Narrowness of Soul, a strange Unthoughtfulness, never considering what are the Attractives, the Motives to Friendship; that 'tis Virtue alone which ought to tye the Knot, and that whoever has it, has an indisputable Right to our Affection; and that the greater, the more perfect it is, the greater, the more fervent ought to be our Love. The Good find themselves united by a secret Sympathy, by an Agreement of Inclinations, a Conformity of Judgments, and a Resemblance of Souls; they all pursue the same Ends, are busied in the same Search, and tend to the same Center.

The Objections which are commonly made against such general Friendships, are, in my Opinion, very weak. They who are for confining it to one, say, That to suppose more, destroys the Notion, and obstructs all the Operations and Offices of it. For Instance, to succour and assist a Friend in his Distress, is an indisputable Duty; but if we put the Case of two such standing in need of our Aid at the same time, and not only so, but desiring Kindnesses, which are inconsistent and repugnant to each other; which way shall we turn our selves? How shall we discharge our Obligations, when our relieving one must be a Prejudice to the other?

Again they say, Suppose a Secret is imparted to us by one of our Friends; if we reveal it, 'tis a base dishonourable Breach of Trust, and unpardonable Violation of Friendship; on the other side, if we do not discover it to our other Friends, we are unfaithful to them; it being a receiv'd Maxim, that in a true and entire Friendship there must be no Reserve.

As for the first Objection, 'tis highly improbable that ever any such Case will happen: Few, or none, have ever met with Misfortunes exactly alike; some Circumstances have been different, something or other has weigh'd down the Scale, there has been some little Disproportion in their Sufferings, and then a Friend so qualified, as I suppose he ought to be, before he deserves that Name, will not repine at the Kindness shewn to another, who needs it more than himself; but allowing their Distress to be equal, yet in that Case a generous Person, one who knows what it is to love, will not be displeas'd at the Assistance given to another of equal Merit, of equal Virtue with himself, but will contentedly wait the Leisure of his Friend, and believe, that what he did was the Result of Reason, and proceeded neither from Partiality nor Neglect: Besides, that Compassion, that Commiseration, which is always a part of his

Character, will incline him to interest himself in the Wellfare of a virtuous Man, and make him rejoice at the Good that's done him.

In answer to the second Objection, give me leave to say, That such Friends as I am speaking of have no Secrets, nothing that they would conceal from one another, nothing that they are asham'd or afraid of having known; they have learn'd to reverence themselves, to have a Regard for their Consciences, and are too well acquainted with the Dignity of their Nature, to do any thing below it, any thing that should raise a conscious Blush, or cause an uneasy Reflexion: In all other Matters, in what concerns their Families or Fortunes, I suppose them to have an equal Interest; and 'tis irrational to talk of perfect Friendships, to believe them to be but one Soul, and at the same time to fancy there will not be an entire Communication of Thoughts: Truth is but one, and as that unites them to it self, so it will also link them to each other, will at once become the Cause and the Object of their Love.

If I may presume to speak my Opinion, I think there is nothing of weight in that Maxim which says, There ought to be no Reserves among Friends; for if my Assertion be granted, there can be no such thing: But if I should so far comply with the Generality of Mankind as to allow it to be true, and that some of my Friends had Matters of moment to impart to me, which they would have conceal'd from the rest, yet in that case it refers only to my self, and to what is properly mine; and in all things of that kind, I'm ready to own, that they have an absolute and indisputable Right: But my Friend's Secrets are not of that number, and ought not to be dispos'd of without their Leave: 'Twould be Robbery in me, to give that to another which is none of my own; they are only deposited in my Breast, and are thought to be safe there; my Fidelity is confided in, and they are believ'd to be as secure in my Custody, as they could have been had they remain'd in their own: What can be baser, what more ignominiously treacherous, more highly dishonourable, than to betray such a Trust, to give up such a Treasure? A good Man would be so far from desiring it, that he would rather abhor me, and shun me as a Monster, if I should but offer to do it: As he would do nothing but what's exactly equitable himself, so he would expect that I should govern my self by the same Rule: But let all that make this Objection assure themselves, that as the Wise and the Virtuous (and 'tis of such alone I've been talking) neither say nor do any thing they would have hid from the

World, so they are far from a useless Curiosity, from having an Inclination to pry into the Concerns of others; their Thoughts and their Time are employ'd in Things much more important, much more necessary, in endeavouring to make each other better, in encreasing their Knowledge, and in preparing themselves for that eternal Happiness, that unexpressible Felicity to which they are jointly hastening.

There are other Mistakes about Friendship, which I think deserve to be taken notice of; as, That in chusing a Friend, we ought not only to regard rigid Virtue and Honesty, but to esteem Sweetness, Liberality, and Obligingness of Humour equally necessary: This I think to be wrong, the two first being only requisite, or to speak more properly, the whole, that we ought to look after, as including in them all the rest: For a Man that's truly vertuous, who acts from a Principle of Justice, and sees a Beauty in it, will always be easy to himself and others, always pleasant, and always doing good Offices; and sure the Conversation of Persons so qualified can never be flat and heavy; where their Virtues are equal, there can be no Disparity in their Dispositions and Humours, no Discontent or Peevishness, no dismal Melancholy, or forbidding Sourness, no distasteful Haughtiness, or brutish Anger; no, where Reason governs there will be no disorderly Passions, no Storms to ruffle the Mind, nor Clouds to overcast it; all will be calm and bright, all harmonious and regular; the Soul will be full of Satisfaction, and take a Complacency in her self; her Joys, like the Rays of the Sun, will diffuse themselves, and from her, as from their Centre, extend to every part of the Circumference, will give a taking Sprightliness to the Actions, a pleasing Vivacity to the Discourse, and an inviting Chearfulness to the Looks.

There is another thing which I think to be a Mistake; and that is, That whenever we cease to love a Friend, we are in danger of mortally hating him; of this Consequence I'm no way assur'd: According to the Notion I have of Friendship, Goodness is the proper Object of Love; wherever it appears, it attracts my Esteem; and those Persons in whom it shines with the greatest Lustre, have the largest share of my Affection, of which it shall not be in the power of any Accident to rob 'em while they continue constant to themselves; but if they deviate from Virtue, if they cease to be what they were when my Kindness for them begun, they have no reason to be angry with me if I withdraw my Affection; 'tis themselves they ought to blame, I'm still the same, still a Lover of that Virtue which they have forsaken, that Truth which they have abandon'd; to those, and not to them, was I united; and as it would be absurd in them to lay the Fault on me, and fancy I have justly deserved their Hatred, when they themselves made the Defection, first broke the sacred Bond, so it would be equally irrational in me to hate them, since 'tis themselves they have injur'd, and not me; that being not to be done without the Concurrence of our own Will. For if we suppose the worst that can happen, that those who were once our dearest Friends, should prove our most inveterate Enemies, that such as once did us obliging Offices, who had the same Care of our Reputation, the same Concern for us as for themselves, and the same Solicitude for our Happiness as for their own, should pursue us with unwearied Malice, load us with Calumnies, and make it their business to shew the utmost Efforts of Spight; yet if we still preserve the inward Calmness and Serenity of our Minds, are still meek, humble, patient, and forgiving, they have done us no Prejudice, inflicted no Evil on us, depriv'd us of nothing that was truly our own, nothing that had an intrinsick Value in it: Besides, all Good Men will consider, that the Bad, as well as the Miserable, have a Right to their Pity, and that their greatest Enemies are to have a share in their Prayers.

There are other Things which deserve to be animadverted on, but I'll wave them, to prevent giving the World occasion to believe, that what I write is only the Result of a contentious Humour, an assuming Vanity, and an Inclination to find Fault; they are Things foreign to my Temper, and I am too sensible of my own Insufficiency to play the Dictator: 'Tis Truth I would find out; to that all my Researches tend: I have no Passions to gratify; and as for Applause, if I had it I should not be the better for it; such visionary Satisfactions, are Things I have no Fondness for: If my Sentiments happen to be wrong, yet I am sure my Aims are right, since I have no farther Design than that of informing my self and others.

I know most People have false Idea's of Things; they think too superficially to think truly; they find it painful to carry on a Train of Thoughts; with this my own Sex are principally chargeable: We are apt to be misled by Appearances, to be govern'd by Fancy, and the impetuous Sallies of a sprightly Imagination, and we find it too laborious to fix them; we are too easily impos'd on, too credulous, too ready to hearken

Line 201. **animadverted**: criticized.

to every soothing Flatterer, every Pretender to Sincerity, and to call such Friends as have not the least Title to that sacred Name; and therefore to prevent my self, and those for whom it becomes me to have a tender Regard, from being deceiv'd, I have, with all the Attention of Mind I am capable of, seriously consider'd what Qualifications are requisite in order to the constituting of a noble, disingag'd, and lasting Friendship, such a Friendship as the most reserved, the strictest Observers of the Rules of Virtue, need not blush to own, and such an one as nothing can lessen, nothing can shake, and which will prove as immortal as the Soul in which 'tis seated.

God is the only desirable Object, as comprehending in himself all the Degrees of Perfection; in him, as in its Source, is whatever we here either love or admire: He is Truth, Goodness, Justice, Beauty, Wisdom, *&c.* In all Created Beings, they are Derivations from him, Streams flowing from him as their Fountain, Irradiations from the inexhaustible Spring of Light: Now as much as we see of these divine Excellencies in those with whom we converse, so much we ought to love them, and by a Parity of Reason, must expect no more Esteem from them than is the just necessary Result of our having those Attractives in our selves, which are the Motives of our Kindness to them.

Would we always resolve to govern our selves by this Principle, and in chusing our Friends act according to the Dictates of right Reason, and never suffer our selves to be guided by Opinion, by the mistaken Sentiments of the Vulgar, the erroneous Notions of the Most, the unconsidering part of Mankind, we should never have occasion to repent our Choice, there not being so much as a possibility of our being mistaken in it. Then external Appearances would not move us; Titles, Grandeur, Wealth, and all those other Trifles which dazzle the Common People, and insensibly engage their Affections, would lose their Force, and prove no Incentives to us.

We should esteem Things according to their real Worth, to their innate Value, and not admire Persons for their Learning, but their Wisdom; not for their Knowledge, but their Virtue; not for being Powerful, but Just; not for being Rich, but Good, nor yet because they are in a Capacity of serving what we falsly call Interest, but because they are Lovers of Truth, and Masters of their Passions: not that I think Learning and Knowledge, and all those other Things which are commonly reckon'd among the Goods of Fortune, ought to be slighted; they are useful, but not necessary Qualifications; the two first embellish and render Conversation instructive as well as agreeable; and when they are join'd with the rest, very much raise and brighten a Character, and place their Possessors on a greater Height, in a more advantageous Light, and render them capable of making their Virtues appear more conspicuous; but if they are Owners only of such Things as are generally known by the Name of contingent Goods, and destitute of necessary ones, they are publick Mischiefs, Enemies to themselves and all the World: Their Learning serves only to heighten their Pride, and increase their Vanity; their Knowledge renders them impertinent, talkative, positive, imposing, impatient of Contradiction, and violent Maintainers of their own Opinions; their Power gives them opportunities of wronging the Innocent, of insulting over the Weak, of oppressing the Poor, and of doing whatever their Ambition, their Avarice, their Malice, and Revenge, shall suggest; and Riches will but feed their Luxury, augment their Intemperance, or else increase their insatiable Desire of grasping more, and by creating a sort of canine Appetite in the Soul, make her miserable amidst the greatest Plenty.

But now if my Friends have Wisdom, if they should happen to have no very considerable share of what the World calls Learning, yet they are capable of advising me, of assisting me in the Conduct of my Life, of telling me what to chuse, and what to avoid; and if they have Virtue, they will disswade me from doing what is ill, be as sollicitously careful of me as of themselves, and keep as constant a Guard over my Words and Actions as over their own, and would be as much troubled to see me faulty, as if they were so themselves: And I dare appeal to any considering Person, whether this would not prove of greater Advantage to me, than if they could lead me through the whole Circle of the Sciences, could explain to me all the abstruse Phænomena of Nature, and make me thoroughly acquainted with all its secret Springs, its inperceptible Movements. If they were just, they would think themselves obliged on all Occasions to do that to me which they would have done to themselves; and as they would not be flatter'd, or dealt insincerely with, would not willingly be slander'd, nor indulge themselves in any thing that should reflect on their Honour, or blacken their Consciences, the same Method they would observe in reference to me: Would no more flatter me than themselves, no more be unfaithful to me than to their own Souls, as soon blast their own Reputations as mine, and have as true a Concern for every thing that relates to me, as if the Case were their own, and all they had dear in the World were at stake, and as they would for every Failure, every Mismanagement, call themselves to a strict Account before the impartial Bar of Reason, and not allow themselves in any thing derogatory to their Character, or contradictory to that Virtue of which they think it their Glory to make a Profession, so they would act the part of Censors to me, and let no Word, no Action of mine, pass unremark'd, nothing unreprov'd that could not stand the severest Test, would make it their Endeavour to brighten my Understanding, to inform my Judgment, to rectify my Will, and throughly awaken all my intellectual Powers: And if they have Goodness, which is a Word of a large Signification, and comprehends in it Piety, Humility, Sincerity, Integrity, and universal Charity, a wishing well to all Mankind, they will endeavour to inspire me with the same Sentiments by which they are govern'd, will labour to make me as pious, as humble, as sincere, upright, and as much pleas'd with doing kind and friendly Offices as themselves.

Now are not these possess'd of the most valuable Treasures? And are they not, though they should happen to be cloath'd in Rags, or confin'd to Cottages, or Prisons, to be prefer'd to the greatest Monarchs on Earth? Such as these are the Friends that I would chuse, and these the Things I would expect from them, and what they may promise themselves from me; for I would desire nothing but what I would return, no Testimonies of Esteem but what I would pay: But alas! where are such Friends to be found. I may please my self with charming Idea's, Court Phantoms of my own creating, and from those Inclinations I find in my own Breast, those innate Propensities to Kindness, which seem to be interwoven with my Being, to be of a piece with my Soul, draw uncommon Schemes of Friendship, of something so fine, so pure, so noble, so exalted, so much beyond whatever the World has yet known of Love, so wholly intellectual, so entirely abstracted from Sense, that I must never hope on this side Heaven to meet with any that will come up to so exact a Model, to so Angelick a Perfection, or at least that will think me worthy of so near a Relation, of such a free, generous, and entire Exchange of Thoughts: But if 'twere ever my good Fortune to be blest with such

Friends as I have been describing, I should be continually afraid of losing them; and if they would resolve to make me compleatly happy, they must have no separate Interest, no Concerns of their own that they would conceal from me, nothing that looks like a Distrust, like a Disregard, like a not reposing an entire Confidence in me; and they must, by observing all the engaging Niceties, all the endearing Punctilio's of Friendship, make it their Business to convince me, that they are really what they pretend to be, there must be no Neglects, no Coldnesses, nothing that may abate the Fervour of the Flame, nothing that may stagger the Belief; Promises must be exactly performed, Services zealously paid, every thing done with an endearing Kindness, an Air of Tenderness, and in a Manner irresistibly winning.

OF LOVE

As there is a Scale of Beings, so there are Degrees of Perfection, Beauties continually flowing from their divine Source in various Measures and Proportions, and dilating themselves through the whole Creation: Wherever we cast our Eyes, we may see them displaying their Charms; by Day shining in the glorious Fountain of Light, by Night glittering in ten thousand Stars; sparkling in Gems, pleasing the Sight in Gold, delighting the Eye in lofty Trees, in the admirable Colours of Fruits and Flowers, in the florid Green of Plants and Grass, and in the amazing Mechanism of Insects and Reptils, those surprizing and inimitable Finenesses which by the help of Glasses are discoverable in their minute Bodies, usefully entertaining it with the exact Proportion of Parts, and the wonderful Variety of Shapes in Birds, Beasts, and Fishes: in these, they appear like little Rivulets; but into Man, the Masterpiece of the visible Creation, they disembogue their scatter'd Streams: We may plainly see all those Excellencies which have been singly Objects of Admiration, uniting themselves in the Humane Nature, which, that it

Line 14. **disembogue**: pour forth at the mouth.

may be the more considerable, has the Superaddition of Reason, which raises it as much above the sensitive Kingdom, as much above Brutes, as they are superior to those who have only a vegetative Life, and they to the inanimate parts of the Creation, which are generally allow'd to be only accidental Concretions of Matter.

Now all these have a Claim to our Regard, according to their respective Values; they are all Participations of Being, and consequently of Beauty; and as they rise higher and higher, and partake more of each, so ought our Esteem to encrease with them: It becomes us awfully to contemplate the Almighty Creator in all his Works, every where to trace his Wisdom and Power: Where they are least conspicuous they challenge Wonder; but where they appear in their full Lustre, they call for both Admiration and Love: The last I take to be a Passion which ought never to be appropriated but to the noblest Objects: To say that we love any thing that is below us, that is of a Rank inferiour to us, is to talk amiss, 'tis a talking without joining Idea's to our Words; or if 'tis true, that we do so, 'tis an irrational Affection.

Indeed God pronounc'd all his Creatures good, as such we ought to look on them, and, as I said before, proportion our Esteem to their Worth; but none of them have any pretence to the lowest degree of our Love but those of our own Species; in them that external Beauty which is seated in the Face, discovers it self in the Shape, in the Symetry of Parts, the Delicacy of the Complexion, the Vivacity and attracting Sweetness of the Eyes, and the Agreeableness of the Air, will authorize our having a Kindness for them, and justify our treating them with Respect; but we must take care that our Esteem be adequate to the Subject, and that it do not degenerate into an indecent Fondness, an ill-grounded Dotage, a foolish Inclination, commonly as transient as its Cause, as little to be rely'd on as those Perfections from whence it springs: We shall do well to consider, that 'tis built on a sandy Foundation, ten thousand Accidents may shake it; but supposing they should not, yet in a short time 'twill totter, and fall of it self; those Charms which support it will fail, Youth will vanish, Age tarnish the brightest Colours, wrinkle the smoothest Skin; Deformity will succeed to Beauty,

---

Line 17. **Superaddition**: addition, above and beyond.

Line 21. **Concretions**: coalesced matter.

Weakness to Strength, and Dulness to the charming Gayety and Sprightliness of greener Years; the most majestick among Mortals, those whose awful Miens imprint Veneration, and enforce Respect, must bend beneath the Load of Years, unavoidably yield to the Infirmities and Decays which necessarily attend a long Life; and such as admir'd them only for those Graces, for those exteriour Beauties, will certainly cease to love them as soon as they are lost, there being nothing left in which their Desires may centre, therefore they follow the wandring Fugitives to each new Face, are in a close pursuit of Things in their Nature transitory, always shifting Places, Things made up of Parts that are ever in Motion, still altering their Forms, and assuming new Figures.

Now what can be more incongruous to our Pretences, more unworthy of intelligent Beings, than to be too much pleas'd with such fleeting Accomplishments, such vanishing Ornaments, which as they are Impresses of that first Beauty, of that original Perfection from whence they proceed, may be allow'd to delight us, to create in us a Complacency for their Possessors, but none of them, strictly speaking, are Objects of Love, that is a Passion much too spiritual, too pure, too exalted, to be prostituted to any thing that is corporeal; 'tis seated in the Mind, and fitted for the Contemplation of intellectual Beauties, it finds Charms in the Understanding, sees Graces in the Soul, infinitely preferable to any that are to be found in the most exquisite Works of Nature: It likes nothing but what is truly amiable, what is really attracting, and what will never cease to be so; scorns to unite it self to any thing which Age can alter, and over which Death can triumph; it chuses what is as immortal as it self; 'tis Truth to which it adheres; Virtue's the Centre to which it tends, from that it derives its Original, and to that alone it owes its Nourishment.

Now this divine Flame can exert it self no where but in Subjects equally good, in Souls govern'd by the same Principles, acting by the same unchangeable Rules; there must be a joint Inclination to Virtue, a like Sense of Honour, the same Notion of Justice, as great an Ardour for Truth, and an exact Conformity of Thoughts; 'twill not reside where there's the least Disparity, where there's any thing impure, or debasing, any thing that can in the least abate its Fervour.

But where shall we find such a Passion, such a happy Agreement! where is that Pair to be found, whose Hearts are fasten'd by such a divine, such an indissoluble Cement, so generous and sublime an Affection? Such Lovers fear no Rivals, admit of no Distrusts, are Strangers to Jealousy, Inconstancy, and all the other Perturbations of Sense: Their Fire burns too bright, is too intense to be extinguish'd, is too ardent to admit of any Coldnesses, any Neglects: They are one, and can no more be unkind to each other than to themselves; are but one Mind, one Soul in different Bodies, and can no more cease to Love, than to Be.

Profane Histories pretend to give us some Instances of perfect Friendships; they boast of a *Pylades,* and an *Orestes,* but we ought to look on this as a Fiction, as a Story, drest up by the Poets, and as little to be credited as that of *Pollux*, who, they tell us, was so kind as to give his Brother an equal share of his Immortality: The greatest Example of this sort that I've met with in any of their Records, is that of *Damon* and *Pythias,* and next to them *Scipio* and *Lælius, Epaminondas* and *Pelopidas, Blosius* and *Tiberius Gracchus* may claim a place: And, for the Honour of my own Sex, give me leave to mention *Hipparchia* and *Crates, Porcia* and *Brutus*, *Sulpitia* and *Lentulus, Arria* and *Petus, Paulina* and *Seneca;*

Line 94. **Profane Histories**: classical myths and legends.

Line 95. **Pylades**: cousin of Orestes who assisted him in his revenge against Clytemnestra; cited as an example of true friendship by Cicero in *Laelius de Amicitia*.

Line 97. **Pollux**: inseparable twin brother of Castor, sons of Jupiter and Leda.

Lines 99–100. **Damon and Pythias**: Damon was a Pythagorean philosopher, whose best friend Pythias was willing to die for him; cited in Cicero's *Tusculan Disputations V.*

Line 100. **Scipio and Lælius**: Laelius was a Roman consul whose friendship with Scipio was cited in Cicero's *Lælius de Amicitia* as the ideal. **Epaminondas and Pelopidas**: Pelopidas was a Theban general who gave away all his wealth because of Epaminondas's influence.

Line 101. **Blosius and Tiberius**: Plutarch mentions Blosius of Cuma as a devoted follower of Tiberius; when questioned by the consuls, Blosius declared that he would have unquestioningly fulfilled any order given to him by Tiberius, including burning Rome.

Lines 102–3. **Hipparchia and Crates**: Hipparchia married the philosopher Crates despite his deformity. **Porcia and Brutus**: Portia, sister of Cato and wife of Brutus, was known for her prudence, wisdom, and conjugal tenderness. After Brutus's death she committed suicide rather than be separated from him.

Line 103. **Sulpitia and Lentulus**: Sulpitia was a poet in the age of Domitian who wrote a poem condemning him for banishing the philosophers from Rome; her connection to Lentulus remains unclear. Lentulus Cornelius was part of the Catilline conspiracy and was convicted in the senate by Cicero and executed. **Arria and Petus**: Arria was the wife of a Roman senator, Petus Cecinna, who was accused of being in a conspiracy against Claudius and ordered sent to Rome by sea. Aria accompanied him and, once at sea, she stabbed herself and presented the sword to her husband, who, inspired by her example, also killed himself (A.D. 42). **Paulina and Seneca**: When Nero commanded the Pythagorean philosopher and his former teacher, Seneca, to destroy himself, his wife Paulina tried to follow his example but was stopped by Nero.

but these are infinitely out-done by two illustrious Names, by a Royal Pair, whose unpresidented Friendship has the Honour to be recorded in the Sacred Writ; I mean *Jonathan* and *David.*

Where was there ever seen a nobler, firmer, a more sacred Union! How admirable was it in its Beginning, its Progress, and its Conclusion! Where shall we meet with one so generous, so humble, so condescending, so tenderly affectionate, so unalterably constant as *Jonathan,* and so reciprocally kind as *David!* Who, without Wonder, can see the Son of a King, the Heir Apparent of a Crown, a Prince bred up amidst the flatteries of a Court, amidst a Crowd of fawning Sycophants, caressing a poor despicable Shepherd, one hardly known in *Israel,* not only giving him those Praises which were due to the Defender of his Country, the Conqueror of the great *Goliath,* but bestowing on him his Heart, himself; the noblest Present he could give, or Love cou'd ask!

That which breeds Envy in narrow groveling Minds, begets Respect in brave and generous Tempers: When he saw that Youth, who was too weak to wear the ponderous Garb of War, who fearless went to meet Gigantick Force, arm'd with no other Weapon but a Sling, return Triumphant, and bringing in his Hand the Trophy of his Victory, his Head, who had bid Defiance to a mighty Host, and with his Looks had almost gain'd the Day, he felt a secret Pleasure in his Mind, the beginning of a growing flame; he admir'd his Courage, gaz'd with Wonder on him, with fix'd Attention heard him speak; each Word encreas'd Esteem, and fan'd the kindling Fire; he found himself urg'd sweetly on, drawn by a delightful Violence to knit his Soul to his; Love firmly ty'd the Knot, and made them one: From that dear moment they had no separate Interest, no Reserves, nothing that they could call their own: *David* to *Jonathan* was dearer far than Empire, than Glory, nay than Life; his only Business was to serve him, his Happiness his whole Concern: When his Merit, join'd with the Acclamations of the People, had made the King his Enemy, he, with the intensest Zeal, became his Advocate, defended his Innocency, and, tho' 'twere with the hazard of his Life, spoke what became a Friend; neither the Threatnings of an angry Father, the

Line 106. **Jonathan and David**: in the Old Testament, the example of perfect friendship: "the soul of Jonathan was knit with the soul of David, and Jonathan loved him as his own soul" (1 Sam. 18:1).

Jealousy of Power, nor yet the Slights and Disregards that constantly attend a Man disgrac'd, and out of Favour with his Soveraign, cou'd make him hide his Thoughts; the Injury done to *David,* the Dishonour thrown upon him by his enrag'd suspicious Father, made him unmindful of himself; his only Care was to secure him, to secure the Man whom he had cause to think was Heaven's peculiar Favourite, and destin'd to wear the Jewish Crown; but with the generous *Jonathan* these Considerations had no Force, his Affection made them all invalid. When full of Grief he went to tell him his Life was sought, and that he must by Flight endeavour to preserve it, how joyful was their Meeting! how loth were they to part! None but such as feel the Agonies of Death, those last dissolving Pangs which separate the Soul and Body, those lov'd Companions, can have a true Idea of their Sorrow: How tenderly did they express their Passion, with what Ardour, what Sincerity, renew their Vows! What Protestations did they make of everlasting Kindness! But when the fatal Minute came, the dire disjoining Moment, how difficult was it to leave each other! how many were the Essays they made! Sighs stop'd their Words, and they could only look their Thoughts, and by Embraces tell the inward Struggles of their Souls, the Pain they felt in being rent asunder! And when 'twas done, how sad were both! What melancholy Thoughts had *Jonathan* when he reflected on the Sufferings of his Friend, those many Hardships, those numerous Dangers, to which he was expos'd! And when he had been pursu'd from place to place by cruel *Saul,* and forc'd at last to make the Wilderness of *Ziph* his Refuge, he found him there; so indefatigably kind is Love, so busy, so inquisitive; it fears no Hazard, declines no Toil, dares any thing, is restless till it can oblige; by it inspir'd, he visited the much wrong'd *David,* the persecuted Innocent; his Friendship still was firm, his Constancy unshaken; the poor, the hated, the forsaken Fugitive, was still as dear to him as if he had been a Monarch, and fill'd the greatest Throne on Earth. O with what Joy did he again behold him, with what transporting Pleasure! How did he strive to alleviate his Grief, and comfort him in his Distress! His Words, like Balm, distill'd themselves into those smarting Wounds his envious Fate had made; he bid him not to fear; told him the God he serv'd would keep him safe, would shield him from

Line 161. **Ziph**: 1 Sam. 23:14.

the Fury of his Father; assur'd him the divine Decree would stand, and that he should possess the Kingdom, should fill the Jewish Throne, and he himself be next to him in Power. The promis'd Exaltation of his Friend did not abate his Love; he could well-pleas'd Descend to let him Rise; and look on his Advancement as his own. O with what Satisfaction did they talk of what should be hereafter! with what Delight confirm their sacred Oaths! How full of Hopes were they the Time would come when they should live together, and undisturb'd enjoy the Sweets of Conversation, the most delicious Banquet of the Mind, that Entertainment which only such a Love as theirs could give, a Passion so refin'd.

But O how blind are Mortals! how far from being able to pry into the Secrets of Futurity! When they believe they've almost reach'd the Goal, they're farthest off. Alas! how sad had been the Parting of *Jonathan* and *David*, had they then known that they must meet no more! Sure Heaven in Kindness to them, conceal'd the fatal Truth; it knew they cou'd not bear the killing News, and kept them still in Hopes of being happy, in expectation of succeeding Bliss, till the retrieveless Blow was given, and *Jonathan* was snatch'd away by Death, till he, together with his Royal Father, fell bravely in the Field of Honour, and nobly died the Victims of their Country. But when the dismal Tidings reach'd the Ears of *David*, what Tongue can tell his Grief! 'twas great beyond Expression: He had lost the whole he lov'd, the best of Friends, one in whom he durst confide, to whom he safely cou'd impart his Thoughts, who with him always shar'd his Joys, and bore an equal Part in every Trouble, or rather took the Burden on himself, was still his kind Adviser, still his Director in every Strait, in every cross Emergency of Fortune. O! in what pathetick Language does he speak his Grief, how elegantly tell his Sorrow! how generously bewail the Death of *Saul!* He ever paid him the Respect due to a Father and a King. The Injuries he did him never rais'd his Passion, or made him do an unbecoming Action: No, so far was he from being guilty of any thing that look'd but like Revenge, or an ambitious Thirst of Empire, that when it was in his Power to kill him, he refus'd it, shun'd, with the utmost Detestation, the very Thoughts of Regicide: He knew that God, who promis'd him a Crown, would, in his own due time, bestow it on him; and as he in his Life rever'd him, so after his Death he treated him with Honour, gave him the Praises due unto his Character, due to the Father of his dearest Friend. Full of Concern for both, full of the tenderest Sentiments that Grief could cause, or Love inspire, he thus express'd his Thoughts, and paid the noblest Tribute to their Fame.

Ah! wretched *Israel!* all thy Beauty's fled!
Thy darling Sons, thy great Defenders dead!
Upon thy Mountains they, lamented, dy'd,
Who for thy sake the worst of Ills defy'd,
Saw Death unmov'd, undaunted met their Fate,
Resolv'd to save, or fall the Victims of the State.

See! low as Earth thy mighty Chiefs are laid,
They who were as superior Pow'rs obey'd;
Who with Majestick Miens, and Airs Divine,
So lately did in glitt'ring Armour shine,
Led on thy Troops, and, full of martial Fire,
Into each Breast did noble Warmth inspire,
Fearless rush'd on, and stem'd the bloody Tide,
Bravely they fought, and then as bravely dy'd.

Let none in *Gath* the dreadful News relate:
With Care conceal the conquer'd Hero's Fate.
May none our Loss in *Askelon* proclaim;
Be silent, all ye busie Tongues of Fame;
Lest with a barbarous Joy, a savage Pride,
Philistine Beauties our just Grief deride;
Lest charming Off-springs of polluted Beds,
Shou'd, with an impious Scorn, erect their Heads;
With artful Dances, and triumphant Lays,
Express their Joy, and their curst *Dagon* praise.

On *Gilboa's* Heights let no more Dew be found,
Let no soft Rain enrich the Rising Ground;
Let them no more a florid Verdure know,

Line 227. **Gath**: the birthplace of David's foe Goliath; David's lament, 2 Sam. 10:20–21.

Line 229. **Askelon**: Ashkelon, Philistine city.

Line 236. **Dagon**: god of the Philistines, half man, half fish.

Line 237. **Gilboa**: range of hills bordering plain of Esdraelon where Saul and Jonathan died.

No more large Crops of springing Plenty show;
No more let Flocks and Herds there Pasture find,
Nothing be left to feed the feather'd Kind;
Nothing be left that can the Priest supply,
Nothing that can on sacred Altars die:
For there the Warriour's Shield was cast away;
For there the Shield of *Saul* neglected lay,
As if no hallow'd Oil had on his lofty Head
Its odorous Drops with Regal Honour spread.

Back from the Feasts of War, the Banquets of the Slain,
The Bow of *Jonathan* did not return in vain;
Nor thence the Sword of *Saul* unglutted came;
Where-e'er he fought, it got him Spoils and Fame.

They both were fraught with Graces all Divine,
Attracting Sweetness did with Greatness join:
The Father laid Authority aside,
The Son made Filial Duty all his Pride.
They mutual Kindness their whole Business made,
And now they undivided rest in Death's calm peaceful Shade.
Not tow'ring Eagles, when by lofty Flights,
They reach'd the Summit of Aerial Heights,
Were half so nimble, half so swift as they,
Nor did fierce Lions with such Strength seize on their trembling Prey.

Ye lovely Daughters of a holy Sire,
Your sparkling Eyes must lose their native Fire;
Tears must obscure those beauteous Orbs of Light;
Your Sovereign has to all your Grief a Right.
In moving Accents mourn o'er vanquish'd *Saul*,
He do's for your intensest Sorrow call;
He, who with tenderest Care did you supply,
Cloath'd you with Scarlet of the richest Dye:
With Gold embroider'd o'er your Garments were,
And glitt'ring Gems adorn'd your flowring Hair.
To these he added many Presents more,
Added Delights to you unknown before.

Amidst the Scene of War, the Horrors of the Day,
How did the Mighty fall a long contested Prey!

Surrounded by their Foes, did full of Wounds expire,
Vast Seas of Blood put out their martial Fire.

O *Jonathan!* thou noblest of thy Kind,
Thy Fate was equal to thy Godlike Mind!
Upon thy Heights on slaughter'd Bodies laid,
Thou hast thy own immortal Trophy made!

O what convulsive Pangs for thee I feel!
Love strikes much deeper than the sharpest Steel:
My Pleasure's gone, my Joys are wholly fled,
All, all is lost, my very Soul is dead:
I'm but the Eccho of my self, a Voice of Woe,
In thee I liv'd, now no Existence know.
While thou wert mine, Heav'n had not sure in store
One dear Delight, one single Blessing more
That I cou'd wish, to heighten my Content:
Fancy it self could nothing more invent:
The whole I cou'd desire in thee I found,
My Life was with continual Raptures crown'd,
And all my Hours but one soft blissful Round:
The Thoughts that thou wert mine made all my Sorrows cease,
Amidst my num'rous Toils gave me a Halcyon Peace;
Contemn'd was ev'ry Danger, ev'ry Pain,
Love made me chearfully the greatest Ills sustain.
When thou wert absent, then my busie Mind
Did in thy dear Remembrance Solace find,
Revolv'd thy Words, on each kind Accent stay'd,
And thy lov'd Image in my Breast survey'd;
Fancy'd thy Eyes each tender Glance return'd,
And with engaging Sweetness for thy *David* mourn'd:
But when thou didst me with thy Presence bless,
O who th' Extatick Transports can express!
Words are too poor, and Language wants a Name
For such a pure, immortal, fervent Flame!
A while I look'd, a while could only gaze,
My Face, my Eyes, my Heart, betray'd my glad Amaze;
My Soul to thine would force her speedy Way,
Panting she stood, and chid her hindring Clay:
Trembling with Joy, I snatch'd thee to my Heart,

Did, with tumultuous Haste, my thronging Thoughts impart:
Troubl'd, thou heard'st me my past Toils relate,
My Suff'rings did a kind Concern create,
And made thee, sighing, blame the Rigour of my Fate.
O with what Pity, what a moving Air,
Did'st thou then vow thou would'st my Hazard's share,
Promis'd eternal Faith, eternal Love,
And kind to me, as my own Soul didst prove;
Nay, kinder far, no Dangers didst decline,
Expos'd thy Life to add a longer Date to mine!
Such an Affection to the World is new,
None can such wond'rous Proofs of Friendship shew!
Not the fair Sex, whom softest Passions move,
Can with such Ardour, such Intenseness love.
But thou art lost! for ever lost to me!
And all I ever priz'd is lost with thee.
Honour, and Fame, and Beauty lose their Charms,
I'm deaf to the harmonious Sound of Arms;
Deaf to the Calls of Glory and of Praise,
I'll near thy Tomb conclude my wretched Days:
In mournful Strains employ my Voice and Lyre,
And, full of Grief, by thy lov'd Corps expire.

How soon, alas! the mighty are destroy'd!
Who can the dreadful Stroke of Fate avoid!
How are they fallen! who but lately stood
Like well-fix'd Rocks, and dar'd the raging Floud!
They who dispers'd their missive Terrors round,
From whom their Foes a swift Destruction found,
Now lie, like common Men, neglected on the Ground.

OF AVARICE

What can be more amazing than to see wise and rational Beings, Beings design'd for the highest and noblest Enjoyments, and richly furnish'd with Faculties fitted for the Contemplation of the greatest, best, and most exalted Objects, wilfully withdraw their Regards from things worthy of themselves, and of that infinite Perfection from whom they derive their Original, and fix them on Earth, on that dull heavy Element, from whence their Bodies, those Prisons of their Souls, those cumbersome Machines in which they act, at first were taken, and by indulging a greedy avaricious Humour, be fond of sinking to the lowest, the most despicable Level, should, before they are necessitated to it by the indisputable Laws of their Creation, the irreversible Decrees of Nature, be in haste to return to it again, uneasie till they are reunited to their primitive Dust! Is it not an unaccountable Madness for such as are Masters of vast Treasures, not to be contented with the bountiful Dividend of Providence? For those that have great Estates to be continually contriving how they shall encrease them? Who can, without wonder mix'd with the highest Detestation, see the generality of Men stick at nothing, though never so base, so injurious, so oppressing, that may promote their Designs? Such as are covetous of Titles, and greedy of Power, what will they not do to gratifie their Desires, to gain what they so eagerly wish for? What vile Offices will they boggle at, what servile Compliances will they not stoop to, what Friend or Kinsman will they not sacrifice, whom will they scruple to ruine, whose Reputation will they not murder, to get or secure the Grandeur, the Honour, the Power, or the Riches they so much prize?

The Poor, whose Lives are one continued Toil, and every Bit of Bread they eat the Purchase of their Sweat, who, wrap'd in Rags, encounter all the Inclemencies of Air, contend with Winter-Storms and Summer-Heats, and, who when tir'd with the laborious Business of the Day, must either make the Earth their Bed, or creep into low squallid Cells, Places as little to be lik'd as Dens of savage Beasts, will play the Villain, flatter, steal and lye, do any thing that's ill to lengthen out a wretched Being, and get a larger Share of those mean things they covet. Such as are rais'd a little higher, can call some fields, some Heaps of Dirt their own, are still conversing with their fellow Brutes, still cultivating every Spot of Earth, considering Night and Day how to encrease their Store, what Crafts to use, what false, sly, undermining Tricks, how to defraud their Neighbours, to trespass on the Rich, and grind the Poor, while those above them make them feel Wrongs as great as those they do, oppress them as much as they do others, and by Ways as equally unjust, as despicably base, rob them of what is their Due, and then prophanely call their lawless Gains the Gift of Heaven, the just Reward of Industry and Prudence: If by a lucky Hit, or a continu'd Series of close Penuries, sordid Methods, by making nuptial Bargains, spunging on the Publick, cajoling weak unthinking Princes, by Rapine, Extortion, Usury, or an excessive Thrift, their wretched Ancestors have damn'd themselves to leave them great and wealthy; they are proud of the Acquest, look big, and value themselves on what they ought to blush at, and strive by ways as altogether ill, as unwarrantably wicked, to add to what they have left them: Wealth thus continued in a Race, they call Gentility, Riches long enjoy'd, they think ennobles Blood, and Gold does make it run more pure: They having nothing properly their own to attract Respect, no shining Qualities to fix the Attention of the Crowd, and gain their Admiration, are forced to seek for something foreign, something that they know will dazzle common Eyes; which being found, they seize it with a voracious Greediness, their Souls stick to it; the more they have, the more they covet, they love it with an unsatisfy'd Desire, continue thirsty at the Fountain, and still with wide stretched Arms, are grasping all that they can reach.

Good God! in this degenerate Age, where are there any to be found entirely free from this accursed Vice! the Young are taught betimes to like it, instructed from their Cradles to be fond of Trifles, to cry for Baubles, like Apes to scamble, scratch and fight for scatter'd Nuts, for Toys as little worth; As they encrease in Years, their Avarice grows with them, their craving Appetite torments them, they still find something to desire; the Objects indeed are various, but the Passion's still the same; that, like their Shadow, grows larger towards the Evening of their Life, gets Ground upon them in their declining Moments, and never leaves them till they are in their Graves, are lost to all the Joys of Sense.

Line 47. **Acquest:** thing acquired. Line 63. **scamble:** struggle for, scramble.

And can there be a more preposterous Folly, a greater Instance of Stupidity, than to be fond of things that cannot long be their's, and slight those real Goods, which, if they please, they may possess for ever? That 'tis the highest Frenzy, every one will own; all with one Voice will blame the griping Usurer, laugh at the meager half-starv'd Wretch, who pines for what's his own, sits hugging of those Bags he dares not open, and makes an Idol of that Wealth, which he should use: Yet all concur to carry on the Farce, each acts a Madman's Part in the great *Bedlam* of the World.

One gets to feed his Pride, another spares to gratifie his Vanity, a third loves Money for it self, loves it with an abstracted Passion; and if he had not Wife, nor Children, Kindred, nor Friends, would still dote on his Heaps, and to encrease them, deny himself all the Conveniences of Life. The Tradesman will use all his Slights, his finest Artifices, to cheat his Customers, will lye and swear, and palm ten thousand Falshoods on them to vend his Goods; his Profit is his God, and Poverty the only Devil he's afraid of. The Mariner will venter on the roughest Sea, contend with rising Surges, deaf'ning Winds and complicated Horrors, nay, slight even Death it self, when Gain's in view: For it, will the Physician meet the greatest Danger, endure the most offensive Stenches, look on the ugliest, the most loathsome Objects; and, what is more, will, with the Patience of a Stoick, a smiling courtly Air, and a respectful Silence, bear with the Impertinence and senseless Jargon of Children, Women, Fools, and Madmen: For it, the Lawyer pleads, it gives an oily Smoothness to his Tongue, endues him with a powerful Elocution, extends his Lungs, and makes him talk with Fire, heightens his Courage, and prompts him on to undertake the blackest Cause; for dear bewitching Gold he'll stretch the Statutes, rack the Law, and often make it speak in the Defence of Guilt; the Client who brings most Guineas with him is ever welcomest, and much more in the right than his Opponent. The Men of Pleasure will rack their Tenants, miserably oppress their poor Dependants, attend whole Mornings at the great Man's Levée, become base whining Supplicants for a Boon, and do whatever is requir'd, for some advantageous Post, for some ambition'd Favour. The fine Lady will be guilty of ten thousand stingy Actions to make a gay Appearance, to outshine her Neighbours; will almost starve her Family, defraud her

Line 77. **Bedlam**: London's notorious madhouse.

Servants, and send the Needy cursing from her Doors, rather than want Supplies for her Diversions, a Fund for *Basset, Ombra, Pickett*, or any other of those Games her Avarice makes her fond of. The Country-Wife will be the Turn-key of her Goal, like *Argus*, still inspect her Under-Brutes, watch all their Motions, observe each Bit they eat, will talk of nothing but the Arts of Saving, and thinks no Knowledge necessary, but what instructs her how to get: She, by a profitable Chymistry, turns all things into Gold, her good Housewifry is the true Elixir, by it she converts Beasts, Birds, Trees, Plants, Flowers, and all the other Products of her Care into the noblest Metal, into that glittering Bullion which she loves so well, that, like *Vespasian*, she would not scruple to extract it from the meanest Things: While she's thus idly busie, her Husband applauds his Fortune, thinks himself happy in having a Partner, whose Intellectuals are commensurate with his own, and who kindly shares with him in the Toil of growing rich: While they are sordidly employ'd in scraping Dirt together, the Soldier takes a more compendious Way of being wealthy; he burns and plunders, wades through Blood for Gain; exposes his Life for Pay, rushes on Cannons, and fearless runs on Points of Swords, for Gold: Nor are they only mercenary Wretches, such as fight for Bread, that are thus greedy; the Great are equally blameworthy; Princes themselves are as avaricious as the poorest of their Subjects: What else makes those that are possess'd of spacious Dominions, of large and flourishing Kingdoms, to be encroaching on the Territories of their Neighbours, still rendring them and their People miserable, and carrying Devastation and Confusion with them where-ever they extend their Arms, and by this means render themselves publick Mischiefs, when they were design'd for universal Blessings.

What were the *Sesostris's*, the *Alexanders*, the *Pompeys*, the *Cæsars*, and all the other celebrated Heroes of Antiquity, together with all the latter Conquerors, the *Tamerlanes*, the *Caliphs*, the *Attila's*, the

Line 106. **Basset, Ombra, Pickett**: popular card games.

Line 108. **Argus**: in Greek myth, a warrior with 100 eyes; Hera used him as a watchman.

Line 132. **Sesostris**: fabled king of Egypt before the Trojan war who invaded Europe and Asia, reign described by Herodotus.

Line 134. **Tamerlane**: Tatar warrior (1336–1405) who conquered Persia and India. **Caliphs**: the chief civil and religious rulers in Mohammedan countries. **Attila**: the Hun, called "The Scourge of God," who conquered much of the Roman empire.

Aureng-Zebs, and all the other Disturbers of the World, but glorious Robbers, illustrious Thieves? And wherein did *Cæsar* differ from the Pirates he executed? He was only mightier, but not less criminal, his Power was an Umbrage for his Faults, and his Lawrels became his Protectors.

How happy was *Sparta* while she despis'd Riches! She had the Honour of being the chiefest, the most valued City of *Greece,* till, in the Reign of *Agis*, Gold and Silver again found a Way thither; and *Lysander*, by bringing in rich Spoils from the Wars, unhappily fill'd her at once with Covetousness and Luxury.

Unfortunate Conquerors! how much better had it been for you never to have been victorious, than to have prov'd the occasional Corrupters of your Country! And how cou'd those things you gave them be properly call'd Goods, since they only serv'd to make their Possessors wicked?

How infinitely preferable is that Poverty, which is accompany'd with Innocency and Content, to Wealth purchas'd by Rapine and Injustice, and kept with Anxiety and Remorse?

What good, nay, what considerate Man would not much rather have chosen to have been the poor just *Aristides*, than the rich impious *Callias;* the Divine *Plato*, than the suspicious, barbarous *Dionysius;* the virtuous *Epaminondas*, than *Alexander* the *Pherean;* the contented

---

Line 135. **Aureng-Zeb**: overthrew Shah Jehan to seize the Indian empire.

Lines 136–37. **Cæsar … Pirates**: according to Plutarch, when the young Julius Caesar was traveling to Rhodes to complete his education, he was seized by pirates; they demanded an insultingly low ransom, which he paid, but he then pursued them and had them crucified.

Line 142. **Agis**: Agis II, king of Sparta; in Plutarch, he is cited for his attempt to reinstitute the austere laws of Lycurgus and divide land equally among the Spartans, which caused him to be assassinated. **Lysander**: famed Spartan commander who captured the Athenian fleet in 405 B.C. and brought the riches back to Sparta.

Lines 153–54. **Aristides … Callias**: an Athenian general, surnamed "The Just," who commanded the forces at Marathon in 490 B.C. and died honored but impoverished; Plutarch cites Callias as the torchbearer of Aristides who disobeyed his order not to plunder the defeated at Marathon, and in fact founded his fortune there.

Line 154. **Dionysius**: Dionysius II, king of Sicily, studied under the philosopher Plato, who urged him to give up supreme power; Dionysius ordered Plato sold as a slave.

Line 155. **Epaminondas**: King of Boeotia, who led the Thebans to victory over the Spartans in 371 B.C. and, according to Plutarch, never told a lie. **Alexander the Pherean**: According to Plutarch and Cicero, he was the tyrant of Thessaly, who took Epaminondas's great friend Pelopidas prisoner.

Marcus Curius, than the greedy, sordid *Perseus?* But the generality of Men are too apt, like the last, to place their Happiness in Riches, to permit Covetousness to be the governing Passion of their Souls, that to which every other Vice must strike Sail.

Nor are the Laity alone chargeable with this reigning Vice; 'tis not contented to erect its Throne in the outward Court of the Temple, in the less holy part of the sacred Edifice, but audaciously enters the *Sanctum Sanctorum*, insolently triumphs over those who by the Dignity of their Function ought to be exempted from its Jurisdiction: Not that all are its Captives; no, there are some who, like the good Angels, keep their Station, still fight under the Banner of the Great Messias, and are so far from yielding the least Subjection to Mammon, that they bravely resist all the Efforts of Avarice, as scorning to have it said, that they are master'd by their Money, are Vassals to their Wealth, who think it their highest Glory to be Almoners to infinite Goodness, to be the Distributors, and not the Ingrossers of the Heavenly Bounty; and who, following the Advice of their Blessed Saviour, are not sollicitous about corruptible Riches, but wisely lay up for themselves such durable Treasures, as will be their's for ever, their's in a future, an eternal State; can bear Poverty, not with a Stoical Apathy, but a Christian Resignation, and contentedly trust Providence with the remaining Moments of their Lives, as not doubting but their kind Benefactor, that God to whom they owe their Being, and who extends his Care to the least, the most inconsiderable Parts of his Creation, who gives Food to the Fowls, Beauty to the flowers of the field, and a delightful Verdure to the Grass, will not neglect the Creatures whom he has vouchsafed to form after his own Image, and who have the Honour to be particularly dedicated to his Service, and to be separated from the rest of Mankind by the distinguishing Characters of Divinity.

But these, alas! are but few, if compar'd with the Multitude; their Number, like that of perfect Animals, being but small, in comparison of

Line 156. **Marcus Curius ... Perseus**: Three times elected consul, Marcus Curius was celebrated by Juvenal in his *Satire* for his frugality and fortitude; Plutarch characterizes Perseus, king of Macedonia, as avaricious.

Line 163. **Sanctum Sanctorum**: holy of holies; reference to the church in general.

Line 170. **Almoners**: agents who distribute money or goods for charity.

those Swarms of Insects, which are every where discoverable throughout the vast Extent of Nature.

'Tis, I fear, a Truth too evident to be deny'd, that too many of them are as greedy as covetous, and as incroaching as any of their poor ignorant Neighbours, more sollicitous for their Tithes, than for the Salvation of their Parishioners, much more busily employ'd in manuring their own Glebe, than in improving the Minds of such as are under their Care; in a Word, as much concern'd for Earth, as it becomes them to be for Heaven.

Religion in all Ages has been the specious Bait, and Priests the luckiest Anglers: In the Heathen World, a blind Zeal, a bigotted Devotion, and a superstitious Dread of Hell, enrich'd their Temples, adorn'd their Shrines, and made their Altars vie with the glittering Canopy of Heaven. Mankind were then immers'd in Vice, inslav'd by their Passions, and influenc'd by sensible Idea's; the Love of sensual Pleasure had taken so deep Root in their Hearts, that nothing was capable of shaking it: They had gross Notions of Good and Evil, and their having them was almost unavoidable, because, the Poets, who were their *Præceptors,* had given their Divinities not only all the Infirmities incident to the Humane Nature, but all those Passions and Vices, to which by a fatal Depravity, a deplorable Depradation, 'twas unhappily subjected.

Who could be more infamous than their *Jupiter,* guilty of greater Enormities than their *Apollo,* their *Mars,* their *Bacchus,* their *Mercury,* and the rest of their Gods? Who more haughty, more passionate, more malicious, revengeful, and jealous than their *Juno,* more shamefully lascivious than their *Venus,* more fierce and bloody than their *Bellona?* Their Deities being such profligate Monsters, 'twas hardly possible that their Worshippers should be vertuous; but there being still left in their Souls some faint Shadows of Truth, some pale Glimmerings of the Celestial Light, some imperfect Notices of their original Purity, they found an inward Principle, an unseen Comptroller of their Actions, something that made them uneasy to themselves, that pall'd their Joys, and fill'd them with disturbing Reflexions, which like frightful Spectres star'd them in the Face amidst their criminal Pursuits; these Terrors were

Line 193. **Glebe**: land belonging to a parish church.

Line 212. **Bellona**: in Roman myth, goddess of war, sister of Mars.

exceedingly increas'd by the Poets, their dismal Description of Hell and those baleful Rivers that surrounded it, the tremendous Forms with which 'twas fill'd, the ghastly howling *Cerberus,* the dreadful Chimæra, the horrid Furies, the fatal Sisters, the inexorable Judges, together with the flaming *Tartarus*, where they were told were to be seen the Giants, the *Danaides*, and with them *Tantalus*, *Ixion*, *Sysiphus*, and all the other poetical Sufferers; these Stories made melancholy Impressions on their Imaginations; they were afraid of the Punishments their Guilt might render them obnoxious to; they were conscious to themselves of their being continually under the severe Inspection of a divine *Nemesis;* were willing to escape the expected Vengeance, and yet at the same time loth to part with their darling Crimes: Of this the Priests took Advantage, and propos'd their making an Attonement by Sacrifices, and put them into a method of rendring the Gods propitious, by erecting magnificent Temples; thus they perswaded them, that they might by external Performances make amends for the Irregularities of their Lives, and complement them into a Connivance at their Faults: By this Artifice, they made themselves considerable, and, like *Phidias*, shar'd in the Honours they had procur'd for them: By their pretended Miracles, their counterfeit Sanctity, and their dubious Oracles, they not only rais'd glorious Structures, and encreas'd their Revenues, but render'd themselves necessary, and made the trembling Multitude obedient to their Precepts: Only a few enlightned Understandings, a few elevated Genius's, saw thro' their Tricks, discover'd their Legerdemain: In those dark Ages, none among them, but a *Socrates*, a *Plato*, and some of their Disciples, were acquainted with the Perfections of the Deity, and knew what would please him; none but such as they, knew that his Temple ought to be a purify'd Heart, and, that virtuous Thoughts, innocent Intentions,

---

Line 224. **fatal Sisters**: the Fates; in classical myth, three sisters who control human destiny.

Line 225. **Tartarus**: an area in Hades where the most impious and guilty were imprisoned.

Line 226. **Danaides**: the 50 daughters of Danaus, king of Argos, who were ordered by their father to kill their husbands on their wedding nights; they were sentenced in Hades to try forever to fill a sieve with water. **Tantalus, Ixion, Sysiphus**: residents of Hades: Tantalus was punished with intense thirst he could never quench; Ixion was bound on a burning wheel; Sisyphus eternally attempted to roll a large stone up a hill.

Line 238. **Phidias:** Greek sculptor commissioned by Pericles to create the bronze statue of Athena Promachose that stood on the Acropolis.

Line 244. **Legerdemain**: deception, sleight of hand.

holy Discourses, just and charitable Actions, were the only acceptable Sacrifices; but 'twas not in their Power to undeceive the People; *Socrates* dy'd in the Attempt, and others found it lost-labour to endeavour to stem the Current: Superstition prevail'd, and every Day made new Conquests; to that we owe some of the greatest Edifices of Antiquity; 'twas that which rais'd the stately Temple of *Belus*, that famous one dedicated to *Diana* at *Ephesus*, and that of *Jupiter* at *Olympia*, together with those so much celebrated in *Greece* and *Rome;* neither did that costly Bigotry expire with those mighty Empires and flourishing Commonwealths mention'd in ancient Story, nor bear the same Date with their Religion; no, it has ever since appear'd on the Stage of the World, and the Priests have still made Use of the same Arts to inrich themselves, and buoy up their Reputation.

In the new-discover'd World, the great Continent of *America,* the *Spaniards* found at *Cusco*, the Metropolis of *Peru*, the wonderful Temple of the Sun, together with the four adjoining ones, of which one was dedicated to the Moon, the second to the Planet *Venus*, the third to Thunder and Lightning, and the fourth to *Iris;* all which, if we may credit History, were admirably Built, and so richly Adorn'd, that they might vie with the finest Structures of Antiquity: With these the Pagods or Temples of *Siam* may claim a place; nor ought those many magnificent Mosques to be forgotten, which are the beautiful Ornaments of several of the Mahometan Cities: All which are undeniable Proofs of the Truth of what I've been asserting; for among those heated Zealots, there was nothing but Smoak, nothing but exterior Shows, their fire did not yield a vital Heat, did not burn bright, their Understandings were obscur'd, thick clammy Fogs, impenetrable Veils of solid Night were plac'd between them and their Reason, they could not discern what was good, nor shun what was ill; what Vice presented as eligible, with that

---

Line 254. **Temple of Belus**: described by Herodotus as one of the most magnificent in the ancient world with golden statues 40 feet high, built to honor an ancient king of Babylon. **famous one**: the temple to Diana at Ephesus in Ionia, believed built by the Amazons; one of the Seven Wonders of the ancient world.

Line 255. **Jupiter at Olympia**: in the Peloponnesus, with a celebrated statue of Jupiter; another of the Seven Wonders.

Line 263. **Cusco**: temple of the sun constructed by the Incas.

Line 266. **Iris**: Greek goddess of the rainbow.

they clos'd, and in all Cases appeal'd to their Senses, and yielded to their decisive Sentence; by them were madly hurried on; and if at any time a rising Doubt check'd their Career, if their Consciences grew troublesome, they this way still'd their Clamours, and hop'd to bribe superior Powers by outward Marks of Veneration: Nor were these the Sentiments only of the Ignorant, the Idolatrous Part of Mankind; they got Footing also among the Jews, among the peculiar Favourites of Heaven, a People preserv'd by Wonders, and conversant with Miracles, instructed by the most sublime of Philosophers, or rather taught by God himself; yet this People, this illuminated Nation, when their great Legislator had been but a while absent from them, found themselves so strongly byass'd by their natural Inclination to Idolatry (and the numerous Divinities they had so lately seen worship'd in *Egypt* being present to their Minds) that they could not be easy without having some sensible Representation to which they might pay their Adoration; this made them apply themselves to *Aaron*, and desire him, with so much Earnestness, to make them Gods. Good Heaven! How quickly did he yield to their Intreaties! What Mischiefs did he bring on his wretched Nation!

The sacred Priest the sensless Mob obey'd;
'Twas *Aaron* who the Golden Folly made:
From *Egypt* he the lov'd Idea brought,
The Calf was then imprest upon his Thought,
There, by his Fancy, so exactly wrought,
That ev'ry Trace unalter'd did remain,
The Lines were deeply carv'd within his Brain;
Thence, by Traduction, lineally convey'd
On all his Sons the spreading Mischief prey'd:
The tainted Stock did dire Effects produce,
Venom was mix'd with all its vital Juice:
Th' impoison'd Juice with Swiftness did ascend,
As quick as Thought to loftiest Boughs extend,
And thence, by subtile Paths, to lower Branches tend,
Did on each Leaf, each slender Fibre seise:
Moses himself encreas'd the curst Disease,
When, by a wondrous Skill, an Art divine,

Line 293. **Aaron**: Exod. 32:1–7.

To Ashes he their *Apis* did calcine,
And with their Liquor mix'd the glitt'ring Dust,
Too much he added to their native Thirst:
The crouding Atoms throng'd into the Brain,
Too close they stuck to be expell'd again:
The sacred Tribe not only Suff'rers were,
Others had in their Guilt an equal Share;
The painful Hunger all alike opprest,
The rav'nous Vultur prey'd on ev'ry Breast,
The Love of Gold its Poison did dilate,
Dispers'd it self throughout the wretched State;
From them into the Christian Church it came;
The Christian Church deserv'd an equal blame,
Too fond it grew of Grandeur, Wealth, & Fame.

For not only the ignorant Pagans, the dull stupid Jews, the foolish deluded Mussulmen, but the enlightned Christians, the Pretenders to more Knowledge, clearer Views, and more elevated Understandings; not only those of the former, but the present Age, have been too much govern'd, too much influenc'd by popular Notions, too much sway'd by Opinion.

What glorious Piles, what vast Buildings, did Superstition raise, in both the Eastern and Western Empires! both at *Constantinople* and *Rome!* What was formerly more august than *St. Sophia!* and what at present more magnificent than *St. Peter's!*

The *Grecian* and *Roman* Clergy took equal Care to provide for themselves and their Religion; the Honour of the Church, and their own private Advantage, went hand in hand; their Interests were too closely link'd ever to be sever'd: they every where had wonderful Harvests; the Bigotry of past Ages pour'd down plentiful Showers of *Manna* on them, and they gather'd it with an indefatigable Toil; and that it might be safe, laid it up in the Ark, put it into a sacred Repository, where 'twas out of Danger of being profan'd, of being touch'd by unhallow'd Hands. By a sort of spiritual Magick, they drew almost all the Wealth of every Coun-

---

Line 313. **Apis**: a god the Egyptians worshiped in the form of an ox in the city-state of Memphis.

Line 328. **Mussulmen**: Muslims. Line 335. **St. Sophia**: Mother church in Constantinople.

Line 341. **Manna**: any needed substance which seems miraculously supplied.

try into which they came within their sacred Circle: By this means the *Caloyers* of Mount *Athos* built, and so richly endowed their Monasteries; and by it the several Orders of the Church have establish'd themselves in almost all Parts of *Europe*, and everywhere amass'd vast Treasures: in *Spain* and *Italy* they have an unlimited Power; and in those two Kingdoms Poverty is everywhere to be seen, except in the Churches, the Palaces of Princes, those of the Pope, and Cardinals, and the other dignified Clergy, together with the Houses of the Religious.

How mean, how dejected are the *Italians!* how much degenerated from their ancient Bravery! How little do they resemble those warlike *Romans* who Conquer'd the World, and gave Law to almost all Mankind! How much has their Country lost of its former Fertility, their Cities of their Beauty, and their Towns of their Riches! Their Altars have ingross'd their Treasures, and those who would be thought the Imitators of an humble suffering Master, of one who while he was here did not think fit to call any thing his own, nay, was so far from being rich, that he had not those common Conveniences of Life which the brute Animals enjoy'd, became Competitors with their Princes, and equal to Crown'd Heads for Wealth and Grandeur: Cou'd an unprejudic'd Spectator take them to be the Successors of poor plain Fishermen, of those Apostles who when they received their sacred Mission, were strictly commanded in all their Journeys, in their long and painful Peregrinations through the World, to take with them neither Silver nor Gold, nor any other Necessaries, but to depend entirely on Providence, and to be contented to receive their Maintenance from the Charity of well-disposed People, from Persons powerfully influenc'd by that Spirit of Love, that tender and endearing Affection which in the Infancy of the Church distinguish'd the Christians from those of all other Religions?

Now 'tis not for such Men as these to pretend to Reform Mankind, to assume the Chair, and act the Dictators: They must first begin at home, must first pull down the Golden Calf which still remains inshrin'd in their Hearts, must sever the glaring Particles, and disperse them among the Needy; shew by their Practice how Riches ought to be used, to whom they ought to be given, and how they may be made Incentives to Virtue, before they preach it to others. They cannot but know, that

Line 347. **Caloyers of Mount Athos:** Greek monks of the order of St. Basil.

Examples have always been more prevalent than Precepts, and that we are sooner prevail'd on by what we see, than by what we hear: A Man who lives the Truths he teaches, cannot fail to inculcate them; they have a resistless Force, and carry Convictions with 'em: We cannot avoid believing those whose Words and Actions are of a piece, and who by the little Regard they have for Riches, make it evident that they are above 'em who use 'em with the same Indifferency that a Passenger does the Conveniences he meets with on the Road, thinks 'em no more his own, no more conducing to his Happiness.

I'm afraid what I have said on this Subject will be misunderstood by the fiery Bigots of all Parties: Such as are warmly engag'd in the Interest of the Establish'd Church, will accuse me of Profaneness and Irreligion for speaking against the Erecting magnificent Edifices for the Worship of God, and both they and the Sectaries will be offended with me for presuming to find fault with them for endeavouring to enrich themselves, and improving the Ignorance and Credulity of the Common People to their secular Advantage: They are all apt to run away with a thing as soon as they have read it, without affording themselves the leisure to examine it, and are not, amidst the Noise and Hurry of their Passions, capable of discerning between Truth and Falshood, and consequently can't make right Judgments: By such I expect to have it said, that what I have writ on this Head is a Satyr on the Clergy in general; they will not allow themselves time to consider, that I have put a Distinction between such as are good, and such as are not so; that to the first I have paid all the Deference due to their Character, have given all the Praises they deserve; and that 'tis the last, those that are the Blemishes of their Order, the Reproaches of their sacred Function, their Antipodes whom they pretend to imitate, and the Reverse of that Master whom they would have the World believe they serve, I take the Liberty to find fault with; 'tis their Avarice I censure, their making Religion a Mask for their Covetousness what I deplore: As for the Aspersions which I doubt will be cast upon me, I assure the Readers if they misinterpret my Words they'll very much wrong me in it; for I can with much Truth affirm, that I am so far from being an Enemy to the worshipping of God in Churches magnificently built and finely adorn'd,

Line 402. **Satyr**: satire.

that I think the Places appropriated to his Service cannot be too august, nor too curiously embellish'd. I consider, that he who is Beauty it self, Perfection in the Abstract, and has been pleas'd to impress some part of his adorable Excellencies on whatever he has made, the whole Universe being a charming Transcript, a fair and dazling Copy of those beautiful Idea's which from all Eternity were in the Divine Intellect, cannot be pleas'd with being worship'd in mean contemptible Places, in Structures inferior to those we build for our selves; this is farther evident to me from the Tabernacle *Moses* was commanded to make, and of which he had the Pattern given him by God himself while he was with him on the Mount: Every thing in it was admirable; the Utensils that belong'd to it, and the Sacerdotal Habits, had peculiar Beauties: How rich were all the Materials, how lively the Colours, how glorious the Gildings, and how curiously wrought, how delicately fine the Embroideries! 'Tis yet more demonstrable from that stupendous Fabrick rais'd by *Solomon*, that surprizing Piece of Architecture, where every thing was exactly Regular, Beautiful, and Magnificent.

There being in the Divine Nature no Vicissitude, no Change, nothing that has the least Resemblance to that Inconstancy of Humour which is to be found among us, 'twere absurd to suppose, that what pleas'd him in those Ages should offend him in this: When he commands us to worship him in Spirit and in Truth, he does not forbid us to join outward Testimonies of Respect with inward and rational Services: The Places in which we pay our Adoration ought doubtless to bear some Analogy to his Nature, to have all the ornamental Graces, all the Finenesses we are capable of bestowing on them; it, in my Opinion, arguing a Want of that due Reverence which it becomes us to have for the Divine Majesty, to let those Edifices which are intended for the Solemnization of his publick Worship, be destitute of handsom Embellishments, of any thing that may be of use to excite Devotion, and demonstrate that profound and awful Veneration which 'tis fit for Creatures to pay to their infinitely great, and unexpressibly bountiful Creator.

I think I have said enough on this Topick to justify my self; I shall only add, that I could wish, that such as have the Honour to attend at

---

Line 427. **Sacerdotal Habits**: priestly garments.

Line 430. **Fabrick ... Solomon**: Solomon's temple, 1 Kings 6–7.

the Altar, would give those that are committed to their Charge, great Idea's of God, endeavour to inspire them with noble and becoming Notions of his incomprehensible Perfections, and make it their Business to banish out of their Minds all slavish Fears, all superstitious Dreads, and make it their Study to raise them from sensible Representations to intellectual Views.

Such among them as strive to do Good, who desire no more than will serve to render their Lives tolerably easy, and who, if they are blest with an Affluence of Wealth, are no farther pleas'd with it than as it puts them in a Capacity of relieving the Indigent, and rewarding the Vertuous, I think I cannot sufficiently esteem; but such as make greater Advances, who for the Propagation of the Christian Faith, and out of the tender Regard they have for such as by their Ignorance and Immorality are in Danger of being everlastingly miserable, chearfully expose themselves to the extremest Poverty, the severest Hardships, and the greatest Hazards that Mankind can be obnoxious to, have not only a Title to my Esteem, but a just Claim to my Admiration.

I have but one thing more to say, which I had forgot to mention sooner, and that is, that I am not against their having handsom Revenues, Settlements independant on the capricious Humour of the People; I am so far from it, that as I would have Churches not only decent, but magnificent, so I would have those who have the Honour to be the Ambassadors of Heaven, not only have enough to render their Lives commodious and pleasant, not only what is sufficient to secure them from Penury and Contempt, but such a Maintenance as may help to support their Character, and which, if they are rais'd to Dignities, may enable them to live suitably to them; but then I would not have their Riches employ'd in aggrandizing their Families, made the Fewel of Vice, laid in as a Fund for Luxury, distributed with a partial Hand, made the Reward of Flattery, appropriated to a Party, or made use of to carry on ambitious Designs, but confer'd with a prudent and distinguishing Bounty.

If I'd a Fortune equal to my Mind,
I like, my bounteous Maker, would be kind,

Line 477. **Fewel**: fuel.

Wou'd spread my Wealth with greedy Pleasure round,
Near me no needy Wretches shou'd be found;
But still the Good shou'd have the largest Share,
Both of my Love, my Riches, and my Care;
For them I'd seek, to their Relief wou'd fly,
Prevent their Prayers, and all their Wants supply.

But since, O my God, thou hast not thought fit to intrust me with such Advantages of being charitable as others are bless'd with, let my Desires supply the Defect of Actions, and let the little I'm capable of doing be acceptable; my Mite have a place in the Treasury, and that Cup of cold Water, which I give with an Eye to thy Honour, and the Order of things, that beautiful Order which thou hast establish'd in the World, receive a joyful *Euge* at the great Day of Retribution.

That Day, when Clangors all Divine,
Shall be the Harbingers of Fate;
When dazling Glories all around shall shine,
And God descend in State:
Officious Clouds shall gladly meet,
Shall croud into one solid Mass beneath his Feet,
That God who here our Flesh was pleas'd to wear,
For us Contempts and Pains to bear,
And all the Frailties of our Nature share;
That God, who fell a Sacrifice of Love,
Now comes with glorious Terror from Above:
He comes! he comes! to judge Mankind!
To judge that World for which he dy'd!
The Good shall still the same kind Saviour find,
The Bad be forc'd to own that Justice which they have defy'd.

2.

See! in the clear expanded Air,
A Throne for him Angelick Forms prepare:
Angelick Forms, whose Number do's transcend
Those sparkling Orbs of Light,
Which give a pleasing Lustre to the Night,
And render even its dusky Horrours bright,

Line 489. **Prevent**: anticipate. Line 498. **Harbingers**: forerunners, announcers.

Which far exceed those num'rous Heaps of Sand,
Which check the Sea, and bound the Land,
And betwixt both the lasting Barriers stand.
He sits sublime, while they attend,
While they their joyful Homage pay,
While they before him humbly bend,
And at his Feet their shining Honours lay,
Refulgent Crowns, which if compar'd with those below,
Like radiant Suns to glimmering Glow-worms show.

3.

At his Command they bid the Dead appear,
Th' affrighted Dead the powerful Mandate hear:
All that have trod the Stage of Life arise,
And on the dread Tribunal fix their Eyes;
The Rich, the Poor, the Princes, and their Slaves,
Come trembling up from their deserted Graves,
From their close Mansions, full of anxious Fear,
They come to breathe superior Air.
Those whose past Lives have pious been,
Who to their Reason calm Submission pay'd,
And ne'er their Passions willingly obey'd,
With less Concern leave their obscure Retreat:
But O! what Tongue their Horrors can repeat,
To whom their Crimes relentless Furies prove,
Who now are curss'd with what they once did love!
They can't the sad Remembrance shun,
But must for ever view the Faults which they have done:
Each do's a *Nemesis* appear,
And each do's justify their Fear:
Not the least Glimpse of Hope remains,
No Joy to mitigate their Pains,
Despair has bound them fast with Adamantine Chains.
They wish, but wish in vain,
They cou'd return to their first Source again,
Back to that Nothing whence they rose,
Or in some deep Abyss cou'd find Repose,
Cou'd in the darkest Shades of Night
Conceal themselves from all revealing Light.

Line 548. **Adamantine**: unyielding, made of the hardest substance.

4.

These he will separate by his Pow'r Divine,
To each their proper Place assign:
And as a Shepherd with the tend'rest Care
His Sheep do's from his Goats divide,
Do's richest Pastures for the first provide,
Lets them exulting feed on his Right-hand,
While on his Left the Goats neglected stand;
So for the Good the noblest Station he'll prepare,
And then in Accents soft as Air,
In the still Voice of gentlest Peace and Love,
That Voice which will extatick Raptures move,
Which welcome to their Souls as chearful Light will prove;
To them he'll with Fraternal Kindness say,
Come ye, whom my Great Father's pleas'd to bless,
Come, and immortal Joys possess,
With Raptures come to that exalted State,
Long præ-ordain'd for you by Fate,
That Kingdom destin'd your's, e're since that Day
On which he did the World's Foundation lay.

5.

For me, when hungry, by Compassion led,
You readily with wholsome Viands fed;
And when the sultry Heat had made me dry,
Did with refreshing Draughts supply;
When wand'ring alone, I sought Relief,
You on my Suff'rings Pity took,
With an endearing Sweetness calm'd my Grief,
And with a kind inviting Look,
A gen'rous Hospitable Air,
Receiv'd the friendless Stranger to your Care.
When I the greatest Poverty endur'd,
When naked bore the Fervour of the Day,
And in the Night, expos'd to piercing Cold, uncover'd lay,
You me with Cloaths from both Extreams secur'd;
And, when in Pain, I languish'd void of Rest,
You kindly came to visit the Distress'd.
When to a Prison I was close confin'd,
You found me out, and with unweary'd Love,

Became the dear Physicians of my Mind:
Like sovereign Balm did your Discourses prove,
Into my Soul they gently were convey'd,
And clos'd those Wounds which cruel Grief had made.

6.

Then shall the Righteous, full of Wonder, say,
When, our dear Saviour, did we thus to Thee!
O how could Thirst and Hunger on Thee prey,
  Who art from all our Frailties free,
Secure from all the Suff'rings of Humanity!
Or how could'st thou, who ev'ry Place dost fill,
  Be any where a Stranger found,
    Thou, who with Glory crown'd,
      Art Lord of all,
The higher Orbs, and this inferior Ball!
Sickness could not its Power to Thee extend,
      On whose Almighty Will,
    Both Causes and Effects depend,
In whose blest Frame, with Harmony Divine,
    The diff'rent Particles combine,
      No noxious Humours there
Are found to mix with poisonous Steams, or with malignant Air.
    Cou'd Space Infinity confine,
Or what's immense be within Limits brought,
What's much too vast for Place, and spreads beyond th' Extent
  of Thought!

7.

Then shall their God from his resplendent Throne
  Thus to th' astonish'd Just reply,
Since I for you left my Celestial Height,
And to my Self your Nature did unite,
Made it my own by that mysterious Tye:
The suff'ring Good as Brethren I esteem,
To me they're dear, my Blood did them redeem;
The suff'ring Good, tho' poor, are priz'd by me,
I can thro' Rags interior Merit see.
Whatever Kindnesses to them you do,
  All the Regards to them you shew,
With an Affection to Mankind unknown,

With an Affection wonderful and new,
I'll take as if design'd for me alone;
And your Reward shall prove
Worthy my Self, and my unbounded Love.

8.

Then turning to the Left, with Looks severe,
With Looks that a Majestick Terror wear,
Depart, he says, depart, ye Curs'd, from me,
From Life and Joy, to everlasting Misery;
To Fire condemn'd, and never-ceasing Pains,
To those dire Realms, where, bound in horrid Chains,
Th'Apostate Prince, and his infernal Train,
Devoted to retrieveless Woes remain.
When Thirst and Hunger, with rapacious Haste,
Upon my fainting Entrails prey'd,
When Sickness did my sinking Spirits waste,
With me you never stay'd:
Not once you strove to lessen my Distress,
Show'd no Desire to make my Suff'rings less:
When dying, with a base insulting Pride,
My Groans you laugh'd at, did my Sighs deride:
When in your Streets I wander'd in the Night,
Helpless and tir'd, you with a scornful Eye,
From me kept off, or turn'd regardless by;
While in Distress you thought you had a Right
To treat me ill, and exercise your Spight:
And, when in Fetters, I neglected lay,
You ne'er did one condoling Visit pay.

9.

Tho' self-condemn'd, th'unhappy Wretches strive
To keep a while their dying Hopes alive;
Low as the Dust their trembling Knees they bend,
And toward Heaven enfeebl'd Arms extend,
With mortal Sadness and dejected Eyes,
Looks where Despair does visibly appear,
Joyn'd with a conscious Shame, and a tormenting Fear;
With fault'ring Lips, and a weak broken Tone,
They to their dreadful Charge reply:
O when, they sighing cry,

Did we so impious prove,
So void of Gratitude and Love?
When did'st thou to this Earth descend,
And in a mean Disguise,
Thy Creatures into Faults surprize?
Since unto us thy Wants were never known,
O let our Ignorance for our Crimes attone:
We never knew thou hungry wert, or dry,
Nor yet bewilder'd in the Glooms of Night;
Nor cou'd we think that thou couldst Garments need,
Could'st need our poor supply,
Who sit'st enthron'd on high,
In Robes of dazling Light,
Robes glorious as the Sun in his Meridian Height:
Or could'st be sick, from whom Health does proceed,
Or made a Prisoner, who dost Nature sway,
And whom superior and inferior Pow'rs obey.

10.

Th' avenging Judge shall then to them reply,
In vain you on your weak Defence rely;
What you've alledg'd can't make your Guilt the less,
You must my Justice, and your Crimes confess:
You knew my Laws, knew their Observers prov'd
My Favourite Care, the Objects that I lov'd:
Yet them you've treated with a barbarous Scorn,
As if they were for your Diversion born,
Left destitute of Pow'r to be your Prey,
Design'd your Slaves, and form'd but to obey;
But know, mistaken Wretches, 'twas on me
You threw the Pain, the Shame, the Infamy;
'Twas me you did despise,
I was the Subject of your Cruelties:
To me th'Indignity was shown,
On me each Obloquy was thrown,
I each Affront resented as my own:

Line 697. **Obloquy**: abuse, derision, detraction.

Then with a Frown that made their Grief compleat,
    Made it as piercing, as 'twas great,
He did once more their dreadful Doom repeat;
His Voice, like Thunder, awful Fear imprest,
It struck a Terrour in each guilty Breast;
It scatter'd Horrour wheresoe'er it came,
And fill'd with dire Amaze the universal Frame:
'Twas heard from Heights above, to Depths below,
None cou'd from it to close Recesses go;
    It was in vain from it to run,
No Place there was where they the dreadful Sound cou'd shun.
Take them, he said, ye Messengers of Fate,
Into the flaming Gulph let them be thrown,
    Where they shall know, when 'tis too late,
        Too late shall own,
Their Business lay in being good alone;
        In Offices of Love,
In being just, compassionate, and kind,
And in a Charity so unconfin'd,
It should it self to all Mankind extend,
And, like my wond'rous Mercy, know no End.
    Past Actions shall torment them there,
        Their Thoughts shall Furies prove,
    Shall fill their anxious Souls with Fear,
    With deep Remorse and black Despair,
    Still shall they lash, and still shall blame,
    Shall still excite an inward Shame;
A Shame, which shall for ever present be,
And like their other Pains, extend to vast Eternity.

11.

    But ye, who liberal were and kind,
    Who made good Works your chiefest Care,
Bestow'd your Alms with an impartial Mind,
    Resolving all that needy were
Shou'd freely of your gen'rous Bounty share;
Who knew no Parties, but to Virtue true,
    Her Vot'ries pity'd in Distress,
Thought a Concern was to their Suff'rings due,
    And strove those Suff'rings to redress,

The noblest way your Kindness did express;
Look'd without Scorn upon their mean Estate,
Defended them from Envy, Pride and Hate,
And buoy'd them up amidst the cross Events of Fate;
Shall now be for your righteous Deeds repay'd,
And hence with Pomp to Heav'nly Seats convey'd,
Where you, with me, shall feast on Joys Divine
Like me, shall with distinguish'd Glory shine.

OF SOLITUDE

Had not Society been that for which we were design'd by infinite Wisdom, there would not have been so strong a Byass in our Inclinations, such Pleasures affix'd to Conversation, such irresistible Charms in agreeable Company; something that by a secret Sympathy, an internal Force, a pleasing sort of Violence, seems to link us to each other, and makes us delight in a mutual Communication of Thoughts, a reciprocal Exchange of Sentiments.

Besides, 'tis not probable that Faculties so bright as ours, were given us to be conceal'd, like Sepulchral Lamps intended only to inlighten Urns, and spread their useless Rays around their small Circumference. Doubtless they were design'd for greater, much nobler Purposes; their Splendour was to be more extensive, like the Sun, to be every where conspicuous: They were to be the Objects of Esteem, to attract Respect and Veneration, by which their Influence might become more prevalent, and they thereby render'd capable of being universal Blessings.

Such as had exalted Understandings, were not to live wholly to themselves, to shine in private, but to be Guides to those of less elevated Sense; the Ignorant, the Novices in Knowledge, to be Scholars to the Masters of Reason; such as had learn'd only the Elements, the first Rudiments of Virtue, were to be instructed both by the Precepts and Examples of such as had made it their long and constant Practice, and who,

Line 9. **Sepulchral**: burial.

by continual Conflicts, had got the Mastery of their Passions, the entire Government of themselves; the Rich were made so, that they might reward Merit, and supply the Necessities of the Poor; the Great were made powerful, that they might become publick Blessings, Defenders of the Distress'd, Protectors of the Innocent, and Revengers of the Injur'd.

From what I've said, it seems evident, that we were not created wholly for our selves, but design'd to be serviceable to each other, to do Good to all within the Circle of our Acquaintance, and some way or other render ourselves useful to those we converse with; for which reason *Solitude* ought never to be our Choice, an active Life including in it much greater Perfection: But if it is our Fortune to live retir'd, to be shut up in a Corner of the World, and deny'd the Pleasures of Conversation, I mean those Delights which naturally result from rational and instructive Discourses, we ought to endeavour to become good Company to our selves, ought to consider, that if we husband our Time well, improve our Abilities, lay in a rich Stock of Knowledge, and by our Diligence and Industry, make a happy Progress in the necessary, as well as the pleasant Parts of Learning, we shall be always agreeably employ'd, and perfectly easie, without calling in auxiliary Aids, be chearful alone, and very entertaining to our selves, without being obliged for any part of our Satisfaction to those Diversions, of which the generality of Mankind are fond.

What can afford a higher, a more masculine Pleasure, a purer, a more transporting Delight, than to retire into our selves, and there curiously and attentively inspect the various Operations of our Souls, compare Idea's, consult our Reason, and view all the Beauties of our Intellect, the inimitable Stroaks of Divine Wisdom, which are visible in our Faculties, and those Participations of infinite Power, which are discoverable in our Wills?

Without us there is nothing but what will be a fit Subject for our Contemplation, and prove a constant and delectable Entertainment. If we look on our Bodies, the Fineness of their Composure, the admirable Symmetry and exact Proportion of their Parts, that Majesty which appears in the Face, that Vivacity which sparkles in the Eye, together with that noble and commanding Air which accompanies every Motion, will afford ample Matter for Meditation: If we extend our View to the sensitive and vegetative Kingdoms, make a strict Scrutiny into the Individuals of each respective Kind, consider their Forms, their

Properties, their Uses, and their peculiar Virtues; and if to these we add the inanimate part of the Creation, and observe Nature as she's there luxuriantly exhibiting her Skill in numberless Productions, we shall find abundant Matter for Thought to work upon; but if we widen our Prospect, and look beyond the narrow Confines of this Globe, we shall be pleasingly confounded with a charming Variety of Objects, be lost in a delightful Maze, shall stray from one Wonder to another, and always find something new, something great, something surprizingly admirable, and every way worthy of that infinite, that incomprehensible Wisdom, to whom they owe their Original.

Thus may we delightfully, as well as advantageously, employ our selves in our Studies, in our Gardens, and in the silent lonely Retirement of a shady Grove.

By Day, the verdent Fields, the lofty Hills, the winding Rivers, the murmuring Brooks, the bleating Flocks, the lowing Herds, the melodious Birds, the beautiful Insects, the pretty little Reptiles, together with the vast Expanse of Heaven, and that glorious Spring of Light which adorns it, and imprints a pleasing Lustre, imparts a delightful Diversity of Colours to every thing on which it shines, will suggest fresh Hints: At Night ten thousand lovely Objects will entertain us, unnumber'd Orbs of Light roll over our Heads, and keep our Thoughts agreeably employ'd.

If at any time we find, that too strict an Attention, too great an Intenseness of Soul, brings a Languor on our Spirits, we may have Recourse to Books; in them (if judiciously chosen) we shall be sure to meet with rational Amusements, something that will instruct, as well as please; will make our Hours slide easily along, and yet prevent their being lost.

Dear to the Gods *Ambrosia* prov'd,
As dear are Books where they're belov'd;
They're still the Mind's delicious Treat,
Its healthful, most substantial Meat;
The Soul's ennobling, sprightly Wine,
Like Nectar sweet, and as Divine:

Line 81. **Languor**: listlessness.

Castalian Springs did ne'er produce
A richer, more spirituous Juice.
When by't inspir'd, we fearless rise,
And, like the Giants, brave the Skies.
Pelion on *Ossa* boldly lay,
From thence both Earth and Sea survey:
On them the huge *Olympus* throw,
Then to the tow'ring Summet go,
Thence take a View of Worlds on High,
From Orb to Orb with Pleasure fly;
Still upward soar, until the Mind
Effects do's in their Causes find,
And them pursue till they unite
In the bless'd Source of Truth and Light.

But none can be thus happy in *Solitude,* unless they have an inward Purity of Mind, their Desires contracted, and their Passions absolutely under the Government of their Reason. Learning without Virtue will not, cannot bestow Felicity: Where there is an internal Disturbance, a Tumult of Thought, a Consciousness of Guilt, and an Anxiousness of Soul, there can be no easie Reflections, no satisfying Pleasures; no, there must be Innocency, Calmness, and a true Understanding of the Value of Things, before the Soul can take a Complacency in herself. To render a private Life truly easie, there must be Piety, as well as humane Knowledge, uncorrupted Morals, as well as an Insight into Nature, a Regardlessness of Wealth, at least no eager Solicitude for it, a being wean'd from the World, from its Vanity, its Applause, its Censure, its Pomp, all that it has of inticing or disturbing, all that it can give, or take away; for without an absolute Independence on all things here, we cannot properly be said to enjoy our selves; and without we do so, we cannot be happy alone.

Give me, O my God, I humbly pray Thee, such Qualifications of Mind as may render me easie in every State, useful to others, and agreeable to my self. When I'm in Company, enable me according to my mean Capacity, to do Good both by my Discourse and my Actions; and

---

Line 92. **Castalian Springs**: in classical myth, a fountain on Mt. Parnassus sacred to the Muses, whose waters inspired one with the gift of poetry.

Line 96. **Pelion on Ossa**: in Greek myth, when the giants attempted to reach heaven, they did so by piling Mt. Pelion on Mt. Ossa; both are mountains in Thessaly.

when I am retir'd from the View of others, and only visible to thy Divine Majesty and my self, let my Thoughts be still employ'd either in bettering my own Mind, or in contemplating thy Works, busy'd in praising, admiring and loving Thee, and in making fresh Discoveries of thy wonderful Wisdom, of that amazing stupendous Skill, which may every where be observ'd throughout the whole Creation, till thou art pleas'd to call me to my Grave, where, while my Body lies, O let my Soul, wash'd clean in the pure Streams of her dear suffering Saviour's Blood, ascend to that bless'd Place, where happy Ghosts possess uninterrupted Joys.

Where new and brighter Objects I shall see,
Objects which with my intellectual Sight agree:
Find Wonders greater than these here below,
And what I see shall with Exactness know:
Shall then no more be to my self confin'd,
But live with Crouds of Spirits ever kind,
Cœlestial Forms from every Passion free,
But Love, blest Bond of their Society;
That sacred Bond, which do's their Hearts unite,
Do's them to Friendship's pleasing Sweets invite,
To Sweets which we can never here possess,
To Joys which only separate Souls can bless;
When freed from Earth, and all its base Alloy,
They taste such Pleasures as shall never cloy;
Pleasures, whose Gust is much too high for Sense,
Too strong, too pure, too lasting, too intense;
Joys to exalted Reason only known,
Of which not here the smallest Glimpse is shown:
What we call Friendship does from Interest rise,
'Tis mean, 'tis vile, 'tis what the Good despise;
Is but a Trade, a Trafficking for Gain.
How few are they who little Tricks disdain,
Scorn wheedling Arts, and uncorrupted Truth maintain?
But those Above, those wise, those spotless Minds,
Are still sincere, it there the noblest welcome finds,
Love reigns supreme, and its diffusive Fire,
Warms every Breast, do's every Heart inspire;

Line 148. **Gust**: taste.

Its Flames still rise, till that dear happy Day,
When Heav'nly Glories all their Pomp display;
When new Delights shall bless their wond'ring Eyes,
And they in shining Bodies mount the Skies,
Shall meet their God in Extasies Divine,
And to his Love each meaner Bliss resign.

INDEX OF FIRST LINES OF POEMS